General Walter Kru

General Walter Krueger

Unsung Hero of the Pacific War

Kevin C. Holzimmer

UNIVERSITY PRESS OF KANSAS

Unless otherwise noted, all photos are courtesy of the National Archives.

First paperback edition published in 2022.

Published by the University Press of Kansas (Lawrence, Kansas 66045), which was organized by the Kansas Board of Regents and is operated and funded by Emporia State University, Fort Hays State University, Kansas State University, Pittsburg State University, the University of Kansas, and Wichita State University

Library of Congress Cataloging-in-Publication Data

Holzimmer, Kevin C.

General Walter Krueger : unsung hero of the Pacific War / Kevin C. Holzimmer.

p. cm. — (Modern war studies)

Includes bibliographical references and index.

ISBN: 978-0-7006-1500-1 (cloth : alk. paper)

ISBN: 978-0-7006-3404-0 (pbk. : alk. paper)

ISBN: 978-0-7006-2660-1 (ebook)

1. Krueger, Walter, 1881–1967. 2. United States. Army—Officers—Biography. 3. Generals—United States—Biography. 4. United States. Army. Sixth Army—History. 5. World War, 1939–1945—Regimental histories—United States. 6. World War, 1939–1945—Pacific Area. I. Title.

U53.K78H65 2007

940.54' 1273092—dc22

[B] 2006032693

British Library Cataloguing-in-Publication Data is available.

Printed in the United States of America

10 9 8 7 6 5 4 3 2 1

The paper used in this publication meets the minimum requirements of the American National Standard for Permanence of Paper for Printed Library Materials Z39.48-1992.

To Kristi

CONTENTS

MAPS

ACKNOWLEDGMENTS

I hope no one who reads this book will fail to read my acknowledgments, because a number of individuals and institutions provided essential assistance, and I would like to publicly thank them. First, I thank the readers of my dissertation, on which this book is based. Collectively and individually, they provided a combination of constructive criticism and encouragement. Through their writing, they have also provided models of historical scholarship. As many before me have acknowledged, the late Dr. Russell F. Weigley ably demonstrated what it is to be a gentleman/scholar. His patient guidance and professional eye for detail without losing the big picture improved dramatically the manuscript and made it much more readable. It was an honor to be one of his students. His unfortunate passing deprived us all of many more years of his first-rate scholarship as well as his friendship. Dr. David Alan Rosenberg also deserves my thanks for his probing questioning and pushing me to think about the "big picture." Dr. David Harrington Watt helped me to look toward other disciplines to improve my historical research and writing. He patiently listened to me as I worked through the graduate process and provided sage advice. Last but certainly not least, Dr. Stanley L. Falk, one of the leading historians of the Pacific War, took an early interest in my work by extending guidance and encouragement. Although all of the members of my committee are leading figures in their own fields, they—without exception—never failed to make time to answer a question or read a draft of a chapter or two.

Several institutions played a key role in the completion of this manuscript. The U.S. Army Center of Military History gave much support via a dissertation fellowship. Former chief of the Research and Analysis Division, Dr. Edward J. Drea, helped me with an encouraging word and constructive criticism at several stages. He also introduced me to several archival sources at the Center of Military History. Dr. Andrew J. Birtle answered many questions and offered much encouragement, as did Brig. Gen. John W. Mountcastle (former chief of Military History) and Dr. Jeffrey J. Clarke (chief historian).

I also extend my sincere thanks to the U.S. Army Military History Institute. It awarded me an advanced research grant that allowed me to conduct a summer of research there. As any historian of the U.S. military can attest, the institute is a virtual treasure chest of information. Mr. John Slonaker answered many questions concerning the holdings of the institute's library. Dr. Richard J. Sommers, Mr. David Keough, and Ms. Pamela A. Cheney made my long hours at the archives a pleasant experience. Their professionalism and courtesy are unsurpassed.

Mr. Alan Aimone and his staff at the archives of the U.S. Military Academy made going through the Walter Krueger Papers a joy. They not only retrieved my requests for materials quickly but answered questions and even sent some materials through the mail.

Dr. Timothy K. Nenninger of the National Archives and Records Administration, College Park, Maryland, pointed me to some records of which I had been unaware. Mr. Mitchell A. Yockelson of the Washington, D.C., branch helped me to locate documents relating to Walter Krueger's early years. I am grateful to both for their assistance.

I must also sincerely extend my gratitude to Temple University. The Graduate School, the Department of History, and the Center for the Study of Force and Diplomacy provided much-appreciated research and writing funds.

A number of other individuals helped me along the way: Dr. Christopher R. Gabel and Mr. James W. Zobel of the MacArthur Memorial and the reviewers of the manuscript for the University Press of Kansas each provided valuable assistance. I also thank Dr. Bruce Vandervort and the *Journal of Military History* for granting me permission to use portions of my article for this book. I would like to name two individuals—both colleagues at Air University—who went out of their way to help me. Dr. J. T. LaSaine not only shared with me his vast knowledge of interwar U.S. national security policy but also allowed me to use some of his own research, included in Chapter 3. Dr. Richard R. Muller commented on earlier drafts and provided constructive criticism and, in addition, has always been a source of inspiration and a role model. In addition, Susan McRory and Susan K. Schott at the University Press of Kansas have been exceptionally professional, as was copyeditor Michelle Asakawa. Michael Briggs has shown incredible patience with a first-time author, and I want to express my appreciation and all of his assistance.

Finally, I would like to thank the members of my family, who all patiently stuck with me to the end: my in-laws, Mr. and Mrs. Douglas Newberry, and my brother-in-law and sister, Dr. and Mrs. David Blinkhorn. I owe the greatest debt to my parents, Dr. and Mrs. Gerald H. Holzimmer. They encouraged my love of history by purchasing all those military books for me when I was young and later on allowed me to pursue my educational goals. For this book, my mother provided valuable research assistance by spending many hours at the photocopier, freeing me to do other work. Similarly, my father has always supported me, no matter what I set out to do, but some of the most memorable times in my life are the hours that he and I have spent fishing on the Florida flats. I do not think he will ever know what these times have meant to me.

My wife, Kristi, also deserves my profound thanks. I'll never be able to return all of the support she has given to me. My two-year-old son, Henry, has also been a great source of encouragement. I am continually amazed by his sense of exploration and discovery. May we both never lose our curiosity about the world around us.

The individuals listed here deserve credit for whatever good comes from this book but not for any of its shortcomings. I alone am responsible for any factual or interpretative errors. The views expressed in this book are my own and do not reflect the views of Air University, U.S. Air Command and Staff College, or any other component of the U.S. government.

INTRODUCTION

At 1200 on 25 January 1946, a large group of U.S. Army generals met for lunch at the Miyako Hotel in Kyoto, Japan. A short time earlier they had just inactivated the formation with which they had fought the forces of Imperial Japan during World War II—the Sixth U.S. Army. In addition to celebrating the end of the Sixth, the generals also gathered to bid farewell to Gen. Walter Krueger. After three years in the Southwest Pacific Area (SWPA) at the head of the Sixth Army, Krueger was calling an end to a forty-eight-year military career and was preparing to return home. Following lunch, Krueger got together "for the last time [with] the large number of officers who had come to bid me farewell." He then proceeded to the Kyoto railroad station where an honor guard of the 33d Infantry Division and elements of the 24th, 32d, and 98th Infantry Divisions as well as the 2d Marine Division met him. Krueger then boarded his train, the *Alamo Limited*, which left the station at 1500.[1]

The next morning, Krueger celebrated his sixty-fifth birthday in the dining car before arriving in Tokyo about noon. At the station, Gen. of the Army Douglas MacArthur's aide de camp, Col. Herbert Wheeler, met Krueger and brought him to the headquarters of the Commander-in-Chief of United States Army Forces in the Pacific and Supreme Commander Allied Forces. There MacArthur himself greeted Krueger and presented him with a Distinguished Service Cross and an additional Oak Leaf Cluster for his Distinguished Service Medal. Krueger then helped celebrate MacArthur's sixty-sixth birthday. After lunch, Krueger exchanged farewells with MacArthur and boarded his train for Yokohama to meet with the commander of the Eighth U.S. Army, Gen. Robert L. Eichelberger; Lt. Gen. Charles P. Hall; and Maj. Gen. William C. Chase, all three of whom had served with Krueger in the SWPA. After all the celebrations and congratulations of the busy afternoon, Krueger relaxed for the next couple of days and prepared to return home.

January 29 was a bittersweet day for General Krueger. On one hand, he was heading home to a wife he had not seen in almost three years. On the other hand, it would be one of the last times he saw many of the people and units that served under his command. One such unit was the 1st Cavalry Division. Before boarding his train—again the *Alamo Limited*—for the trip to Yokosuka, he inspected an honor guard from the division, which he considered one of the very best of the Sixth Army. As Krueger boarded the train, the division's band appropriately played "Deep in the Heart of Texas" and "California, Here I Come!" At Yokosuka, he boarded the battleship U.S.S. *New Jersey* for the long journey across the Pacific to San Francisco. The usually stoic Krueger recalled that the ceremonies "started a eulogy of my services that brought tears to my eyes." Over the next seven days, the U.S.S. *New Jersey* cruised along the twenty-ninth parallel, where the weather was warm but cloudy and the seas rough. The cruise allowed Krueger to reflect on his long and distinguished army career, as there was little else to do beyond reading, writing letters, and watching movies in the evening.[2]

At 0815 on 10 February 10, the mighty battleship steamed under the Golden Gate Bridge and anchored in San Francisco Bay. "It was a beautiful day," Krueger's trans-Pacific diary notes, "with quite a lot of color as several 'welcoming boats' came out to meet the NJ." The next several days were busy ones for Krueger as he met the press, attended a cocktail party, and hosted a "steady flow of visitors" to his room at the St. Francis Hotel. An intensely private and introverted individual, Krueger must have been worn out by the publicity and entertaining before he finally left San Francisco for San Antonio, Texas, on a "hard flight which at times necessitated an altitude of nearly 20,000 feet and oxygen."[3]

The residents of San Antonio rolled out the red carpet for one of their most famous citizens. They not only organized a parade but also had purchased a gift for Krueger—a brand new 1946 Pontiac. When Krueger arrived home on 13 February 1945, he was greeted not only by his wife and family but also by Texas governor Coke Stevenson; San Antonio mayor Gus B. Mauermann; Lt. Gen. Jonathan M. Wainwright, the commander who had led the surrender of the U.S. Army in the Philippines in 1942; and Lt. Gen. Herbert J. Brees, his old Third Army commander. Shortly after standing for a seventeen-gun salute, Krueger inspected an honor guard from the 2d Infantry Division, which he had commanded in the late 1930s. Krueger and the welcoming party then headed for Alamo Plaza. There, a crowd greeted the Sixth Army commander and enjoyed a forty-five–minute parade of marching, music, and pageantry. San Antonio had given Krueger a fitting welcome, for under his leadership, the Sixth Army had been one of the most successful army formations of the war. It had formed in the early months of 1943 and conducted approximately twenty-one successful operations in two years across thousands of miles of ocean and jungle-covered terrain. Unfortunately, unlike many other high-level World War II commanders, Krueger would quickly fade away from the public eye.[4]

Although Walter Krueger received slight but positive wartime exposure, history has been generally unkind to him. Writers—whether professional historians, official U.S. Army historians, or popular writers—have followed two patterns when assessing Krueger's contributions to the war against Japan.[5] The first school is highly critical, suggesting that he was a plodding, indecisive, and cautious ground commander.[6] Other authors have simply ignored altogether Krueger's contributions to the American war effort during World War II. Many works on war either fail to mention him or provide a cursory treatment of his accomplishments. The reader of these authors' works, if they learned of Krueger's existence at all, could well get the impression that he played only a minor role in the war.[7] Only five article-length works have assessed Krueger's career, including William M. Leary's chapter in *We Shall Return! MacArthur's Commanders and the Defeat of Japan*.[8] In short, no systematic analysis of Krueger's important career has yet emerged, and the current image that does exist stems largely from negative inquiries that treat Krueger only indirectly. Most authors have arrived at their conclusions while examining a related topic such as the Pacific War in general or one of Krueger's colleagues. These works address the topic of Krueger's career without taking the necessary biographical approach.

With this study I hope to fill a glaring gap in American military historiography by examining the career of Walter Krueger, specifically his role in World War II. My approach—not surprising in a biography—is chronological, which I believe is especially important in assessing Krueger's performance in World War II. Some of the most recent works on the campaigns of World War II take an operationally sequential approach to events in SWPA, as if Krueger had the luxury of beginning one new operation when he neatly finished his previous one, giving the impression that he was only dealing with one operation at a time. This method does not provide for the reader all of the complexity and difficulty of conducting military operations in the Southwest Pacific. However, by taking a strict chronological approach, one in which his operations are laid chronologically, one may see that operations overlapped one another and this proved to be a significant factor that shaped his generalship. This biography also situates Krueger within the context of military operations—logistics, MacArthur's leadership, the joint environment, topography, and so on—as they unfolded, to determine his role in shaping events in SWPA. In other words, I view events during the war from Krueger's vantage point. This is not to say, however, that it will tell his story in a necessarily sympathetic manner, rather than purely empathetic. There is plenty about which to critique Krueger. His personality was often abrasive and he could be overly critical of his principal commanders. These issues—along with others—will also be addressed.

Within this chronological approach, I will explore three broad themes. The first theme involves Krueger's personal life and personality. On these points, the researcher will inevitably face problems. The Krueger papers at the United States Military Academy at West Point, New York, do not contain many documents that shed much light on Krueger the man or the positions he held about a great many issues. Krueger wrote to his wife, Grace, while away from home, but none of these letters has survived.[9] Furthermore, he never kept a personal diary during World War II, and he refused to write his memoirs after the war. Instead, he insisted upon writing a history of the Sixth U.S. Army, which relied heavily on after-action reports.[10] Simply put, he was a man who stubbornly refused to make a record of many of his personal views. Nevertheless, one may construct a view of his personality through use of what does exist of his personal correspondence and through the views of his friends, particularly Fay W. Brabson. The portrait that emerges of Krueger is of a man who was driven, impatient, competitive, aggressive, ambitious, and sensitive to criticism; was often seen as aloof and distant; and possessed a forceful and at times overbearing personality.

The second theme of the book concerns Krueger's ideas about command. Several major consistent and recurring themes run through the course of his career. The art of command may be defined as, in the words of Harold R. Winton, "the ability of the commander to direct the efforts of his units to the accomplishment of a mission and was generally felt to require a combination of intellectual and psychological qualities particularly adapted to the conduct of war."[11] An analysis of Krueger's contribution to the tactical and operational doctrinal debates of the early twentieth century and his role in leading the Third U.S. Army in the General Headquarters Maneuvers of 1941 allows the historian a window through which to gain further insights into the evolution of U.S. Army doctrine. Recently, two schools of thought have emerged in the historiography concerning interwar U.S. Army doctrine. The first suggests that the U.S. Army was doctrinally ill-equipped at the start of the war, while the admittedly much smaller other school contends that the U.S. Army had developed an operational doctrine, one much more modern than many have previously believed.[12] As will be seen, the present study supports that by late 1941 the U.S. Army indeed had a sophisticated operational level doctrine and, furthermore, that Walter Krueger was vital to its formulation. Coming so late in the interwar era, however, the doctrine was not widely disseminated—in particular because the army had more pressing concerns, such as the day-to-day concerns of rehabilitating a military force that had suffered from years of national apathy and neglect. In fact, Krueger successfully adopted this doctrine—designed as it was to the American or European continent—to the very different topographical situation of the Southwest Pacific.

The third—and most central—theme of this biography is that Walter Krueger was far from the methodical, slow-moving, and overly cautious commander of most examinations of him. Krueger could be aggressive when he needed to be, but he was also in many instances constrained by incomplete intelligence, logistical constraints, and a commanding officer who insisted upon speedy operations often for illegitimate military reasons and in the face of many legitimate military risks. Viewed from a larger vantage point, this study adds to the recent historiographical reexamination of Gen. Douglas MacArthur during World War II. This body of scholarship sheds much deserved light on MacArthur's lieutenants and their valuable efforts in SWPA. In the end, their contributions were essential in the war against Japan.[13] Krueger is no exception, and as the chief coordinator of the Allied military effort in SPWA, his contributions were significant.

Although my focus is on Walter Krueger, I also address the larger themes of U.S. military history. Krueger was, after all, just one representative of a much larger system. Therefore, this study will seek to understand some of the broader historiographical issues of U.S. involvement in World War II through an examination of one influential and important military figure. It will seek to understand, for instance, some of the "whys" of the U.S. victory over Japan.[14]

The book is organized into three parts. Part I covers Krueger's life and career prior to World War II with the intent of analyzing the experiences that ultimately would prepare him for his role as commander of the Sixth Army. Whereas his earlier years are difficult to document, Krueger's career becomes easier to follow as he earned more and more responsibility, especially after the mid-1930s. Particularly useful are the records of the U.S. Army's General Headquarters Maneuvers of 1941, during which Krueger's Third Army played a key role, as well as items in the Walter Krueger Papers. Housed at the National Archives in College Park, Maryland, and at the U.S. Army Military History Institute at Carlisle Barracks, Pennsylvania, the operational records of the maneuvers provide a detailed picture of Krueger as an army commander during simulated wartime conditions. From his decisions and actions in the autumn of 1941, one can begin to discern the type of army commander Krueger would become during World War II.

Part II analyzes Krueger's time in charge of the Sixth Army during World War II. For insight into his role in SWPA, this study—in addition to a strict chronological approach—will take a multifaceted examination of all the factors that influenced Krueger as an operational leader: the doctrinal side of the war (the aspect of war that provided a blueprint to operate an army), the tactical side of the war (the level underneath the Sixth Army), the military-strategy side as dictated by MacArthur (the level above Krueger), and the logistical side of the war (the level of war that helped to sustain the Sixth Army). Throughout the war, tactical situations at the regimental level or logistical shortages at the divisional level, for example, played significant roles in Krueger's decision making and shaped the course of the battle. Only by examining many of the forces that influenced Krueger, including MacArthur's command philosophy, logistics, American military thought and doctrine, the personalities of the principal military leaders in SWPA, and the tactical side of the war, as well as Krueger's own experiences, can the historian accurately evaluate Krueger as commander of the Sixth Army. Fortunately, the history of his army is well documented. The National Archives, the Walter Krueger Papers, and the U.S. Army Military History Institute contain much material about Krueger and his Sixth Army.

Part III covers Krueger's retirement years, which were marked by sadness and disappointment. This last part also summarizes the themes and goals of the study.

I hope to demonstrate that Krueger's role in World War II was larger and more important than is usually acknowledged. While MacArthur (and to a much lesser extent, Eichelberger) has received much of the attention, Krueger nevertheless was a vital component in the American victory, providing the operational leadership to the army's Pacific campaigns. Because of his ironlike will and his cutting-edge work in formulating an operational doctrine, Krueger breathed life into the Pacific War strategy and made sure it was executed successfully. As a result of extensive prewar preparation, he successfully forged and led a large combined-arms and joint effort in the Pacific theater, bringing together the infantry, armor, artillery, navy, and air force. In short, Krueger played a large role in the defeat of Japan, one usually overlooked or minimized by historians.

Part I

The Making of a General Officer: 1881–1943

Chapter 1

From Germany to the Philippines, 1881–1903

Walter Krueger's career path differed greatly from others of his generation, and he was perhaps one of the most unlikely candidates to become a general officer in the early twentieth-century U.S. Army. Most army officers of Krueger's time had been born in the United States, with the largest single group (33.4 percent) from the Midwest. During the interwar period, foreign-born officers made up only 2.5 percent of the officer corps even though 17 percent of the white male population were foreign born. Just over 70 percent of the generals included in one important study of that period had graduated from the United States Military Academy at West Point, New York. About half of the entire officer corps were West Pointers, and their percentage increased with time after World War I. Most officers (67.6 percent) had earned post–high school degrees, and 87.2 percent of generals held degrees from institutions of higher education. "In broad strokes," the study concludes,

> a composite American Army officer of the period between the World Wars emerges. He was almost forty years old and, more likely, a veteran of World War I. He probably spoke with a Midwestern accent or a Southern drawl. Chances are that he graduated from either West Point or a civilian college. (If he were a general, a West Point graduation was much more likely.) And he had probably attended at least one army school. Finally, there was almost a one-third possibility that he had had enlisted experience.[1]

Not much of Krueger's career resembles that of this "composite soldier." First, Krueger was of European birth, one of only two foreign-born U.S. generals in the entire interwar period; the other was General Ben Lear, who had been born in Canada.[2] Second, he never graduated from high school and never attended West Point or even obtained a college degree. Last, unlike two-thirds of his fellow officers, he had extensive enlisted experience. He started his long army career by dropping out of high school and joining the military during the Spanish-American War. His stint in the army spanned six decades, beginning as a private and ending as a four-star general while in an assignment that would prove to be the pinnacle of his long career: command of the Sixth U.S. Army during World War II. Krueger spent over forty years in the army preparing for just such a command. His preparation consisted of several elements: self-study, prior enlisted service, experience in the Philippine Insurrection and World War I, time in the U.S. Army's school system (as a student, instructor, and writer), and finally service as an army commander in the General Headquarters Maneuvers of 1941. These experiences provided Krueger with the tools he would need to become a successful army commander.

Krueger was born on 26 January 1881 in Flatow, Germany. His father, Julius O. H. Krüger, was a prominent landowner who served as an army officer during the Franco-Prussian War of 1870–1871. In 1880 Julius married Anna Hasse, the daughter of a physician. When Julius died several years later, Anna packed up her three children and moved to the United States. She settled in St. Louis, Missouri, the hometown of her maternal uncle, Edward Nixdorff, a well-known brewer. Anna soon married a Lutheran minister, Emil Carl Schmidt, also an immigrant. The Schmidts made their home some fifty miles east of St. Louis in Washington County, Illinois.[3]

At some point in the early 1890s, Schmidt moved his family to Madison, Indiana, a town on the Ohio River with a population of approximately 8,000 residents. Swept up in the dramatic rise of big business during the Gilded Age, Madison was one of many small Midwestern cities that stood on the verge of vast social, economic, and political change. The aggressive national industrial trusts threatened the city by purchasing several of the locally owned manufacturing businesses. Local manufacturers flourished as well, such as those in the brewing and milling industries. In short, Madison was a bustling, but small, industrial city.[4]

Carl Schmidt, whom city residents called "Herr Schmidt," took the pastorate of the Evangelical Lutheran Church in Madison as well as a church across the river in Carroll County, Kentucky. Described as a man of "great energy and determination" as well as "autocratic and high tempered," Schmidt was a demanding stepfather. Though the young Krueger had begun his education in Germany at the age of five, his real education started in America under the tutelage of his stepfather. Schmidt taught Walter mathematics and languages, while his mother taught him to play the piano. Schmidt also inculcated in young Walter a discipline toward life and a passion for knowledge, both of which became hallmarks of his personal and professional life. Throughout his life, Krueger devoted himself to learning. "If my father had a hobby," Krueger's son, Walter Krueger Jr., remembered, "it was work. He enjoyed work. He always had a den in our home wherever we lived, and was at his desk in this den during most waking hours of the day, when he was at home, throughout his life. He had a large library in several languages and read voraciously."[5]

The home, of course, was not the only source of education for Krueger. He first attended the Upper Seminary School while in Madison and then attended the Cincinnati Technical High School of Cincinnati, Ohio. Cincinnati Technical School prepared young men to become, among other things, carpenters, butchers, and bricklayers. At the age of fifteen, Krueger apparently elected to become a blacksmith, since his mother refused to let him pursue his adolescent ambition of becoming a naval officer by attending the U.S. Naval Academy at Annapolis, Maryland. "She was," he recalled, "afraid for me on the water."[6]

Cuba and the Philippines

Nearing graduation in 1897, Krueger decided to make an eight-inch-square picture frame out of wrought iron to complete the requirements for graduation. However, fate played a decisive role in Krueger's life at this juncture. With the United States on the verge of war with Spain, the patriotism and nationalism that swept the nation in the late 1890s deeply affected the impressionable young man. Without waiting to see if his instructor had accepted his picture frame, Krueger enlisted in the U.S. Army in order to fight in the Spanish-American War. As the *Cincinnati Times Star* reported nearly fifty years later, "He finished [his project], liked it, presented it to his brawny instructor. He left town, went to war—never came back, probably never knew it was accepted, certainly never saw it again. Probably never needed it to prove his excellence as a smithy."[7]

Krueger and some of his classmates joined the army on 17 June 1898 after witnessing the 6th Infantry Regiment drill at Fort Thomas, just across the Ohio River. The pageantry of the army, combined with the nationalist feelings of the country, offered the young men more excitement than their classes in the various trades could provide. Military excitement and glory, however, would be deferred, because only a month after Krueger enlisted, the Spanish defenders of Santiago de Cuba surrendered.[8]

A young enlisted man such as Krueger must have faced a mixture of emotions near the turn of the century. On one hand, the nation was infused with the possibilities of an awakened sense of nationalism. The Spanish-American War provided a source of pride and patriotism for the many Americans who supported the conflict. In addition, many young soldiers, like Krueger, could take pride in the fact that the war proved to be the first U.S. military victory over a European nation in over eighty years.[9] On the other hand, Krueger must also have heard of the many problems the army was facing. Whereas the Spanish army in Cuba surrendered largely because of its terrible living conditions, the American forces hardly fared any better. By the beginning of July, both Spanish and American soldiers were facing a life-threatening situation.[10] In the ensuing occupation of Cuba, the situation for American troops did not materially improve. Maj. Gen. William R. Shafter's V Corps, totaling 20,000 men, was not in the best of shape when it started the trip home on 7 August 1898. On the eve of the victory that propelled the United States into world power status, malaria, yellow fever, and dysentery struck the U.S. troops in Cuba. Although the conditions of Shafter's troops slowly improved, sickness remained a major problem. In late July and early August, the V Corps finally set sail for the United States, while the last of the contingent, composed of the severely sick, left Cuba near the end of August. To relieve the beleaguered and decimated V Corps, the War Department sent the volunteers from the 11 May 1898 Act for garrison duty, including Krueger's 2d Volunteer Infantry Regiment. By the time Krueger and his fellow infantrymen arrived in Santiago de Cuba, various diseases still incapacitated a significant portion of the American army. On 27 July, more than 4,000 troops, a fifth of the overall total in Cuba, occupied hospital beds. Though yellow fever was feared most, malaria contributed more to debilitate the Americans than any other disease.[11]

In all, Krueger spent approximately eight months in the Santiago de Cuba region with the 2d Volunteer Infantry, ultimately earning the rank of sergeant. After being mustered out of the army on 18 February 1899, he returned home to Ohio, deciding to pursue a career as a civil engineer rather than a blacksmith. However, many of his friends and acquaintances reenlisted for service in the Philippines to fight Emilio Aguinaldo's Republican insurgency. Deciding to forego a career in engineering, Krueger also reenlisted in June 1899 and was shipped off to the Philippines as a private with Company M of the 2d Battalion/12th Infantry Regiment.[12]

Upon arriving in the Philippines in the closing week of June, Krueger and the other soldiers of Company M participated in the twenty-five-mile pursuit of Aguinaldo from Angeles to Tarlac between August and November 1899. Krueger's regiment—commanded by Brig. Gen. Joseph "Fighting Joe" Wheeler—was attached to Maj. Gen. Arthur MacArthur's 2d Infantry Division of Maj. Gen. Elwell S. Otis's VIII Corps. After the hostilities commenced early in February 1899, Otis had sent MacArthur's forces north from Manila in an effort to defeat the insurgent forces along the strategically significant Manila-Dagupan railroad, which ran through the central Luzon plain and formed the lifeline of the insurgent defenses. In early spring, however, the offensive became bogged down at San Fernando by the onset of the rainy season and the corps commander's cautious nature. As new regiments arrived from the United States, including the 12th Infantry, MacArthur continued his offensive despite the poor campaigning weather, finally resulting in the capture of Tarlac in November. Despite MacArthur's success, Otis's overall operation failed to catch Aguinaldo. Facing the steady northern advance of the U.S. Army, Aguinaldo gave up on the conventional tactics that served him so poorly and instead adopted guerrilla warfare in autumn of that year. Otis, however, declared victory, while the Republican Army waged war from its own hometowns. From late 1899 to May 1900 (when Otis left the Philippines), Otis spread out his army to protect various important points throughout the Philippines. For Krueger and the other soldiers of the 2d Division, this meant garrison duty, protecting railroad lines, and patrolling over 100 towns and villages. Often these patrols would result in engagements during which the insurgents would flee, preferring to harass unsuspecting patrols or outposts.[13]

Lessons Learned as an Enlisted Man

The war proved to be a difficult experience for the American soldiers who fought in the Philippines. The extreme tropical climate and weather caused most of the difficulties. Campaigning throughout the rainy season and an unusually wet November, the soldiers encountered roads and trails that were nearly impossible to traverse. "The men ate, slept, and marched in the drizzle and downpour," Kenneth Ray Young writes of the November 1899 campaign. "Their perpetually wet clothes slowly rotted on their backs. Rifles rusted, and all the equipment was covered with a thin coat of mildew. When it was not raining, the sun baked the ground, and the air became heavy with humidity as the temperature hovered around ninety degrees by 6 a.m. The men gasped for breath like fish out of water."[14] These conditions had obvious negative effects on the combat readiness of U.S. troops. The combination of mud, water, and heat sapped the endurance of the soldiers, many of whom suffered from heat exhaustion. In addition, many tropical diseases—such as cholera, dysentery, malaria, and typhoid—contributed to the misery of the American ranks. In one regiment during the month of May 1899, for instance, 45 percent of the men were reported sick. Later on that year in November, Krueger's own company had the least number of sick in the 12th Infantry. By Krueger's own calculation, 37 percent were incapacitated, a total of 28 men. While he had been fortunate not to get sick himself, the situation left an enduring mark: "I have been very lucky in not being laid up with disease so far, and I cannot be too thankful for it. It is a pitiful sight to see some formerly strong healthy men now merely crawling along, a living skeleton."[15]

Exacerbating the situation were critical shortages of food and equipment at various times throughout the campaign. Often the men of the 2d Battalion/12th Regiment, for example, went without food. While the logistics of the U.S. Army had improved dramatically since the Spanish-American War, not all of the problems were overcome. This situation, along with memories of conditions in Cuba, made an indelible impression upon Walter Krueger. As an enlisted man, he witnessed and experienced firsthand what happens when food and supplies do not get through to the front lines. It not only reduces fighting efficiency but lowers morale as well. "Years ago in the Philippines," he later remembered, "I went without food and other supplies, and I know what it is to be hungry; then and there I resolved that if I ever had the say-so my men would never be without enough to eat." Indeed, years later, Krueger made the conditions and well-being of the troops under his command a high priority. Once, while commander of the Third U.S. Army, he told a group of officers, "I have such a high regard for our men that there is something within me [that] turns around when I see they [enlisted soldiers] are not being handled right." Part of Krueger's philosophy concerning enlisted men was that if they needed correction, he would never raise his voice to them. Instead, he would talk to them in a calm and reassuring voice, making sure they understood what was wrong and why it was important to correct the problem. Officers were a different story, and on many occasions Krueger would hold them accountable for the poor performance of their soldiers. Consequently, he received the respect and admiration of many of those who served with him, especially when he commanded the Sixth U.S. Army during World War II. Many veterans of the Sixth Army who had personal contact with Krueger told similar stories of his concern for them and their comrades.[16]

One such soldier described his encounter with the Sixth Army commander during an inspection at dusk in 1944 at Hollandia, Netherlands New Guinea. Krueger surprised an officer as his men were preparing for the invasion of Leyte. "It was almost dark and I directed the beam of my flashlight into his face as he approached, and then begged his pardon when I recognized his rank," the officer remembered thirty-two years later. "He put me at ease at once and spoke in a quiet, friendly manner. He asked about the spirit of my men, the condition of our equipment, and my personal feelings concerning the mission ahead and then he left. … In those few minutes, in the dark, he made an impression on me that I have remembered all of these years."[17]

Maj. Gen. William C. Chase could also attest to Krueger's concern for his soldiers, in particular the food situation. Commander of the 38th Infantry

Division during World War II, Chase recalled both Krueger's expectations and his reaction to those whom he felt did not give enough attention to their soldiers' well-being:

> Above all, he [Krueger] insisted that officers of all ranks take care of their men. His specialty was to descend unheralded and unannounced on kitchens at any time of day or night, and they had better be spotless or the general's wrath was enormous. He loved to take the meat saw apart because he could almost always find a piece of old meat somewhere in the apparatus. Some cook dubbed him with the nickname "Meat Saw," which seemed so appropriate that it was adopted somewhat generally—and very quietly.[18]

A Career in the Army

During his post in the Philippines Krueger decided to make the army his career. Having risen through the ranks to become a sergeant on 26 June 1901, he was asked if he would take the examination for a commission. "I demurred," he recalled. "I still had no idea of making the army a career. But I figured that as long as I was in I might as well get the best, however little that might be." Although he thought he had "flunked gloriously," on 1 July 1901 he received his commission as a second lieutenant and was assigned to the 30th Infantry Regiment and sent to the island of Marinduque, located off the northeast coast of Mindoro.[19]

Krueger held a number of assignments as a member of the 30th Infantry, including quartermaster, engineer officer, ordnance officer, signal officer, disbursing officer of civil funds, postmaster, exchange officer, a member of the general court-martial in Manila, and commander of Company K. Though undoubtedly busy with his duties, Krueger nevertheless found time to utilize his passion for learning by preparing for and passing several examinations covering such topics as infantry drill regulations, the manual of guard duty, and small arms firing regulations. He was not necessarily demonstrating any extraordinary talents that would separate him from his peers at this point in his life, but one can discern the beginnings of a life-long pattern in Krueger's military career—self-study as a means to success. Whereas many officers in the Old Army had an anti-intellectual bias against advanced military schooling or even self-improvement, Krueger sought to further his education when the opportunity presented itself.[20]

Although he held a number of ordinary positions for a second lieutenant, not everything was so routine for him. One of his most unpleasant assignments was that of guarding military prisoners on Malahi Island in the Laguna de Bay. Isolated and hostile, Malahi Island became one of the most forbidding areas in the Philippines. Located on the island was a lake so contaminated that even bathing in it was considered unsafe. The prison itself was nearly as toxic. Behind its walls resided the worst prisoners of the U.S. Army, deserters and murders. Another second lieutenant detailed to the prison was George C. Marshall Jr. Years later, from the comfort of his home in Leesburg, Virginia, Marshall remembered the terrible conditions of the prison:

> The prisoners were the dregs of the army of the Philippine Insurrection. They were the toughest crowd of men I have ever seen. You had to count them twice each night. To go through the barracks there where they were lying stark naked on these gold metal cots without any sheets—we didn't use sheets, any of us, at that time—it was a very depressing sight. The kitchen—I saw a man attacked there with a cleaver.... We were not there very long because we were relieved by the Seventh Infantry from the States. Their depression when they saw the place was very great. Our elation when we left was even greater.[21]

Krueger and Marshall met at the prison, and Krueger later recalled his introduction to the future Chief of Staff: "In view of the strenuous guard duty we had an officer of the guard and the officer of the day. On this occasion Marshall was the officer of the guard and I had the other duty. He was newly arrived and was beautifully turned out in his uniform. I had been there several years and was not so well turned out. He asked where we slept. I pointed to a corner of the shack on some straw. I could imagine how he felt." For his part, Marshall remembered Krueger as all business. "He is of typical German stock," he recalled, "thorough, hard-working, ambitious, and devoid of humor."[22]

Though busy with his duties, Krueger still had time for relaxation and other pursuits. Consequently, just as Krueger's professional life was beginning to take shape in the first few years of the twentieth century, so too was his personal life. In 1903 he met his future wife, Grace Aileen Norvell. Traveling to the Philippines to visit her sister (the wife of an army chaplain), Grace had enjoyed a happy and religious upbringing. She eventually fitted the role of army wife superbly. "She was sincerely and dearly loved by everybody," her youngest son remembered. "Women as well as men were crazy about her. ... She was a great army wife, devoted and loyal to my father, a great support to him. And she was a dear darling mother. Wives of younger officers were always at ease with her. She had a very happy disposition, a good sense of humor, poise, and she was a real lady in every respect."[23]

Fortunately for Krueger and his fellow soldiers, their tour of duty at Malahi Island lasted just under one year. With the duties at Malahi completed, the 30th Infantry Regiment was shipped back to the United States in December 1903. The first twenty-two years of Krueger's life had brought him to several diverse places around the globe and had established two important characteristics in his life and work. The first was a passion for learning. (Later in his career, he would make a name for himself by being a self-made and self-educated army officer as well as an expert in tactics.) The second was his knowledge of the concerns of the average soldier in the front lines. This firsthand experience included participating in a war that had caught the United States by surprise. The nation sent its army into war unprepared, without sufficient food or proper equipment. Krueger promised himself that if he occupied a position of responsibility, he would make the well-being of his troops a higher priority than his commanding officers had done when he was an enlisted man. It is no wonder that enlisted men later considered him a "soldier's soldier."[24]

Chapter 2

Education of a Tactician, 1903–1920

In December 1903, Walter Krueger and the 30th Infantry Regiment traveled back to the United States and arrived at Fort Crook, Nebraska. Krueger held a variety of jobs, including acting battalion adjutant of the 3d Battalion. Within a few days of receiving the battalion adjutant's position, Krueger also became the battalion quartermaster and commissary. He worked at his new responsibilities for only a month before he received a two-month leave of absence, effective 10 September 1904, in order to marry Grace Norvell.[1]

After his leave, the newly married Krueger served as judge advocate for court-martial trials for the 30th Regiment, but in late July 1905 he learned that his career would be taking an important step forward when his regimental commander selected him to attend the Infantry and Cavalry School at Fort Leavenworth, Kansas. With this, the young second lieutenant embarked on a series of traditional but important assignments in the U.S. Army.

Infantry and Cavalry School

By 1904, selection to attend the Infantry and Cavalry School at Fort Leavenworth had emerged as a badge of honor within the ranks of the officer corps. The commandant, Brig. Gen. J. Franklin Bell, had recently reorganized the school into two one-year programs. The Infantry and Cavalry School covered the basics of the military profession, such as military engineering, military law, foreign languages, military art, and even the handling of units up to the divisional level. Once this year of study was completed, only the top half of the class continued to the second year, the Army Staff College, which taught military art, General Staff duties, logistics, and the operational employment of units up to an army corps.[2]

Students found the atmosphere of the school competitive and stressful, particularly in the first year as the officers competed for the limited number of slots allocated to the Staff College. "Everyone worked hard," Krueger recalled. "I would fall across my bed when I came from class. We didn't average six hours sleep." He persevered, however, graduated with honors, and was one of the students who moved on to the second year at Leavenworth. In addition to excelling at the Infantry and Cavalry School, Krueger pinned on the silver bars of a first lieutenant before beginning his studies at the Staff College.[3]

In all, Krueger and his classmates valued and benefited from the Infantry and Cavalry School experience, despite the long days. Among the school's most important contributions was the development of the student's critical and analytical skills. For Krueger, the Leavenworth experience only reinforced his longtime love of learning. In this sense, his experience was a positive one. He adapted well to the army's postgraduate school despite never having attended college or even graduated from high school. The Leavenworth programs therefore provided a structure and framework for Krueger's intellectual and academic interests.

In addition, the Leavenworth schools modeled "safe" leadership, whereby a "safe" U.S. Army officer understood the doctrine and techniques of his institution and shared with his colleagues a common understanding of how to wage war American-style. Furthermore, the professional military education that officers received at Fort Leavenworth inculcated the importance of teamwork. By experiencing the same curriculum, graduates possessed a mutual frame of reference and ability to work smoothly with one another. Krueger was one of the first generation of officers who was schooled in this "safe" leadership. The distinctive stamp of Fort Leavenworth would stand out clearly during World War I, when senior officers recognized a "Leavenworth clique" within the ranks of their staff officers.[4]

Because Krueger attended the Infantry and Cavalry School as American tactical doctrine was evolving, he witnessed the army's transition from the old rigid and linear system of tactics to the flexible and open-order tactics embodied in the *Infantry Drill Regulation, 1911*. Concurrent with the attention on loose-order tactics was an emphasis on the psychological component of leadership. With the modern battlefield dominated by weapons of unprecedented lethality, instructors taught their students about the value of a leader's grasp of the human element during the heat of battle. A good leader knew how to motivate and psychologically prepare his men for the realities of warfare, while the poor leader neglected such matters.[5] Fort Leavenworth's teachings served to reinforce Krueger's own views on the subject that had formed from his experiences in Cuba and the Philippines.

After graduating from the Army Staff College, Krueger took a well-deserved rest with the help of a two-month leave of absence. At the end of this break, he joined the 23d Infantry Regiment at Fort Ontario, New York, to which he had been transferred in October 1907. Over the next several years,

Krueger held a number of positions, including an assignment on a general court-martial to an instructor at the Officers Garrison School. After he had served only a few weeks as an educator, he was selected by his commander, Col. Philip Reade, to lead a group consisting of 1st Lt. Fay W. Brabson, 2d Lt. W. T. MacMillan, and three other officers from two different regiments for "Progressive Military Map Work" in Manila, Philippines. Krueger worked on the topographical map project through the hot summer months, during which he began a life-long personal friendship with Brabson, who had been at Fort Leavenworth a year before Krueger.[6]

Brabson described Krueger as, among other things, an impatient man. Whether concerned with something as important as work or as simple as waiting for dinner at a restaurant, Krueger became discouraged and frustrated by delays. Brabson explained his friend's impatience as a result of both his ambition and energy, which often led to impulsive behavior. "Krueger has more energy than nearly any man I know," Brabson wrote. He "has lots of ability but gets people under him impatient because of his restlessness. Too he is somewhat impulsive and will on the spur of a moment and as an afterthought order something that will cause endless bother to the one doing it and when in fact Krueger had no idea of using what he had ordered." In addition, Krueger was extremely competitive and worked hard, driving those around him to work hard as well. Brabson wrote of one instance in which Krueger extended office hours. "From a comparative estimate," Brabson complained, "I am very strongly of the opinion that Krueger drove his section entirely too fast even their extra hours of hard work and all considered." When the six-man team finished its work, Krueger remained in the Philippines with the Military Information Division for one year before returning home in June 1909. Krueger's second exposure to the Philippine Islands had allowed him to study its geography and terrain. Such analysis would obviously come in handy when Krueger traveled back to Leyte and Luzon in thirty-six years.[7]

Upon returning to the United States, Krueger returned to professional military education by teaching both Spanish and German at Fort Leavenworth. Although fluent in German, Spanish, and French, Krueger found teaching difficult, as many of the students had no prior second language education. Consequently, as the senior instructor of the Department of Languages, Capt. Arthur Thayer, wrote in his report for the 1909–1910 academic year, "The ultimate progress of such [instruction], in the short course of forty-five lessons, can hardly be deemed sufficient to say that they have a working knowledge of the language." Nevertheless, Thayer found Krueger's performance, as well as that of Krueger's colleagues, "highly satisfactory; their close attention to work, their ability, and their patience produced as good results as could reasonably be expected."[8] Of Krueger's work at the Staff College, Thayer wrote in 1911, "Progress of this class, generally satisfactory. All work showed interest and zeal. All members acquired accuracy and facility in translating." Some members even developed a "fairly accurate conversational fluency."[9]

As well as teaching at the Army Service Schools, Krueger worked with America's militia system. As part of the Dick Act of 1903 and its modification of 1908, the army became responsible not only for arming the National Guard of the United States but also for training it. The army consequently spent much time and effort in preparing the militia for war, and nearly all regular army officers, including Krueger, worked with citizen training programs during the summer months. Krueger taught officers of the organized infantry at Camp Benjamin Harrison in Indiana and at Pine Camp, New York.[10]

The Writer

Krueger also found time to research and write. He published a translation of Immanuel's *Regimental War Game* as well as a translation of a foreign article on European artillery, entitled "The French and German Field Artillery: A Comparison" by Lt. Gen. H. Rohne. He next wrote an article that focused on desertions in the U.S. Army, looking at the problem—characteristically—from the enlisted man's point of view. In "Desertions and the Enlistment Oath" he argued that because desertions "have reached an enormous figure in the last few years," the army had to pay more attention to the psychological motivations of new recruits. Krueger argued that many desertions originated at the very beginning of the soldier's army career: the enlistment oath. According to Krueger, an enlisted man had to take the oath of enlistment in a recruiting office, "the interior of which is usually as cheerless and unprepossessing as the exterior, and, after the preliminary matters, the physical examination, etc., are settled, the oath is administered without ceremony, without due solemnity, and in a perfunctory manner." In short, the current enlistment oath, Krueger continued, is "meaningless." "Under these circumstances," he asked, "how can we expect the enlisted man to regard the profession of arms as a noble one, how can we expect him to regard the oath of enlistment as a sacred pledge, and his service to his country as a sacred duty?"[11]

Instead of making the enlistment oath a perfunctory component of enlistment, Krueger believed that the army needed to utilize it as an indoctrination device and should look to other organizations for ideas on how to make the oath a symbol of a recruit's commitment to the army and his country. Specifically looking at organized religion, he argued that humans are most easily "reached" through the sense of vision:

> The early religions recognized this fact; they recognized that the multitude could be reached through the sense of sight better than though [*sic*] any other agency, and their worship was adapted accordingly. The creeds, in which argument was substituted for outward forms, appealed to the highly intelligent, to the intellectual classes, while those retaining all outward forms, pomp and ceremony, the symbolisms of early religions, appeal to the masses and also to a great many of the more intelligent. The power of ritual and ceremony cannot be over-estimated.

In other words, to stem the tide of an increasing number of desertions, the army had to start adopting some of the techniques and pageantry of religious and secret orders, because, he reasoned, the oath must be worthy of the vocation. "Should not the man who at any moment might have to lay down his life for his country be initiated, be sworn in with due solemnity, with proper ceremony?" he asked. "Would not the solemnity attending such initiation (enlistment) cause the oath to stand out more clearly in all its sacredness, and would not the oath be regarded with more reverence than is now the case where it is an oath in many instances simply because a penalty is provided for its violation? Surely it would." Simply put, Krueger argued that an enlisted man was not likely to desert if he were convinced that his duty in the army was worthy of his utmost attention and commitment *through* a ceremony rich with tradition, symbolism, and solemnity. "Would not this ceremony make every man taking the oath feel that he was actually joining something; would not his innermost being feel a thrill when he places his hand on the folds of the glorious emblem of our country and swears to defend that flag even unto death?"[12] Clearly, Krueger failed to analyze and come to terms with the complex mix of reasons why men desert their military units, offering one solution. Within a short time of completing this article, Krueger embarked on his largest written work: the translation of Wilhelm Balck's two-volume tactical manual.[13] Balck's manual is an important work that attempted to come to terms—as did the U.S. Army's *Infantry Drill Regulations, 1911*—with the lethality of defensive firepower in such wars as the American Civil War, the Crimean War, and the Russo-Japanese War. After first stating that "tactics is psychology," Balck—who commanded a German division during World War I—acknowledged that human spirit would no longer be sufficient in the twentieth century: "The self-sacrificing spirit and firmly rooted discipline of the troops found an insurmountable obstacle in the rapid fire of unshaken infantry. The war experiences of our regiments show that bullets quickly write a new tactics, demolish superannuated formations and create new ones." Balck stressed the psychological dimension of war because of the fear on the part of many military leaders that the end of close-order formations would also lead to the end of discipline within the ranks of the common soldier while facing an increasingly deadly battlefield. With this in mind, Balck warned his readers that "a doctrine of tactics which does not properly appreciate the psychological element stagnates in lifeless pedantry."[14] However, Balck moved beyond just an emphasis on élan and the human element and urged armies to adopt open-ordered tactics, reserving close-order formations for training and drill. In fact, he argued that the entire attack should be carried out in a skirmish line:

> In extended order, infantry can most easily surmount obstacles, cross difficult terrain, and take the fullest advantage of the accidents of the ground, as cover against hostile fire and as rifle rests. In extended order, infantry is, moreover, able to develop its fire power most effectively, while at the same time offering the smallest possible targets to the hostile projectiles. Thus the *skirmish line* is the principal combat formation of infantry; by means of it a combat is initiated and carried through to the end.[15]

Krueger's translation of Balck's two-volume *Tactics* was timely, for it appeared in the same year as the publication of the army's important *Infantry Drill Regulations, 1911*. There were many parallels between the two, and *Tactics* reinforced the changing state of tactics as represented in the drill regulations. Both manuals stressed the employment of infantry in extended order and expected unit commanders as well as individual soldiers to act with considerable freedom and initiative. Predetermined and prescribed formations, rigidly carried out despite circumstances, were discouraged. In both systems, drill was used primarily as a technique to instill discipline and the basics of tactics and weaponry.[16]

With the publication of the translation of Balck's *Tactics*, Krueger's reputation as an expert tactician began to take shape. However, Krueger found the writing process taxing. In fact, he thought that with the publication of *Tactics*, his translating career was over. Unless he was "forced or driven to it," Krueger wrote to Brabson, he would not undertake such a project, for the gain was "scarcely worth the trouble."[17]

In October 1911, Krueger learned that in six months' time he would be relieved of his teaching responsibilities at the Army Service Schools. Until the United States entered World War I, he remained in the eastern half of the United States, continuing his role, in various ways, as an instructor for the army. He was assigned to the 3d Infantry Regiment and transferred to Madison Barracks, New York, where his ordinary duties were punctuated with an assignment as the aide-de-camp for the military attachés of the Connecticut Maneuver Campaign of 10–19 August 1912.[18]

The Mexican Border and World War I

With the outbreak of World War I, the War Department asked Krueger to become an observer with the German Army. He could not, however, accept the position. Grace Norvell, Krueger's mother-in-law, had moved in with the couple. Consequently, the Kruegers could not have afforded the added expense of relocating to Berlin.[19]

Instead, the U.S. Army sent Krueger to the 10th Infantry of the Pennsylvania National Guard as an inspector-instructor in 1914 and two years later promoted him to captain. His time with the 10th Infantry was not all routine training, however, especially after tension between the United States and Mexico rose when Gen. Jacinto B. Treviño warned that if Gen. John J. Pershing's troops advanced farther south into Mexico, his forces would attack American troops. Pershing bluntly replied that under no circumstances would he or his army yield to Treviño's demands. With tensions strained, it became obvious to all observers that the American forces along the Mexican border would be inadequate in the event of a war. President Woodrow Wilson then ordered the National Guard into federal service on 18 June 1916 to support Pershing. The next day, National Guard units began assembling all over the United States, preparing for the move to the Southwest. Since no Guardsmen ever fought against any Mexican troops, they spent most of their time training, marching, and honing their marksmanship. Finally, in February 1917, the Guard started to return home after some seven months of duty. Krueger remained with the national militia with posts in Pennsylvania, Alabama, West Virginia, and Washington, D.C. He helped the Guard with a wide variety of tasks—for example, assisting with setting up campsites, railroad construction, securing requisitions, and establishing an officers' school at the University of Pittsburgh. "Everything," he wrote, "that is humanly possible to foresee has been done by myself by making others get busy."[20]

His experience with the militia, in combination with the outbreak of World War I in Europe, led Krueger, along with many others, to closely examine the state of U.S. military preparedness. After lengthy reflection, he did not like what he saw. In attempting to reconcile the problems of modern warfare as outlined in *Tactics* and the American military tradition, Krueger published an article in the March 1917 issue of *Infantry Journal*, entitled "Preparedness." In this seven-page article, Krueger looked at what type of military system the United States should adopt. He rejected proposals to adopt a Swiss-type military system with its reliance on citizen soldiers, an issue that was much debated within the U.S. Army. Instead, Krueger resurrected arguments first introduced by Emory Upton in the late nineteenth-century U.S. Army, specifically denigrating the competency of the citizen soldier: "The trouble is that our people still believe, in spite of the handwriting on the wall, that military amateurs are practically as good as professionals.... This is at the root of all our military problems. This belief must be eradicated before we can hope to have anything in the way of real preparedness."[21]

Krueger advocated a national conscription of 125,000 men per year, with each new conscript serving for two years, giving the army a strength of 250,000 men. After serving two years with "the colors," each young man would "pass to the 1st Reserve, in which he would remain three years, then to the 2d Reserve, where he would remain for two years, thus completing his seven years' period of service. While he is in the 1st Reserve, he would be required to report each year for one month of training. While in the 2d Reserve, he would be required to report each year for fifteen days of training."[22]

Krueger's article did not have much to say about the state of the U.S. officer corps. He simply advised that any soldier could take an examination for a commission as a second lieutenant after his two-year term of service with the regular army. The individual could either serve in the regular army or with the National Reserve. With the Reserve, the officer would follow a scheduled series of promotions. If electing to pursue a career as an officer in the regular army, the newly commissioned officer "would of course rise from grade to grade practically as is now the case."[23]

Krueger was thus an Uptonian in regard to the crucial issue of military preparedness. In several important ways, Krueger was even more Uptonian than other, more notable army leaders. Whereas some envisioned important contributions the citizen soldier could make, Krueger, in contrast, saw none. While not criticizing explicitly the concept of democracy or any American institution, Krueger nevertheless believed that age-old American concepts of the citizen soldier were simply unable to defend the United States adequately. Only through conscription and a two-tiered reserve system did Krueger believe that the country could prepare itself for a major European-style war.[24] In his opinion, the nation should not adopt universal training (using the regular army to instruct citizen soldiers) but universal service (using conscription so that, in effect, all citizens get regular army training). Furthermore, he believed that his system was not at all antagonistic to democracy. In fact, it was more in line with democratic principles than the contemporary one. Attempting to square his plan with the current American system, Krueger argued in a lecture at the Army Service Schools that

> in conclusion it might be well to point out that Germany's strength does not rest upon the organization of its army, although that has been and still is a model for its friends as well as for its foes, but upon its military system, universal service, abhorred by republics, but nevertheless the most democratic system imaginable. Universal service is Germany's greatest and best safeguard against war, for in it every class of society suffers and has its pursuits interfered with. High and low, rich and poor, noblemen and peasant, priest and layman, all must serve, and no one is excused. The Germans are, indeed, a "Nation in arms," and it is safe to say that, should war come, as it surely will, Germany will give a good account of herself.[25]

As much as he tried, however, Krueger could not persuade many Americans that universal service was compatible with American values. Like those Uptonians before and after him, Krueger was not sensitive to the underlying suspicions that Americans had toward conscription and the encroachment of the military into U.S. society. Instead, his attempt to change American values to fulfill military needs demonstrated how out of touch the Uptonian approach to military policy actually was.[26]

Continued work with the militia as a mustering officer only reinforced his position on the American system of preparedness, though his association with the National Guard would provide him with the promotion he so desperately wanted. Four days before President Wilson received a declaration of war precipitating the nation's entry into World War I, a conflicted Krueger wrote to his friend Fay Brabson that he hoped "that the proposed scheme for universal SERVICE (remember I'm an opponent of universal training) will go through for that in my opinion is the best thing for the country, though it will mean that I shall not have the honor of being colonel of the volunteer outfit."[27]

Whatever his personal views regarding the citizen soldier, Krueger was enough of a professional to work within the system. Shortly after the United States entered World War I, Krueger worked in the Bureau of Military Affairs along with Brabson. The two labored hard on the problem of "militia conversion," making citizen soldiers into warriors who were fit for overseas duty. The task taxed and frustrated Krueger, who suspected political machinations and weak leadership within the bureau wasted his efforts.[28]

Krueger remained in the Bureau of Military Affairs through the summer of 1917, unsure of what the future held for him. For a time he thought he would be attending the Army War College, but the army decided to send Krueger to Camp Zachary Taylor in Kentucky as the 84th National Guard Division's G-3 (operations) officer.[29]

During his stint as G-3 of the 84th Division, Krueger returned to translating foreign military manuals, this time publishing Julius K. L. Mertens's *Tactics and Technique of River Crossings*. "The translator," Krueger wrote in his preface, "had hoped to retire from the field after completing Volumes I and II of Balck's *Tactics*, but a request made to him to give another tactical work to our army, coupled with the worth of the subject matter and its great importance in the present world war, prompted him to reconsider his decision."[30] The Army Corps of Engineers had requested the work with the hope that it would be of assistance in World War I.

In November 1917, at the same time the division started training exercises, Krueger, now a temporary major (as of 5 August 1917), became its acting chief of staff. He remained so until February 1918, when he received a transfer overseas to attend the American Expeditionary Forces (AEF) General Staff School in Langres, France. The leader of the AEF, Gen. John J. Pershing, and his staff established the school to instruct and bring up to date many officers who never had any formal or specific staff training. In practice, even officers who graduated from the schools at Fort Leavenworth often attended Langres, because the specific curriculum between the two schools differed slightly. Whereas the Infantry and Cavalry School and the Army Staff College provided foundational and broad tactical, operational, and staff instruction, Langres prepared its graduates with specific and practical knowledge they would use immediately upon graduation. In the end, Langres proved successful in training American officers for the staff and combat duties that would soon face them.[31]

In May 1918, Krueger and the other officers at Langres learned that any soldier whose division was not under orders to make the trip to France was to return to the United States. Since the 84th Division was still stateside, Krueger therefore would have to go back to its base, now located at Camp Sherman, Ohio. The War Department, however, kept Krueger in France with the AEF by transferring him in June to the 26th Infantry Division, the New England National Guard division. Krueger's new division was in the vicinity of the Chemin des Dames, near Toul, where it had been since early March. The division had participated in its first battle on 20 April, repulsing a German assault after suffering 669 casualties. The months of May and June were relatively quiet for the New Englanders, except for one German raid. Krueger served for a time as the division's operations officer and earned a temporary promotion to lieutenant colonel. During his time as G-3, Krueger kept in close daily contact with the various divisional units. Additionally, he made frequent personal inspections of the front-line troops. In the last few days of June, the division left the Chemin des Dames sector and headed to the northwest of Château-Thierry, where it was to take part in the Allied Aisne-Marne offensive.[32]

Krueger, however, would not take part in the offensive in any meaningful capacity. Rumors around AEF headquarters and throughout the American lines pointed to French unhappiness with Krueger's presence with Allied forces. According to several sources, the French distrusted Krueger because he was German born. Consequently, the French government requested that he be sent back to the United States. Apparently responding to French pressure, the AEF shipped Krueger home to be reunited with the 84th Infantry Division at Camp Sherman, Ohio. Missing out on the opportunity to contribute directly to the war effort disappointed Krueger, but he concluded that things could be worse for him. Writing to a friend with the AEF, Krueger commented, "I would of course be glad to be with you, but then I'm rather glad not to be tied down at the Staff College."[33]

Krueger and the men of the 84th Infantry believed they would never get to France. Unexpectedly, in August 1918, orders came to prepare for the movement overseas. Thus Krueger was "quietly returned" to France without the French government's knowledge. Krueger expressed mixed feelings about the new posting: "My own case," he wrote in the autumn of 1918, "is not particularly desirable. … Of course I'd like … to be where there is something doing and feel perfectly capable to keep in the doing but don't know anyone who wants me badly enough to ask for me. … Anyway I hope I'll get somewhere where they are doing things."[34]

Krueger again did not have to wait very long, for on 17 October 1918 the AEF ordered him to report for duty with the Tank Corps as its chief of staff. He quickly found the job both rewarding and frustrating. Because the Tank Corps was a new branch, Krueger believed that it could provide an avenue for promotion and advancement. However, as the chief of staff, he was tied to his desk for most of the day, which he did not particularly enjoy. He wrote to his friend Fay Brabson,

> I was ordered up here as Chief of Staff, GHQ Tank Corps, a pretty big job, full of possibilities, but also involving a lot of desk work, which, as you know, I don't like. Should the war continue the Tank Corps would offer a dandy field for anyone, but as it is, anyone coming in would of course not be able to start at the top.… All the ranking officers in the T.C. [Tank Corps] are youngsters—years our juniors and older more experienced ones are badly needed of course. There is nothing much in it for a G.S. [General Staff]

> officer aside from the C. of S. [chief of staff], as far as rank is concerned, so a transfer to the T.C. is the only thing that offers a chance for promotion.[35]

Krueger's hopes for promotion with the Tank Corps evaporated with the announcement of an armistice in the early days of November. On 10 November 1918, one day before the Germans signed the cease-fire, the AEF reassigned Krueger to the Army Service School at Langres for teaching duty. Within a few months he again was transferred, and for the next several months Krueger bounced from job to job. On 4 January 1919, he joined the VI U.S. Corps as its G-3 officer, pleased with his new job. "Hope they leave me there for a while," he wrote shortly before assuming this new post, "at least long enough to enable me to make good."[36]

"They" did not. The War Department disbanded the VI Corps that April. Krueger next made a lateral move to the IV U.S. Corps and received the temporary rank of colonel. He stayed with the corps until 11 May, when it too was terminated. Although he spent only five short months as the operations officer with a corps, Krueger was convinced that he had finally found his niche. "My work as G-3 of a corps is interesting and suits me tip top. As long as we keep a large force over here, I would like to stay for the experiences. For it is the only army that I've ever seen, and perhaps ever will see. Desk work does not appeal to me very much."[37]

For Krueger as well as the rest of the AEF, the Great War was over. Like many of his colleagues, Krueger had advanced rapidly in wartime rank, but on 30 June 1920, he reverted back to his permanent rank of captain. The following day, he received the permanent rank of major. For his service in the war, Krueger earned the Distinguished Service Medal in 1919.[38]

Major Krueger felt uncertain about the next few years. Like many who had fought in the war, he asked questions concerning the future of the nation as well as his own. Specifically, he wondered if America had learned the lessons he attempted to teach in his "Preparedness" article of 1917:

> No one seems to know what will happen to the old regular army, and I don't care to guess. I wonder if we will be foolish enough to go back to our old defenselessness—I hope not. It will all depend very largely upon what visions our returning legions take home with them. We of the army, … I'm afraid, have mighty little influence one way or another, though we ought to be heard. We are all too apt to live in the past and … having won most people will be inclined to say 'Look what we accomplished'—'we licked them after raising a splendid army in a short time; what we've done once we

> can do again and therefore why have any large measure of preparedness?' But I hope for the best and that the good sense of our people will prevail over hysteria.

Krueger, in short, believed that the officer corps of the U.S. Army had a responsibility to prevent the nation from slipping back into complacency and reliance on its citizen soldiers for national defense.

The years between 1903 and 1920 constituted an important period in Krueger's professional life, setting in motion the patterns that would influence his career within the army. He spent his early years as an officer at Fort Leavenworth during a time when it was the focal point of the army's attempts to come to terms with modern industrial warfare. Through his years as a student, instructor, and translator/author, Krueger established himself as one of the army's tactical leaders and best-educated officers.[39] His work contributed to official army doctrine, as established in *Field Service Regulations, 1911*. Furthermore, he learned at the Infantry and Cavalry School and Army Service School the operations of the modern army staff. Fort Leavenworth graduates would apply their knowledge and make "significant contributions," as one historian has commented, during World War I.[40]

During the war itself, Krueger gained valuable experience in staff work, preferring a position as an operations officer or chief of staff of a corps headquarters. The war, moreover, served only to reinforce his position on the capability of the United States when it relied on its militia for national defense. In order to be properly prepared, Krueger asserted that the nation needed to adopt universal service. Through advancing such arguments, which were strongly at odds with American culture and values, Krueger demonstrated how out of touch members of the U.S. Army could be when formulating U.S. military policy. Finally, Krueger's personality as an officer was firmly established during this time. He was, above all, ambitious and energetic. He continually sought avenues for promotion and advancement. Whatever his particular position, everyone agreed that he was hard-working and determined. In fact, some believed that he pushed himself and his staff too hard. All of his experiences at Fort Leavenworth and in World War I were but a beginning. Throughout the next two decades, Krueger would advance rapidly to the top of the army leadership based on the attributes and expertise he demonstrated at this early stage of his career.

Chapter 3

Preparation for High Command, 1920–1938

Following the close of World War I, Walter Krueger and the rest of the U.S. Army returned home to an uncertain future. The nation was retreating from the idealism of the Progressive era and President Woodrow Wilson's international crusade to bring democracy to the world. This return to "normalcy" also included an antimilitaristic spirit. Throughout the 1920s and 1930s, the nation's anti-idealistic mentality, pacifist inclination, memories of the horrors and futility of the so-called Great War, and the Great Depression all worked against the military's efforts to prepare for future wars by denying it badly needed funds and reducing its numbers to an authorized peacetime strength of 280,000 men, only a small fraction of its wartime peak.[1]

While this rejection of all things military must have surely disheartened many (if not all) officers as they witnessed their prospects for promotions dwindle, Krueger rode through the hard times with hard work and determination, and, consequently, he steadily rose in both responsibility and rank. He found his avenue for advancement, as he had earlier in his career, through education. Building on his reputation as a tactical expert, Krueger attended and then taught at both the navy and army's senior military schools—the Naval and Army War Colleges. As the country moved through the 1920s and 1930s and approached World War II, he moved from an academic position to one of actually preparing the nation for war through his posting to the Army War Plans Division of the War Department General Staff. The period saw Krueger's rise from an instructor at one of the army's branch schools to brigadier general in charge of charting the army's course in future conflicts.

From the vantage point of the summer of 1919, Krueger—like the army he served—faced doubt and uncertainty. As the United States turned toward the postwar period, it had little need for its army or, for that matter, an officer whose areas of expertise were tactics and corps operations. Consequently, Krueger struggled to find his own niche with the ranks. After returning to the United States on 22 June 1919, Krueger, with a tinge of sarcasm, told a friend that he had been "'specially' selected" to teach at the Infantry School at Camp

Benning, Georgia. He was appointed no doubt for his tactical expertise, but to him it was a puzzle: "Why I was picked out for that is a mystery to me—but I suppose no one else wanted the job." If forced to teach again—a prospect that did not at all please him—he would have preferred a job that utilized his recent experiences as corps operations officer (G-3), perhaps at the Army Service Schools at Fort Leavenworth, Kansas. "I did not want to go to school again nor to instruct in anything," he complained, "but would have preferred Leavenworth to any other, because I'm at least conversant—I think—with staff work." Fortunately for Krueger, he remained at Camp Benning only for a year.[2]

Krueger's next assignment led him to Camp Funston, Kansas, to command the 55th Infantry Regiment. He soon learned that the army had selected him to attend the Army War College in Washington, D.C.[3]

The Army War College instituted several changes for Krueger's class of 1921 in lieu of the perceived deficiencies of the American officer in the First World War. The postwar Army War College sought to provide a comprehensive approach to the problem of modern industrial warfare. Above all, it wanted to teach the prospective leaders of the army that wars no longer could be won through the mobilization of just the army. Now, a nation had to prepare its industry, agriculture sector, manpower, and transportation as well. At the behest of the new director of the War Plans Division, Brig. Gen. William G. Haan, Maj. Gen. James W. McAndrew—the first commandant after World War I—added a new dimension to the curriculum beyond just an emphasis on general staff duties. Haan wanted the college to address the subject of command more thoroughly than it had been doing. He further suggested that the line separating the functions of command and General Staff duties should be clearly delineated and explored. McAndrew, therefore, added a two-month period of study entitled the "Command Course."[4]

Many officers who attended the Army War College found the curriculum difficult and challenging. Ten members of the class of 1920 did not finish—more than 11 percent of the entire class. In Krueger's class, two did not graduate, and not all who completed the course did so with good grades. Upon graduating, students would be recommended for service based on the quality of their work. Three categories of service were prescribed for graduates: high command, General Staff duties, and special qualifications. Most were placed in one of the departments of the General Staff, such as the Operations or Personnel Divisions. Krueger's name appeared on a short list of officers who earned a spot on both the high command and on the General Staff lists. In addition, he was also recommended to become an instructor at the college.

In all, the class of 1921 was a successful one. Thirty-one of the eighty-seven students became general officers by 1936.[5]

Krueger found his year at the Army War College difficult but rewarding. "The work at the [General] Staff College," he wrote to Fay Brabson, "is intensely interesting and requires an immense lot of work on the part of anyone sufficiently interested in the subject matter to put his best into it." Despite the workload, he still had time to ponder what the future might hold for him, and by March 1921, he remained—as he was in 1919—pessimistic. He feared that his promotion to permanent lieutenant colonel would be delayed because of the U.S. Senate's failure to confirm a list of general officers. The next month, however, the Senate accepted a new list of general officers, thereby creating a vacancy for Krueger's promotion.[6]

Promotion was not the only issue that concerned Krueger; so too did the assignment process. Based on his experience, he suspected that he would either remain at the War College or be transferred to another school as an instructor. Krueger had had enough of teaching. He considered himself first and foremost a soldier and, in particular, wanted to return to a corps headquarters. "As to my fortunes upon completing the course—I have no idea," he wrote to Brabson while still a student. "My personal preference is of course to go to a corps area headquarters—but, although I have no reason to believe that I have done well so far in the course—I have no means of knowing how and on what basis selections for various details are made. Therefore—everything is in the lap of the God's [*sic*] and aside from my repugnance against any work to make me an instructor any where, I shall not meddle with my destiny."[7]

Unfortunately for Krueger, his next assignment was as an instructor at the Army War College, which was still in the midst of change after restarting in the wake of World War I. He taught the "Art of Command" course as well as others, contributing lectures on a variety of subjects. His views in these lectures were shaped, in part, by a four-month trip he made to Germany in early 1922 after he was transferred to the college's Historical Section. He was one of the first Americans provided admission to the German War Archives after the war. As a result of this access, several of his lectures dealt with various aspects of the German loss in the war.[8]

Through these lectures, Krueger developed several themes that became hallmarks of his own ideas about command. The first examined war from a broad national perspective. Krueger believed that to wage a successful war, a nation had to be unified. His ideas appear to have been largely shaped by an examination of Germany's performance during the war. In his 1922 lecture titled "Observations and Reflections on the Situation in Germany," he argued that the sources of Germany's defeat could be found in the deep class antagonisms between the "governing classes" and the working classes. According to Krueger, while the governing classes prospered because of the industrial revolution, the same types of benefits did not extend to the masses. In time, the asymmetrical distribution of wealth and privileges created deep social unrest, and the working classes eventually came to resent bitterly those who governed, including the military. The Great War only exacerbated these social tensions. As the war dragged on, the working classes, tired of the bloody war and wretched living conditions, revolted against the upper classes in the fall of 1918, because they came to recognize that Germany had begun the war for economic reasons—reasons that only benefited the wealthy. Krueger therefore believed that national unity was important for any nation that resorted to war, and it was a theme that he—as well as many of his generation—repeated numerous times and in numerous different venues throughout the interwar period.[9]

Krueger would maintain his concern for national harmony throughout his career, especially when he came into a position in which he could influence and shape U.S. national security policy, first as executive officer of the War Plans Division (WPD) and then as assistant chief of staff of the WPD. In a review of Capt. William S. Pye's manuscript entitled "Joint Army and Navy Operations, Part I," for example, Krueger—who at the time worked at the WPD—wrote that

> to my mind the state policy of a nation is essentially a crystallization or summation—usually wholly subconscious so far as the mass of people is concerned—of their hopes and aspirations. ... If the aims and aspirations of a people are not commensurate with the physical power it can bring to bear against an opponent, it is sure to be defeated. In other words, there must be a harmonious balance between the aims of a people and its power to attain those aims. To my mind nothing more clearly demonstrates this principle than Germany's example in the late war.[10]

The next major theme Krueger developed as an instructor at the Army War College was the importance of having a decentralized command system during times of war. Krueger believed that the United States had much to learn from Germany's performance in the recent war. Specifically, the German military system—while not acting in harmony with a majority of Germans—nevertheless received high marks for its decentralized command system. "Its most admirable feature was undoubtedly decentralization of effort," Krueger argued in his lecture entitled "Military System of the German Empire." "Very wide decentralization was the rule in every branch of the system, the Germans fully appreciating that organization consists after all of nothing but the distribution of labor and that, to insure adequate results, labor must be suitably distributed, responsibility for its performance must be fixed, and power commensurate with that responsibility must be allotted."[11]

Decentralization should not just reside in the Ministry of War and the General Staff but in the lower command echelons as well. In a WPD conference held at the Army War College on 12 January 1922, Krueger suggested that in writing a "basic war plan," commanders in the field must be given wide latitude to formulate operational and tactical plans to fulfill their missions. "Needless to say," Krueger stated, "the Basic Plan must indicate the general mission as well as the mission of the various forces employed, in sufficient detail to enable widely separated forces to cooperate directly or indirectly toward the attainment of the object of the war. But the plan must not attempt to prescribe the execution of the operations determined upon."[12]

Once a nation entered a conflict unified and with a decentralized command structure, Krueger believed that the only course was direct offensive action with the intent of annihilating the enemy forces. Hannibal, the "Father of Strategy," he argued, offered some of the best examples of offensive action:

> Mere victory was not sufficient for Hannibal; he desired annihilation. That is why he always attacked his opponent in flank and rear and invariably sought to cut off his retreat. His tactical handling of troops—especially of cavalry—was superb, his Cannae a masterpiece of tactics. He thoroughly understood that the offensive alone leads to decisive success and that rapidity, activity and surprise are its vital elements. While his opponents constantly violated the principles of economy of forces, superiority and cooperation, he kept his forces in hand and invariably assured himself the superiority at the decisive point.[13]

Although emphasizing offensive action for the purposes of annihilating the enemy, Krueger's studies led him to conclude that a successful leader applies these principles in a flexible manner. In his only lecture on military operations at the Army War College, Krueger stressed that "the principles of war are in themselves as simple and easily comprehended as they are difficult of application and execution. That they are immutable is a hackneyed phrase accepted as irrefutable." Using the well-known battle of Cannae (216 B.C.), Krueger argued that Hannibal, in his defeat of the Romans, violated many of the principles of war:

> A perfect, annihilating battle had been fought, remarkable chiefly because, contrary to all theory, it had been won by an inferior over a superior force. "A concentric maneuver is improper for the weaker force," says Clausewitz; "it must not attempt an envelopment on both flanks, simultaneously," says Napoleon. Hannibal, however, violated both maxims and won, because he was opposed by a Varro and was clever enough to take advantage of the opportunity that Fortune had placed in his hands. Hannibal's tactics at the battle Cannae are superb, both in conception and execution, constituting a masterpiece of which military history furnishes but few equal and no superior examples.[14]

While endeavoring to annihilate their enemy, commanders needed to remain flexible with their plans—even if it meant violating widely held military principles.

The final major theme Krueger developed in his year of lecturing at the Army War College was always to take into account the "human factor" in war. He was impressed by the ways in which Hannibal cared for the well-being of his men. No doubt linking his own experience in Cuba and the Philippines as an enlisted man with his study of history, Krueger stressed that in taking care of his men, Hannibal was able to forge an army that defeated a numerically superior force. "His knowledge of human nature and the power he wielded over men were marvelous and are shown by his incomparable control over an army knit together neither by ties of race, religion nor love of country, an army which not even in the worst of times mutinied against him. He cared for their wants—his supply system being always excellent—[and] shared their privations."[15]

Through formulating these five themes—the importance of national, governmental, and military policy convergence during war; the importance of a decentralized command; the importance of pursuing a strategy of annihilation through vigorous offensive action; the importance of having flexible war plans; and the importance of acknowledging the "human factor"—as well as others, Krueger earned a reputation as a keen observer of military issues. In fact, the General Staff decided that Krueger's lectures on Germany were so useful that they should be reproduced and sent to all general officers, the General Staff, and the General Service Schools.[16] It should be noted that Krueger reflected many of the ideas that were circulating throughout the army during the interwar period and were not necessarily new or original. However, he presented his arguments coherently, in a well-presented, and—if giving his ideas orally—forceful manner. In other words, he was an articulate exponent of the conventional wisdom. It was on this basis, as opposed to any new or original body of ideas, that Krueger earned his reputation as a military intellectual.[17]

Before the academic year ended, the assistant chief of staff of the War Plans Division, Brig. Gen. Briant H. Wells, requested Krueger's services. Wells had worked with Krueger during World War I in the IV Corps. Undoubtedly, Krueger's performance as the corps's operations officer had caught the eye of Wells, who was then the corps's chief of staff.[18]

Shortly after his arrival at WPD, Krueger traveled to several corps areas to gather information on two war plans. Wells selected Krueger to work on Special Plan Blue, a mobilization plan for the United States in the event of an internal emergency, and Special Plan Green, in the event of a war against Mexico. Krueger had experience with Special Plan Blue. He worked on a similar plan—War Plan White—as a student at the Army War College.[19]

In addition to developing Special Plan Blue, Krueger and Lt. Col. Asa L. Singleton, also of WPD, traveled to the Panama Canal Zone to gather information on the readiness of the canal's defenses through observing joint army and navy exercises. Leaving New York on 15 January 1923, they spent about one month in Panama, and in late April 1923, Krueger prepared a report of his findings. His recommendations for improving the defenses of the Panama Canal Zone included such topics as mine equipment and bombproof shelters.[20]

Upon his return to the United States, Krueger was assigned to the Joint Army and Navy Planning Committee (JPC), which was created by the Joint Army and Navy Board (JB). Formed in 1903 by the Secretary of the Navy and the Secretary of War, the Joint Board promoted interservice cooperation and coordination and dealt mainly with developing various war plans. Because the board was composed of the chief of staff, the deputy chief of staff, the chief of the War Plans Division, the chief and assistant chief of Naval Operations, and the director of the War Plans Division, its members found it difficult to work at their normal, high-level positions while also coordinating army-navy plans. Consequently, the Joint Board established the Joint Planning Committee—composed of at least three officers from WPD and three officers from the War Plans Division of the Office of the Chief of Naval Operations.[21]

The JPC conducted research and wrote studies at the request of the JB as well as initiated studies on its own. To create a spirit of cooperation and coordination between the two services, the committee was informal. It met approximately once a week and reached its decisions through consensus. Through their association with the committee, officers such as Walter Krueger gained firsthand knowledge of interservice issues of command and operations. Army officers, for instance, received valuable insight into the strengths and weaknesses of naval operations, including terminology and modes of operation. Krueger not only obtained such knowledge during his time with the JPC but met several naval officers with whom he would work during World War II.[22]

During his tenure on the JPC, Krueger continued to help plan the defense of the Panama Canal. In addition, he contributed to War Plan Tan (Cuba) and War Plan Orange (Japan). Krueger's association with War Plan Orange (WPO) turned out to be an important part of his interwar education, containing an analysis of the strengths and weaknesses of Imperial Japan. Krueger's involvement in WPO exposed him to many facets of campaign planning. Among the more important aspects of the plan, the "estimate of the situation" stood out as particularly valuable. In this section, planners attempted "to understand the reasons for taking any action specified in the plan." The plan also included the number and types of forces to be used in the operation, specific objectives for the forces to achieve, and a time line "by which the various measures proposed in the Basic Plan are to be completed."[23]

Throughout the 1920s and 1930s, the WPD continually revised its war plans, including WPO, as the international and domestic environments changed. The joint-planning process was highly political, with interservice and intraservice factions bargaining to inject their particular views in the final draft. By the time Krueger joined the committee, it was again assessing its plans for a war against Japan and, in fact, was already formulating an estimate of the enemy. In the event of a war with Japan, the JPC predicted, the United States would need to establish a strong naval force in the western Pacific Ocean before Japan could be defeated. The JPC also believed that the best route for an American offensive was through the Japanese Mandated Islands. Krueger contributed to this estimate and helped write several drafts of the war plan before the final was accepted by the JB on 15 August 1924. It held an optimistic view, boldly avowing that the United States would take immediate offensive action in the event of war. Krueger and the other authors divided the war into three phases. Phase One covered the initial period of war, during which the Japanese were expected to overrun U.S. territory in the Western Pacific, including parts of the Philippines. The second phase anticipated the time when the United States would deploy its forces across the Pacific Ocean in preparation for Phase Three. Once its forces were established in the Western Pacific, the United States would force Japan into capitulation through an air and naval blockade. While the planners believed the war would be "a long war," overall, they stressed aggressive, offensive action: "Operations should be conducted with boldness from the earliest stage of the war and the initiative sought in all operations."[24] WPO 1924 has been described justly as unrealistic. For instance, it called for an expeditionary force of 50,000 troops to arrive in Oahu, Hawaii, by D+10 and then leave the Hawaiian Islands by D+14. Although its logic might have been sound—"it being understood that the promptest possible reinforcement of Manila Bay is of the greatest military and naval importance"[25]—the force Krueger and the other planners earmarked for embarkation from the West Coast on the first day of war represented one-third of the entire U.S. Army. Indeed WP0 1924 was—as one historian of WPO suggests—"really more a statement of hopes than a realistic appraisal of what could be done."[26]

The unrealistic projections of WPO 1924 reflect the acute bureaucratic wrangling between the navy and army in the early 1920s over military strategy in the Pacific as well as the reality of American politics. For WPO planners, the Philippine Islands were the center of U.S. strategic interests in the Far East, and they determined that Japanese forces would surely target the islands soon after the outbreak of any hostilities between the two countries. WPO correctly predicted that the Japanese would easily overrun the undermanned U.S. defenses there, due, in large part, to the provisions of the Washington Conference of 1921–1922. Political and military leaders, however, could not publicly admit that they would not be able to adequately defend American interests in the Philippines. In the 1920s, consequently, WPO began to reflect this political reality and, at the same time, ignored military fact by assuming that the U.S. forces stationed in the Philippines could withstand a Japanese attack (or at least hold on to Manila Bay until reinforcements arrived) to form a base from which future offensive operations would be launched. Furthermore, the navy firmly believed that the army garrison in the Philippines should hold out as long as possible, biding time for the navy to marshal its fleet. The army, for its part—especially Gen. Leonard Wood—rejected the navy's vision and called for the strengthening of the army's Philippine presence or an outright withdrawal from the islands. With all of these competing and—in several instances—contradictory requirements and missions, it is no wonder that Krueger and the rest of the WPO planners produced such an unsatisfactory document.[27]

Krueger also worked on the army's specific portion of the joint WPO—the Army Strategical Plan Orange. It too took an optimistic and unrealistic view of how the United States should respond in the face of a Japanese move against the Philippine Islands. It is difficult to fathom—given his earnest views on the importance of national harmony during wartime—that Krueger would endorse such a strategy in light of the fact that the United States clearly would not fund its military requirements. But he argued that the plan should not be taken as a final statement of army plans but instead should be viewed as a document to spur additional thinking and debate on the subject. He concluded,

"In my judgment the plan constitutes a suitable basis for development and I therefore submit it with the recommendation that it be approved."[28]

Nevertheless, Krueger acknowledged the weakness of the army plan, writing that "the Plan as submitted is consistent with the Joint Army and Navy Orange Plan approved by the Secretary of War and the Secretary of the Navy. Although a great amount of work was been given to its preparation, it contains no doubt many small errors and inconsistencies and perhaps a few large ones." Krueger's comments betray the degree to which the army itself approached the subject of war planning. Some at the time had argued that the army could only plan on the basis of concrete studies on mobilization from the various staffs in the army, specifically the operations (G-3) and logistics (G-4) sections. Only after such careful mobilization plans could the WPD then develop war plans. Another faction—which included Krueger—suggested that army plans like Army Strategical Plan Orange were "by no means final" but rather were "designed to form merely a basis for development."[29] Unfortunately, it is difficult to determine if, in fact, Krueger actually believed the bold and optimistic plans to race across the Pacific Ocean should form the basis of U.S. war planning. In light of his previous studies on German war effort in World War I, it is unlikely that he believed in the practical utility of such grandiose plans, based as they were on a major disconnect of military strategy that sought to quickly regain the Philippines and a national military policy based on limited military capabilities. Indeed, within nine years, Krueger would revisit this issue by arguing—along with other military leaders—that the United States needed to adopt more realistic national and military policies that included objectives much more in alignment with military capabilities.

In addition to working on WPO, Krueger took part in a wide variety of activities. For example, he returned periodically to the Army War College to lecture about miscellaneous topics, including a talk on the function of the War Plans Division. Moreover, he continued his work on plans for mobilization, traveling throughout various corps areas during September 1923. He also observed several military maneuvers. One such exercise attempted to demonstrate the Air Service's effectiveness against naval units by conducting bombing tests against several battleships off the coast of Cape Hatteras, North Carolina. In addition, Krueger traveled to Hawaii in March 1925 to observe joint army and navy maneuvers.[30]

Krueger's work with WPO and various army–navy–Air Service exercises provided a solid foundation for his next assignment. On 13 March 1925, at his own request, the army sent Krueger to the Naval War College. In the early 1920s the War Department, in an attempt to foster interservice cooperation and understanding, determined that the army should send officers to serve on navy staffs and that the navy should likewise send its officers to gain experience with army staffs. As part of this practice, WPD wanted these officers first to attend both the Army and Naval War Colleges. Army officers who went through such an education would eventually end up on the General Staff, specifically the War Plans Division.[31]

The Naval War College covered many of the same subjects—policy, strategy, command, and economics—as the Army War College. Like its army counterpart, the Naval War College also employed war games and problems, but unlike the Army War College, it used these pedagogical methods, in part, to study military situations from a joint army-navy perspective. Krueger and the other army officers detailed to Newport, Rhode Island, had to write several theses and participate in naval war games as well. Krueger, for instance, had to complete tactical problems involving a hypothetical war between Japan and the United States. In the first tactical problem, he had to locate a Japanese fleet "and bring it to decisive action in order to assure the safe operation of our convoys between Pearl Harbor, Guam, and Manila." Other problems had him take the position of a Japanese commander, who is instructed to "destroy the Blue [American] convoy, in order to immobilize the Blue Fleet." Overall, his year at Newport exposed Krueger to the specific issues involved in naval operations as well as the nature of joint operations.[32]

Krueger also had the opportunity to read, think, and write about the important issue of *command* in one of his Naval War College theses. To define the word, he used the analogy that command "is to military forces what the head is to the human body." He suggested that there were several functions of a military command. The first was to organize and prepare for combat the forces under the charge of the commander. "Organization alone," Krueger continued, "will not suffice, however, for the constituent elements of the military force will still lack the cohesion, skill and self-confidence necessary to enable them to function effectively alone or collectively in carrying out the will of the COMMAND. . . . Cohesion is produced by discipline, which may be defined as that subconscious obedience that is essential to all military control."[33]

But how exactly does one achieve discipline? Krueger maintained that it had to be earned by the commander from the soldiers under his care. Consequently, a wise officer had to skillfully employ a variety of incentives and rewards. The "best discipline has always been that which consisted largely of willing obedience resulting from personal pride, esprit de corps, sense of duty, loyalty to the commander, patriotism, or religious fanaticism," he wrote. "This kind of discipline is best taught by inculcating habits of obedience, self-control, and coordination; by meting out wise rewards and just punishments; by creating mutual confidence and esteem; and finally, by precept and example." In other words, officers had to think carefully about the ways in which they attempted to instill discipline. They had to move beyond just demanding it through "extremely harsh means" but rather develop it through positive reinforcement.[34]

In addition to discipline and cohesion, a commander had to, as his main objective, forge his troops into a sword, capable of decisive military action. For Krueger, training was the key to creating a formidable fighting unit: "To make a military force really effective, it must, like the sword-blade, acquire a sharp edge—skill, and a fine point—self-confidence. This, as in the case of cohesion, is the province of training. Without such training, organization, cohesion, and valor would be ineffective."[35]

The second function of command was to make sure that the whole organization functioned smoothly and effectively through indoctrination and training. Making clear references to the purpose of his Fort Leavenworth experience, Krueger argued that a commander needed to indoctrinate his staff with a "common language" to assure "uniformity of understanding." Krueger explained that: "Without DOCTRINE, supervision and coordination, teamwork and cooperation, and unity of action are difficult if not impossible. Doctrine knits all parts of the military force together in intellectual bonds, and assures that each part will work intelligently for the interests of the others and of the whole."[36]

The final three functions of a commander concerned administration and supply, planning, and execution of a battle plan. "To summarize," he wrote, "it may be said then that the functions of the COMMAND consist of organizing, training and indoctrination, administering and supplying, planning and executing. It performs these functions no matter how simple or complex; the dominant factor in it, the master mind, is that of a single individual, the commander. 'From him must flow the energy that wields the weapon, the enthusiasm that nerves the human mass, the organized military group, to the supreme effort in the battlefield.'"[37]

Having recognized and explored the principles of command, Krueger next addressed the attributes and characteristics of a successful commander: "So much for the theory of COMMAND in the abstract." He sought to "discover what the qualities are that have made commanders succeed and to endeavor to emulate them."[38]

Krueger suggested that the great commanders throughout history, such as Napoleon and Commodore Horatio Nelson, had "cool heads." Even in the most frantic of times, they resisted the temptation to become "over-excited." This mentality also extended to good times as well. A capable leader, in short, would never lead himself to "be intoxicated by good nor bewildered by bad news."[39]

A great commander also had a rare combination of boldness and prudence. Quoting Hans Delbrück, Krueger wrote that "no matter how recklessly he challenges fate again and again, he by no means rushes headlong and aimlessly into the unknown, but knows perfectly where he must call a halt, turns from the offensive to the defensive, takes the risk of the enemy attacking him in his turn and at the same time endeavors to supplement his victory through policy." He further elaborated that good leaders also have "decision and good sense." They possess the "ability to form a clear resolution without hesitation, and to put it into execution."[40] This particular attribute would become a hallmark of his time in the World War II, when his decisions attempted to mitigate what he and his staff perceived were his superior's unwarranted risks for no particular military benefit. Indeed, Krueger's leadership in World War II sought to strike a balance between Gen. Douglas MacArthur's sometimes emotional decisions and the U.S. Army's overall desire to conduct speedy military operations. It was this skill—developed in part while at the Naval War College—that served him well as commander of the Sixth U.S. Army and made him an extremely effective military commander.

Krueger further recognized that another important feature of command was unity. "Although COMMAND, as already stated, implies 'unity,' that is, the exclusive right or power to control the forces entrusted to it, something more is required in order that success may be assured, to wit, UNITY OF COMMAND, by which is meant the right or power of the COMMAND to control all the forces that can and must be made available for the purpose of attaining that success."[41] Even before attending the Naval War College, Krueger spent many hours thinking about the problems as well as the benefits of joint navy-army operations, and therefore it was natural that these ideas held a prominent role in his thesis. In fact, of the many topics he dealt with, the principle of unity of command was one of the most important. While a Naval War College student, Krueger articulated his differences with the War Department's 1921 nine principles of war as published in *War Department Training Regulations No. 10–5: Doctrines, Principles, and Methods*.[42] Specifically, he did not agree with the principle of cooperation, which was a form of command that did not of rely on a single joint commander but was, in the words of historian William Felix Atwater, "a form of command whereby neither the Army commander nor the Navy commander would be placed in an inferior position or be placed under the command of the other."[43] Command issues, therefore, would be settled by agreement and compromise between the two rather than by issuance of an order. Ostensibly for Krueger, the concept of cooperation was just too vague and was dependent on the various commanders involved who often had their own separate concerns and goals. "Our own history is full of examples of the absence of unity of command and of the disastrous consequences flowing therefrom," Krueger wrote. "We need only recall the days of the Civil War. Independent armies were in every field from the very start. In 1861, when [Brig. Gen. Irvin] McDowell was advancing toward Centreville, [Pennsylvania, Maj. Gen. Robert] Patterson was in the Shenandoah Valley, [Maj. Gen. George B.] McClellan in West Virginia, and other forces were scattered about elsewhere. No attempt was made to place all forces in the East under one commander. Was it surprising that McDowell was defeated in consequence at Bull Run? For three years the Northern Armies were conducted without unity of command and the cost of this neglect, in blood and treasure, was enormous."[44]

Drawing such conclusions from not only the American Civil War but also the Seven Years' War, Krueger argued that the army had to adopt the principle of *unity of command* as opposed to *cooperation* because of the seemingly obvious advantages of the former over the latter. "If unity of command is of such vital importance, why then, it may well be asked, is it not applied to the army and navy of each country?" he asked. "The answer is simple. Armies and fleets do not, as a rule, operate together, their respective spheres of activity being usually far removed from each other. When armies and fleets do operate together, however, unity of command or, at the very least, unity of strategic direction, should undoubtedly be provided."[45]

Finally, after discussing the characteristics of great commanders and the conditions under which they had to work, Krueger ended his thesis with a discussion of exactly how a leader had to manage his staff. The general staff—the "staff agency designed to relieve the commander of as much of the burden of carrying on the functions of command as possible"—worked, according to Krueger, in the name of the commander and should not be considered "as anything other than the brain cells of the commander, acting solely as part of his dominating personality. These brain cells are one and all controlled by and subject to his brain cell that expresses his will. Their acts are never their own acts, but his acts, being either actually sanctioned by him or accepted by him as acts performed by his alter ego, the general staff."[46]

In order to make sure that the staff runs properly, Krueger advocated the acquisition of a strong and forceful chief of staff, who "is the chief adviser and personal representative of the commander. He assists the commander in the supervision and coordination of the command and should enjoy his complete confidence and a considerable degree of independence in the performance of his duties. He is responsible for the working of the whole staff, and, under the orders of his commander, for the control and coordination of the operations of the troops." Therefore, the chief of staff, along with the assistant chiefs of staff (G-1, G-2, G-3, and G-4), should be given "a great deal of latitude in the performance of his duties, this latitude extending even to the issue of orders in the commander's name, in case of necessity, without prior reference to him."[47]

In the main, Krueger's ideas of command are similar to those of the U.S. Army's between the two world wars. In his examination of the army's conception of command during the interwar period, Harold R. Winton suggests five dominating characteristics: the role of the commander as "the single animating force and solely responsible agent of and for his command," the commander's "will" as being the one of the most important characteristics he could possess, the ability to manage and understand "complex situations," the necessity of a commander to care for his troops, and, finally, a commitment to bringing operations to a quick conclusion.[48] Of these, Krueger emphasized, in one form or another, the first four but not the last—bringing operations to a quick conclusion. To Krueger's mind, bringing military operations to an end as quickly as possible was not the most important issue. Attaining military and national objectives were. His later actions would indicate that he refused to conflate speed with the attainment of higher level objectives.

Interestingly, however, an issue that Winton suggests the U.S. Army did not emphasize during the interwar army was "the Moltkean ideal of giving one's subordinates sufficient freedom of action to allow them to take action in war's fluid environment that was responsive both to the dictates of the immediate situation and the framework of the higher commander's will."[49] Krueger placed great value in providing subordinates, specifically the chief of staff, the autonomy to execute the commander's orders. Apart from this significant issue, Krueger's ideas of command largely reflect those of his contemporaries throughout the interwar era. The Naval War College administration thought highly of Krueger's essay and later used it as a required text for its correspondence course. It was also used at the school after World War II.[50]

In addition to the topic of command, Krueger revisited an issue that would increasingly dominate his thinking of war during the interwar period: the importance of national unity. When he first seriously considered this theme at the Army War College, he did so by looking at historical examples of different countries—Germany and Carthage. At Newport, he wrote a thesis—entitled "Policy"—that focused on the policy of the United States. This paper provided the foundation for how he interpreted the role of the United States in the world both during his time at the Naval War College and later, during his second stint in the War Plans Division in the mid-1930s.[51] His thesis reflects a realist analysis of international relations and the acceptance of the Clausewitzian definition of war as being a servant of policy. At the heart of his examination was the notion of national policy. He divided this term into two components: domestic policy and foreign policy. The relationship between these two was extremely important for both the politician and the military officer. "It goes without saying," he wrote, "that Domestic Policy and Foreign Policy must be adequately balanced and that Politics and Diplomacy must be in step with each other, must be closely harmonized, otherwise the interests of the nation will suffer."[52] It was in this study that he applied the notion of national harmony to the United States after he had earlier applied it to Germany and Carthage.

After making many naval contacts, gaining a detailed education of naval strategy and tactics, revisiting War Plan Orange, and refining his thinking about the issue of command, Krueger graduated from the Naval War College in May 1926.[53] Overall, Krueger found his year there a profitable experience. Upon leaving Newport, however, he continued to feel that his chances for promotion and advancement in the infantry "were practically nil." Consequently, Krueger decided to transfer to the Air Corps, and in early 1927 he attended the Army Air Corps Primary Flying School at Brooks Field in San Antonio, Texas. He felt strange attempting to earn his wings at the age of 46 as well as "leaving the arm that I've served in for 28 years. But I came to the decision after mature consideration and only hope that I'll make the grade. If I do, it will be at least one thing that I shall be able to point to with pride as something that has not been done by anyone else at such an advanced age as mine."[54]

Krueger believed he was making "adequate progress" at Brooks Field. "Whether that will continue," he wrote, "remains to be seen, but it is my earnest hope and desire that it will." As much as he tried, Krueger's time at the flying school did not turn out as he had hoped. It represented one of the few failures in his professional life. Not only was he hospitalized for several weeks with neuritis in his right arm (which obviously hampered his time there) but he also failed in his bid to become a pilot. Ultimately, Krueger's age kept him from achieving his wings. His evaluator—Lt. Claire L. Chennault—failed Krueger because, as Walter Krueger Jr. remembers, Chennault "didn't want an old man to kill himself."[55]

Understandably, Krueger met this setback with disappointment. As with earlier career disappointments, however, he tried to remain philosophical and confident in his abilities:

> I tried to make the grade, but it was no use. Though I did better, perhaps, than any one expected, I could not indefinitely continue to do as well as a

> twenty-year old youngster, and it is upon the capacity and performance of such a youngster that the flying course of our air corps is based. I think that it would have been a good plan for the A.C. [Air Corps] to let me get by anyway, even if I could not fly as well as a youngster, for I could have been of considerable value to that corps. The personnel at Brooks Field wanted me to make the grade, but the authorities in Washington were apparently unwilling to make any concession. However, I learned a great deal, even though I failed to get a military pilot's license. Failure in itself is, however, unpalatable to me.[56]

After his time at Brooks Field, the War Department offered him a job in the historical section in Berlin, Germany, but he declined "in consideration for" his mother-in-law, who continued to live with the Kruegers and, he admitted, "is getting very old and is at present extremely feeble." Krueger instead was sent, "to make my chagrin even worse," to the headquarters of the Seventh Corps Area, where he was assistant to the National Guard officer. Krueger did not think highly of the National Guard, and to add insult to injury, he noted that usually it was "a job that is held, where filled at all, by a lieutenant or a captain." In short, the job offered no challenge, especially for an ambitious officer who had just graduated from the Naval War College. "So here I am," he wrote to Brabson, "with practically nothing to do, wondering whether I am going to be left here for four years or whether I am going to be used for some better job than this. I would not mind particularly, if I were stationed farther east, because Jimmie [his older son] is on duty at Fort Humphries, and Walter, jr. [his younger son], is at West Point, but as it is, we shall have mighty little chance of seeing either of them. However, no doubt I should not kick, for, after all, I have had a good many choice details and should be glad to have a bum one for a change."[57]

Fortunately for Krueger, his time at Seventh Corps Area did not last all that long. In December 1927 the War Department gave him the opportunity to return to the Naval War College, this time as an instructor. The corps area commander, however, wanted Krueger to remain at his headquarters, and Krueger frankly did not believe that he would be released. Only intervention by Gen. Charles P. Summerall, the chief of staff, freed Krueger to return to Newport. Under the circumstances and as expected, Krueger was "glad" to receive his new assignment.[58]

As a faculty member, Krueger served in the Department of Operations and taught classes on joint operations, strategy, World War I, command and staff, and army command. For the latter two courses, he revisited and expanded on several issues of command addressed in his 1925 Naval War College thesis. During the 1930–1931 academic year, for instance, he confronted the topic of joint operations and doctrine. As he had done in his thesis, Krueger disagreed with the army's nine principles of war. In a 9 July 1931 memorandum to the Naval War College chief of staff, Krueger argued, "Ever since the so-called Nine Principles of War were promulgated in our Service, many well-informed officers have questioned their soundness and usefulness. The serious doubts that I myself entertained in regard to these principles have finally become convictions." His main objection to the nine principles of war was that they might lead an uninformed commander to believe that success in war is as easy as simply applying several rules of war. "It is clear," he explained, "that a theory of war which teaches that the mere correct application of a set of precepts, such as the so-called Nine Principles of War, will ensure success, is unsound and even dangerous, since it inevitably leads to an entire misconception of the true nature and character of war." Although he thought that the principle of the objective and the principle of superiority were the only two that were "immutable" and "fundamental," Krueger maintained the other seven were "not principles at all, if that term is intended to mean fundamental truths or laws that always obtain and to which there are no exceptions."[59]

Krueger criticized how the army asserted that cooperation was one of the paramount conditions for success in war but did not take sufficient steps to implement it. "This doctrine is much easier to preach than to carry out, for history shows that it was only too often honored in the breach rather than in the observance." Six years after he had first brought up the problems of disunity of command in joint operations, Krueger continued to ring the warning bells for the army, only this time as an instructor. He incorporated his beliefs in his lectures, specifically in the command course. He advised his students that if the army and navy were not going to formalize the issues of command in joint operations, then the two services should make every effort to understand each other to ensure bilateral cooperation. "The two services must have a common, definite understanding of their respective functions in national defense and of the best method for attaining coordination in operations," he wrote. In short, "THEY MUST SPEAK THE SAME LANGUAGE." The warnings, however, again fell on deaf ears, and the War and Navy Departments decided to stick with the concept of cooperation over unity of command. Ironically, Gen. Douglas MacArthur later would give Krueger the primary responsibility to make his joint operations—based on cooperation—run smoothly and effectively.[60] During this time Krueger also participated in the development of a joint exercise at the behest of the presidents of the Naval and Army War Colleges. Operations Problem VI, which had begun in 1928, required students over the course of a month to examine all of the various aspects—including naval, ground, and air operations—of transporting ground forces overseas to assault a defended location. A variation of War Plan Orange, it asked students to capture Luzon (the chief island of the Philippines) to form a base from which U.S. forces would then isolate Japan. As the army's sole faculty member at Newport, Krueger was one of Operations Problem VI's biggest supporters, and he considered many of the various aspects of joint army-navy-air operations in the context of a Blue-Orange (U.S.-Japanese) conflict.[61]

Through many of his lectures, Krueger attempted to raise awareness of joint army-navy operations. At one such lecture on landing operations, his friend Fay Brabson was in attendance. Although not everyone present agreed with Krueger's assessment of the value of landing operations, others, including Brabson, found his ideas intriguing. "He is a great student, has a keen mind, is an analyst, [and] has sound judgment," Brabson wrote in his diary of Krueger's lecture, "but he is a poor speaker." He continued, "With all his idiosyncrasies he is an earnest true character with a good mind and indomitable energy. He said he told his boys [Jimmie and Walter Jr.] that whatever they started he counted on them to finish regardless of obstacles and pain."[62]

Krueger enjoyed his time at the Naval War College, especially in light of his displeasure with his previous assignment. While he appreciated a job that provided him the opportunity to do something meaningful, he still could not yet get over his failure at the Army Air Corps Primary Flying School. "We have a lovely place here and are very comfortable," he wrote. "My work is both interesting and, I think, profitable, although my failure to make the grade in the air corps still sticks in my bones. I'll probably never get over it entirely."[63]

After one year as a student at the Army War College, another year as an instructor there, three years at the War Plans Division, and five years at the Naval War College as both student and instructor, Krueger returned to commanding troops in June 1932, when he became the commanding officer of the 6th Infantry Regiment and Jefferson Barracks, Missouri. Just over a month after receiving his new appointment, Krueger pinned on the rank of full colonel on 1 August 1932.

Krueger was happy to be back in command of troops despite the position's challenges. In addition to his other responsibilities, he was in charge of a large concentration of the Civilian Conservation Corps.[64] "Naturally, I was delighted to get this fine command, though the matter of commanding is getting more and more difficult from year to year," he explained to Brabson. "There are so many ways in which a C.O. [commanding officer] can stub his toe that he never knows whether he will make a success of it or go down in the records as a failure. However, fortunately nothing keeps me awake at night;

I do my best at all times and all else is in the lap of the Gods. One thing I should like to add, however, I am blessed with a fine body of officers and men, and if anything is wrong here, it is pretty sure to be my own fault."[65]

Overall, Krueger's two years in Missouri were satisfying ones. Along with his professional accomplishments, all seemed to be well with his family. His mother-in-law was doing quite well, "surprisingly so" according to Krueger. His younger son, Walter Jr., had recently married, and his other son, Jimmie, was stationed in Manila. His daughter, Dorothy, was still living at home and was "turning heads of young lieutenants, much to my regret."[66]

Back in command of troops, Krueger again put into action his ideas concerning the care and well being of his enlisted force. He regularly visited soldiers in the hospital and encouraged the members of his unit to attend religious services. He also tried to attend church services while he was in command of troops, though he did not do so at other times in his life. Nevertheless, according to his son Walter Jr., Krueger was a religious man, "as those who knew him well will attest." Even while at church, Krueger demanded a "neat, clean bearing and appearance, with leather and insignia shined." After one church service, Krueger approached the chaplain, telling him how much he enjoyed the sermon. He then added, "But don't let me see you preaching in that pulpit again with those dirty crosses."[67]

Despite being away from an intellectual environment for the first time in six years, Krueger, as was his nature, continued to read, write, and lecture on topics that interested him. The issue of the U.S. military and American society became a particular interest. He had held strong reservations against the militia system on the eve of World War I and had rejected the American system of a volunteer militia while advocating a policy of universal conscription. Krueger believed that the regular army, not the citizen soldier, should be the heart of the U.S. military establishment. But by at least 1936, he had modified his ideas on the subject.[68]

In a lecture in St. Louis, Missouri, Krueger outlined his revised thoughts concerning the military of the United States. He argued that it "was not until 1920 that we finally adopted a military policy that gave us a good army, THE ARMY OF THE UNITED STATES, with its three components, the REGULAR ARMY, the NATIONAL GUARD, AND THE ORGANIZED RESERVES." For most of its history, U.S. military policy relied on the Federal Militia Act of 1792, which "was worthless, since it virtually transferred the war powers of the Congress to the states and even went so far as to require individual militiamen to provide their own arms, equipment and mounts. As constituted this militia was purely a state force." In times of war, the militia, "in so far as it was organized, being purely a state force," would be called to aid the regular army. With words that echoed his 1917 "Preparedness" article, Krueger concluded, "The system was inefficient and extremely costly and with our entry into world affairs might at any moment have brought us to brink of disaster. It is not too much to say that the system cost almost more than it was worth."[69]

The passage of the Dick Act of 1903, Krueger continued, signaled the beginning of the end of this old system and ushered in a new and improved (albeit imperfect) one. The act "was the first attempt to systematically organize the militia of the United States into a balanced force, and to make some provision for its use by the Federal Government in case of emergencies." However, it restricted presidential authority by limiting the length of service and prohibiting the militia's use beyond the territorial limits of the United States.[70]

A combination of the National Defense Act of 1916, the harsh realities of World War I, and the National Defense Act of 1920 built on and enhanced the foundation laid by the Dick Act. The two national defense acts and the world war created a federalized National Guard "and gave it a more uniform and efficient organization" by insuring federal supervision over the National Guard and the Reserves through arming, training, equipping, and supplying the two organizations, thereby giving the United States "for the first time in our history a sound military policy."[71]

At the age of fifty-one, Krueger in 1932 believed that his chances of becoming a general officer had all but ended. With the prospect of retiring a colonel, Krueger wrote, "I shall not worry and eat my heart out; life has been good to me—I have been happy and my work has always absorbed my energies—and I could not complain even if I were eventually to pass out of the picture as a colonel. … After all," he asserted, "just thirty four years ago I did not know a single solitary soul in the whole army, and now I am in command of once of the finest regiments and posts of that army—I love it all."[72]

Although Krueger may have believed that his career in the army was facing a dead end, the War Department had other ideas. In late 1933, Brig. Gen. Charles E. Kilbourne wrote to Krueger to ask him if he would like to rejoin the WPD as its executive officer: "I am anxious to maintain here a strong division of strong men," Kilbourne wrote, "especially as our working members have been reduced to 9 (10 including myself). I especially need an executive knowing all the ropes and competent to handle relations with the Navy in the Joint Planning Committee. My present force … are [*sic*], I believe, too junior in rank." Kilbourne emphasized an important feature of the way in which WPD operated: "We try here to let each member of the division develop the best there is in him. Rank doesn't count among ourselves. I frequently yield my own opinion and judgment to that of the officer especially responsible for a given task. And I'm frequently glad that I did. I'd want you to maintain the same attitude and feel sure you can." Obviously, Krueger's experience at the Naval War College and his rank played a large role in Kilbourne's desire to have him join WPD.[73]

To entice Krueger to join him in Washington, Kilbourne suggested that the move would greatly benefit his career. "You would fill the bill admirably," Kilbourne wrote. "Also in your present position I think the detail would be favorable to your chances for advancement. That is I believe the detail would be of advantage to the War Dept., to this division and to you."[74]

The effects Kilbourne's arguments had on Krueger's decision are unclear. However, the opportunity to take a position that would aid his career was too good to pass up, and on 19 January 1934 he was detailed as a member of the General Staff. "I was very much gratified to be asked to go back to the War Plans Division and shall work my head off to make a success of my job," Krueger wrote to Brabson. "The W.P. Div. is the only G.S. [General Staff] Div. that appeals to me. However, I shall leave my regiment and Jefferson Barracks with keen regret. My work here have [*sic*] been all absorbing—but I love it."[75]

Krueger reported to the WPD on 20 July 1934. One of his duties as the executive officer was to review all of the various war plans. The most important and relevant war plan, War Plan Orange, had changed little since Krueger had left WPD in 1925. Although WPD revised WPO in 1928, its basic tenants remained the same. Following a Japanese invasion of the Philippines, American planners called on U.S. forces to hold Bataan and Corregidor while the navy prepared for an advance across the central Pacific with reinforcements. Despite obvious weaknesses, such as exactly how the U.S. Navy could reach the Philippines through the Imperial Japanese Navy, WPO reflected optimism in certain military circles throughout the early 1930s about the possibility of U.S. forces holding Manila Bay until support arrived from Hawaii.[76]

However, a shift in U.S. war-planning strategy began in the mid-1930s as a result of the appointment of three important individuals. Adm. William H. Standley and Capt. Samuel W. Bryant were named chief of Naval Operations and director of the Naval War Plans Division, respectively. Rather than support the optimistic assumptions that had provided the foundation of WPO 1924, both men admitted that the United States could not hold Manila Bay. Instead, they wanted to concentrate American efforts on capturing Truk in the Japanese-mandated Caroline Islands to use as a base for future operations against Japan. Equally important for the reshaping of U.S. war plans was the replacement of Kilbourne as chief of WPD with Brig. Gen. Stanley D. Embick on 12 March 1935. Embick firmly believed that the United States should rethink its strategic interests in the Far East. Instead of being a strategic asset, he wrote, the Philippines "have become a military liability of a constantly increasing gravity. To carry out the present Orange Plan—with its provisions for the early dispatch of our fleet to Philippine waters—would be literally an act of madness."[77]

This environment was substantially different from the one Krueger had left in 1925. Working for an assistant chief of staff who was articulate and dissented from the conventional view of the role of the Philippines in U.S. defense, as well as working with naval leaders who were themselves skeptical of holding on to Manila, emboldened Krueger to interject his own views on aligning national policy and military capability. Almost three months before he arrived in Washington, Krueger wrote a letter to Capt. Wilbur R. Van Auken, with whom he had served as an instructor at the Naval War College. Krueger foreshadowed some of the issues he would tackle after returning to WPD. Although he argued with great emphasis concerning the necessity of military officers to keep out of the affairs of civilian leaders and grand strategy, Krueger nevertheless admitted, "I do not mean to assert that we should not thoroughly appreciate and do our part to bring about, let us say for example, a toning down of certain policies, because of the absence of the necessary military power to attain them in war; or that we should not exert all our efforts toward adequate political, diplomatic, economic and moral preparations to meet the possible or probable war."[78] Even before returning to WPD, Krueger was already thinking along the lines of Standley, Bryant, and, more important, Embick.

It is not surprising, then, that his work at WPD would reflect a cautionary and realistic tone. In a memorandum dated 28 October 1935, Krueger examined the ends, ways, and means of U.S. involvement in the Philippines, a technique similar to his earlier work on the harmony of national policy. By looking at the situation in the Far East via both national policy and foreign policy, Krueger argued that the conventional wisdom of U.S. policy toward the Philippines was built on faulty assumptions—in particular, that the Philippines "are of great economic and strategic value to us." His assessment led him in a completely different direction: "The economic value to us of the islands was never material and will, in any event, cease to be a determining factor once independence becomes effective [granted by the Tydings-McDuffie Act of 1934]." These views reflected an increasingly isolationist sentiment within the army throughout the 1930s.[79]

Krueger's comments betrayed his continuing doubt about U.S. military policy. His work with the War Department demonstrates his attempt to instill harmony between U.S. defense commitments and American economic realities. These ideas share much in common with Krueger's boss, Stanley Embick, who for many years argued that the United States would find defending the Philippine Islands difficult.[80]

Despite the vocalized beliefs of Krueger, Embick, Standley, Bryant, and many other military planners, civilian leaders in Washington, D.C., still held that the Philippines were vital to American interests. Consequently, WPO continued to include the concept of Philippine defense. The four officers, however, influenced future versions of WPO by managing to scale back the type of offensive the United States would fight in order to recapture the Philippines. They successfully brought U.S. strategy back from its optimism and bold offensive action of the 1920s, instead calling for caution. As Embick put it on 2 December 1935, "The best that could be hoped would be that wise counsels would prevail, that our people would acquiesce in the temporary loss of the Philippine Islands, and that the dispatch of our battle fleet to the Far East would be delayed for the two or three years needed for its augmentation to a strength expressive of our potential military capabilities."[81]

With this shift in naval and army war-planning leadership along with a changing international situation, the Navy and War Departments reexamined WPO, revising it in May 1935 and again a year later. The committee sent a memorandum in the spring of 1935, signed by Krueger, to the JB outlining its suggestions for a revised WPO. The JPC believed that in the event of a Japanese invasion, U.S. forces in the Philippines should be expected to maintain control of only Manila Bay, and they should expect no immediate reinforcements. This requirement was reduced further in the 1936 revision, when planners determined that only the entrance to Manila Bay should be held. The navy exerted its influence by arguing that any return to the Philippines would require a steady and progressive advance through the Marshall and Caroline Islands. These changes in WPO reflected an acceptance that any return to the Philippines would take years instead of months to complete. Krueger's work in highlighting the weaknesses of the U.S. position in the Philippines no doubt played a large role in these revisions.[82]

These modifications, however, represented more of a compromise between the navy and army than anything else and demonstrated the continued split of opinion over national and military policy concerning the Far East. Whereas navy officials believed there was little reason to reassess U.S. policy, army leaders held this as an important goal. Krueger and the other army members of the JPC believed that the granting of Philippine independence necessitated a complete reexamination of policy. In addition, the army JPC members were "firmly convinced that this re-examination should not be predicated upon, nor coupled with, any estimate made in connection with the War Plan–Orange, since this might result in that War Plan exercising an undue and unsound influence upon national policy." The Krueger-led contingent continued to stress that the existing plans placed "impossible responsibilities" upon the army.[83]

Despite the army-navy compromises in the 1935 and 1936 revisions, Krueger remained unsatisfied with War Plan Orange. In a 28 October 1937 memorandum, Krueger—now chief of WPD as of May 1936, which led to his promotion to brigadier general—suggested that the 1928 version of WPO (amended) was no longer applicable in the current national and international environment, for the plan provided the president with only one option—to adopt the Central Pacific offensive, a costly military option the Depression-gripped nation could scarcely afford. Krueger wrote:

> It is also probable that the war envisaged in the plan under discussion will involve the maximum war effort of the United States. Unless, however, our people felt that their vital interests were at stake, and this is improbable, we could scarcely expect them to support an offensive war such as that envisaged in this plan. Moreover, we are today in the midst of a profound social revolution which has gradually gained more and more in extent during the past decade. Hence, the staggering toll of such a war as that envisaged in the plan might well strain our political and social structure beyond the breaking point. In any case, what would we gain, even if we were victorious, if America were ruined in the process?[84]

He suggested therefore the creation of a new plan that was flexible and reflected American economic realities as well as military contingency. One may detect the theme of national unity once again in Krueger's work, but now he possessed the opportunity to actually influence military policy.[85]

He continued with this theme in a 22 November 1937 memorandum. Utilizing Clausewitzian language, Krueger argued that "the first and most critical decision which the statesmen and the highest military authority must make in connection with any war is to determine the nature of the war. This requires that they ask themselves what is the political object of the war, what are the international and domestic conditions, and what are the issues at stake from the point of view of each of the probable belligerents." To answer these questions, Krueger suggested that the statesmen/military authority determine whether the war is limited or unlimited. Unlimited war is "war whose purpose is to crush the enemy so utterly that he will accept any terms, does not depend upon the desires of statesmen and military leaders, but almost wholly upon the peoples of the nations concerned." Unlimited war, according to Krueger, has many dangers for the nation seeking such a decision. It may simply be beyond the capabilities of the nation. "The conclusion to be drawn from the foregoing," he warned, "is obvious: the war effort made must be in harmony with the issues involved, unless the nation is too weak to have any choice." After discussing the definitions of unlimited/limited war, he used it to analyze the situation of the United States in 1937. He suggested that the United States needed two types of plans: a strategic concentration plan and a strategic operations plan. Furthermore, he noted that only the first one should be a detailed plan, while the latter should "only indicate in a general way what is to be done and what we hope to accomplish with the means available.... In view of the lack of clearness that, so far as we are concerned, is sure to prevail until a late moment in regard to the political object of the war, it is evident that our Joint Basic War Plan Orange can not well extend beyond the strategic concentration."[86]

Clearly, this memo and the one of 28 October 1937 reflect an increasingly tense international situation in the Far East as a result of Japan's war in China as well as increasingly tense discussions between the army and navy over the character of a war with Japan.[87] The navy was ready to adopt an aggressive war of naval economic strangulation against Japan, relegating the army to garrison duty. Three-decades–old differences in the conception of national defense between the two services came to the surface and increasingly shaped U.S. strategy. The navy had for some thirty years advocated a Central Pacific offensive against Japan, whether it be a quick offensive one or one that took many years and emphasized economic warfare. The army, in comparison, increasingly sought to defend the United States with the establishment of the Hawaii-Panama-Alaska defensive triangle. Neither the JB nor the JPC, consequently, could reach a consensus on War Plan Orange. After continued haggling, the two services reached an agreement in February 1938 only after the board requested the intervention of Deputy Chief of Staff Embick and Rear Adm. James O. Richardson.[88] Meanwhile, Krueger and Embick—among others—sought to downplay the Philippines in U.S. national policy and strategy. In particular, Krueger's contribution to the army position included the notion of flexibility and creating a foreign policy that was in harmony with domestic policy. He feared that the navy's conception of WPO committed the United States to one type of war, one that omitted other types of offense strategies. Furthermore, it smacked of placing military requirements in front of political objectives. If war came, he warned, the U.S. armed services could only give the president one option before the political objectives were even formulated. In addition, he argued—like Embick—that the United States could simply not defend the Philippines. Doing so ignored national priorities and would be a financial burden the nation could not afford to shoulder. Placing so much emphasis on military priorities (i.e., the protection of the Philippines) threatened the delicate and harmonious balance between foreign and domestic policy, a balance that was necessary for national security itself.

Partly in response to Krueger's memorandums, the JB directed the JPC in November 1937 to reassess the nation's plans for war with Japan. Within two weeks, however, the committee reached an impasse between its army and navy members. The resultant document was a compromise between the two positions. The navy retained the Central Pacific drive but at the expense of adopting the army's cautious timetable. While there would be a naval thrust through the Central Pacific, it would take place later rather than sooner and would be less ambitious by virtue of the army's insistence on protecting the strategic triangle of Hawaii-Panama-Alaska and reducing the resources it would contribute to the operation. The 1938 version of the war plan reflected Krueger's call for flexibility in the means the United States could employ against Imperial Japan. Created with the Great Depression in mind, the new WPO sought to devise a means to an end that reflected the nation's financial realties. "The result," Louis Morton writes, "was a broad statement of strategy calling for 'military and economic pressure,' increasing in severity until 'the national objective,' the defeat of Japan, was attained."[89]

In addition to his work with War Plan Orange, Krueger upon his return to the War Plans Division had the opportunity to deal with other military issues. For instance, he had the occasion to contribute to the army's ongoing debate surrounding joint operational doctrine among all of the services and branches. As he had maintained in his Naval War College thesis "Command," Krueger continued to call for the principle of unity of command for all services and branches of the armed services. In regard to air power, he clearly believed that an independent air force could not operate on its own whether it was supporting ground or naval units. Not able to survive independently, air units, Krueger thought, were one vital component of a larger joint combined-arms force. He believed, for example, that more emphasis should be given to the "development of a doctrine to govern such covering operations and their coordination with naval operations." Although he was an infantry officer, Krueger recognized the importance of centralized control of airpower, and he argued that parceling out air assets would only "fitter away air forces which could be much better controlled and much more effectively used under command of Corps, and preferably Army, Commanders only."[90]

Krueger also weighed in on the issue of mechanized cavalry. In the late 1930s, many in the army were debating whether the cavalry should maintain its allegiance to the horse or embrace mechanization. Some even wanted to establish a mechanized cavalry division. In 1936–1937, the U.S. Army Command and General Staff School produced a text that explored the organization, mission, and tactics of the proposed division. It prescribed that the division should be a combined-arms force, capable of independent operations. Krueger, however, voiced his opposition to such an organization for both doctrinal and economic reasons. In an April 1937 memorandum, the chief of WPD maintained that "in my opinion, the primary function of the Cavalry Division is screening and reconnaissance. This requires mobility, coupled with only enough fighting power to do the job. Each of the organizations proposed is too large and appears to sacrifice mobility to fighting power." In other words, Krueger believed that every branch and service had a particular place to play in a combined-arms force. He did not—as some have charged—deny the importance of armor, mobility, or combined-arms. Indeed, Krueger was an enthusiastic armor advocate, which he would demonstrate a few years later at the helm of the Third Army. What he did object to was adding functions to the cavalry above and beyond its traditional role of reconnaissance and screening. Consequently, Krueger did not accept the argument that the cavalry division should be designed for independent action. Neither cavalry nor the air force, nor for that matter any other branch, could or should try to act independently. They should be utilized as part of a large combined-arms force in which each service's or branch's strengths would be utilized while their weaknesses were minimized. The particular role of each branch of the army also made sound economic sense as well. In the late 1930s, the army could hardly afford to fund redundant fighting units, no matter how doctrinally sound they might be. In short, it was not the mechanization of cavalry that Krueger decried. Rather it was creating a division so big that it eclipsed the mission for which it was initially designed.[91]

On 1 July 1938, Krueger left WPD and returned to commanding troops, this time in command of the 16th Infantry Brigade at Fort George G. Meade, Maryland. His years in staff positions were over, and from here on he would command troops. Henceforth, his assignments included experimenting with a new divisional structure, and he was being groomed for corps command by the commander of the Third Army and his old WPD chief, Maj. Gen. Stanley C. Embick. His tenure as chief of WPD had capped a period during which he worked largely at the theoretical foundations of his profession and rose in rank from major to brigadier general.

His career throughout these years was important in several respects. At the Army War College, the Naval War College, and the War Plans Division, he studied the complexities of a war against Japan. Along the way, he also forged important relationships with naval officers, many of whom he would work with during World War II.

Furthermore, Krueger became familiar with virtually all aspects of army function and organization. As chief of WPD, he had to deal with all of the members of the General Staff (G-1, G-2, G-3, and G-4) with their accompanying bureaucratic fighting. As a result of its function of preparing war plans for the nation, WPD has been described as the foundation of the General Staff, since it necessarily had to deal with all aspects of army organization. This ability to work cooperatively with others—specifically with members of the sister services—would play a significant role in Krueger's success during World War II.[92]

Of this era of Krueger's career, Fay W. Brabson succinctly wrote,

> A high light of General Krueger's career following World War I was the period he spent at the Naval War College. There, with his felicity for succinct statement and the clarity he brought to the subject through the use of tables, he did much to crystallize command policies that should apply to the Navy and to the Army when working together. Later as a member of the War Plans Division of the General Staff he worked with officers of both services on joint planning problems. In both those assignments General Krueger's realism and sound common sense impressed in an exceptionally favorable way the policy-making officers of the Army and Navy.[93]

Finally, throughout these important years, Krueger worked out the theoretical basis for how he would command in wartime. Five factors made up his concept of command, developed through both experience and reflection. First, Krueger always took the opportunity to learn and prepare his mind for command. He had a passion not only for learning but for his profession. An early attribute of Krueger, the inclination to study and learn, was further developed under the tutelage of his stepfather. Upon entering the officer corps, Krueger took every opportunity—on the U.S. Army's time or his own—to approach the study of war and warfare primarily through historical analysis, always training his intellect for the challenges of command. Educational preparation would, in turn, help develop for the commander the proper psychological attributes, the second aspect of his command philosophy. A military leader needed to be the animating and dominating spirit of his command, the one who gives both purpose and meaning to the unit. To this end, cooperation among the services could never replace the efficiency and efficacy of unity of command. It was the duty of those at the highest civilian and military levels to ensure that the officer in the field operated under such conditions and was not hindered by the diffuse notion of cooperation. Furthermore, a commander needed to develop a cool head, allowing nothing to stir up his emotions. Likewise, Krueger believed that in all a commander did, he needed to be flexible. Whether developing war plans or executing them, Krueger thought flexibility was key. For instance, he had no patience for those who rigidly applied the "so-called nine principles"[94] of war.

Third, while believing the officer needed both the responsibility and authority to command, Krueger also maintained that the commander had to create a decentralized command structure that allowed his subordinates to complete their missions in their own way. A strong and competent staff was vital in this regard, as it worked the details of administration and control, allowing the commander to keep himself above the mass of details and instead free to concentrate on strategy.

Fourth, a commander had a responsibility to those who obeyed his orders. Krueger continually underscored the need to look after the well-being of his soldiers. Based on his experience as a volunteer as well as his study of some of the great captains of history, Krueger understood the importance of making sure that the basic needs of the troops were met and that they were fully trained and prepared for their military mission.

Finally, once it was determined that the nation had called for its armed forces to proceed into battle, Krueger believed that all efforts should be made to create a plan that emphasized aggressive offensive action. Hannibal's performance at Cannae epitomized for Krueger military action that was bold and offensive as well as creatively and imaginatively conceived. Furthermore, Krueger did not think that offensive action alone would always bring success. To the contrary, he believed in weighing costs against possible benefits. He applied his thinking about such matters at all levels of war, from the tactical to the strategic. Through his study of history, for example, he continually stressed that a nation's success in war depended on its ability to harmonize domestic and foreign policies. As a member of WPD from 1935 to 1938, during the depths of the Great Depression, he urged the army to create war plans and a military organization that, once implemented, would not bankrupt the nation and create social and political chaos. In regard to War Plan Orange, his understanding of the important relationship among economics, military policy, and national will explains his unwillingness to adopt a quick offensive to save the Philippines in the mid-1930s. But his thinking about the nature of foreign policy during this time was also a product of his association with Stanley D. Embick, who profoundly influenced Krueger as well many other army war planners. Moreover, Krueger's thinking was spurred by powerful challenges from the navy, whose members wanted an offensive strategy against Japan by employing economic warfare. Furthermore, his ideas on weighing costs versus benefits also contribute to the operational level of war and are particularly helpful in examining operational art. A commander at this level must translate tactical success to strategic objectives. Krueger recognized this and never wanted to conduct military operations that might hinder strategic success. High-level commanders, for instance, will not rush into a situation without adequate intelligence and will recognize the culminating point of their attack.

By 1938, Krueger had formulated the broad outlines of his five aspects of command—thorough educational preparation; proper psychological characteristics, including being the dominate force of the unit, possessing a cool head, and flexibility; creating a decentralized command structure; taking care of the soldiers; and valuing aggressive and bold offensive action and continually balancing this bold and aggressive military action against possible costs and anticipated gains. Whereas the nineteen years from 1919 to 1938 allowed Krueger to explore the theoretical aspects of command, the next several years allowed him to implement what he had learned. During the following five years, Krueger would become one of the army's leading operational commanders, who not only helped to modernize the United States Army in the face of new modes of warfare but then helped to train an army for overseas duty during the opening stages of World War II.

Chapter 4

Training with the Third Army, 1938–1943

The United States of the 1920s had an army hardly worthy of a world power with global responsibilities, and the army of the late 1930s was scarcely any better. In many respects, it was still an army besieged, badly hampered in its efforts to keep abreast of the profound changes taking place in the art of war. The stock market crash of 1929 forced the nation to adopt stringent financial measures. The Depression-era presidents demanded that the various branches and institutions of government adapt their individual budgets and activities accordingly. In 1929, for example, President Herbert Hoover asked the War Department to make "extensive reductions in the cost of the Army in all or any of its components or activities."[1]

Along with the strong antimilitaristic temperament of many Americans,[2] the Great Depression made it difficult for the War Department to justify the continuation of a costly modernization program that included acquiring new weapons such as tanks and airplanes. Forced to cut its budget by the president and Congress, the army had to decide what programs to scale back or even eliminate altogether. Vigorous debate within the army ensued, which focused on exactly what programs should enjoy continued funding. Throughout the disagreements, almost all officers accepted one basic principle: the most important part of the army was its personnel. Consequently, as the army scaled back its purchases of new weapons, the War Department ultimately opposed any attempts to reduce the number of soldiers or officers throughout the ranks.[3]

The effects of the Depression, the widespread pacifist mood, and the army's own budgetary decisions all had a debilitating effect on the army and its ability to wage war. The army relied on mostly World War I-era equipment throughout much of the 1930s, and tactical and operational doctrine suffered as a result. Lacking the new generation of weapons, it could not experiment with the improving capabilities of the tank and airplane. Furthermore, the army was increasingly involved in the Depression-fighting programs of the New Deal, such as the Civilian Conservation Corps. Ultimately, historian

Russell F. Weigley writes, "For the most part … the early 1930's saw the conditions of the Army go from bad to worse."[4]

Despite the severe economic depression afflicting the army, Walter Krueger—like many other committed officers—did what he could to prepare the nation for any military contingency. Specifically, he helped to create an operational doctrine virtually out of nothing. In contrast to the period from 1919 to 1938, in which Krueger had helped to produce joint army-navy war plans, from 1938 to 1943 he was integral in developing new forms of army organization, experimenting with large-unit doctrine, and, after the United States entered World War II, training American troops for overseas military duty.

Upon being released from his duties as chief of the Army War Plans Division, Krueger looked back on the past few years with fondness. In some respects he regretted leaving, because, he wrote, "I love the work and the fine fellows with whom I have the good fortune to be associated. If I have succeeded in handling W.P.D. [War Plans Division], the credit is in my judgment very largely due to them."[5]

Second Division Tests

In September 1938, Krueger took command of the 16th Infantry Brigade at Fort George Meade, Maryland, for a brief period of only five months. At Fort Meade, he received his second star before again moving, this time to Fort Sam Houston, Texas, to command the 2d Infantry Division in March 1939.

The relocation to Fort Sam Houston brought with it some excitement, because as commander of the 2d Infantry Division, Krueger would be propelled into the center of the army's efforts to modernize its organization and for the next two years would help to formulate the nation's embryonic operational doctrine.[6] Heretofore, the U.S. Army primarily had concentrated on both ends of operational doctrine: strategy and tactics. As the army moved toward World War II, therefore, it not only had to create an army but also had to draft a comprehensive operational doctrine. In most cases, however, the process of creating the doctrine lost out to the time, effort, and expense of actually establishing the army. That the strategic and tactical doctrines contradicted each other further complicated the story. The strategic doctrine emphasized defeating the adversary with overwhelming power, but at the tactical level, the army attempted to instill the mindset of mobility and maneuver through lightly armed troops. How the army intended to use a lightly armed force to crush an enemy with overwhelming power was never spelled out and caused confusion. It left corps and army commanders in a tough spot. Indeed the

American way of war possessed two distinct legacies, which led the army in two different directions.[7] Consequently, those officers who built this emerging army (especially those at the corps and army command levels) had to synthesize these two divergent doctrines and forge an operational doctrine out of necessity. As one of the principal trainers of the new army, Krueger was at the forefront of forming a new operational doctrine while working as the 2d Infantry Division commander and later as a corps and army commander.

Also in a state of change in the late 1930s and early 1940s was the army's organizational structure of its fighting units. In the late 1920s, the War Department—as a result of overseas developments concerning motorization, mechanization, and organization—had sought to reorganize the infantry regiment and, more important, the division to be more in line with the doctrine of mobility and maneuver. Out of this interest came several studies that suggested the army adopt a "triangular" infantry division. All subunits within the new formation contained three elements. Three sections composed a squad, three squads composed a platoon, three platoons composed a company, three companies composed a battalion, three battalions composed a regiment, and three regiments composed a division of approximately 16,000 troops. The old division, composed of four regiments (hence the name "square") and totaling about 28,000 men, was designed for a war of attrition and stability, in which firepower and sheer numbers of soldiers were paramount considerations. With improvements in the internal combustion engine throughout the 1920s, tactical and operational mobility became a more important factor in modern warfare. To help bring high mobility to the battlefield through the triangular organization, the War Department also instituted the concept of pooling. It took all supporting elements from the division and placed them in the corps or even army headquarters. Whereas the infantry division of old was a fundamental player in a military strategy of overwhelming power, the army now wanted a lean infantry division, one more akin to a war of maneuver, possessing high mobility and unhindered with nonessential support elements.[8]

The triangular division meant that the corps and army would now be the agents to put into practice the strategy of overwhelming power. Clearly, the newly designed division did not have its predecessor's capability for sustained combat. Indeed, discussions in the various service journals of applying the art of overwhelming power focused on corps and armies.[9]

The 2d Infantry Division conducted initial tests from 15 September to 15 November 1938 and was observed by Brig. Gen. Walter C. Short on behalf of the chief of staff. Except for some experimentation with the teletype, the 2d Provisional Infantry Division (PID) did not conduct any large-scale testing of either motorization or triangularization between the 1938 test and late 1939.

When Krueger took command of the division in March 1939, full-scale testing resumed. Right from his arrival in Texas, Krueger became involved with plans to test the renamed "Provisional 2d Division" (P2D). He assembled the various units of the division—the 9th, 20th, and 23d Infantry Regiments—at the Leon Springs Military Reservation, twenty miles northwest of San Antonio, ahead of schedule and then conducted the actual test through the end of September.[10]

All of the preparation and testing kept Krueger busy. "The work is extremely interesting," he remarked to his friend Fay Brabson, "and keeps me going at a fast rate, but I'm outdoors so much that I seem to thrive on it." Despite the magnitude of his task—while still assembling his division in mid-July—he remained confident that by September he would have enough data compiled to make a complete assessment of the triangular structure.[11]

Because the War Department had stripped the division of many of its support capabilities, Krueger concluded that the division would have difficulty sustaining itself in combat. Responding to the War Department's request to comment on what type of reinforcements the triangular division would need when acting alone, Krueger was not at all optimistic. In almost all supporting echelons, the P2D commander believed that the division needed to be reinforced. Although a corps echelon normally handled hospitalization, for example, Krueger suggested that the division needed one 250-bed hospital company. He argued that in a war of mobility, when a division might be called upon for independent action, a corps might not be able to provide proper medical care to subordinate formations. "When a division is detached," he wrote, "hospitalization and evacuation by the corps will probably not be as regular and as prompt as is the case when the division is operating with the corps. Consequently, additional beds and hospital facilities must be available in the division." In addition, Krueger found the division deficient in maintenance and motor transportation. All in all, Krueger determined that the previous estimates of the division's range were too optimistic. He calculated that the division could travel only 75 miles in one day, far short of earlier estimates of 130 miles.[12]

Despite their many differences over the P2D, Krueger and the War Department agreed on several other matters of organization. He believed, for instance, that the division should not include organic air (i.e., specifically attached to a division), antiaircraft, and tank units, leaving these elements to higher echelons, which would dole out these units to specific infantry divisions only when necessary. He did see, however, the need for increased antitank measures. At the time, the army's antitank weapons were completely obsolete, relying on the .50-caliber machine gun and the 37mm gun. The

P2D had eighteen .50-caliber machine guns for front area defense, thirteen for local defense for the field artillery, and eighteen motorized 37mm guns to meet attacks against the flanks. Not able to control the types of weapons allocated for his use, Krueger became concerned with the number of weapons in his division and concluded, "Organic guns are considered inadequate to cover such an area when the division is acting alone." He suggested that eighteen more 37mm guns be assigned to the division, thereby providing a total of sixty-seven antitank guns. The additional eighteen 37mm guns, he advised, should be organized into an antimechanized company with its platoons arranged similar to the antitank platoons of each infantry regiment.[13]

On 18 December 1939, the War Department ordered Krueger and the commanding generals of the 1st, 3d, 5th, and 6th Infantry Divisions—which were also converting into triangular divisions after the preliminary tests of the 2d Infantry Division—to "secure additional views on recently approved organizations and to test them under widely differing conditions of terrain and climate." They were to examine all aspects of their divisions including organization, mobility, tactics, supply, and reinforcements. All tests and reports were due 30 June 1940.[14]

Around this same time, Krueger accrued some additional responsibilities. In conjunction with commanding the 2d Infantry Division, Krueger took charge of the IX Corps (Provisional) on 31 January 1940. The Third Army commander, Maj. Gen. Stanley D. Embick, Krueger's old boss at the Army War Plans Division, created the provisional corps to participate in Third Army maneuvers in the spring of 1940. This set of exercises, as well as others, eventually would prepare the army to participate in the largest peacetime maneuvers in U.S. history—the General Headquarters (GHQ) maneuvers of the fall of 1941—by moving progressively from basic soldiering skills to the operations of larger units.[15]

Throughout the first few months of 1940, Krueger spent much of his time with his provisional corps, and by 20 March, he had selected all of his corps headquarters personnel, organized them into a formal headquarters, and sent a corps command post to observe the 2d Infantry Division maneuvers in April. As commander of both the 2d Infantry Division and the IX Corps during the army maneuvers, Krueger was in a unique position to judge the merits of the new divisional structure and the way it operated in a corps.[16]

After completing a series of maneuvers in January 1940, putting his troops through several weeks of target practice, and conducting more preliminary maneuvers that February, Krueger again put the 2d Infantry Division through its paces in April 1940 at the Leon Springs Military Reservation. Reporting his conclusions, he repeated his earlier warnings of the operational limitations of the triangular division. When asked by the War Department if the division "is adequate for sustained offensive action for a period of 48 to 72 hours," he responded that the "*maximum period for sustained action with the present peace strength is 48 hours*" (Krueger's emphasis). After two days, the division would need to halt offensive actions primarily because of fatigue at all echelons. With a minimum of supply and support elements in the streamlined triangular division, officers and enlisted men alike would not last beyond forty-eight hours under combat conditions. "Infantry rifle companies are too small to perform required combat missions," Krueger wrote. "Losses from fatigue, simulated casualties, and other normal causes weaken the organization so that remaining personnel obtain no rest because of multiplicity of duties even during lulls in action." To alleviate such circumstances, he recommended, for instance, an increase in the number of personnel and equipment for the division's engineers. "In preparation for and during the several advances and withdrawals made by the division in the maneuvers, the units of the Engineer Battalion were required to operate over large areas, dispersed in small groups, and to work continuously," he wrote. "At the end of 36 hours, all men were practically exhausted and incapable of further useful work. The necessity for an increase in personnel to provide additional work units and reserves was evident." In addition to more personnel, Krueger suggested that the division possess more motorized transport for the engineer battalion.[17]

As a result of his findings, Krueger once again questioned the fundamental assumptions of the War Department. In the War Department's directive of 18 December 1939 that initiated further testing of the new divisional structure, the army reminded its division commanders of the current doctrine concerning the role of divisions and corps in combat: "The Triangular Division is intended to have organic means to function as an *interior* division of a larger unit. It has minimum means for supply, evacuation, and maintenance. It is important that this concept be kept in mind when evaluating the results of tests and experiments. It is expected that the triangular division will be reinforced when detached or on an exposed flank; such reinforcements may include anti-tank, reconnaissance, and service units." In other words, the triangular division was designed solely to be the fighting portion of an army corps, with the latter providing the majority of service and supply functions. It would be modified only when acting independently, but this would not be standard operating procedure.[18]

Recognizing the division's weaknesses when operating autonomously, Krueger stated that "in general, the division should be given combat and service units similar to those organically in the Army Corps." Even when the division was attacking "on a narrow front with flanks secure" as part of a corps,

Krueger believed that it needed additional units, specifically one regiment of 75mm guns, one regiment of 155mm howitzers, one antitank battalion (with "weapons preferably larger than 37-mm gun"), and one antiaircraft battalion.[19]

Krueger, moreover, found fault with the standard divisional artillery weapon: the 75mm gun, which, he stated, "is not a satisfactory weapon for the close support of fast-moving modern infantry." Instead, based on his own experience and his understanding of the war in Europe, he preferred the 105mm howitzer:

> The 105-mm howitzer is considered the ideal weapon because it has the power and the trajectory to cope with all targets with which the division will normally be confronted, including hostile artillery.... The adoption of the 105-mm howitzer would conform to the trend toward larger calibers for close support artillery weapons, a practice which has apparently been very successful in Europe in recent months.[20]

On other aspects of firepower, Krueger found the division adequate. Theoretically, with the use of improved infantry arms, such as the M-1 Garand semiautomatic rifle, the triangular division could produce as much firepower as its old square counterpart, even with fewer men. Throughout the 1940 divisional tests, Krueger determined that "more power is available on the same frontage, or the same power is present on a wider frontage. Detached elements and security forces are able to offer more effective resistance for the number of men engaged." While unable to engage in sustained combat for any length of time, the division could, nevertheless, produce ample amounts of firepower. "Increased small arms fire," Krueger concluded, "had increased the rapidity and scope of tactical operations of the division."[21]

After approximately ten years of study, the War Department formally adopted the triangular division during the 1940 fiscal year. The army believed it had found a suitable replacement for the old World War I-era square division, and in adopting the new configuration it gave greater import to mobility than to manpower and firepower. The triangular division represented a move toward operational mobility without a significant loss of firepower.[22]

Krueger's findings, specifically his "Special Report based on Field Service Test of the Provisional 2d Division conducted by the 2d Division, U.S. Army" of September 1939, cast doubt on some of the War Department's fundamental assumptions for the triangular division. While the army wanted a division with the ability to engage in a war of high mobility, it neglected to provide the division with the proper manpower and material support to wage such combat. Even assuming that the division had to operate "for a limited time beyond supporting distance of other ground forces," Krueger found the division incapable of sustained action without substantial reinforcements. In the face of such warnings, the War Department believed that the division would be able to operate with the corps providing supply and service operations. In fact, the army believed—completely reversing Krueger's logic—that the more independently the division operated, the less supply and service echelons it should have. "It is even more necessary for the independent division to remain foot-loose than it is for the division when part of a corps," Eighth Corps Area commander Maj. Gen. Herbert J. Brees wrote. "The principle of relieving it from all service functions that can be performed by a higher echelon should be adhered to." But as historian Robert Stewart Cameron correctly points out, to tie a division so closely to its corps negated the very type of mobile combat that the army wanted to adopt: "Reducing the personnel and support elements, however, increased the division's dependence upon reserve and rear echelon formations, thereby interfering with its ability to wage the war of maneuver for which it was intended."[23]

IX Corps Exercises

With the 2d Infantry Division tests completed, Krueger turned his attention to his IX Corps (Provisional), which was about to face the Third Army's other formation, Maj. Gen. Walter C. Short's IV Corps, in a mock war. The Third Army designed its spring 1940 maneuvers "to train the new type of corps, composed of triangular divisions, in concentrations over long distances against a mobile enemy, and in maneuver under combat conditions, both alone and coupled with combat aviation and mechanized forces." Previous exercises in 1936 and 1938 had examined the possibility that the Third Army—based in Texas—would participate in the defense of the U.S. southern border against invasion. With much of the world at war in early 1940, the War Department now focused on preparing its army for combat overseas in the type of mobile operations that characterized the first year of the war. Consequently, the War Department wanted to maximize the learning process by finding the most competent commanders to engage in the mock battles, and it believed that the two corps commanders selected were best able to fulfill their assignments. "I know Short well; he is a very able, determined, and rather stubborn type," Chief of Staff General George C. Marshall wrote in a letter to Embick. "Incidentally, Krueger, with a different complexion, is much the same sort. Both of them are aggressive, energetic, and to a certain extent, self-opinionated. Both of them, I believe, are leaders with a sufficient understanding of mobile army operations to produce valuable results. You will probably find them 'head on' regarding many considerations brought up by results of maneuvers."[24]

During the period between 28 April and 6 May, IX Corps conducted its own exercises, "designed to develop team play between the several elements of the Corps and to train the staffs of all units in conducting large-scale operations in the field." The exercises covered both offensive and defensive operations. After three days' rest, the corps was ready to participate in the Third Army maneuvers, scheduled to commence at daylight on 9 May.[25]

The IX Corps (Provisional) consisted of the 2d Infantry Division, the 1st Cavalry Division, and the 4th Cavalry Regiment and was for the purposes of the exercise was called the Red Army. The IV Corps, or Blue Army, had the 1st, 5th, and 6th Infantry Divisions plus the Provisional Tank Brigade, which was commanded by Brig. Gen. Bruce Magruder and had two light tank battalions from the 66th and 68th Infantry (Tank) Regiments and a company of medium tanks from the 67th Infantry (Tank) Regiment. Throughout the exercises, Blue enjoyed numerical superiority; Short's corps had roughly 40,000 men whereas Krueger's corps had about 30,000. Both forces met in the Sabine River area of Texas and Louisiana during the month of April. The maneuver area included over 1.7 million acres of land on both sides of the Sabine, including 259,400 acres of the Kisatchie National Forest.[26]

Throughout the maneuvers, which lasted through 25 May, many of the newspaper headlines praised the exercises as progressive, calling the military operations "smooth" and claiming the army was testing the "blitzkrieg" method of warfare. However, during the postmaneuver critiques, army leaders pointed to the many fundamental errors made by both sides. Numerous small-unit commanders, for instance, failed to provide adequate reconnaissance. In addition, Brees, commander of the Eighth Corps Area, pointed out that both too many infantry and cavalry units were road-bound, while Krueger commented that most commanders treated the exercises as map maneuvers and "failed to go out and look at the ground."[27]

Brees also fired some highly public comments directed at the senior leaders of the maneuvers that were reported by the *New York Times*. He criticized commanders on both sides for stretching thin their reconnaissance, while also faulting them for emphasizing the tempo and mechanics of operations rather than focusing on implementing sound tactics.[28] Brees's critique created a stir among the senior leaders, including Krueger. The fact that Brees made his comments public only served to compound the problem. General George C. Marshall later recalled, "In addition, he made rather caustic reference to the leadership of the older generals. Further, this was mimeographed and released to the press." Consequently, Marshall moved to change the way in which postmaneuver critiques were handled. For starters, critiques of senior commanders were no longer to be made in front of junior officers. "As a matter of fact," Marshall told Lt. Gen. Lesley J. McNair, "it might even be desirable to confine the portion of such critique to the two commanders themselves, and possibly their chiefs of staff. Certainly, such a critique should not be open to the public or released to the press."[29]

Despite these deficiencies, Krueger and the other high-level leaders were able to test and evaluate how the army's new divisional structure fit with existing doctrine. Krueger concluded that the army relied too heavily on maneuver and mobility to bring about decision on the battlefield without heeding other aspects of sound tactics. In his after-action report, the commander of the IX Corps remarked that

> The exercises as a whole indicated to me that we are too prone to accept the envelopment or turning movement per se as the most effective form of attack. Such operations are, however, effective only if the attacker has a considerable superiority and utilizes it to hold the defender so firmly in position as to prevent him from withdrawing.... Therefore, if the attacker engages the defender so firmly in front as to pin him to the ground while the enveloping or turning force moves against or around his flank, the stage is set for a serious defeat of the defender's forces.[30]

Krueger's comments strike to the heart of the problems of the army's interwar emphasis on an organization and tactical doctrine built on mobility and maneuver up to the divisional level, on the one hand, and a strategy of power at the large-unit level, on the other hand. The triangular division was meant to be a component of a corps yet conceived to carry out a war of overwhelming power. The obvious contradiction created problems, particularly at the division level. Krueger commented,

> The triangular division is a battle unit and when so employed is a strong, cohesive striking force with a great deal of power. The corps is essentially a tactical unit designed to control and give direction to the battle units assigned to it. I consider it unsound to disperse the division by combat teams over a wide front in an attack. Coordination of effort is almost certain to be missing and control by the division command will be difficult if not impossible. ... But this is not intended to mean that a combat team should not be used in an enveloping or turning movement. If so used, however, communication and other facilities must be assigned to such combat teams.[31]

Consequently, as he had while in command of the 2d Infantry Division, Krueger recommended that the number of riflemen in each division be increased "substantially." "The rifle strength of the divisions is too low, and runs dangerously close to the acceptance of the theory that the rifleman is provided merely in order that he may support the heavy weapons in getting into position," Krueger wrote. "I am firmly convinced on the contrary that the most important factor in battle, in the last analysis, is the rifleman, and that heavy weapons and all other auxiliary means must support him in getting into position from which he can assault the enemy."[32]

The maneuvers made clear the transitional state of the army. Men on horseback, for instance, fought alongside armored vehicles. Similarly, the tactical and strategic doctrines still reflected different sets of traditions and assumptions. Krueger's comments had underscored the absence of a concept of an operational level of war that bridged the contradictory tactical and strategic doctrines. In short, the army needed more practice in the art of war, and the Third Army's May 1940 exercise was just the start. For future maneuvers, Krueger suggested that the army include more combined-arms training: "The participation of all arms in future maneuvers is desirable in order that all may become familiar with the capabilities and limitations of the several arms."[33]

As the spring maneuvers ended, the army became more and more concerned with events in Europe. On 10 May, German forces had brought their war to the west by invading the Low Countries and France. By the time the Third Army completed its corps-vs.-corps maneuvers, Belgium was on the verge of collapse, British forces had their backs to the sea at Dunkirk, and the heart of France awaited the final thrust of the Wehrmacht. The United States responded to the German juggernaut, in part, by beginning to look more closely at preparing the National Guard. Consequently, the War Department used its next set of maneuvers—scheduled for August 1940—not to test doctrine or organization but to provide training to its newest members. "The primary purpose was to give training in field service and combined operations to divisions, regiments, and smaller units," Krueger wrote in his postmaneuver remarks. "They were not a test of higher commanders and staffs in their operative functions and ability to make sound decisions."[34]

The Third Army set aside the entire month of August 1940 for this purpose. The first week was allotted for the concentration of both regular army and National Guard units, and this was followed by six days of small unit and division training. Actual army maneuvers were scheduled for 17–20 August, and the entire exercise period ended with the usual critique and analysis by the various high-level participants and observers.[35]

As part of the maneuvers, Brees gave command of the VIII Corps to

Krueger on 27 June. His corps (Blue) was to face the IV Corps (Red) under the command of Maj. Gen. Albert H. Blanding. The exercise included a "war" between the two corps. The objective was similar to that of the May 1940 maneuvers, with Krueger commanding a hostile force that was to "invade" western Louisiana from Texas across the Sabine. His goal was to secure the bridges of the Red River near Alexandria.[36]

Unlike its predecessor, the August 1940 maneuvers were not successful. According to Krueger, to throw National Guard units into large-scale maneuvers without adequate training—in this case, two weeks' worth—was simply a waste of time not only for the Guardsmen but the regulars as well. A lack of basic soldiering skills hampered the Guardsmen's efforts to acquire a familiarity with the army's tactical doctrine. Sanitation conditions around National Guard camps, for example, were poor, particularly around kitchens, latrines, and bivouac areas. While the overall health of the regular army was excellent, National Guard units suffered "many cases of mild heat exhaustion and gastro enteritis," the VIII Corps maneuver report recounted. "This was partly due to excessive heat and humidity and partly to lack of proper supervision and discipline in unseasoned troops. There was also excessive indulgence in drinking of beer and soft drinks and eating of candy."[37]

Other aspects of National Guard performance warranted criticism as well. Motor traffic suffered from a lack of road discipline as trucks congregated at certain points, thereby creating large congested areas. Although march discipline improved throughout the maneuver period, "bunching of motor vehicles continued." In addition, routes were often not clearly marked, leading to further confusion. In at least one case, ration trucks did not reach their units because of the failure to post road signs.[38]

To help integrate the National Guard units into the regular army, Krueger suggested that National Guard units should not be thrown immediately into large-unit exercises. Rather, they should be first equipped with the latest equipment and "be given intensive training leading progressively from basic training of individual and minor units to the higher units, discipline and hardening being stressed."[39]

Other problems arose that were beyond the purview of the National Guard. The list included insufficient numbers of corps troops, no military police, and no medical or engineer units. A lack of permanent corps personnel further exacerbated the situation. Corps troops were continually transferred from one unit to another. In his critique, Blanding commented that "the principal lesson learned from the maneuver is the vital necessity of getting the necessary equipment for training and having continued training in the field. Corps staffs should be permanently organized and trained to function as a team."[40]

For the next two years, Krueger remained with the Third Army as a corps commander, largely helping to train National Guard units. Throughout this time, the command and organization of the Third Army underwent significant changes. The first occurred when Brees, now a lieutenant general, replaced Embick as commander of the Third Army at midnight 30 September 1940. A letter from the War Department, dated 3 October 1940, instructed all field commanders, including Brees, to devote "the maximum time" to training and as little time as possible to administrative affairs. Despite the priority of training, the regular army remained hampered by shortages of both qualified officers and training equipment, including supplies as basic as targets for small-arms practice.[41]

Just as the Third Army experienced transformation, the training and administrative organization of the army changed as well. On 3 October 1940, Marshall reorganized the army, attempting to make the training of the National Guard more efficient. The National Defense Act of 1920 had divided the United States into nine geographical zones, each one the responsibility of a single corps area command. Initially, corps areas were supposed to take charge of mobilizing manpower within its zone during national emergencies as well as training the U.S. Army in peacetime. Throughout the years, personnel shortages hampered the army, forcing some of the corps area headquarters to function as army headquarters as well. As the army sought to modernize, it had to overhaul this now awkward command arrangement.[42]

Based largely on the recommendations of McNair, Marshall's reorganization separated all corps areas from army commands. It gave to the corps areas the responsibility for administrative duties and requisitioning supplies for the formations within their geographical zones. Free from the burden of such duties, the armies, corps, and divisions were to concentrate on training and tactical matters. At the same time the War Department reorganized the army, it also named Krueger formal commander of the VIII Corps, although he had been the de facto commander for more than three months.[43]

Third Army and the GHQ Maneuvers

For a time, it appeared that Krueger's position as commander of VIII Corps would be brief. Shortly after he received his new command, the War Department considered him along with Short, now in charge of the First Corps Area, as a possible replacement for the retiring Lt. Gen. Charles D. Herron, commanding general of the Hawaiian Department. "For reasons on this side of the water," Marshall wrote Herron in December 1940, "it appears desirable to send Walter Short to Hawaii instead of Krueger, and for the same reason it appears best to make the transfer at an earlier date than originally intended. Therefore, Short will probably be relieved as a tactical commander in the early part of January and ordered to Hawaii." Marshall had other plans for Krueger. "Krueger, incidentally, I expect to hold for the command of the Third Army on Brees's retirement in the late spring."[44] Unfortunately, Marshall's reasons for selecting Short instead of Krueger are not clear.[45] Nevertheless, one is left to wonder what Krueger's fate would have been if he had been in Hawaii when the Japanese attacked Pearl Harbor instead of Short.

Within several months, Marshall made his decision final concerning Krueger's appointment as commander of the Third Army. Brees himself, who was scheduled to retire on 30 June 1941, probably aided the chief of staff's decision. He suggested to Marshall that considering the "strenuous projected summer program," including the Third Army's participation in the army's largest peacetime maneuvers in history, he would retire ahead of schedule "on or about May 15th." Furthermore, Brees recommended—despite his unfavorable appraisal of the VIII Corps commander's performance in the May 1940 exercises—that Krueger replace him, since Krueger was "the most logical candidate for this Army job."[46]

In mid-April 1941, Marshall confided to Krueger in a lengthy and insightful letter, "I do not anticipate any difficulty in securing approval for your promotion to command of the Third Army, and I will try to settle the matter within the next few days, so that you can be certain as to your course for the immediate future." With Krueger's approval almost a certainty, Marshall proceeded in his letter to offer some direct and frank criticism of the VIII Corps commander. First writing that he had "been well aware of your mental ability and of your tremendous capacity and willingness for hard work," Marshall went on to present three specific comments on Krueger as a military officer, all of which were noted for the "purpose of the efficient development of the Third Army."[47]

The first, and the one "that possibly exercises the dominant influence I am troubled about," Marshall remarked, centered on Krueger's inability to accept criticism. "You are a man of decided opinions, along with great ability cultivated through many years of hard work, and as a partial result of this there has grown up the impression that you have a hard time hearing other people's views and adapting them to your own use—and that you are evidently unaware of this reaction of yours," Marshall wrote. "In the big picture of this emergency, you will have to follow another pattern if the best results are to be obtained."[48]

Similarly, Marshall singled out Krueger's "sensitiveness to possible or assumed criticism involved in any suggestions, coupled with your reaction to any course of action which you think might involve you unfavorably. There is much these days that those at the top have to take on the chin, and I must be certain that you will carry your full burden of the task in a self-effacing manner." Finally, Marshall claimed that there is an "impression from a number of directions" that Krueger had a difficult time working with a "policy" if he did not fully and wholeheartedly agree with it.[49]

Apparently, Marshall had in mind Krueger's reaction to the May 1940 maneuvers. It was obvious that Krueger did not accept Brees's criticism of his performance, and Krueger's strong and determined personality was a matter of concern on the verge of his promotion to army commander. Marshall, therefore, had legitimate concerns whether the VIII Corps commander could handle the large jump in responsibility to that of an army commander. After all, Krueger had one of the most important jobs in the army: training it. While forging a modern army to match the performance of the Wehrmacht, Marshall had to make sure that his commanders could assimilate a large range of lessons and views from a variety of sources.

Krueger responded respectfully to Marshall's candid remarks by stating, "I offer neither explanation nor excuse, but accept your comments without reservation, in the same spirit in which they were offered, and will profit by them. I appreciate fully that, no matter in what capacity I may serve, I must obviate the impressions to which you refer. ... You shall have no cause hereafter for anxiety on my account in this connection."[50] Whether his reaction was based on true sincerity, pure ambition, or a combination of the two, Krueger's response reflected his determination to flourish in his profession. As he and Fay Brabson had discussed on many occasions beginning almost forty years earlier, to become and then succeed as a general officer was Krueger's goal, and he was not going to let this opportunity slip by.

In seeking the approval of Secretary of War Henry L. Stimson, Marshall sent the 14 April letter to Krueger as well as his own memorandum to the longtime Republican statesman. In it, Marshall told Stimson that "General Krueger is a few weeks my junior in years, and was my senior in rank. He has been one of the intellectuals of the Army; is a very hard worker; is one of the German type." Highlighting the prospects for Krueger if he were not given the Third Army, Marshall concluded, "If Krueger is passed over, I am inclined to think his efficiency as a corps commander would be affected."[51]

On 5 May 1941, Marshall formally notified Krueger that he had "received a clearance from the Secretary of War in the matter of your appointment as Commander of the Third Army on the relief of General Brees May 15th, and

I thought you would like to know without further delay." At the same time he received his new command, Krueger also earned his third star. Krueger commented, "I realize how big the task is, and now that I am commanding the Third Army, I realize what a terrific responsibility it is. I am not worried about responsibility. It will not keep me awake. Whether I have enough energy and punch to carry on indefinitely the future will show."[52]

Krueger immediately prepared for the GHQ army-vs.-army maneuvers later in the year. The preparatory work included identifying and bringing to the Third Army qualified personnel. He requested the services of Lt. Col. Dwight D. Eisenhower, who was then serving as the chief of staff of the IX Army Corps. Reflecting his views of the ideal chief of staff, Krueger believed that Eisenhower would fit perfectly, writing to Marshall that "in my judgment, that position demands a younger man, one possessing broad vision, progressive ideas, a thorough grasp of the magnitude of the problems involved in handling an Army, and lots of initiative and resourcefulness. Lieutenant Colonel Dwight D. Eisenhower, Infantry, is such a man." After arriving at Third Army, Krueger instructed Eisenhower to organize its staff. Normally, Krueger kept Eisenhower close to headquarters while he went into the field to see for himself the progress of the army's training, because, as Krueger remembered, "I wanted a man there to look after things. I always felt that the commander or his CofS [chief of staff] should always be at headquarters."[53]

Charged with developing the skills of commanders in leading large units, the Third Army continued with its training program in western Louisiana. Within two weeks of assuming command of Third Army, Krueger supervised a series of corps maneuvers beginning with the VIII Corps (2–13 June), the V Corps (16–27 June), and the IV Corps (11–23 August). These corps maneuvers were followed by corps-vs.-corps maneuver that pitted the V Corps against the VIII Corps in late August. With the period of corps training completed, Krueger turned his attention to his army headquarters, first with a command-post exercise and then with a series of field maneuvers that placed IV Corps against a makeshift Third Army, consisting of the V and VIII Corps (4–9 September). All of these exercises were conducted in western Louisiana.[54] Throughout these two and one-half months of training, Krueger continually stressed two points. First, he wanted his army to become skilled in the technical side of operations. Time and time again, he demanded proficiency in such subjects as traffic control, concealment and camouflage, tactics of small units, infantry-artillery liaison, transmission of information and orders, simplification of staff procedures, defense methods against tanks and aircraft, feeding of men, and resupply of ammunition. Though the army made steady progress, he underscored the need to eliminate repeated mistakes. After one of the last exercises before the GHQ maneuvers, Krueger ominously remarked in his critique to various Third Army personnel, "If you will take the trouble to read over the notes of past critiques, you will be struck with the consistency with which many technical criticisms have been repeated.... Over and over, general and specific criticisms have been leveled at the proficiency of troop commanders with respect to these matters. There can be no doubt that, *so far as mere talking can assure*, all our senior officers and staffs—at least, *all officers present in this room are conversant with the standards demanded in the Third Army*" (Krueger's emphasis).[55]

Krueger also stressed the importance of aggressive offensive and defensive action through coordination of all available arms. At all levels, he preached that in order to ensure success, a commander needed to have a detailed understanding of the enemy through a careful reconnaissance effort; focus his thoughts on a singular objective; devise a plan that emphasizes speed, aggression, and power; issue simple but effective orders; and provide his subordinates with the freedom to execute the plan. In regard to tank and antitank warfare, for example, Krueger stated:

> The most effective use of armored forces and of their natural foes, the massed anti-tank formations, can be attained only through thoughtful planning and perfect technique. There must be continuous reconnaissance to determine the practicability of the terrain for the use of armored forces. If this is done, then the direction of their attack should be such as to strike at a vital area or element in order to make their use worth while. To barge ahead, gain local successes in numerous places and then be stopped by a natural obstacle, is a waste of power.[56]

Of course, to make the attack work, all of the elements under the commander had to work together, using some predetermined common method. It was incumbent on a commanding officer to make sure that all components functioned as a single entity. "The utmost coordination is necessary in a unit as large as a corps if it is to function in an effective manner," Krueger stated. "Only through coordination can its full force be used."[57]

With his Third Army trained and ready for further testing, Krueger's next challenge was the GHQ maneuvers, scheduled to start on 15 September 1941. Since the Third Army was already in Louisiana, there was no long travel time to the maneuver area, which covered 30,000 square miles in both Louisiana and east Texas. The Third Army's assembly area was just north of Krueger's headquarters in Lake Charles.[58]

While Krueger was clearly an able trainer and educator who continually stressed the essential aspects of soldiering and aggressive offensive action, he and his staff nevertheless encountered difficulties as they prepared for the impending maneuvers. Both the Second and Third Armies were charting new ground, and Krueger and his staff were unsure as to exactly how they should best set up their headquarters. Eisenhower commented that "since none of us has ever functioned on an Army Staff in such large maneuvers, we are having some difficulty in deciding just how many individuals are needed in each section.... I'm trying to find out what would constitute a reasonable employment and stick to that."[59]

With Krueger's personality, ambition, and desire to succeed, it is not surprising that he committed all of the resources he could to the upcoming maneuvers. In fact, he went so far that McNair had to rein him in. In a letter to Krueger written on 5 June 1941, McNair laid it on the line:

> Your gang there seems to have the idea of anticipating every possible need in connection with signal communication and providing for it completely beforehand, even to the extent of constructing elaborate and costly pole lines. For example, there is a demand for a pole line between Lake Charles and Shreveport, which would cost $200,000 and would be paid for by the government at a rate of $61,000 a year—believe it or not. This proposal, to my mind, is preposterous, and would be a gross and wholly unjustified misuse of government money.

McNair further criticized Krueger's headquarters, which he characterized as "an elaborate, permanent set-up," which belied the fact that the Third Army's presence in the Lake Charles region was, in fact, temporary. McNair concluded, "I am quite willing to make available to the armies such troop units and means as would be reasonable in active operations, if such means are at all obtainable. What I am objecting to is the preparation of facilities, far in advance of the maneuvers, under conditions which are one hundred percent artificial."[60]

Krueger's opponent in the GHQ maneuvers would be Lt. Gen. Ben Lear's Second Army, which had to travel almost 200 miles to Louisiana from Alabama. Lear was a conventional soldier, one not particularly accustomed to modern military operations. While he could at times be creative in terms of planning, Lear could not execute his plans in a timely fashion because of his insistence on thorough preparation. Adding to his trouble as an operational commander, he was—as one historian has commented—a "stickler for spit and polish who criticized freely and abrasively."[61]

The Second Army (Red) would participate in the maneuver with fewer men than the Third (Blue) but possessed armored superiority. Lear's army contained the VII Corps, composed of the 27th, 33d, and 6th Divisions and the 107th Cavalry Regiment, and the I Armored Corps, which possessed a powerful mechanized force of the 1st and 2d Armored Divisions. Krueger's army, in contrast, consisted of the VIII Corps (2d, 45th, and 36th Infantry Divisions and the 113th Cavalry Regiment), the IV Corps (31st, 43d, and 38th Infantry Divisions), and the V Corps (32d, 34th, and 37th Infantry Divisions and the 106th Cavalry Regiment). Third Army also had the services of the 1st Cavalry Division, three antitank groups, and the 1st Tank Group, composed of two light tank battalions, which served as reserves. Supporting the ground forces, each side shared approximately 500 combat aircraft. The participants of the GHQ maneuvers totaled eighteen divisions organized into five corps of approximately 600,000 men.[62]

During the first phase of the maneuvers, the Second Army took position west of the Red River, and the Third Army assembled in southern Louisiana between De Ridder and Oadale. GHQ provided strategic direction to both armies by issuing operating instructions. Lear was ordered to invade Blue territory by moving across the Red River at 0500 on 15 September. His mission was simple: destroy the Blue Army near Lake Charles. Consequently, he ordered his VII Corps to cross the Red River and establish positions on its western bank. Once this was accomplished, he wanted to send his highly mobile I Armored Corps all the way to the Sabine River, where it would then head southeast to the flank and rear of Krueger's army.[63]

Similarly, GHQ ordered Krueger into offensive action. He was told that enemy forces were most likely moving toward the Red River. His mission then was to advance northward and destroy the Red Army. Krueger, therefore, planned to align his army with the VIII Corps on the left, the IV Corps in the middle, and the V Corps on the right and move them all vigorously to the northeast. He hoped to pin Lear's forces against the Red River and annihilate them.[64]

With speed that belied its composition,[65] Krueger's infantry army dashed forward and located the invading Red force. By nightfall, his reconnaissance units had ascertained much of Lear's position. It was clear to Krueger that Red's I Armored Corps had moved far to the east, as the 2d Armored Division reached positions between the Sabine River and Many, Louisiana. With an armored attack threatening his left flank, Krueger sent the 1st Antitank Group to the VIII Corps. Lear's other corps, however, did not quite achieve the same success. The VII Corps faced difficulty moving across the Red River, thanks in part to Blue air raids against key crossing points. Largely because of the trouble the Second Army had in getting all of its elements deployed, the first day of the maneuvers ended with the momentum in Krueger's favor. Despite

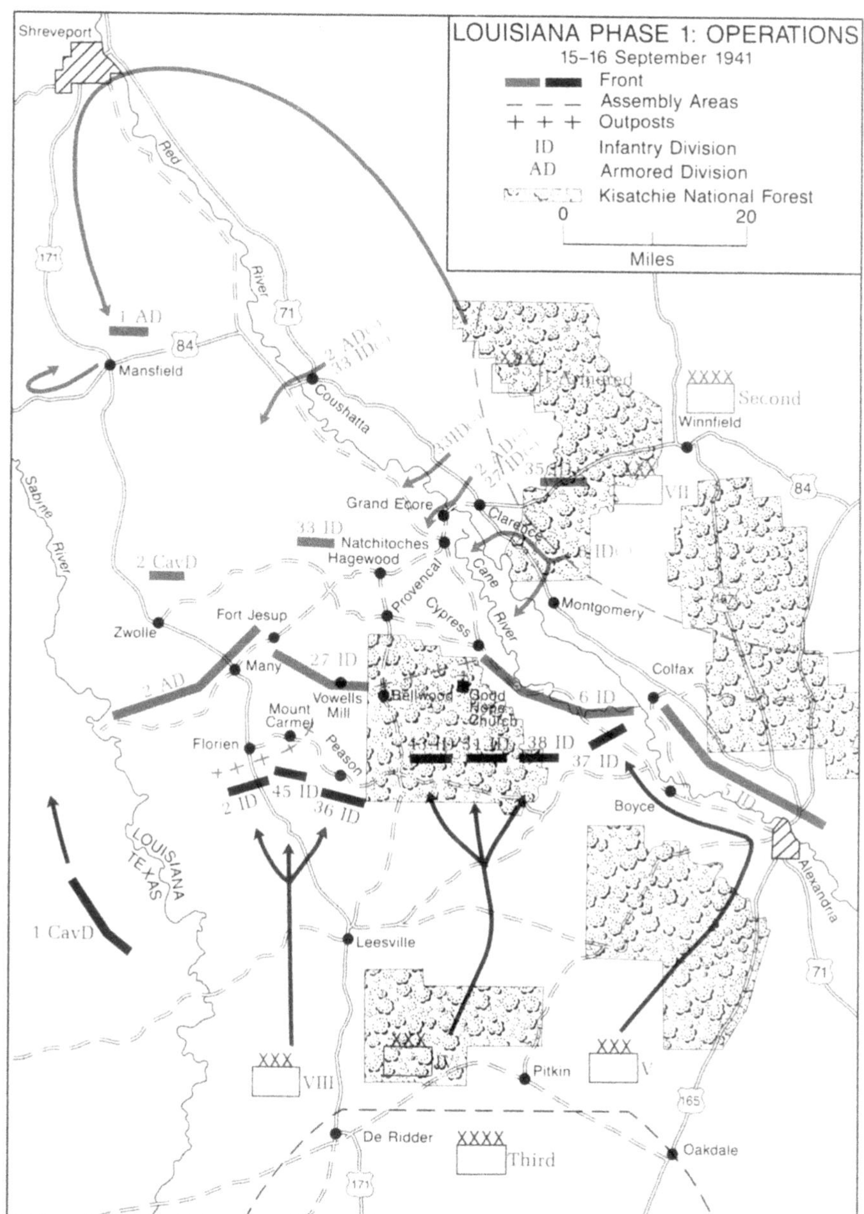

Map 1. GHQ Maneuvers of 1941: Phase One, 15–16 September 1941
Source: Christopher R. Gabel, *The U.S. Army GHQ Maneuvers of 1941* (Washington, D.C.: Center of Military History, United States Army, 1992), 66.

having superior mobility, Lear labored in springing his plan and had to spend the night with the knowledge that many of his divisions were defending overextended fronts. The 6th Infantry Division alone held a line of thirty miles extending between the Louisiana towns of Cypress and Colfax.[66]

The following day witnessed engagements that Krueger used to buy valuable time so that he could reposition his army. Realizing that Lear had pushed some of his forces all the way to the Sabine River the previous day, Krueger wanted to swing his army from facing the northeast to the northwest, in order establish his lines parallel with those of the Second Army. In the west, the VIII Corps, with the assistance of antitank units, pushed the 2d Armored Division back. Meanwhile, the IV Corps and the 1st Tank Group moved forward and engaged the 6th Infantry Division. As a result of the day's events, Lear postponed the planned strike by the I Armored Corps to 18 September.[67]

One would expect that Lear would have spent 17 September shoring up his positions by establishing a more favorable posture from which to launch his flanking attack. Strangely, however, most of his forces spent the day immobile. The only activity was in the east, where the 2d Armored Division unsuccessfully attempted to push forward as a prelude to the next day's offensive. The Second Army's predicament was only made worse with losses elsewhere along the front. Krueger was surprised by Lear's inactivity and ordered his army to assault the Second Army's positions. In the center as well as the east, Krueger's forces pushed the Red Army back, in the case of the 6th Infantry Division some six miles.[68]

Despite losing ground on 17 September, Lear still planned to launch his attack the next day, so that on the day of the Red Army's big offensive strike, most I Armored Corps's forces were curiously divided and scattered throughout the Second Army's lines in an attempt to stabilize Red positions against increasing Blue pressure. This situation left the I Armored Corps's mission largely on the shoulders of the 2d Armored Division, which launched its attack as scheduled at 0600. The VIII Corps, however, deployed its reinforced antitank units and eventually wore down the advancing columns. In the absence of proper combined-arms support, the Red tanks faltered, advancing at most ten miles. Meanwhile, the 1st Armored Division, after a long delay due to its activities of the previous day, struck the center of Blue lines in the vicinity of Kisatchie National Forest. Forced to operate in terrain generally unsuited for armored warfare, the 1st became bogged down and virtually ceased to function as an effective mechanized unit.[69]

Realizing that Lear's offensive was grinding to a halt, Krueger decided to seize the initiative and launched his own attack on 19 September. He sent his 37th and 38th Infantry Divisions northward against Red's left flank.

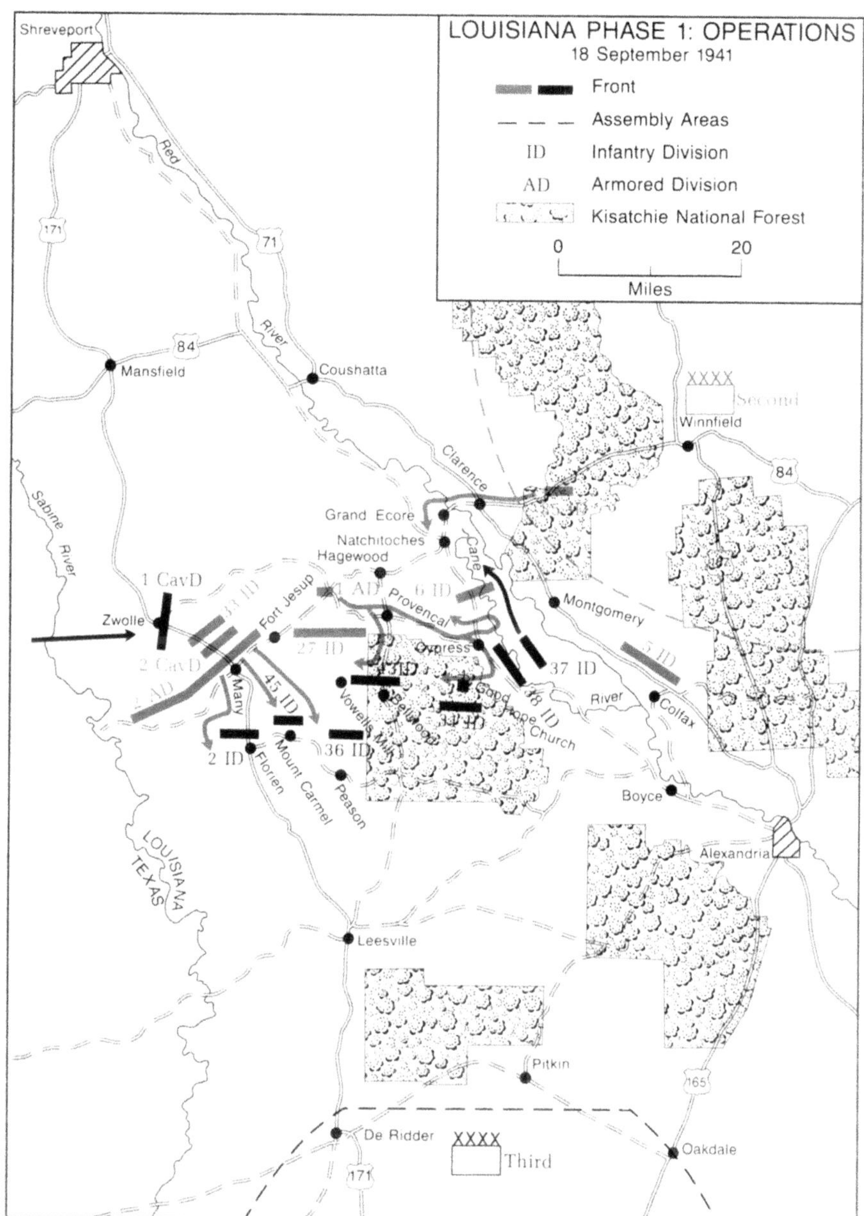

Map 2. GHQ Maneuvers of 1941: Phase One, 18 September 1941
Source: Christopher R. Gabel, *The U.S. Army GHQ Maneuvers of 1941* (Washington, D.C.: Center of Military History, United States Army, 1992), 78.

The two divisions pushed through Red's VII Corps and threatened to cut off the Second Army from its crossing points over the Red River. More central in Krueger's plans, however, was an assault by the 1st Cavalry Division to the rear and right of the Second Army's position near Zwolle, Louisiana. Although this attack was temporarily called to a halt because of "impending" Red armored attacks near the Florian-Peason-Toro area, it resumed the following day.[70]

Keeping in mind his own critique of the May 1941 maneuvers concerning the failure by many commanders to execute a turning movement successfully, Krueger wanted to make sure that he did not imprudently send the flanking force into the enemy's rear areas without pinning down the frontline divisions first. The Blue IV and V Corps, therefore, pushed forward, producing measurable results. Although primarily a holding movement, the V Corps's attack captured Natchitoches, and according to Krueger, "the bulk of the 1st Cavalry was moving on ZWOLLE-MANY." These events propelled the Blue commander to alter his plan slightly by committing the reserves of the IV Corps to pierce the center of the Red lines. While the 1st Cavalry Division continued its flanking attack in the Red right flank, the 34th Infantry would lead a combined-arms assault against the center of the Second Army. Krueger recalled that "I decided to resume the attack on Friday morning [19 September], the weight of attack to be directed against the Red left and center." Preceded by tanks, bombers, and artillery fire, the 34th Infantry Division stuck in the direction of Robeline early that day. Krueger then was applying pressure along the Red front, while he sprang a two-pronged attack, the first aimed at Zwolle and the second at Robeline. In addition to the two pincers, the formations whose objective was to hold Lear's army in place also aggressively advanced. Units of the IV and V Corps moved in a northwesterly direction as the Second Army retreated and attempted to reorganize its defensive positions. Under these circumstances, the war's conclusion seemed clear, and at 1530 on 19 September, GHQ called an end to Phase 1 of the maneuvers.[71]

Throughout the first phase of the GHQ maneuvers, Krueger, unlike Lear, demonstrated that his own brand of operational planning was based on seizing the initiative and aggressively pursuing his objective. He was able to combine the army's two separate tactical and strategic doctrines into a successful mode of operation. Using the less mobile foot infantry to fix the enemy, he concentrated his mobile elements along with his air power to form mobile combined-arms formations to strike at the rear and flanks of the enemy. He also demonstrated flexibility and a willingness to change plans when circumstances dictated such an alteration. When I Armored Corps, for example, threatened his left flank on 16 September, he changed the axis of his advance.

Instead of moving to the northeast, he rotated his army and pushed to the northwest instead. According to Christopher R. Gabel, Krueger's "reaction was swift and vigorous." Likewise, when he realized that Lear's army was committed to its existing course on 18 September, Krueger unleashed his own offensive that eventually led to the collapse of Red's left flank. In this first phase, Krueger's army was given a defensive mission, but he responded by staging, as historian Francis G. Smith writes, a "blitz defense."[72]

The second phase of the maneuvers began at 1200 on 24 September. Before this war started, however, GHQ reconstituted the two armies. It decided to give the Third Army an almost two-to-one advantage in manpower by assigning it the I Armored Corps headquarters and the 2d Armored Division. The Red Army received two of the three available antitank groups as well as other troops. McNair wanted to test a small army's ability to defend itself against an army that possessed greater mobility and greater numbers of infantry and tanks. This time around and unlike the previous phase, the Second Army had a purely defensive mission—to defend Shreveport—while the Third Army's objective was, of course, to capture it.[73]

Facing this difficult situation, Lear planned a defense in depth. Placing four of his divisions on the front lines and three in reserve, he created a series of parallel defensive lines. He included in his plan the phased withdrawal of his army from one defensive line to the next in the hope that such a strategy would eventually wear down his opponent until "reinforcements" arrived on 30 September. Krueger, in contrast, planned an aggressive offensive strategy that relied on envelopment. He proposed to send his three infantry corps northward from their staging area between Bon Weir and a point south of Alexandria in order to engage and fix the enemy. Once the Second Army had been pinned down, he wanted to send the I Armored Corps along with the 2d Infantry Division, acting as army reserve, presumably against a weak spot in the enemy lines.[74]

Almost immediately upon the start of the maneuvers, Lear began his general withdrawal, during which he ordered the demolition of all railroad bridges and river-crossing points. Nevertheless, Blue forces succeeded in advancing approximately twenty miles. Much of the same activity occupied the second day's events as well. However, because his "reinforcements" would not arrive for five days, Lear could not just trade space for time. Eventually, he would need to hold his ground at some point. Consequently, he decided to halt in the morning hours of the third day, 26 September, when his army was about thirty to forty miles north of their original positions.[75]

By late 25 September, a frustrated Krueger was trying to decide just how to force the Second Army into combat. In the afternoon, he elected to

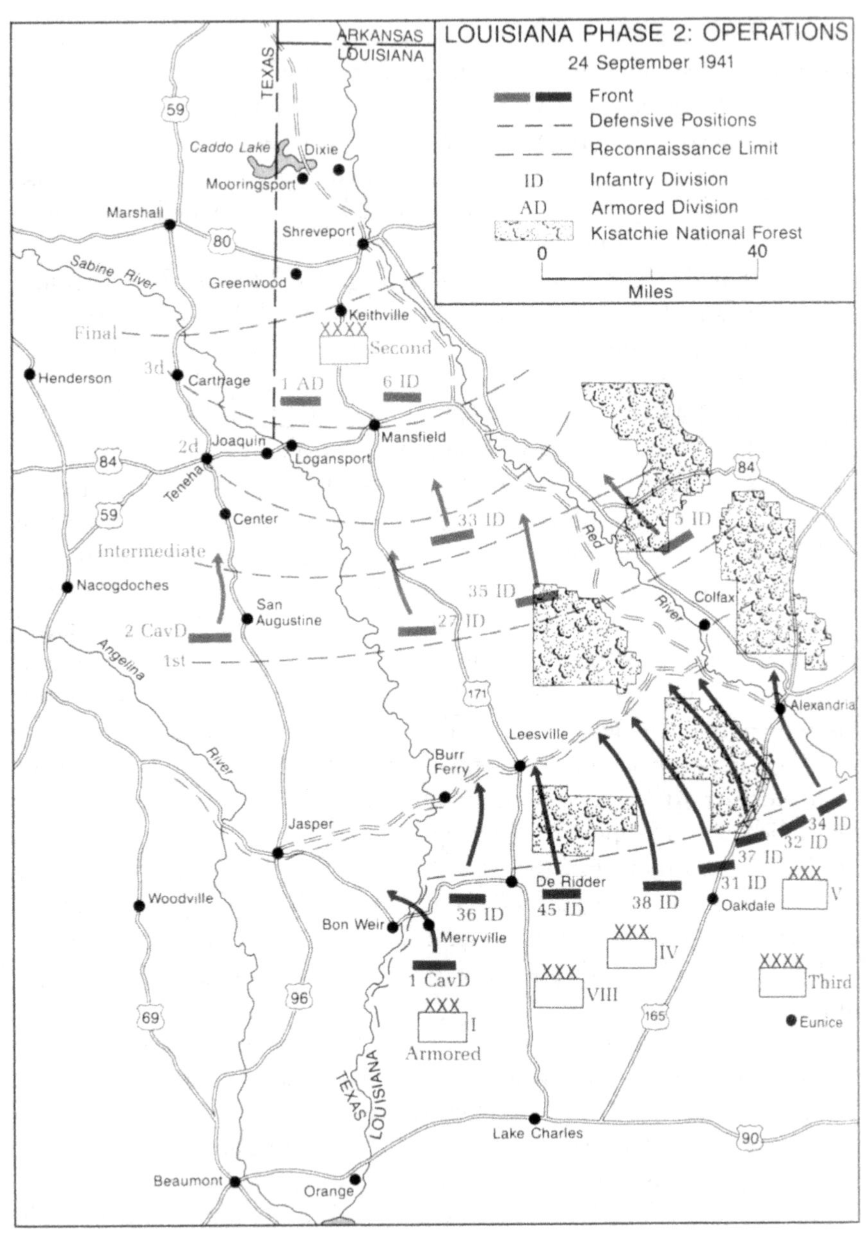

Map 3. GHQ Maneuvers of 1941: Phase Two, 24 September 1941
Source: Christopher R. Gabel, *The U.S. Army GHQ Maneuvers of 1941* (Washington, D.C.: Center of Military History, United States Army, 1992), 98.

commit his I Armored Corps and sent it along with the 2d Infantry Division to a staging area near Leesville. He ordered the IV, V, and VIII Corps to continue their pursuit of Red forces, while the I Armored Corps was going to attack from its positions near Leesville. After he learned that the Red Army had ceased its northward retreat, Krueger quickly altered the plan to take advantage of the situation. At approximately 1730, while in the field at Lake Charles, he devised his new plan and sent it to Eisenhower for distribution. He wanted his three infantry corps to maintain their advance, not to catch the withdrawing Red Army, but to fix it, while he sent the I Armored Corps along with the 3d Air Task Force "to the west bank of the Sabine River after nightfall, [to] advance north and operate against Red right and rear."[76]

The commander of I Armored Corps, Maj. Gen. Charles S. Scott, divided his forces into two groups. The first (consisting of the 41st Infantry Regiment of the 2d Armored Division and various other attached units) took an extended route to Shreveport through Texas. The other group (made up of the 2d Armored Brigade and the 2d Infantry Division) took a much shorter path, with the objective of severing the links between Shreveport and Red's VII Corps. The I Armored Corps made excellent progress throughout the first day despite Red's attempt to delay its progress with continued reliance on demolitions and delaying tactics. With the flamboyant 2d Armored Division commander Maj. Gen. George S. Patton Jr. in charge, the outer column advanced about 200 miles, while the inner column traveled approximately 100 miles.[77]

Because Lear curiously did not seem to be responding to the armored envelopment on his right flank, the I Armored Corps persisted in its attack throughout 27 September. Patton's force swept up and behind Red's defenses of Shreveport, and the inner column advanced past Teneha and turned into the Second Army's right flank, north of the VII Corps. Meanwhile, Blue's three other corps successfully prevented the VII Corps from falling back by engaging its frontline divisions.[78]

The following day brought additional bad news for Lear. The VIII Corps drove through Red's mainline of defenses and into Mansfield, where heavy fighting ensued. The I Armored Corps closed on Shreveport, dispensing with Lear's scattered and poorly organized defensive measures. Although the battle for Shreveport was far from over, based on the previous three days' events, McNair decided that the exercise had fulfilled its purpose and terminated it late that afternoon.[79]

Although GHQ believed that the maneuvers were a success, postmaneuver critiques focused on the key deficiencies still prevalent throughout the army. At the top of the list was the glaring lack of qualified leaders. During the

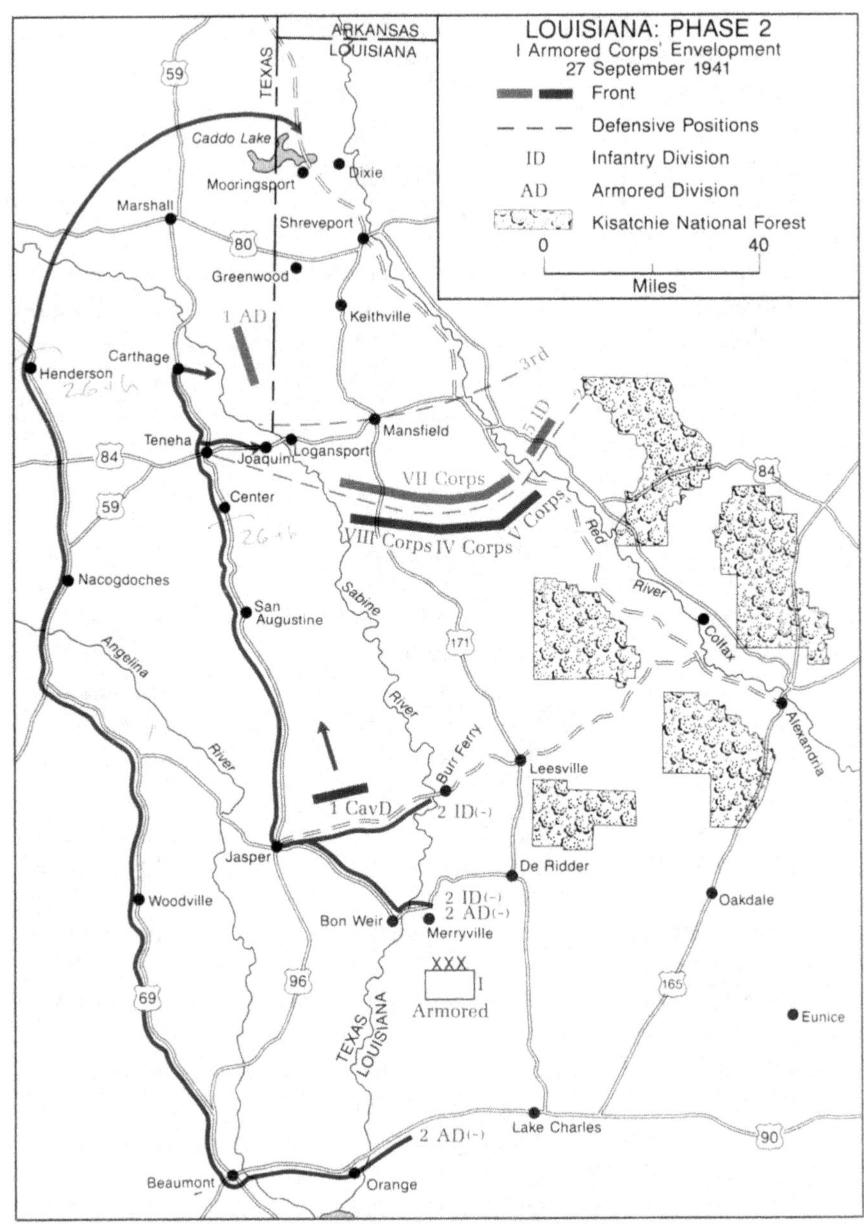

Map 4. GHQ Maneuvers of 1941: Phase Two, 27 September 1941
Source: Christopher R. Gabel, *The U.S. Army GHQ Maneuvers of 1941* (Washington, D.C.: Center of Military History, United States Army, 1992), 104.

months that followed the maneuvers, both Krueger and McNair spent much time in ridding the ranks of incompetent officers and replacing them with experienced and well-trained officers who could continue molding the army into a combat-ready fighting force. The maneuvers thus helped to identify those individuals who were qualified for higher command.[80]

The newspapers of the time celebrated the Third Army's conduct of the maneuvers, especially its dramatic envelopment of the Second Army's western flank. Over time, Eisenhower, who was still Krueger's chief of staff, was credited for the Third Army's success. The GHQ deputy director of the maneuver, Brig. Gen. Mark W. Clark, for example, claimed that Eisenhower planned the I Armored Corps's exploits. For his part, Eisenhower rejected the acclaim, writing that "shortly afterward, I was given unsought publicity in a newspaper column whose author attributed credit to me that should have gone to General Krueger. I still have no idea why I became the target for his praise." Despite this admission, Eisenhower remains widely believed to have been the true architect of Third Army operations, even though more than sixteen years after the maneuvers, Krueger commented unequivocally that he, not Eisenhower, was the author of all Third Army plans. Historians, furthermore, have generally argued that Eisenhower was the key to the Third Army's success and that the 2d Armored Division's exploits were formulaic, in that the division had performed a similar maneuver in a previous exercise.[81]

Philosophy of Command

Although the 2d Armored Division's activities have been overemphasized and over dramatized, its operations are symbolic. During both the GHQ maneuvers of 1941 and later in World War II, according to many contemporaries and subsequent commentators, Krueger's successes came in spite of him or as a result of those who worked with him. Though the armies under his command (both in the maneuvers and later in World War II) were successful, he still has not received credit for their accomplishments. The debate suggests that historians need to reexamine Krueger's method of operation as commander of an army, especially in light of the historiographical trend that tags him as methodical and plodding.[82]

His ideas of formulating, writing, and disseminating operating plans revolved around the principle of simplicity. Unlike the prescriptions in official War Department publications such as *Manual for the Commander of Large Units*, he viewed his job as providing his corps and divisional commanders with general directions and then allowing them to fulfill their objectives with minimal interference from above. At an August 1941 conference of Third

Army commanders, Krueger informed his subordinates what to expect from him in the upcoming maneuvers: "My idea is—I do not like to give detailed instructions. My idea could be put in a very few words, and have the staff work it out." He liked to work directly, and if possible, face to face with his senior commanders:

> An army order on any action is going to be very brief. That will go only to large independent unit commanders. ... When such an order is pending, before it is issued I will have a conference with the various commanders if it is possible to do, and give them a picture and hand them the order. "My concept for this operation is thus and so." Everybody will know. Carry on without having it described in great detail. I have placed a great deal of reliance in the confidence of senior commanders in each other.[83]

Throughout the fall maneuvers, Krueger consistently put into practice his ideas of issuing orders, many of which date back to his days at the War Colleges. In the second phase, for instance, he sent the I Armored Corps on its flanking attack on Shreveport by issuing simple verbal orders after talking to the corps commander personally.

It is also clear from his theory and practice of command that Krueger formulated Third Army plans and was *the dominant* influence in his headquarters, another aspect of command to which Krueger had given quite some thought. Specifically with regard to the 2d Armored Division's famous advance on Shreveport in the second phase of the maneuvers, Krueger would not have allowed a colonel, no matter how bright, to run his headquarters or make major decisions, especially in light of his strong, often overbearing personality, which often led others to describe him as "typical German."[84]

Krueger's actual plans were aggressive and progressive, just as the actual forms of his orders were clear and simple. He advocated the use of combined-arms attacks—including air units, artillery, tanks, and infantry—relying primarily on enveloping movements. The composition of a particular force had to include all the branches of the army in supporting roles. Combined arms weighed heavily in his concept of force structure. "There must be," he simply said, "close integration of all units."[85]

If provided the proper ingredients, Krueger advocated the creation of an armored force for use in independent missions. "I will probably use such armored force as I have got," he said prior to the GHQ maneuvers, "by attacking on a narrow front–to find out where the weak spots are and take all the tanks on a narrow front, preceded by dive bombers and followed by a mobile division, and go right through. If I can possibly do it, I am going to make the other fellow dance to my tune." In his opinion, the experience of the exercises only confirmed his ideas of combined-arms and armored operations. "I was again impressed with the absolute necessity of having armored forces closely supported by other troops," he remarked. "An armored spear head is nothing but a figure of speech when the going is really bad. In any case, I believe careful consideration should be given to the proposition of normally having a motorized division form part of an armored corps."[86]

Once the proper organization was established, it was important, according to Krueger, to use it in an aggressive manner, no matter what the size. The overall objective must be the annihilation of the enemy, usually through enveloping or turning movements. "The use of cover, maneuver, skillful use of supporting weapons, and exploitation of the possibilities of flanking fire are all too frequently neglected," Krueger stated about small-unit tactics. "When an organization meets opposition, even if the enemy is employing only hit-and-run tactics, the leader of every unit down to the small must immediately concern himself with ways and means for speeding up the general advance rather than merely with methods for *driving back* the small detachment facing him.... Efforts must be made to capture or to annihilate the enemy by action against his flanks and rear."[87]

The principles of aggressive tactics that sought to annihilate the enemy also applied to larger formations. Krueger maintained that

> this principle applies not only to isolated minor actions, but to major actions as well, in fact to all phases of combat, inclusive of hand-to-hand conflict. All commanders must ponder these questions; those commanding minor units must constantly practice combining automatic, mortars, rifles, machine guns, bayonets and grenades in such a way as to annihilate the enemy. When the sum total of the plus results of these small actions along a general front markedly exceeds the minus ones—then victory will be won. But these plus results can be obtained only through skill—daring—leadership—resourcefulness.[88]

Krueger's philosophy of command was consistent with his actions in the fall 1941 maneuvers. Given the proper allocation of infantry, aircraft, tanks, and artillery, as in the second phase, Krueger created a combined-arms force under the command of I Armored Corps and provided it a mission of striking deep into enemy territory after his two infantry corps had fixed the main body of the Second Army. "Since it was desirable to have the Armored Force operate independently, the 2d Division was motorized and attached to form the Provisional I Armored Corps, a highly mobile and powerful striking force," he recounted in his postmaneuver comments. "This arrangement had every advantage, whether the Armored Corps was used straight ahead in a breakthrough, or in a turning movement." Even without the benefit of large tank formations, as in the first phase, he placed his limited armored resources to support the drive of the 34th Infantry Division in a knifelike penetration of the Second Army's front lines.[89]

Krueger was helping to create nothing less than a de facto operational doctrine based on highly mobile combined-arms attacks and relying on maneuver to annihilate the enemy. Krueger's actions in the GHQ maneuvers of 1941 illustrate this emerging doctrine and provide a stark contrast to the older attritional strategic doctrine executed by Lear. In the first phase, Lear squandered his superior armored force in piecemeal attacks. He preferred to utilize a strategy of overwhelming power along the entire front rather than attempting to employ his army in operations based on flanking or enveloping movements. Lear failed to commit his forces with initiative and aggressiveness, and he diluted the firepower of his armored units by scattering them throughout his army. Krueger, meanwhile, aggressively reoriented his supposedly immobile infantry army and then launched a flanking and penetration attack against the stationary Second Army. The second phase demonstrated that with an armored corps, Krueger utilized all of his advantages to launch an even more daring raid. In the contest between Second and Third Armies, the commander of the latter demonstrated a firm grasp of modern military operations, while the leader of the former failed to appreciate the power of combined-arms formations by frittering them away all along his front and did not appreciate the increased pace and tempo of motorized operations.[90]

Not more than three months before the entrance of the United States into World War II, Krueger was helping to bring to life an operational doctrine that did not even exist only several years earlier. Krueger attempted to bridge the two disparate tactical and strategic doctrines by building on the strengths of the two. By using the less-mobile infantry elements of his army, he fixed the enemy's position; he then used the more mobile and heavier firepower of the armored and triangular divisions to make the decisive flanking attack. The army, however, had not yet completed conversion of the infantry divisions from the square to the triangular formations. The four army commanders in the GHQ maneuvers of 1941 had to make do primarily with square infantry divisions or specialty corps, such as the I Armored Corps, neither of which was to see action overseas during the war. If the triangular division had been used on a wide basis, perhaps its many deficiencies (which Krueger pointed to earlier when he was 2d Infantry Division commander) would have become more apparent. Nevertheless, the operational doctrine represented in the 1941 *Field Service Regulations* and brought into existence for the first time under Krueger's direction was applicable to the future force structure. The foremost historian of the GHQ maneuvers states:

> Only one of the field armies involved in the maneuvers clearly anticipated the operational art that would characterize American operations in World War II—Krueger's Third Army, where Eisenhower served as chief of staff. Krueger fought on a broad front, yet retained a high degree of responsiveness owing to his skillful use of motor transport and to the latitude that he afforded his subordinates. His powerful operations were clear and straightforward, and they produced maximum results at minimum risk.[91]

Thus, Krueger not only utilized the broad principles laid out in *Field Service Regulations* 1941 to formulate his specific plans for his Third Army in the GHQ maneuvers of 1941 but also anticipated the formal operational doctrine espoused in FM 100-15, *Field Service Regulations: Larger Units*, published in June 1942, which provided official guidance to commanders of formations above divisions.

Chronic problems at the small-unit level continued to plague the maneuvers.[92] However, this was another justification the War Department gave to the exercises. As Marshall told a U.S. senator who criticized the maneuvers because of all of the mistakes made, "My God, Senator, that's the reason I do it. I want the mistake down in Louisiana, not over in Europe, and the only way to do this thing is to try it out, and if it doesn't work, find out what we need to make it work." Krueger's job then was to introduce the army—especially its newest members—to the new tactics and doctrines based on mobile combined-arms formations. In fact, the army previously had very little instruction in this type of warfare, which was particularly true for the National Guard units. "These maneuvers, then, gave us the first chance we have ever had of coordinating infantry, artillery, armored forces, anti-tank forces, antiaircraft forces and air forces of magnitude," Krueger wrote in a letter to Maj. Gen. Edward F. McGlachlin Jr. "Although difficult, the coordination of all the arms was extremely interesting, but, what was more important, it provided us with an experience that otherwise we never would have had."[93]

Just as Krueger made an impact on operational doctrine, he made an equal impression on the officers and men who served under him. He was constantly on the move throughout the maneuvers, conducting inspections, observing his men, and teaching tactics and other aspects of soldiering. One of the National Guard divisions that served in the Third Army was the 45th Infantry Division, which was stationed at Camp Barkeley, near Abilene, Texas, and composed of units from Oklahoma, Arizona, Colorado, and New Mexico.

The commander of Camp Barkeley happened to be Col. Fay W. Brabson. After arriving back at Camp Barkeley upon the completion of the GHQ maneuvers, the 45th Infantry Division commander, Maj. Gen. William S. Key, told Brabson that "Krueger's energy in [the] maneuvers was unbelievable and that Krueger had left quite a lasting impression upon the personnel of the Division."[94]

Indeed, many of the enlisted men of the National Guard remembered Krueger taking his concern for their welfare to the extremes. Bill Mauldin was a member of the 45th Infantry Division during the maneuvers and recorded his surprise at Krueger's acute interest in the performance of army boots: "It is an awesome experience when a man with three stars on each shoulder steps out of the bushes and demands to see your bare feet."[95]

Trainer for the Army

For the next two years, Krueger and the Third Army continued to direct their energies toward training an unprepared army for war. In fact, Krueger asserted, "In a word, I regard our training mission at the moment as being of paramount importance." However, his efforts were both hampered and intensified by the December 1941 Japanese attack on Pearl Harbor, Hawaii. The increasing flow of new personnel—at one point, 10,000 soldiers arrived at Third Army per month—created a flood of untrained officers. After extensive inspection, Krueger determined that "entirely too many officers lacked adequate knowledge of what I called the 'Vulgar part of Soldiering,' such as general housekeeping, kitchen management, sanitation, care of weapons, supplies, stores, transportation and so on."[96]

This situation must have frustrated Krueger immensely, because he considered leadership a crucial component of the army. "Yet good leadership is the most difficult thing to produce," he explained in 1942, "for it requires inherent qualities of character, of initiative, of energy, of resourcefulness, and tenacity that every human being is not endowed with. Moreover, good leadership requires a high degree of skill, both technical and tactical, to make the most of every situation." Concluding that merely demanding quality leadership would be inadequate to correct the situation, he set up the Third Army Junior Officers Training Center (JOTC) at Camp Bullis, Texas.[97]

Eventually dubbed "Krueger Tech," the JOTC treated the student officers as enlisted men and covered purely practical subjects such as using the compass, administration, field sanitation, supply operations, and small-unit tactics. The six-week course proved successful and marked improvement in basic soldiering skills and conduct. Krueger particularly enjoyed the fact that the training was difficult and rigorous. On one occasion, he asked the commandant of the JOTC if the school had a rainy day schedule and was pleased with the short answer: "Yes, raincoats." The school was so successful that the Fourth Army and various other formations inquired about establishing similar schools in their respective camps. The Third Army's JOTC, nevertheless, lasted only until four classes had graduated, in part because the Officer Candidate Schools finally started to churn out competent officers, and Krueger needed to focus his energy on the upcoming series of Third Army maneuvers in 1942.[98]

The maneuvers of 1942 were only corps maneuvers, with the VIII Corps conducting its exercises from 4 August to 19 September, and the IV Corps conducting its own from 22 September to 8 November. The two corps concentrated on offensive and defensive problems involving rivers and air–ground cooperation in the attack. These maneuvers further refined the basic techniques that the army would encounter in Europe and Africa. Still, they were far from flawless, as Krueger wrote to his new chief of staff, Brig. Gen. Alfred M. Gruenther:

> The maneuvers have gone pretty well, though, as you will see from my critiques when they reach you, many things are done wrong and need material improvement. ... Shortcomings in minor tactics and discipline, and what, as you know, I usually call the vulgar part of soldiering, still leaves much to be desired. Throughout, however, constant improvement was made in these matters, and I am confident that the outfits left the maneuver area in much better shape in these respects than when the maneuvers began.[99]

One of the problems in tactics that particularly frustrated Krueger was the tendency many commanders had for dispersing their forces in piecemeal attacks instead of conserving their strength for decisive assaults:

> One thing that I am afraid I have not been able entirely to correct is the predisposition of commanders to fritter away troops in more or less complex schemes instead of using a simple plan and striking with all they have at the critical point and the critical time—all this in spite of the fact that the experience of all warfare indicates that a commander cannot possibly be too strong at the decisive point at the decisive time.[100]

As he had in the GHQ maneuver of 1941, Krueger again demonstrated his commitment to the principle of aggressive and offensive action, this time as a teacher instead of a practitioner.

Despite steady progress, several considerations—outside of Krueger's control—hampered the Third Army's training program. The effects had far reaching and unfortunate consequences for the future combat performance of the U.S. Army. The first factor was the resources the Third Army had to commit to defend the Gulf Coast and the southern border. At the request of the War Department, Third Army headquarters ordered its subordinate commands to "expect surprise" and to "understand their mission of instantaneous readiness to carry out their mission of protection against any kind of raiding force." Over the course of the next several months, the Third Army devoted almost all of its attention not to training but to the possibility of invasion from the south.[101]

The constant shuffling of units in and out of Third Army, furthermore, made the establishment of teamwork difficult if not impossible. Four divisions and one corps left the Third Army in the first quarter of 1942, and twelve new divisions and two new corps were attached. At the end of December 1941, the Third Army could count among its members 240,165 men. Four months later, it had only 174,520 soldiers. By 30 June 1942, the numerical strength of Third Army was 199,367, and by 31 December 1942, it was 331,192. Officers, enlisted men, and formations came and went with great frequency in a short period of time, which had an obvious and detrimental impact on training the army.[102]

Acute shortages of up-to-date equipment, moreover, impeded any attempt to create an army well versed in the complexities of modern warfare. The Great Depression was largely responsible for this situation, only made worse for the Third Army after the United States entered the war. By the beginning of 1942, stateside divisions received only 50 percent of their authorized equipment, and nondivisional units obtained only 20 percent. Material resources were stretched even further when the War Department made daily requests of equipment for overseas duty. The shortage of essential equipment, such as tanks, aircraft, machine guns, and ammunition, impeded the army's ability to train its formations in combined-arms warfare. Because of this situation, training methods too often included lectures, discussions, and conferences instead of hands-on rehearsals with up-to-date equipment. Not until late 1943 would production meet the needs of both combat and training.[103]

Compounding the problems that protecting the southern border from surprise attacks and shortages of personnel and equipment had on the Third Army's training program was a lack of time. From 1939 to 1942, the U.S. Army not only had to raise an army virtually out of thin air but also had to design, test, and produce new equipment such as a new medium tank;[104] devise, test, and implement a new divisional organization; and lay out and attempt to perfect a new form of operational warfare. All of this occurred within the short period of approximately three years and against the backdrop of the lingering effects of the Great Depression. It is surprising that the army did as well as it did in creating a force to wage war under these handicaps.[105]

It is not surprising, then, that Krueger believed he would end the war (and possibly his career) training the U.S. Army for combat duty. As much as he would have liked to be detailed to an overseas post, he felt that his age would ultimately prevent that from happening. "There's nothing that I should like better than to have a command at the front," he wrote to one of his old instructors at the Infantry and Cavalry School in Fort Leavenworth, Kansas. "I should love to try to 'rommel' Rommel. However, I am sure that younger men will be selected for tasks of that nature, in fact for all combat commands. I shall be 62 this coming January [1943], and though I am in perfect health, can stand a lot of hardship and people tell me I look and act ten years younger than my age, I do not delude myself."[106]

It was then a great shock when on 13 January 1943, while inspecting the 89th Infantry Division at Camp Carson, Colorado, Krueger received a radiogram from Gen. Douglas MacArthur, commander in chief of the Southwest Pacific Area that stated: "I have just recommended to Chief of Staff that you and the Third Army Headquarters be transferred to this area. I am particularly anxious to have you with me at this critical time."[107]

Throughout the period of 1938–1943, Walter Krueger had been at the forefront of creating the American army that was to fight in the Second World War. Despite facing great obstacles—the austere financial era of the Great Depression, a lack of adequate time, a lack of equipment, contradictory tactical and strategic doctrines, and an absence of an operational level of warfare until the early 1940s—Krueger led the army's efforts to modernize its divisional structure (even pointing out its weaknesses) and fashion an operational doctrine suitable for army-level operations.[108] Through these efforts and, more specifically, through his participation in the GHQ maneuvers of 1941, he demonstrated a thorough understanding of army operations based on combined arms, aggressiveness, and mobility. With MacArthur's invitation, Krueger had the opportunity to put into practice his ideas of command—ideas that had occupied much of his earlier career.

All of Krueger's training, as well as that of the rest of the army, had focused on a European-style war that emphasized warfare in wide-open spaces. Virtually no one in the U.S. Army had prepared for jungle warfare with all of its difficulties.[109] The question was, then, could Krueger make the transition to command an army under completely different circumstances from those for which he had trained?

Part II

Operational Leadership in the Southwest Pacific Area: 1943–1945

Chapter 5

New Britain, May 1943–February 1944

Although Lt. Gen. Walter Krueger was one of the U.S. Army's most experienced officers, he faced many difficult challenges upon arriving in the Southwest Pacific Area (SWPA). He not only had to confront Gen. Douglas MacArthur's impatient drive to the Philippine Islands but also had to learn to work with several strong, disparate, and often incompatible personalities. Furthermore, while proving that he was at the forefront of the emerging U.S. operational doctrine for fighting in open country based on his work in Louisiana, Krueger was not at all familiar with operating an army in an unfriendly jungle terrain, although he had fought in such an environment forty years before. Thus, Krueger's first set of operations, collectively known as Operation CARTWHEEL, would provide him with much-needed experience. He would use the period from May 1943 to February 1944 to become adjusted to warfare in the unique Pacific Theater and prepare for the campaigns that would follow.

On 13 January 1943, while visiting Camp Gruber, Oklahoma, and the 85th Infantry Division, Krueger received a telephone call from the commanding general of the Army Ground Forces, Lt. Gen. Lesley J. McNair. Because McNair was hard of hearing, Col. Clyde D. Eddleman—Third Army's operations officer—remembers Krueger "chased everyone out of the division headquarters … so he could yell back at McNair." Hearing problems aside, McNair told Krueger that the War Department had accepted MacArthur's request and instructed him to travel to Washington the next day. Once in the nation's capital, Krueger learned that although the War Department approved MacArthur's request for him, it declined the SWPA commander's petition for the Third Army. Instead, the army instructed Krueger he would lead the new Sixth Army, which would have an authorized strength of approximately half of the current table of organization for a headquarters of an army.[1]

To the Pacific

In his official radio message to the War Department, MacArthur spelled out his justification for requesting Krueger: "Experience indicates the necessity for a tactical organization of an American Army. In the absence of such an echelon the burden has been carried by GHQ [General Headquarters]. I recommend the U.S. Third Army under General Krueger, which would provide an able commander and an efficient operating organization. I am especially anxious to have Krueger because of my long and intimate association with him."[2]

Despite MacArthur's characterization of his relationship with Krueger as "long and intimate," in fact, the two men did not have a close personal or professional association with one another. They first met each other in Manila in 1903, and while they both taught at Fort Leavenworth in 1909, one had little to do with the other. The next time they worked together was in the War Department when Krueger was in the War Plans Division and MacArthur was chief of staff. Krueger recalled, "That he should have remembered me well and favorably enough to ask for my services in SWPA was as remarkable as it was flattering."[3]

The real reasons why MacArthur selected Krueger for this command are not entirely clear. After all, the SWPA commander already had an extremely competent commander in Lt. Gen. Robert L. Eichelberger, an Ohioan who had been a veteran of the Siberian Expedition and commanded MacArthur's Buna campaign in late 1942. After the long struggle for "bloody Buna," however, MacArthur decided he needed someone else to command his forces in battle. There are four reasons MacArthur most likely selected Krueger over Eichelberger. First, MacArthur was displeased with Eichelberger's performance at Buna at several levels. Apparently he believed Eichelberger had wasted time and incurred too many casualties in taking the village. In addition, and perhaps more important, Eichelberger seemed too willing to accept the credit and the accompanying public adulation for the victory in Papua. He had his own press officer and provided the media with access to himself as well as his staff. Finally, Eichelberger appeared to be disloyal to his immediate superior by working behind MacArthur's back to secure a Congressional Medal of Honor for himself and Distinguished Service Crosses for members of his command. In Krueger, MacArthur found an officer who had a long track record of being quiet and publicity-shy.[4]

In addition, Krueger's tactical and operational skills most likely attracted MacArthur. Besides his insistence on fast-paced operations, MacArthur gave much freedom of action to his commanders to plan and execute his missions and rarely interfered in an operation once it had begun. However, he did meddle in terms of continually changing the timetables for various operations (mainly by moving them forward) as well as constantly shuffling around the forces to be used in each operation.[5] It is unlikely, therefore, that given the wide latitude in planning and execution that he gave to his subordinates he would hand over the reins of his only army to a commander in whom he did not have full confidence, or to one who possessed an overly cautious nature, in light of his desire to return to the Philippines as quickly as possible. Krueger's performance in the GHQ maneuvers of 1941 and subsequent training with the Third Army most likely cemented in MacArthur's mind that Krueger was a first-rate commander, one who could successfully take his army back to the Philippines.[6]

In sum, MacArthur's decision to bring Krueger to SWPA was probably based both on MacArthur's concerns about Eichelberger's performance at Buna and personality, and on Krueger's military expertise. Vice Adm. Daniel E. Barbey, commander of the VII Amphibious Force in SWPA, best summarized MacArthur's decision by writing, "What his [Krueger's] seniors wanted done, he wanted done—and well. He had an excellent military reputation. [And] He shunned publicity, which was all to the good in the Southwest Pacific."[7] Krueger's appointment effectively put Eichelberger out of a job from March 1943 to March 1944 and became the seed of a bitter relationship. Eichelberger resented losing an opportunity to command an army, which he took personally.

Returning to his Third Army headquarters at Fort Sam Houston, Texas, on 21 January, Krueger wasted no time in forming the headquarters for his new army. MacArthur activated the Sixth Army on 25 January 1943, with the majority of the personnel for the new army coming from the Third Army, the Headquarters, Headquarters Company, and Headquarters Special Troops. In addition to building the basic elements of the new army, Krueger and his staff prepared to make the required long trip to Australia. Krueger and the advance party, including Brig. Gen. George Honnen (chief of staff), Col. George S. Price (G-1), Col. Horton V. White (G-2), Eddleman (G-3), and Col. Kenneth Pierce (G-4), left San Antonio on 2 February 1943 and arrived at Amberley Airfield near Brisbane on 7 February. Unfortunately, the move was marred by tragedy. Two days after arriving Down Under, Krueger learned that a plane carrying additional members of his staff had crashed off the coast of Canton Island. Apparently the pilot miscalculated his altitude on the landing and crashed approximately one and half miles offshore. All but three of the twenty-one passengers died.[8]

On 16 February 1943, MacArthur officially placed Krueger in command of the Sixth Army and established its headquarters at Camp Columbia, about ten miles west of Brisbane. MacArthur also designated the Sixth Army as Alamo Force. Under normal circumstances, Krueger's army would have come under Australian Gen. Sir Thomas Albert Blamey's authority. MacArthur, however, circumvented this problem of having an American formation under the command of a foreign officer by creating a task force from Krueger's army, which would then serve directly under GHQ SWPA.[9]

Upon arriving, Krueger inspected the various units under his command, which consisted of I Corps and its 32d and 41st Infantry Divisions, the 1st Marine Division, the 2d Engineer Special Brigade, the 503d Parachute Infantry Regiment, the 158th Infantry Regiment, the 98th Field Artillery (Pack) Battalion, the 40th and 41st Antiaircraft Brigades, and, a few months later, the 1st Cavalry Division and the 24th Infantry Division.[10]

Krueger confronted several major factors that would influence Sixth Army operations. One of his first concerns was the effect of the tropical conditions on his troops. He later recalled, "The prevalence of malaria gave me serious concern." Noting that "drastic measures" were necessary to combat the disease, he set up a rehabilitation center under the direction of Col. Frank LaRue at Rockhampton, in which "a large number of men were cured of malaria and returned to duty."[11]

Krueger also believed that SWPA held its own unique logistical problems. For starters, the "very considerable" distances from the Australian ports and New Guinea varied from 700 to 2,200 miles by air. Complicating the distance was that Australian port facilities were "inadequate to meet the heavy demands" of offensive operations in SWPA. The ports lacked the proper equipment, storage facilities, and stevedores. "All of these conditions contributed to delay the unloading and loading of vessels, and caused a serious backlog of shipping and congestion in the various Australian harbors," Krueger complained. "The worst instance occurred at Townsville where once 185 vessels were simultaneously in port awaiting discharge, with just eight docks available." In addition to the distances and poor dock facilities, logistics were hampered by the deficient railroad system throughout Australia. Several of the Australian states, for example, had different gauges, "which entailed unloading and reloading at each state boundary."[12]

Finally, Krueger also noted the unique topography of SWPA. Tactics and the newly developed operational doctrine of the U.S. Army assumed that any combat would take place where mobility and firepower would predominate—open country. The 1941 edition of the *Field Service Regulations*, for instance, contained just over two pages of instruction on jungle combat. The focus of the interwar army was clearly on another European war, not a war fought against the Japanese in the jungles in SWPA.[13] Krueger had his work cut out for him.

Although he had been at the forefront of creating an operational doctrine for a European-style war and had worked at planning at the strategic level for War Plan Orange, Krueger had not devoted much, if any, thought to the tactical or operational problems of jungle warfare until he arrived in Australia. As if believing there existed a standard and typical form of warfare, Krueger observed,

> Conditions in SWPA were in short unique. They differed radically from those normally encountered in war. They did not permit an army to conduct its operations with roads and railroads behind it as a line of communications except on Luzon, and even there to a limited extent only. Moreover, the conditions caused each major headquarters to be echeloned in great depth, with its elements separated by great distances, so that the only ready communication between them was by radio.[14]

His comment betrays an army that was so focused on warfare in open country that any diversion from the type of combat it envisioned was classified as an aberration, almost deviant. The Japanese did not decide to meet the United States on the field of battle of the U.S. Army's choosing. It was therefore paramount that Krueger adjust to a whole new way of fighting.

To understand fully the implications of these five important conditions—the effects of the tropical climate on the conditions of his troops, distances, dock facilities, the poor state of railroad transportation, and the jungle terrain—on the practice of warfare in SWPA, Krueger met with the various unit commanders. He also visited the Jungle Training School at Canungra at the end of February to see firsthand how American troops were preparing for upcoming operations. In addition to going out to the field, Krueger and his staff read and studied the many reports generated by SWPA organizations covering the first year of the war. The Sixth Army, for instance, obtained copies of Eichelberger's report on the Buna campaign, which Krueger found "most interesting and instructive."[15]

Along with acclimating himself—literally and figuratively—to his new environment, Krueger had to become familiar with MacArthur's strategic plans for SWPA. MacArthur had put the plans on temporary hold while U.S. forces struggled at Buna but had since opened them up for review, even as the Papuan campaign was winding down. MacArthur continued to worry (just as he had in 1942) about how the war would play out in his theater. He anxiously waited for clarification from the political and military leaders in Washington as to exactly how Allied forces in the Pacific Theater would conduct the war against Japan. Would the president decide to commit SWPA forces to an advance up the northern coast of New Guinea to the Philippines, or would the bulk of the American effort be devoted to a naval thrust through the Central Pacific Ocean? MacArthur had good reason to believe that the U.S. Navy option was the preferred course of action in Washington. Consequently, all of his strategic plans—almost from the beginning—envisioned keeping military operations in his theater one step ahead of those in the Central Pacific. Speed became the foundation of his strategic vision.

In February, MacArthur asked Krueger to review the plans for Operation ELKTON, which covered operations against the large Japanese military complex at Rabaul, New Britain. From his careful reading of MacArthur's plan, Krueger immediately recognized MacArthur's desire to return to the Philippines. Furthermore, he discerned that the plans—predicated as they were on the utmost speed without consideration of available forces—could cause problems from an operational perspective. Specifically, Krueger highlighted the proposed simultaneous assaults at Wewak, New Guinea, and Kavieng, New Ireland. Krueger warned that

> this makes each operation contingent upon the other, and ignores the imponderables. Yet no one can foresee whether these operations can be started simultaneously. If they do not start at the same time, as now planned, however, the effect will be unfortunate, whereas if the plan were made more flexible by permitting either of these operations to start when ready, advantage could be taken of the situation then existing. Hence I see no reason why either operation should not start when it can do so.[16]

Once again, Krueger emphasized the theme of flexibility as well as the need to weigh operations against potential costs, both hallmarks of his command style.

Krueger also suggested that the plan did not clearly articulate the importance of the Vitiaz Strait, the waterway between the Huon Peninsula on New Guinea and the western tip of New Britain. Although Phase Two of ELKTON called for the American forces to advance along the northeast coast of New Guinea to the Vitiaz Strait, Krueger noted that "this idea is not included with sufficient definiteness in Phase II of the plan proper." He believed ELKTON I to be overall "sound" but, nevertheless, in effect called for a main effort to control the Vitiaz Strait, which, once secured, "will greatly reduce the risk involved in all our contemplated subsequent operations, in particular those northwest through the Solomons." Krueger envisioned a simpler plan than the one MacArthur had conceived. MacArthur was, in his opinion, unnecessarily dispersing scarce U.S. forces by attempting to capture Gasmata, which was not vital for securing Vitiaz Strait. Instead, Krueger wanted to isolate Gasmata with air and naval units and then concentrate forces solely against Vitiaz Strait, which would then open the opportunity for an attack against the Admiralty Islands, an eventual and vital objective for the neutralization of Rabaul.[17]

The revision of ELKTON did not take into account Krueger's criticisms. Instead, ELKTON II was virtually the same as the first version, the only major difference being the type of forces used. MacArthur submitted this plan to the Joint Chiefs of Staff (JCS) in March 1943, and in a 28 March 1943 directive the JCS instructed MacArthur essentially to carry out Phase Two of ELKTON. MacArthur was ordered to seize the Kiriwina and Woodlark Islands, just off of the northeast end of New Guinea; the Lae-Salamaua-Finschhafen-Madang region of New Guinea; and the western portion of New Britain. Adm. William "Bull" Halsey's forces—"operating under general directives" of MacArthur—were to advance up the Solomon Islands to Bougainville. These measures would place U.S. forces in a position to launch the final assault on Rabaul, which, because of the lack of resources, would have to wait until 1944.

Armed with JCS authorization, MacArthur began working on the details of his plan, which, by the end of April, had evolved into Operation CARTWHEEL. It involved approximately thirteen operations by Southwest Pacific Area (SWPA) and South Pacific (SOPAC) forces over the span of eight months. MacArthur issued his general offensive plan for CARTWHEEL on 6 May. The first set of operations involved a SOPAC drive into New Georgia and Santa Isabel and the occupation by SWPA forces of two small islands located between 100 and 150 miles off the southeastern tip of New Guinea. The two islands—Kiriwina and Woodlark—offered perfect locations for airstrips, from which Lt. Gen. George C. Kenney's Fifth U.S. Air Force could strike Rabaul. Following the capture of these islands, GHQ SWPA then intended to seize portions of New Guinea and New Britain, all paving the way for an eventual assault on Rabaul.[18]

Operation CHRONICLE: *Kiriwina and Woodlark Islands*

MacArthur turned to Krueger's Alamo Force to initiate SWPA's part in CARTWHEEL. Krueger's role as commander of the Sixth Army and Alamo put him in one of the most important positions within SWPA. Unfortunately, there existed no unity of command in SWPA under MacArthur. Instead,

Krueger was given the task of *coordinating* the three services. Once directed by MacArthur to begin a military operation (such a directive contained objectives and the forces to be employed), Krueger was responsible for planning; integrating all air, sea, and ground forces involved; supervising its execution; and developing the captured area for future efforts. "Krueger's authority to co-ordinate planning," the official U.S. Army historian observed, "gave him a pre-eminent position; he was first among equals."[19]

GHQ SWPA ordered Alamo Force to prepare for the occupation of Kiriwina and Woodlark Islands, code-named CHRONICLE, on 7 May, although actual planning had started four days earlier. Facing his first operation as commander of an army, Krueger, according to his operations officer, displayed a bit of apprehension. Consequently, Krueger planned the operation with the utmost care and detail.[20]

The first order of business was to establish links with the other services, particularly Vice Adm. Barbey's VII Amphibious Force, which provided Krueger the amphibious assault expertise he would need over the next few years. Krueger requested that the VII Amphibious Force send representatives who could speak and make decisions on behalf of their commander. Barbey accordingly sent Commanders M. T. Farrar and Bern Anderson, both of whom assisted with the coordination of planning.[21]

Krueger's final plan, submitted to GHQ SWPA on 29 May, envisioned landing the 112th Cavalry Regiment, code-named LEATHERBACK Task Force (TF) and commanded by Col. Julian W. Cunningham, on the Guasopa Peninsula on the southeast tip of Woodlark Island. Another task force, code-named BYPRODUCT, and its 158th Infantry Regiment (both commanded by Col. J. Prugh Herndon) were to land on Kiriwina Island. In the days leading up to D-day, Krueger moved HQ Alamo Force to Milne Bay in order to better supervise the operation. HQ Sixth Army, meanwhile, remained in Australia at Camp Columbia.[22]

Because Woodlark and Kiriwina held no Japanese defenders, Krueger decided to send advance parties of engineers before the main task forces. Landing on 23 June, these teams searched the islands to ensure no enemy were present, identified exact landing sites, removed coral obstructions from channels, established outposts, began erecting island defenses, and prepared trails and roads.[23]

On the surface, CHRONICLE should have been an easy operation. Nevertheless, Krueger immediately faced many difficulties that would continually plague his operations for the next year. The first concerned the state of SWPA shipping. Through many interservice conferences, the Sixth Army commander learned that many of the transport ships had arrived in the Southwest

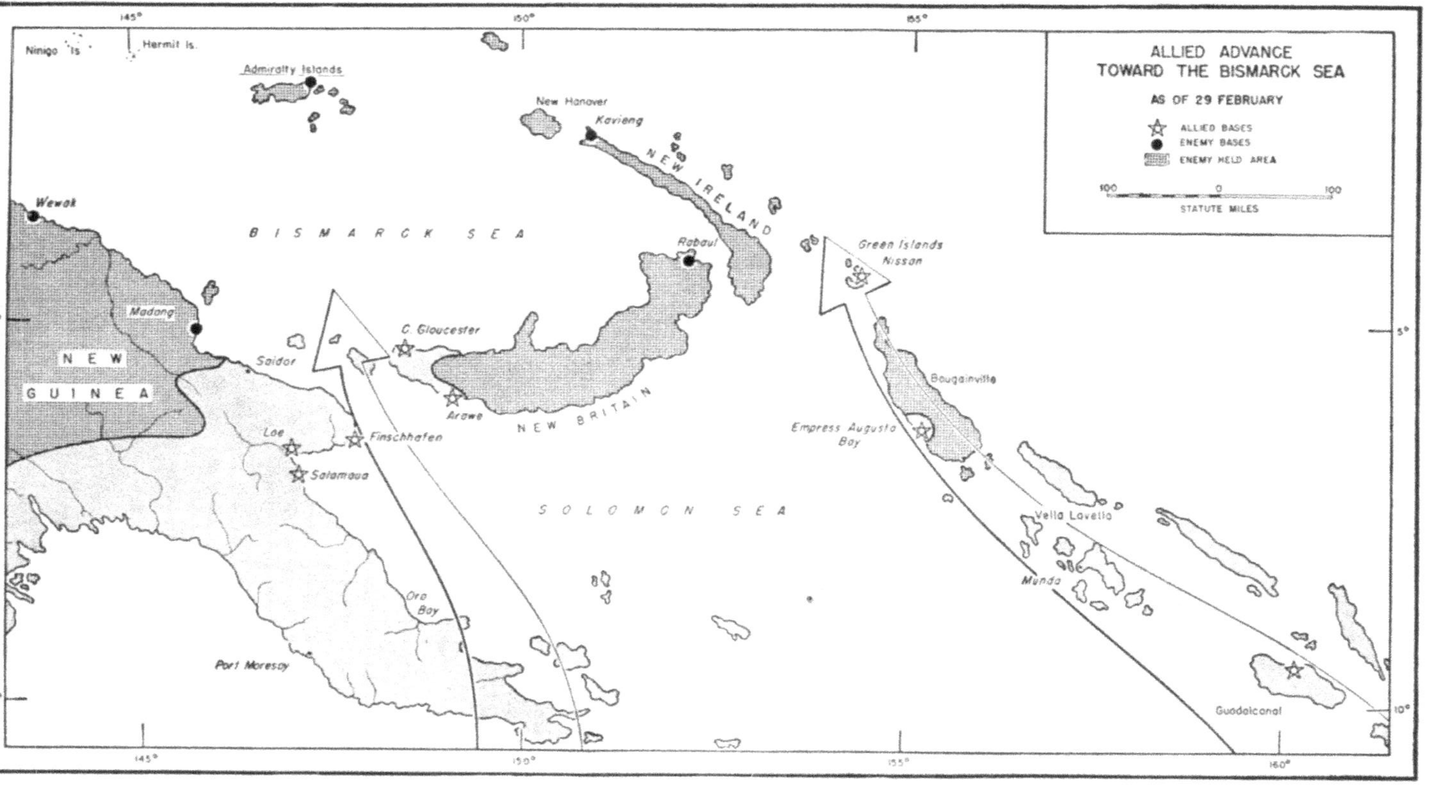

Map 5. The Operation CARTWHEEL Area
Source: U.S. Army, Historical Division, *The Admiralties: Operations of the 1st Cavalry Division, 29 February–18 May 1944* (Washington, D.C.: Government Printing Office, 1946), 2.

Pacific Area in poor condition and were unfit for duty. As a result, Barbey's VII Amphibious Force had to request additional ships. The lack of quality transports meant that there would be no ships available for any contingencies once the operation was underway.[24]

The inadequacies of the SWPA staging base at Milne Bay further complicated Krueger's supply plan for CHRONICLE. In fact, Krueger convened a special conference to address this issue. Krueger, Kenney, Barbey, and other high-level officers in SWPA attended the one-day meeting and discussed such problems as the limited loading facilities and impassable roads. The unloading facilities, for instance, were so bad that the combat units stationed there—scheduled for Operation CHRONICLE—had to sacrifice some of their time for combat training in order to unload ships. To alleviate the difficulties, Krueger recommended a special committee provide suggestions on how to improve the conditions at Milne Bay so that CHRONICLE could be launched with little or no delay. Many doubted that Milne Bay could be turned into a successful staging base before 30 June, the day when Krueger's men would seize Woodlark and Kiriwina.[25]

Making Krueger's work even more difficult was MacArthur's dual organization of the Sixth Army and Alamo Force. In explaining just how unwieldy this arrangement could be, Krueger later wrote,

> Up to the Leyte Campaign, the inherent difficulties faced by my dual headquarters in planning and administration were aggravated by the command set-up, which was a novel one to say the least. Until the matter was corrected, I had administrative authority command over all Sixth Army troops, but exercised operational command over those only which were alotted [*sic*] to Alamo Force. As Commanding General Alamo Force, I had no administrative authority, not even courts-martial jurisdiction, over the Sixth Army troops in that force, except in my capacity as Commanding General Sixth Army. Moreover, when U.S. Army units not belonging to Sixth Army were allotted to Alamo Force, I had neither administrative command nor courts-martial jurisdiction over them, not even as Commanding General Sixth Army.[26]

Eventually these problems were alleviated by MacArthur, but the system—described by Krueger as "extremely complicated and burdensome"—continued to hinder Krueger's exercise of command until MacArthur finally disbanded Alamo Force in September 1944.[27]

Despite warnings from Krueger and others about the need to improve Milne Bay, GHQ SWPA nevertheless steadfastly maintained the need to remain on schedule. MacArthur's G-3, Maj. Gen. Stephen J. Chamberlin, stated at the 24 May conference that the operation could not start later than the 30 June deadline. To the contrary, he even suggested that it should start sooner so that the SWPA timetable would not be delayed. However, on 25 May, the Sixth Army notified Chamberlin that delays were likely and that the earliest possible date was in fact 30 June.[28]

In addition to logistical complications, Kenney warned Krueger that air support would be difficult because of the distances involved. He pointed out that his airplanes would simply not have enough fuel to provide adequate air cover and instead suggested that he could bomb nearby Japanese air bases so that the enemy could not launch a counterattack. Krueger then decided the landings should take place at night, during which time enemy bombers and naval units would have difficulty spotting the SWPA invasion force. Despite these precautions, the lack of air cover caused some anxiety throughout SWPA.[29]

Krueger nonetheless guided Operation CHRONICLE to a successful conclusion, glitches and all: the amphibious landing got mixed up, and heavy rains hampered both the off-loading of supplies and the construction of the airfield. Krueger traveled to Kiriwina on 11 July to see for himself the condition of the island and the progress of engineering duties. He did not like what he saw. Three days after arriving, Krueger sacked the TF commander, replacing him with Col. John T. Murray. For his part, Herndon complained that he did not have enough heavy equipment or engineers, more of which came after his relief. Despite such hardships, BYPRODUCT TF completed both the necessary roads and a 5,000-yard runway by the end of July, and by 18 August, the 79th Squadron of the Royal Australian Air Force began operations from Kiriwina.[30]

Compared to BYPRODUCT TF's experience, LEATHERBACK TF's operation against Woodlark Island proceeded more smoothly. The first echelon arrived off the landing site on the Guasopa Peninsula in two parts on 30 June and 1 July (the first from Townsville and the second from Milne Bay) in four APDs (high-speed destroyer transports), six LCIs (landing craft, infantry), and six LSTs (landing ship, tanks). The only major problem throughout the two days came when the APDs attempted to unload. One had difficulty negotiating a narrow channel and went aground. According to the CHRONICLE historical report, troops did not follow "carefully laid plans," and the ships were "unloaded with difficulty and confusion." Despite this setback, by 0600 on 1 July all ships had been emptied and the shore cleared; work on the airfield began the next day. Throughout the next several weeks, LEATHERBACK TF worked on the construction of its airstrip and island defenses.[31]

Although involving virtually no Japanese opposition, Operation CHRONICLE provided the perfect opportunity for Krueger to experiment with the intricate and complex nature of amphibious warfare. As a result, Krueger drew several conclusions from his army's experiences. First, it was essential to plan fully for all aspects of an operation, from operational battle plans to the proper way to load a cargo ship. Krueger, his staff, and Barbey's VII Amphibious Force had planned CHRONICLE so thoroughly that the methods of preparing and transferring troops, supplies, and equipment became the basis for the standard operating procedures for future amphibious operations. It was also important, in Krueger's view, that once plans were completed they should not be changed or altered, since modifications "upset schedules and are disastrous to efficient operation." Although he had always preached the virtues of flexibility, the complexities of joint operations in SWPA meant that any alterations of shipping arrangements would only delay and sow confusion into any operation.[32]

Furthermore, Krueger emphasized the need for a clearly defined unity of command, especially during the landing phases of an amphibious assault. He pointed out, for instance, that during the Woodlark operation, "Landing troops failed to follow carefully laid plans for unloading these APDs, and consequently, they were unloaded with difficulty and confusion." Only with a clearly defined chain of command could this situation improve in future operations. "The shore party commander must be given complete control of the entire beach area," he argued, "and must be responsible to the task force commander only. Each member of the party must have a thorough knowledge of his own particular duty and clearly understand the chain of command." Perhaps not surprisingly, for Krueger this meant that the assault phase should be under army control. The navy's responsibility would extend only to transporting the army to the beaches. Unfortunately for the Alamo Force commander, MacArthur ultimately sided with Adm. Thomas C. Kinkaid, the commander of the Seventh U.S. Fleet, who maintained that the naval task force commander should be in charge during the transportation and assault phases, while the army commander would take command only after the troops had established a beachhead.[33]

Another lesson Krueger learned from CHRONICLE was the absolute necessity for thorough training, covering even the most minute tasks. Krueger particularly emphasized advanced preparation for shore parties. "Prior training in landing operations and in loading and unloading landing craft," he stressed, "is essential."[34]

Finally, Krueger called for more spare parts for all motor vehicles and engineering equipment. "Vehicles and equipment," he pointed out, "were dead lined due to the lack of parts and construction was correspondingly delayed. Ordinary reserves of spare parts allotted to equipment in the United States and the mainland of Australia are entirely inadequate in the operational areas of this theater. They must be at least tripled." Krueger believed the U.S. Army had to adjust quickly to the heavy toll that the tropical climate imposed on weapons and equipment.[35]

Once he officially terminated Operation CHRONICLE on 5 August, Krueger turned his attention back to the poor logistical facilities in the Southwest Pacific Area, particularly those at Milne Bay and Oro Bay, located just to the south of Buna. As usual, the most important factor involved with these bases was time. MacArthur needed them as soon as possible to continue Operation CARTWHEEL. After studying the two areas, Krueger's staff devised a plan to improve their capabilities. Utilizing the labor of American soldiers and engineers along with New Guinea natives, Alamo Force efforts focused on the basics, including clearing jungle roads and paths, raising bridges, and building docks, hospitals, and shelters. Under Krueger's watchful eye, the two bases started to turn around before 15 August, at which time U.S. Army Services of Supply took over responsibility for them.[36]

The rehabilitation of Milne and Oro Bays was only a first step. Krueger still had formidable logistical obstacles to overcome. Alamo Force still experienced severe shortages of many critical items, such as warehouse, laundry, bakery, salvage, and engineer equipment; field ranges; and mess outfits. On 28 September, Krueger was given the opportunity to discuss these problems with the head of the U.S. Army Service Forces, Lt. Gen. Brehon B. Somervell, when he traveled to HQ Alamo Force as part of an inspection tour of SWPA and SOPAC. Krueger singled out the need for more service troops, better mail service, heavy engineering equipment, and three times the amount of spare parts then available. Despite all of Krueger's efforts, however, right up until the end of the war SWPA experienced critical material shortages.[37]

Operation DEXTERITY: Cape Gloucester and Arawe

Whatever the logistical circumstances of SWPA and Alamo Force, MacArthur demanded that his operations proceed without delay. Consequently, Krueger and his staff had to begin preparations for their next role in Operation CARTWHEEL. Even before the Kiriwina and Woodlark Islands missions were completed, GHQ SWPA informed Krueger to prepare for Operation DEXTERITY, the occupation of Gasmata and Cape Gloucester.[38] The seizure of both would place western New Britain under American control. In conjunction with Alamo Force's establishing positions on New Britain, an Australian force under the direction of Gen. Sir Thomas Blamey would advance up the northern coast of New Guinea to capture the Huon Peninsula. These two operations would place the Vitiaz Strait under Allied control and bring Kenney's air force closer to Rabaul.[39]

Along with logistical problems and time constraints, Krueger faced a difficult intelligence situation. With good reason, Krueger believed he could not rely solely on the intelligence that GHQ SWPA G-2 (intelligence) gave him, despite having access to intercepted and decrypted Japanese messages (ULTRA) that often provided accurate estimates of enemy strength. He studied the U.S. Army's retaking of the Aleutians, where, expecting a powerful and entrenched Japanese defensive force, Lt. Gen. John L. Dewitt, commander of the Western Defense Command, attacked Kiska with 35,000 troops after bombing the island for six weeks only to find the Japanese had withdrawn from the island some fourteen days before. From the start, Krueger recognized the unique role intelligence would play in his theater.[40]

Already contemplating devising his own means to gather information, a rather bizarre incident on the verge of launching DEXTERITY only confirmed Krueger's suspicions that he could no longer rely solely on traditional intelligence-gathering methods. Krueger learned that just as he wanted to know more about the conditions of the Japanese as well as the topography of New Britain, Vice Adm. Barbey was trying to obtain hydrographic data for the amphibious approach and landing. To fulfill the needs of both Alamo Force and VII Amphibious Force, Krueger and Barbey joined together to deploy a combined army-navy reconnaissance team, called the VII Amphibious Force Special Service Unit #1. The unit set off for New Britain on a mission lasting ten days in the first week of October. On the last day of its mission, communications broke down between the members of the unit and the PT boat that was preparing to pick them up. The rendezvous never occurred, and, consequently, Service Unit #1 waited on the island for an additional eleven days. Finally rescued on 27 October, the team—near starvation and exhausted—returned to Milne Bay, where it was debriefed by the navy, which then curiously put the army representative on the team, Lt. Milton Beckworth, on a boat and took him on a four-day cruise, ostensibly against his will, in an attempt to prevent him from going to HQ Alamo Force to present his findings. Beckworth eventually returned to Cape Cretin, where he told his story. Upon hearing of the VII Amphibious Force Special Service Unit #1's experience on the island and Beckworth's ordeal, Krueger grew more and more concerned with the navy's lack of cooperation.[41]

The limitations of GHQ SWPA intelligence and the lack of genuine army-navy collaboration led Krueger to create his own reconnaissance force, which served directly under him. On 20 October 1943, he wrote to the commanding general of the 1st Cavalry Division, Maj. Gen. Innis P. Swift, that "I have for some time had under serious consideration the establishment of a training center, on general lines like the one above [referring to his Junior Officers' Training Center, or "Krueger Tech"], but for an entirely different object, that is, to develop a small group of selected officers and men for use as special scouts, trained to get information of the terrain and/or hostile dispositions near, in, or even behind the enemy's lines; or to take out enemy posts or gun positions; or to undertake demolitions and so on." He asked Swift to locate an officer to command the school, preferably a colonel.[42]

The curriculum of the school—lasting six weeks—included the use of rubber boats, intelligence gathering, scouting and patrolling, navigation, survival, communications, weapons, and physical conditioning. Krueger wanted only the best soldiers to make it to graduation and, therefore, insisted that the school be challenging. "The course ... will be entirely practical, and intensive," he explained to Swift. "By a very severe weeding-out process I hope to be able to get a highly trained group of young officers and men, and shall be entirely satisfied if a mere ten per cent of each class make the No. 1 grade." Eventually, the school graduated ten classes from December 1943 to the end of the war, and Alamo Scout teams conducted 106 reconnaissance missions and liberated two prison camps.[43]

Gathered from a variety of sources, Krueger's intelligence estimated the Japanese garrison at Cape Gloucester at 3,000 to 4,000 men and at Gasmata, between 1,000 and 1,500 men. With these numbers, he next set out to work on a plan. In fact, even before he obtained reliable figures on Japanese strength, Alamo Force had made substantial progress on the plan for Operation DEXTERITY. MacArthur, anxious to have one operation proceed after another without delay, had his staff begin working on the details of DEXTERITY while Alamo Force focused on Operation CHRONICLE. In typical fashion, MacArthur issued the targets, the units involved, and the dates, this time giving Krueger the 1st Marine Division, the 32d Infantry Division, and the 503d Parachute Infantry Regiment. He directed Krueger to send the 126th Regimental Combat Team (RCT) of the 32d Infantry Division—now recovering from an earlier and exhausting mission—against the Japanese airfield at Gasmata in southern New Britain. Next, MacArthur targeted Cape Gloucester with the 1st Marine Division and the 503d Parachute Infantry Regiment. The dates were 14 November for the former and 20 November for the latter.[44]

In what became a virtual standard operating procedure, GHQ SWPA next met with the staff of Alamo Force to discuss the plan. Through these particular discussions, members of Alamo Force successfully persuaded MacArthur to allow the participating units to locate their staging areas closer to their target areas. GHQ SWPA issued its final operating instructions on 22 September, after which Krueger and his staff worked on their own operational plans.[45]

On 28 September, Krueger sent the first draft of his plan to GHQ SWPA for approval. Following MacArthur's strategic suggestions, Krueger decided to send Brig. Gen. Clarence A. Martin's 126th RCT/32d Infantry Division to capture Gasmata. After the Gasmata assault, Krueger was next going to use the 1st Marine Division, commanded by Maj. Gen. William H. Rupertus, against the 3,000 to 4,000 Japanese who held the airfield of Cape Gloucester. The plan specifically envisioned the main landing by Combat Team C (built around the 7th Marine Regiment, less one battalion) on the east coast of the cape. Meanwhile, the regiment's other battalion would land on the west coast near the village of Tauali to block the Japanese from either reinforcing the cape or escaping to the south. Supporting the marines was the 503d Parachute Regiment, which would make its drop near the airdrome at dawn of D-day. While the leathernecks on the west coast set up defensive positions, Combat Team C and the 503d would make a coordinated assault on the airfield. GHQ SWPA approved the plan on 14 October.[46]

Over the next few weeks, it became apparent that the Japanese decided to make a stand in the Cape Gloucester area by funneling more soldiers into the area. Alamo Force estimated that by December, the Japanese had between 5,668 and 9,344 men there, while the 1st Marine Division came up with numbers between 8,400 and 12,076.[47]

With Japanese reinforcements arriving in western New Britain, Krueger decided to counter by strengthening the invasion force for Cape Gloucester (code-named BACKHANDER TF). On 2 November, Krueger, Rupertus, Barbey, and Eddleman gathered at HQ 1st Marine Division on Goodenough Island for a conference to determine just what changes they needed to make as a result of the additional Japanese. Eddleman suggested to Krueger that the entire Combat Team C—including the battalion scheduled to land on the west coast—be instead landed on the east coast and followed by the 503d. For the landing against Tauali, Eddleman advised using an entire RCT, the 1st Marine Division's Combat Team B, which was built around the 1st Marine Regiment/1st Marine Division. Those present agreed with his suggestions, and several days later Krueger received authority from MacArthur to use the additional forces.[48]

Along with the growing number of Japanese troops in the target area, Krueger cast a suspicious eye on MacArthur's schedule. The Alamo Force commander believed that such a timetable was too inflexible. In a 12 November letter to MacArthur, he noted that the amphibious attack on Cape

Gloucester followed the one at Gasmata by only six days. If the first operation faltered, the second would have to be delayed, since there were no shipping reserves. In addition, operations had stretched the VII Amphibious Force thin, as Barbey's force was responsible for supplying Australian forces in their push to capture the Huon Peninsula. The Australians would not be finished until 20 November, leaving little time for its ships to make it back to the staging areas of Milne Bay to train with the assault units. Persuaded by Krueger's points, MacArthur delayed the DEXTERITY landings by a month.[49]

The postponement of the operation did not solve all of Krueger's problems. Kenney began having doubts about the Gasmata phase. After reviewing geographical reports, Kenney doubted that the terrain would allow suitable airfield development. Furthermore, the operation would require the employment of long-range fighters, which were in such short supply that Kenney would commit to air support only for the landing phase of the operation.[50]

Kenney's reservations led to a conference on 19 November during which he laid out the limitations and potential problems about the Gasmata portion of Operation DEXTERITY. The results of the meeting led Krueger's staff to conclude that SWPA forces could expect high casualty rates and sustained damage to material and equipment. Consequently, the attendees suggested to MacArthur that he cancel the Gasmata landing. MacArthur agreed, and SWPA leaders met yet again, this time on 21 November, to select a replacement. The naval representatives suggested that an area should be taken that would allow them to build a PT boat base. After looking at many different locations, the various staffs agreed on Arawe—approximately seventy-five miles to the west of Gasmata—as the most appropriate substitution, and the members of the conference relayed their findings to MacArthur, who then approved the change.[51]

In addition to changing the target, MacArthur altered the forces involved. He decided to return the 126th Infantry Regiment, scheduled to assault Gasmata, to the 32d Infantry Division. For the operation against Arawe, Krueger set up DIRECTOR TF, composed of the 112th Cavalry Regiment, the 148th Field Artillery Battalion, the 59th Engineer Company, and various other supporting units. Both the 112th Cavalry Regiment and DIRECTOR TF were commanded by Julian W. Cunningham, now a brigadier general. Krueger essentially assigned three objectives to DIRECTOR TF. The first, and most important, was to draw Japanese attention from the main American landing at Cape Gloucester. The second was to set up a defensive perimeter and then establish contacts with American forces at Cape Gloucester. Last, Krueger wanted Cunningham to assist the navy in building a patrol boat base in the Arawe area. D-day was set for 15 December.[52]

Meanwhile, Alamo Force and the 1st Marine Division revisited the Cape Gloucester plan. Specifically, the 503d Parachute Infantry Regiment's participation in the BACKHANDER operation concerned them. Rupertus, for instance, feared that if poor weather prevented the deployment of the paratroopers, his task force would lack the manpower to take its objective. In fact, he even hinted at the ability of the Japanese to seriously threaten his force, writing, "If the weather is bad, then the jumper boys won't be there to help me & I'll be on the beach with a measly C.T. [combat team]" Furthermore, the use of the 503d would require the use of precious airfields, which meant, in turn, that fewer bombers could support the landings.[53]

The issue came to a head during a 14 December conference called by the SWPA commander to discuss the target date of the operations as well as his own concerns about the proposed use of the 503d Parachute Infantry Regiment. MacArthur opened the conference by stating that he was doubting his decision to employ the paratroopers, arguing that using the unit against the type of enemy anticipated would result in high American casualties. When MacArthur asked those in attendance how they liked the operation, the 1st Marine Division's operations officer, Lt. Col. Edwin A. Pollock, responded, "We don't like it." He not only indicated that he disliked the scheme of maneuver that involved two separate landings and then having both units move to the airdrome but also made clear his displeasure over the employment of the paratroopers.[54]

When it was Rupertus's turn to speak, he voiced his concerns not with the scheme of maneuver but over the issue of manpower. If the 503d was dropped from the operation, he feared that his task force would be severely undermanned. In fact, Rupertus argued that he was counting on the paratroopers to help him meet Alamo's ambitious objective. If the paratroopers were withdrawn, he stated that the sole RCT landing at Cape Gloucester would have to set up a defensive perimeter on D-day and wait for reinforcements to complete the mission the following day. Rupertus concluded by stating that withdrawing the paratroopers would be a great mistake and would give the initiative to the enemy.[55]

Krueger responded by asserting that while he agreed with MacArthur's fears over the use of paratroopers, he did not want to abandon the plan of maneuver; after all, Krueger included the 503d Parachute Infantry Regiment drop because GHQ SWPA had included the unit for use in Operation DEXTERITY. Consequently, as Krueger pointed out, "the plan was made to fit the forces so assigned." With MacArthur doubting the utility of using the 503d, the Sixth Army commander suggested a compromise in which another force would replace the 503d. After a brief discussion, MacArthur agreed and canceled the 503d's jump. To make up for the loss in manpower, Krueger looked to the only source of troops available: Combat Team B, which was scheduled to land at Green Beach just to the west of Cape Gloucester. Krueger decided to land the 2d Battalion/1st Marine Regiment in its place, but because this force was considerably smaller than the original, its mission was simplified accordingly. Its assignment was to establish defensive positions along the coastal track to prevent the Japanese from reinforcing Cape Gloucester or from escaping to the south. It would not participate in the actual assault on the airdrome. The main effort would come from the east coast landing. The plan for this phase called for the entire Combat Team C (roughly 3,500 men) to land on the east coast and establish a beachhead, while Combat Team B (minus the 2d Battalion) was to land soon thereafter and move along the coast to seize the airfield.[56]

Krueger based his plan for the Cape Gloucester phase of DEXTERITY on the forces given to him by GHQ SWPA and the notion of aggressive movement. Originally given two marine RCTs and the 503d, Krueger had to make do with far less and drew up plans that took advantage of the forces provided. Despite the difficulties of operating a task force in the jungle, Krueger wanted to utilize two axes of advance. His plan involved a double envelopment of Cape Gloucester even though he did not really like the idea of relying on a paratroop drop in the jungle as a necessary component of his plan. When MacArthur decided to scrap the 503d's part, Krueger *had* to streamline the plan to a single thrust out of sheer necessity and not because the marines were pressuring him. With only two RCTs, there were simply not enough forces to complete the double envelopment from both the east and west.

By early December, then, Krueger had for the most part finished planning for the landing against Arawe, and by mid-December he had completed planning for the Cape Gloucester operation as well. He next turned his attention toward getting his forces ready for the upcoming battle. But just as the troops of Alamo Force prepared for the Arawe operation, MacArthur decided on 10 December that Krueger should begin preparations for an assault on Saidor, on the northern edge of the Huon Peninsula and defended by Lt. Gen. Hatazo Adachi's Eighteenth Army. Saidor's importance lay in its airstrip as well as its position in the Australian effort to secure the Huon Peninsula. An American attack on Saidor would seal the Huon Peninsula from any Japanese attempt to reinforce the units there locked in combat with the Australian 9th Infantry Division.[57]

After MacArthur made his decision concerning Saidor (code-named MICHAELMAS), the SWPA commander traveled to Alamo Force headquarters—one day before the start of the Arawe operation—to discuss this future mission.[58]

As in the past, the most pressing concern revolved around logistics. With two operations already scheduled (Arawe and Cape Gloucester), where would Alamo get the extra shipping necessary to transport and supply the Saidor TF? Weighing such factors, MacArthur decided to base the Saidor operation on the outcome of the Cape Gloucester operation. Once Alamo Force had the situation well in hand there, the MICHAELMAS operation would be executed. Nevertheless, MacArthur named 2 January 1944 as D-day.[59]

In the midst of adjusting to the changes to the BACKHANDER plan and the addition of the Saidor operation, Krueger still had to oversee the assault on Arawe, still on schedule for 15 December. At 1600 of 13 December and under the watchful eyes of both Krueger and MacArthur, the 112th Cavalry Regiment began loading on their transports from beaches on Goodenough Island and set sail at 2400 of the same day. After a day's journey, DIRECTOR TF reached its destination at approximately 0300 of 15 December. The landing force faced scattered resistance; the majority of enemy troops—about two companies—had moved off the peninsula after the 2d Squadron made their assault, and by 1430, the Americans cleared the peninsula and set up a defensive perimeter.[60]

Secure in the knowledge that his troops were safely ashore at Arawe (and shortly after completing the changes in plans for the Cape Gloucester operation), Krueger turned his attention the next day to preparing the Saidor task force for its mission. He selected Brig. Gen. Clarence A. Martin, who led the 126th Infantry Regimental Combat Team of the 32d Infantry Division, as task force commander. The choice was a natural one since the 126th was originally scheduled to assault Gasmata in the original DEXTERITY plans. The bulk of MICHAELMAS TF was staged at Goodenough Island, although its supporting units were scattered throughout the Southwest Pacific Area.[61]

Since there was little time between MacArthur's announcement and D-day (just over twenty days), a full reconnaissance was not possible. Therefore, Alamo Force had to get its information about terrain and suitable landing sites solely through aerial photographs. Three beaches were chosen—Red, White, and Blue. Although the beaches were rocky, the ground behind them was dry, and they were close to the airfield.[62]

On 22 December, Krueger issued his formal operations order after a rather short planning period. It called for Vice Adm. Barbey's fleet to transport Martin's task force to the three beaches from its staging area on Goodenough Island. The 126th Infantry Regiment would land its 3d Battalion on Red Beach as the 2d Battalion landed one of its companies at White Beach and another at Blue. The 1st Battalion would then land on White Beach at

H+30 minutes. Once ashore, the MICHAELMAS TF would move inland to capture the airstrip and then set up a defensive perimeter.[63]

Martin decided to land his 7,000 men with as much surprise as possible. This meant that H-hour for MICHAELMAS was set earlier (0700) than normal and thus would allow a limited preinvasion bombardment. Naval fire would last only twenty minutes, while the air force would bomb and strafe inland later in the day.[64]

With the broad planning for Saidor completed by 23 December, Krueger made final preparations for the upcoming Cape Gloucester assault. On 24 December, he moved his command post (CP) from Goodenough Island to Cape Cretin, on the southeastern corner of the Huon Peninsula. Then on 2 February 1944 he moved HQ Alamo Force and HQ Sixth Army to Cape Cretin, thereby finally establishing a unified headquarters. The next day he traveled to Combat Team B's staging area in Finschhafen to supervise its last-minute preparations for the assault on Cape Gloucester.[65]

While the marines successfully executed their mission at Tauali, both of Rupertus's combat teams landed at Cape Gloucester in the absence of significant enemy opposition. With both task force perimeters secured on the first night, Rupertus looked forward to resuming his offensive the next day. Although his overall objective was the capture of the airfield, he nevertheless was concerned with the Japanese opposition that faced the western edge of his beachhead. He feared that a strong attack against the 7th Marine Regiment might threaten not only the beachhead but also the rear of the 1st Marine Regiment's offensive against the airfield. His plan of utilizing 3d Battalion/7th Marine Regiment as the reserve for the 1st Marine Regiment was no longer tenable, since it was essential that the battalion be used for beachhead defense. Consequently, in the evening hours of 26 December, Rupertus sent Krueger a message, requesting that the 5th Marine Regiment (scheduled to assault Rooke and Long Islands in Vitiaz Strait) be released for service for BACKHANDER.[66]

The Alamo Force commander and Rupertus had agreed before D-day that two battalions of the 5th Marine Regiment would be available if the marine commander requested reinforcements. Consequently, Krueger sent orders at 0751 on 27 December that the 1st and 2d Battalions of the 5th Marine Regiment move out. Bad weather, however, prevented Barbey from receiving the news until late in the day. The marines therefore could not load up, leave their staging area, and still hope to reach their destination by 28 December. Because he did not want to move the troops during daylight (which might expose them and his transports to Japanese air attacks), Barbey further delayed the movement another twenty-four hours. The two battalions finally embarked at 2100 on 28 December.[67]

When Rupertus discovered that Krueger was sending the reinforcements, the division chief dispatched an urgent request that the remainder of the regiment be delivered. He argued that increased pressure on his beachhead perimeter made the full employment of his division necessary. Krueger saw no reason not to send Rupertus the additional battalion, telling him that he "had no intention to deprive you of its use."[68]

With the additional manpower, Rupertus wrestled control over the cape. On the afternoon of 29 December, Rupertus sent word of his accomplishment to Krueger: "First Marine Division presents to you as an early New Year gift the complete airdrome of Cape Gloucester. Situation well in hand due to fighting spirit of troops, the usual Marine luck and the help of God. Both Strips occupied at noon. Consolidating perimeter defense around drome. Rupertus grinning to Krueger."[69]

Throughout the next several weeks, the marine division secured its position, extensively patrolled the area, and refurbished the airfield. With the enemy threat to Cape Gloucester ended, Rupertus then sent elements of his division to Rooke Island on 12 February but found that island devoid of any Japanese. The 1st Marine Division also pushed south to clear the far western quadrant of New Britain.[70]

While the battle for Cape Gloucester unfolded, Krueger remained at his command post at Cape Cretin, even though he would have preferred to have visited the 1st Marine Division during its operation. But he had other concerns that kept him at HQ Alamo Force. "Although I was anxious to see the progress of the operations at Cape Gloucester," he explained, "I was obliged to defer my visit until the Saidor operation was well under way."[71]

Operation DEXTERITY: *Saidor*

In fact, Krueger was forced to deal with MICHAELMAS before he would have liked. As the date drew near, Krueger had grave doubts about the ability to meet MacArthur's 2 January D-day. Consequently, Krueger made an effort to change MacArthur's mind. He warned that the projected D-day would jeopardize ongoing operations, especially Cape Gloucester, which was not yet in U.S. hands. Furthermore, he argued that Barbey had not yet approved the plan for the amphibious phase of the operation that had already been worked out by Alamo Force and VII Amphibious Force representatives. "I consider it," Krueger concluded, "highly desirable to launch the MICHAELMAS operations now scheduled, and troops are ready; but in view of the factors pointed out herein I must regretfully advise deferment of the operation, or at least deferment of the decision to launch that operation." Krueger's counsel fell on deaf ears; Alamo Force would hit the beaches of Saidor on 2 January, ready or not.[72]

In light of the circumstances in SWPA in the last few months of 1943, Krueger had legitimate concerns over the early launch of MICHAELMAS. As much as the Saidor operation presented hardships for the army, the particular burden lay on Barbey and his VII Amphibious Force. "By that time," Barbey wrote, "I was physically and mentally exhausted from many last-minute arrangements for Cape Gloucester and hardly in a mood to give concentrated attention to the preparations for another operation, and my staff was in the same condition."[73]

Furthermore, Barbey's transports would be operating on a tight shipping schedule. His ships would have to participate in the assault for BACKHANDER on 26 December, travel over 300 miles back to Goodenough Island to repair damaged vehicles, have towing gear inspected, refuel, load the MICHAELMAS TF and its supplies by 31 December, and get underway by 1 January. There would be little room for error. "There was neither time nor ships available for practice landings or full-scale rehearsals," Barbey later explained. "As it was, we would be hard-pressed to get enough undamaged ships back from Cape Gloucester in time to complete the loading on the thirty-first."[74]

Despite the problems involved, MacArthur insisted on maintaining his timetable, and in light of Barbey's delay in approving the Alamo shipping schedule and amphibious assault plans, he had Admiral Kinkaid inform Barbey "that every effort should be made to meet [the] projected date and that all naval resource[s] of area are at his disposal for that purpose." Furthermore, MacArthur notified Krueger, "I am most anxious that if humanly possible this operation take place as scheduled. Its capture will have a vital strategic effect which will be lost if materially postponed. It amounts to the exploitation of New Britain landings and would have to be accomplished promptly in order to reap full benefit."[75]

With MacArthur's mind made up, Krueger continued his preparations in light of the enormous complexities involved. On 28 December, Krueger reluctantly ordered the commander of MICHAELMAS TF to prepare for the D-day of 2 January.[76]

Under great pressure, Barbey's force made it back to Goodenough Island after the landings at Cape Gloucester. The troops of Martin's 126th RCT were, in Barbey's words, in "excellent spirits" and were "fresh, and with new equipment." The same could not be said for his sailors. The "crews of the ships which carried them," he pointed out, "were a tired lot worn out from the grueling runs to Gloucester and the frequent air attacks." Nevertheless, the task force set sail on schedule at 0830 on 31 December aboard six LSTs.[77]

Fortunately for the men of Martin's MICHAELMAS TF, the rainy and overcast sky that greeted them did not turn out to be an omen. To the contrary, the GIs met no opposition and quickly turned their attention toward base development.[78]

But even as the Americans were gaining control of Saidor, Krueger had reason to fear the situation at Arawe. On 6 January, Cunningham reported to Krueger that his troops had found evidence that the Japanese had established positions 400 to 500 yards in front of the American main line of resistance. Because mortar and artillery fire had not stopped the Japanese, Cunningham asked the Alamo Force commander for additional troops as well as armor support to launch a strike against enemy positions.[79]

Determining that an assault by the men of the 112th Cavalry Regiment alone would incur "unnecessary losses," Krueger immediately sent F Company/158th Infantry Regiment and B Company of the 1st Tank Battalion/1st Marine Division, which arrived by 10 January. With the additional firepower, Cunningham devised a plan to extend his defensive perimeter forward by approximately 1,000 yards. The attack—launched at 0900 on 16 January—began with strikes by Consolidated B-24 Liberators and B-25s, which dropped eighty-seven tons of bombs. After this intense twenty-minute air assault, the artillery and mortars opened fire for thirty minutes. The main attack pushed off at 0950 with the tanks in the lead followed by infantrymen and cavalrymen. Employing this well-coordinated attack, DIRECTOR TF achieved its objective at 1300. Faced with such an attack, the Japanese commander, Maj. Masamitsu Komori, withdrew and offered the Americans no more resistance.[80]

Lessons Learned from Operations CHRONICLE *and* DEXTERITY

Krueger officially terminated the operations at Arawe, Saidor, and Cape Gloucester on 10 February 1944, signaling the end of the Sixth Army's role in Operation DEXTERITY and the completion of Phase Two of CARTWHEEL. Viewed separately, the five amphibious operations produced mixed results. The Royal Australian Air Force flew operations from Kiriwina Island, while Woodlark Island was used primarily for SWPA flank protection. Arawe and Cape Gloucester never proved to be important bases for future Allied operations. No PT base was ever built at Arawe, and by the time the airstrip at Cape Gloucester and Saidor were completed, SWPA and SOPAC forces had accomplished all of the tasks for which the airdromes were supposed to support. In the end, these airfields were used primarily as emergency runways.[81]

Strategically, however, CARTWHEEL was extremely successful. By accomplishing Phase Two, Krueger's forces had established an Allied presence on the southern and western edges of the 100,000-strong Japanese garrison at Rabaul. In addition, the seizure of Saidor had split the Japanese Eighteenth Army in New Guinea in half by separating the 41st Division at Madang from the 20th and 51st Divisions at Sio. Consequently, its commander ordered the latter two divisions—already in poor condition—to march approximately 200 miles west to Madang. Illness, starvation, and the stress of the movement in the harsh jungle terrain of New Guinea took their toll. Combined, the two formations had about 14,000 soldiers in December 1943, but by the time they reached Madang by 1 March 1944, only 9,300 had survived.[82]

In short, Alamo Force's participation in CARTWHEEL dealt a serious blow to the Japanese Eighth Area Army at Rabaul and the Japanese Eighteenth Army on New Guinea. Krueger summarized his army's strategic success by writing:

> The Arawe and Cape Gloucester operations had cleared western New Britain of the enemy, threatened Rabaul and given us additional airdrome sites and control of Vitiaz Strait. The Saidor operation exploited these successes, protected the left flank of Alamo Force and completed the encirclement and destruction of the Japanese forces trapped on Huon Peninsula. Moreover, the development of an airdrome and base at Saidor brought pressure to bear on the Japanese strongholds at Madang and Alexishafen. Upon completing DEXTERITY Operation, SWPA forces were thus in an excellent position to undertake such further operations as the CinC [commander in chief] desired.[83]

CARTWHEEL was also a success at the tactical and operational level. Although the U.S. Army possessed little jungle warfare experience, Krueger quickly adapted the standard doctrine to the new environment in which he found himself. He profited from the army's and marines' experiences throughout the first two years of the war by reading about and studying various battles, such as Buna and Guadalcanal. Consequently, he wholeheartedly advocated the use of tanks in the jungles of the South Pacific and dispatched what armored units he had to those commanders who required them, even though prewar army manuals discounted their use in the jungle. But he did not rely solely on armor. Krueger used all the branches of the army plus the two other services to apply a combined-arms force against the enemy.

At the operational level, he discovered that many important aspects of the army's operational doctrine could be effectively applied to the Southwest Pacific Area. He specifically wanted to institute maneuvers despite the difficult terrain. Without insisting on aggressive movement, he feared that it would be all too easy for his various task forces to become complacent with a slow and methodical pace. Under such circumstances, his men could become easy targets for Japanese counterattacks. Krueger, for example, did not want the marines at Cape Gloucester to waste precious time establishing a beachhead before moving inland. He knew all too well that the Japanese would use the jungle to their advantage by building a defensive perimeter if the Americans did not move off the beach quickly. It was hard enough to maneuver through the jungles, swamps, and mountains without the added burden of facing entrenched Japanese defenders.

Applying tactics and an operational art originally designed on the open country of the United States to the closed spaces of the jungles of the South Pacific did not occur easily or quickly, but was rather a product of long hours of hard work and an efficient staff. Right from the start and even before Operation CHRONICLE, Krueger set in place a daily routine of preparing for each operation, a pattern he had advocated and used for years as commander of the Third U.S. Army. He later recalled, "After studying the directive of the Commander-in-Chief covering a particular operation, and weighing available information, I usually indicated in a general way what I desired my troops to do, and then left my staff free to work out the details in collaboration with the staff representatives of the naval and air forces involved, but was kept constantly informed of the progress being made in planning, and made decisions when necessary."[84] Thus, Krueger strove to provide his organization wide latitude in executing his broad directives. He believed that if he had injected himself into the detailed planning work of his staff, it would have inevitably stifled "free discussion and to that extent [hampered] progress." "In my opinion," Krueger concluded, "the commander should remain aloof from detailed planning as far as practicable, keep an open mind, and be ready to make decisions if and when required."[85]

The vital link between Krueger and his planning staff was the chief of staff. Through his chief of staff, Krueger kept in touch with all aspects of his army. "As a rule, the Chief of Staff reported to me each morning, and at other times when necessary, and informed me of anything of importance that had happened," Krueger explained. "At these meetings we discussed all matters that required action and I gave such instructions regarding them as were necessary." In fact, the position was, in the words of one of the Sixth Army's chiefs of staff, "General Krueger's alter ego." The job was particularly important considering the unique requirements of army operations in SWPA. Because the vast distances of the Pacific scattered the operations of the Sixth Army and made command and communication difficult, Krueger had to spend a significant portion of his time traveling. During these absences from his headquarters, it was Krueger's rule to have his chief of staff remain behind to make decisions on his behalf.[86]

Krueger's relationship with his chief of staff, however, was tested throughout his first year and a half in SWPA, during which three individuals held the position. Krueger's first chief of staff was Brig. Gen. George Honnen, who came to the Sixth Army with Krueger from the Third Army. After two months in SWPA, Honnen's health succumbed to the pressures of war. Honnen spent the months of April, May, and June 1943 in and out of an army hospital for treatment and, much to Krueger's regret, was finally ordered to the United States on 18 June.[87]

Brig. Gen. Edwin D. Patrick, who came over from Adm. Halsey's staff, replaced Honnen. Bored with and unfulfilled by his duties in the South Pacific, Patrick was glad to get the call from Krueger in late June. Although he was pleased to be back with the army, Patrick's term as chief of staff did not turn out as he expected. Patrick did not have the personality to be a mediator between Krueger and his staff. Over time, this situation caused friction within the HQ Sixth Army, and Patrick was replaced on 10 May 1944 by his deputy, Col. George H. Decker (later promoted to brigadier general). "Patrick was an able officer," Decker later explained, "but he didn't have the ability to get along with General Krueger, and he didn't really soften the blows that came from on high. He would more or less pass them onto the staff, and this caused a bit of resentment; and finally it became, I think, a situation that General Krueger thought should be corrected so he assigned General Patrick to command a regimental combat team."[88]

According to the Sixth Army operations officer, Col. Eddleman, Decker proved to be a more-than-competent chief of staff. In fact, in his opinion, the Sixth Army staff operated best under Decker's direction. Commissioned as a second lieutenant in the Regular Army in 1924 and a graduate of the Command and General Staff College, Decker successfully softened Krueger's oftentimes blunt critiques of subordinates. "When I got something from General Krueger to pass on to the staff, I'd usually call the principal staff [officer] ... in and talk to him about it and explore with him the 'in's and 'out's and determine then if what General Krueger had dictated could really be done in a way that would be helpful to the Army."[89]

Far from a "yes man," Decker—a future U.S. Army chief of staff—made sure that Krueger heard all sides of an issue, even if it meant telling him that a particular directive was not workable. Consequently, members of the Sixth Army staff felt as if they were valuable elements of a team rather than just automatons that mechanically carried out orders. Decker remembered,

> In some cases, the staff officer would have objections to certain things, and I would go back and talk to General Krueger about it and get his decision. I'd say [for example], "Sam Sturgis, the engineer, had a great many problems; and they were real problems." ... Sometimes I'd take Sam with me and say, "Sam would like to point out something in regard to this," and then General Krueger would make his decision. In this way it kept the staff from feeling that they were being directed to do things that were beyond their capabilities.[90]

Another important member of Krueger's staff was Eddleman, Sixth Army's G-3 and eventual vice chief of staff of the U.S. Army. In addition to meeting with his chief of staff, Krueger held daily conferences with a member of the G-3 section—either Eddleman or one of his officers—usually after breakfast. It was at these discussions that Krueger provided Eddleman with his ideas concerning ongoing operations or planning for future ones. Eddleman translated Krueger's ideas into action through the work of the Joint Planning Group, composed of representatives of the army, navy, and air force. "In order to permit the fullest and freest discussion by the Joint Planning Group, I never injected myself into its deliberations, but kept unobtrusively in the background, though in close touch through Colonel Eddleman, to whom I made such suggestions from time to time as I deemed necessary," Krueger later explained. "Final agreement on the joint plan was reserved for a commanders' conference, though all spade work had as a rule been done by the joint planners by the time the commanders met."[91]

The CHRONICLE and DEXTERITY Operations, conducted from 22 June 1943–10 February 1944, were important on several levels. On the strategic level, MacArthur's offensive against the Japanese, specifically targeting the Japanese stronghold of Rabaul on New Britain, had achieved many objectives. Conducted by the Sixth Army (Alamo Force), the assault on the five different locations secured the Vitiaz and Dampier Straits and the southern end of New Britain, helped to place the Solomon Sea under Allied control, acquired the southern end of New Britain, threatened the southern and western flanks of Rabaul, and caused Japan's Eighteenth Army to retreat up the coast of New Guinea.

Operations CHRONICLE and DEXTERITY were equally important for Krueger's development as Sixth Army commander. Above all else, he was gradually introduced to the effects that MacArthur's desire to return to the Philippine Islands as quickly as possible would have on army operations. The planning for the assault on Saidor while the Arawe and Cape Gloucester operations were as yet unfinished foreshadowed what Krueger would encounter as he fought up the New Guinea coast. During this time, Krueger would be involved in the planning of as many as five simultaneous operations. The prelude of CARTWHEEL allowed him to learn about the complexities of warfare in SWPA before meeting much greater challenges.

In addition, Krueger earned experience leading an army under the peculiar conditions of a tropical environment. Although highly skilled in conducting operations in open country, he, like the rest of the army, never had prepared for jungle combat. CHRONICLE and DEXTERITY combined to provide adequate and gradual training for him and his staff. They had to adjust to the impact the great distances had on logistics, command, and communication; the special health considerations required by the army in a tropical setting; and the way in which the U.S. Army had to apply its tactical and operational doctrine to jungle and mountainous terrain. In all this, Krueger was successful. He quickly learned that the basic tenets of U.S. military doctrine worked. Even though the jungle restricted movement, units still had to maneuver as components of a combined-arms force. This, in Krueger's view, was the key to victory in future battles.

Chapter 6

The Fight for New Guinea, Part I: February–May 1944

Gen. Douglas MacArthur could justifiably be proud of what he had accomplished in the early phase of CARTWHEEL, the American offensive against the Japanese stronghold of Rabaul, New Britain. By early 1944, Lt. Gen. Walter Krueger and Alamo Force had seized control of western New Britain and provided airbases from which Lt. Gen. George C. Kenney's Fifth Air Force could continue its air assault against the Japanese stationed in Rabaul. The American and Allied zone of control had advanced approximately 300 miles, resulting in 3,833 Japanese troops killed in action (KIA) and 367 captured. At the same time, Alamo Force recorded 484 KIA, 1,307 wounded in action (WIA), and 16 missing in action (MIA).[1]

As impressive as MacArthur's statistics were, the navy could boast of even more progress. Starting in November 1943, Adm. Chester W. Nimitz's forces captured the Gilbert Islands, and by February 1944 they had driven 2,000 miles to the Marshall Islands. "In the process," Stanley L. Falk writes, "Nimitz had bypassed scores of Japanese islands and their garrisons, leaving them isolated and cut off from supply, reinforcement, or escape. He had leaped forward roughly twice as far in eight months as MacArthur had in nearly two years."[2]

MacArthur had good reason to worry about Nimitz's success, especially in terms of U.S. strategy after Operation CARTWHEEL. Nimitz's progress, he feared, might prompt the Combined Chiefs of Staff (CCS) to give Nimitz the main responsibility of defeating Japan. Heretofore, Washington had not made an overarching declaration of U.S. strategy in the Pacific, instead preferring to craft strategy in very small increments. The CCS made strategy on the fly: approving relatively small campaigns in each Pacific area, awaiting the results, and then approving another round of operations. The final objective was clear—the defeat of Japan—but how that objective was to be achieved was a source of much debate. Would Nimitz's drive into the Gilbert and Marshall Islands convince the CCS to commit American resources to a single offensive drive against Japan—through the central Pacific? Such a strategy would logically end with an invasion of Formosa (now Taiwan)—bypassing the Philippines—before the final assault on Japan itself. Unfortunately, the CCS still had not settled any of these issues by late 1943 or early 1944. At the Sextant Conference (November–December 1943), for instance, the CCS authorized MacArthur to continue with CARTWHEEL and then proceed to move up the northern coast of New Guinea, stopping once he reached the Vogelkop Peninsula. Meanwhile, the U.S. Navy was told to drive farther west, into the Marianas. The debate over the Philippines versus Formosa was delayed.

For his part, MacArthur had figured out how to best defeat Japan almost from the moment he fled Corregidor in early 1942. To his way of thinking, the Philippine Islands—specifically Luzon—were the key to success, not Formosa. He searched for any way to bolster his case for the liberation of the Philippines. Operations in his theater were opportunities to prove that his conception of the war against Japan held the most promise for a quick and efficient end to the war. To demonstrate this, MacArthur wanted to outpace his naval counterparts to the north. He constantly searched for opportunities to extend the range of his military operations. With renewed vigor, MacArthur thus launched his 1944 campaigns on New Britain and New Guinea, viewing both with a redoubled sense of urgency. Any delay or setback might deter the CCS from ever authorizing him to return to the Philippines. MacArthur therefore placed immense pressure on his subordinates, specifically Krueger, to proceed as quickly as possible. As was noted earlier, MacArthur had a tendency to consider a particular operation over well before it actually was, and then to order Krueger to initiate another one. In this sense, Krueger not only operated between strategy and tactics (by executing MacArthur's strategic vision) but also had to reconcile MacArthur's optimistic timetable to the tactical realities of combat on New Guinea. The experience gained in DEXTERITY would serve Krueger not only in completing CARTWHEEL but in the operations beyond.

Although the CCS was unsure whether to move into the Philippines or Formosa, it remained committed to CARTWHEEL. With this in mind, MacArthur instructed Krueger on 23 November 1943 to prepare for an assault on the Admiralty Islands and New Ireland to be followed by an attack on Hansa Bay. This order was clarified on 13 February 1944, directing Krueger to prepare to hit the Admiralties on 1 April 1944 with the reinforced 1st Cavalry Division, code-named BREWER Task Force.[3]

The Admiralty Islands

The Admiralty Islands consist of two main islands, Los Negros and Manus, and a dozen or so inconsequential ones. Los Negros is the smaller of the two and boasted Momote airdrome with airstrips extending to 5,000 feet.

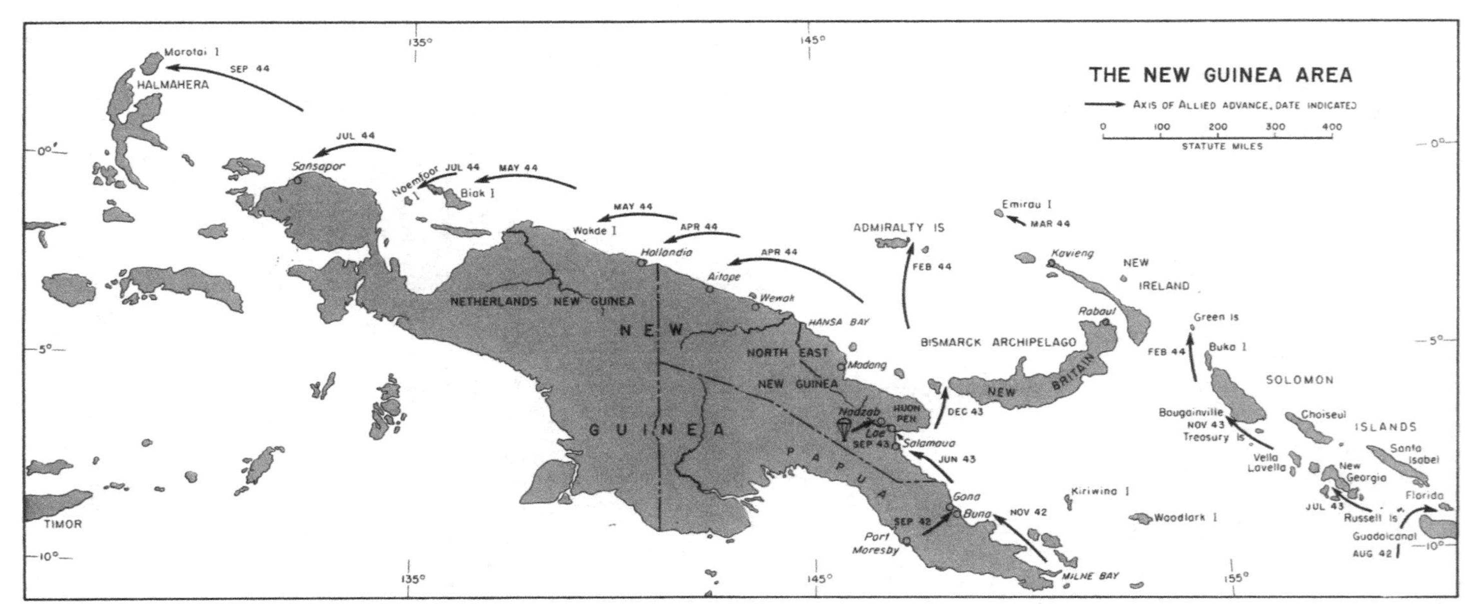

Map 6. The New Guinea Campaign
Source: Maurice Matloff, ed. *American Military History* (Washington, D.C.: Office of the Chief of Military History, U.S. Army, 1969), 505.

To the west of Los Negros, separated by the Loniu Passage, lies Manus. Approximately forty-nine miles long and sixteen miles wide, Manus boasts an interior—like most islands in this theater—that is mountainous and jungle-covered, and mangrove swamps shroud most of its shore. The two islands form Seeadler Harbor, a perfect sanctuary for the navy's ships. It is six miles wide, twenty miles long, and 120 feet deep. With their harbor and airfield, the Admiralties represented the last phase in the encirclement and neutralization of Rabaul. Taking the two islands, in the words of MacArthur, would be like putting "the cork in the bottle."[4]

Krueger immediately began preparations. The usual planning meetings began between members of Krueger's own staff and the representatives of Kenney's air force and Admiral Kinkaid's navy, much of which was devoted to supplying the forces engaged at Saidor. Most of the detailed planning undertaken by Krueger involved coordinating the three services into an effective joint force. As happened in previous operations, Krueger had to weigh the often competing interests and viewpoints of the navy and army. Through intensive discussions, Krueger's team selected to land BREWER TF inside Seeadler Harbor. To be sure, there were many risks to this plan, but it was the best landing site for such a large force. By 23 February 1944, Krueger had successfully coordinated all of the joint staff work as well as finalized his own army plans.[5]

Krueger's schedule, however, was about to change. On 24 February, he received an "urgent" radiogram that instructed him to prepare for an "immediate reconnaissance in force of Los Negros Island in the vicinity of Momote air strip." In his constant search for ways to speed up his operations, MacArthur had seized on some intelligence given to him by Kenney. Throughout the first half of February, Fifth Air Force planes had been targeting Japanese positions in both the Admiralties and New Ireland, and in the midst of this bombing campaign, Kenney's pilots believed that the Japanese had evacuated Los Negros. Recalling his pilots' reports, Kenney wrote that a "reconnaissance plane had flown at a low altitude all over the island for half an hour. No one had fired a shot at it. There was still a heap of dirt in front of the Jap field hospital door that had been piled there two days before by the bombing. There had been no washing on the lines for three days. In short, Los Negros was ripe for the picking." With this intelligence in hand, MacArthur ordered Krueger to prepare the reconnaissance in force to land on Los Negros on 29 February, over a month ahead of schedule.[6]

Faced with a dramatically changed mission and schedule, many of MacArthur's lieutenants were understandably upset with the reconnaissance-in-force idea. Vice Adm. Barbey, for one, was delighted with the original

Admiralty timetable. With the rushed Saidor operation fresh in his mind, Barbey believed that the original Manus operation provided him the necessary time to prepare his amphibious force. "It was quite satisfying," Barbey wrote, "to have almost ten weeks to prepare for the Admiralty landing." Then bad news arrived in the form of MacArthur's new directive, which "changed everything" and forced the staff of the VII Amphibious Force to improvise under unfavorable conditions. Barbey later recalled:

> The old "hurry up" was with us again. Within the next 3 days we would have to prepare another set of landing plans in conjunction with the Army, find some APDs not too far away and get them to Oro Bay, load them with troops, provide them with destroyer escorts and have them under way for an amphibious assault in the Admiralties, 500 miles to the north. It was quite a job.[7]

Krueger did not like the reconnaissance in force, either. Not only was he disturbed that MacArthur had pushed forward the landing by over a month, reduced the number of soldiers involved, and scaled down the aerial and naval preparation; but, in Krueger's view, GHQ SWPA had misread the intelligence estimates. Whereas the Fifth Air Force maintained that the Japanese had abandoned the Admiralties, Krueger's own G-2, Col. Horton V. White, calculated that 4,500 Japanese soldiers remained. Krueger also relied on MacArthur's own intelligence officer, Maj. Gen. Charles A. Willoughby, who used ULTRA (intelligence produced by decrypting enemy communication) to determine that the Japanese had elements of the 17th Division, the 1st Battalion/1st Independent Regiment, elements of the 38th Division, and various other units throughout the Admiralties, amounting to 3,250–4,000 troops.[8]

To gain more information on the enemy troops and their dispositions, Krueger deployed his Alamo Scouts. He had planned to deploy them prior to the original Admiralty operation on 1 April 1944. In fact, a group of scouts, led by Lt. John R. C. McGowen, was about to embark on its mission for the original Admiralty operation when the soldiers were called back to get their updated assignment. Krueger ordered his scouts to the eastern side of Los Negros to gain information on Hyane Harbor, the Alamo Force landing site. The day before the Alamo Scouts boarded their plane (26 February), Krueger wished them well and stressed to them that their success on this mission (the Scouts' first) was important to the future of the Alamo Scouts as well as to the Admiralty operation. Once ashore, McGowen and his team found three machine gun nests, 200 yards of trenches, and evidence of activity, including signs that the Japanese were improving their defenses. In short, McGowen reported, Los Negros was "lousy with Japs."[9]

None of Krueger's own estimates led him to the conclusion that the Japanese no longer defended the Admiralties. To the contrary, it seemed they were ready for a fight. Despite the information from his own G-2 and Krueger's Alamo Scouts, MacArthur remained steadfast in his commitment to the reconnaissance in force. Krueger, therefore, spent the five short days between the moment he received MacArthur's message of 24 February and D-day reworking Alamo Force plans. MacArthur ordered the 1st Cavalry Division to make up BREWER TF, the same outfit scheduled for the original landing. Still employing the old square organization, the 1st Cavalry Division was dismounted and commanded by Maj. Gen. Innis P. Swift, who was also in charge of the task force.

In addition to the conflicting views of enemy strength on the Admiralties, Krueger had to dramatically alter his existing plans, specifically in terms of the unknowns that his forces would encounter. In a 25 February 1944 planning conference, the many competing joint issues came to the surface. Brig. Gen. William C. Chase, commander of the reconnaissance force, for example, expressed his doubts that the island was free of Japanese defenders. If the enemy intended to hold Los Negros, Chase speculated his force would have a difficult time defending itself or, if the situation significantly deteriorated, getting off the island. As a result, Rear Adm. William M. Fechteler, commander of the attack force, assured Chase that the navy would not withdraw from the island until the mission was successfully completed.[10]

The decision to scale down the forces also forced Krueger to make special arrangements in the operational command of the assault force. Unlike other joint operations, in which the naval commander led the army units as well as the naval forces until a beachhead was firmly established, Fechteler would remain in charge of the reconnaissance-in-force phase of the operation as well. Upon the termination of the reconnaissance, Chase would then take over shore operations. Barbey feared that employing the standard operating procedure could cause undue confusion in case the army had to withdraw from the island in an emergency by forcing too many changes in command.[11]

In addition to intelligence and command arrangements, Krueger faced a more fundamental issue. He and the other commanders had to determine for themselves exactly the objectives of the reconnaissance in force. The attendees of the 25 February conference, for instance, were not too sure about the exact meaning of MacArthur's 24 February memo. The radio message advised Alamo Force to include in the reconnaissance force fifty pioneer troops,who would rehabilitate Momote airdrome.[12] This suggestion prompted considerable confusion. Should the reconnaissance force be responsible for rebuilding the airdrome? Should follow-up engineering units do the work? In short, exactly *when* should the engineering work be done? What was the overall mission of the reconnaissance in force? Faced with a lack of consensus on intelligence, hastily altered command arrangements, and vague mission objectives, Krueger had just reasons to be concerned about BREWER.

The lack of transports ultimately helped to focus the mission. Although Barbey possessed several LSTs (landing ship, tanks), LCIs (landing craft, infantry), and LCTs (landing craft, tanks), these vessels could not be used since they were too slow to make MacArthur's D-day. They would arrive at Los Negros at a later date, and so Barbey had to use APDs (high-speed transports). "Only 3 APDs were available," Barbey recalled, "and they could carry a total of 510 troops, and that was not enough by nearly half. The 9 available destroyers would have to do double duty as troop transports, although they were totally unsuited for this role." These ships had very limited cargo space and could carry only 1,026 men altogether. This meant that the reconnaissance force could bring with it only small quantities of supplies. Barbey later wrote, "Only the lightest equipment—no vehicles or even kitchen gear—was carried and the men were restricted to bare essentials." Not only would it be impossible to send with BREWER TF sufficient supplies, but because the slower transports would take several days to reach Los Negros, if Chase ran into trouble his force could not be immediately reinforced. In the event of heavy enemy opposition, the difficult task of withdrawal would be the only option open to the 1st Cavalry Division.[13]

Despite such limitations, the members of the 25 February 1944 conference tried to reach a consensus concerning the type of equipment to send with BREWER TF. Initially, discussion centered on sending a construction battalion in three LSTs to Los Negros a day or two after the reconnaissance force landed, but this was unsatisfactory to most of the assembled officers. Instead, the talk quickly turned to figuring out how to supply BREWER TF with enough engineering equipment to repair the airstrip with the reconnaissance force on 29 February. Specifically, Col. Clyde D. Eddleman, Krueger's operation officer (G-3), suggested sending in the new LSD (landing ship, dock) *Carter Hall*, which was capable of carrying and unloading all types of motor vehicles, such as tanks and bulldozers. Barbey claimed that the only way to get the airstrip up and running in the shortest period of time was to bring in heavy equipment as well as other provisions with the *Carter Hall*, since no other ship available could accommodate such engineering provisions. The problem was that the LSD, according to Barbey, could not unload at any beach save the one at Seeadler Harbor, although the landing site was Hyane Harbor.[14]

Another problem with the plan was the fact that the airdrome would require much more work than either the army or naval staff realized. According to Maj. Gen. Ennis Whitehead, the Fifth Air Force's preinvasion bombardment with 1,000-pound bombs would make large craters, and he did not think that repairs "would be too rapid." In other words, to bring Momote airstrip to operational readiness, BREWER TF would need much more equipment and engineers than what was being discussed at the conference.[15]

With the requirements for repairing the airstrip spiraling higher and higher both in terms of men and equipment, it eventually became clear that it was not possible to bring in sufficient equipment to rebuild the airstrip with the naval transports then available. Consequently, the discussion turned back to focusing on the main objective of BREWER: a reconnaissance in force of Los Negros and securing Momote airstrip.[16]

Over the next two days, Krueger and his staff continued to work on the plan, resulting in Field Order No. 10. Dated 27 February, the order divided BREWER TF into two echelons. The first, commanded by Chase, was composed of the 2d Squadron/5th Cavalry Regiment, Battery B/99th Artillery Battalion (less two gun sections), 673d Antiaircraft Machine Gun Battery, Reconnaissance Platoon/HQ Troop of the 1st Cavalry Brigade, a communications platoon, a reconnaissance platoon, a medical squadron, a portable surgical hospital, and naval and Allied Air Forces (AAF) liaison parties. This reconnaissance in force was ordered to land on the southern end of Hyane Harbor and move onto Momote airdrome. If Chase encountered no significant Japanese resistance, Krueger ordered him to hold the airstrip for the second echelon, which contained not only additional combat personnel but engineers as well. Under the direction of Col. Hugh Hoffman, this force—numbering 2,700 men—included the 1st Squadron of the 5th Cavalry Regiment, the 99th Field Artillery Battalion (less two gun sections), 1st Platoon of A Troop/8th Engineer Squadron, and the 40th Construction Battalion (U.S. Navy), along with antiaircraft units and signal troops. In effect, Krueger clarified MacArthur's radio message of 24 February, which suggested that Chase rebuild Momote airstrip. Because of the damage that would be inflicted on the airstrip by SWPA warplanes, the amount of men and material necessary to fix the airstrip, and the lack of sufficient transport ships, Chase's initial echelon could not include an adequate number of engineers and equipment in the initial reconnaissance force. Instead, they would be in the follow-up echelon aboard six LSTs and two LCMs (landing craft, mechanized).[17]

The same day Krueger released Field Order No. 10, the first echelon of BREWER TF loaded onto its three APDs at Oro Bay; it left at 0645 on 28 February. The trip to Los Negros was uneventful, except for the late arrival of MacArthur and Kinkaid, who joined the convoy aboard the light cruiser *Phoenix* at 1326.[18]

BREWER TF reached Los Negros in the early morning hours of 29 February under a cloudy and rainy sky. Thirty-five minutes prior to H-hour, the escorting destroyers opened fire on their predetermined targets as the first wave of the reconnaissance force boarded its twelve LCPRs (landing craft, personnel, ramped). Because of the inclement weather, the air force's participation was restricted to sporadic bombing and strafing runs by B-24s and B-25s. The first wave landed at H+2 minutes and received only slight enemy fire. The second wave, however, came under heavy machine-gun fire. As a result, two destroyers moved in and silenced the enemy, paving the way not only for the safe landing of the second wave but also the third wave, which hit the beaches at H+30 minutes.[19]

The enemy fire against the second wave notwithstanding, the Japanese offered no serious or organized resistance against the 1st Cavalry Division's landing, since the main strength of the Japanese garrison was deployed to the north to protect Momote airfield and Seeadler Harbor. By 0900, a defensive perimeter was established 300 yards inland, and fifty minutes later BREWER TF seized Momote airdrome. Realizing that his 1,000-man force could not hold the entire Momote airdrome, Chase pulled his task force into a small area, covering the northeast section of the airstrip. Throughout the afternoon, the Americans dug their defensive positions, which the soldiers found difficult because much of Los Negros was coral and also due to the lack of barbed wire.[20]

Such defensive preparations were necessary. When notified of the American landing, the commander of the Japanese Eighth Area Army, Gen. Hitoshi Imamura, ordered the troops on Los Negros to launch an all-out attack. The commander of the Japanese forces on Los Negros, Col. Yoshio Ezaki, therefore sent the 1st Battalion of the 229th Infantry Regiment, stationed around Momote airdrome, to annihilate the enemy force. Employing machine-gun attacks and infiltration tactics, Ezaki's force initiated its assault at dusk. Throughout the night and early morning hours of 1 March, the battle raged, with some Japanese soldiers penetrating the American lines and attacking rear areas, precipitating hand-to-hand fighting. By daylight, however, BREWER TF repulsed the Japanese counterattack.[21]

As the battle on Los Negros developed, MacArthur, who had visited the landing beaches at approximately 1600 on 29 February, traveled back to HQ Sixth Army at Cape Cretin. Arriving early on 1 March, the SWPA commander expressed his satisfaction with the operation and told Krueger to exploit the landing with whatever force was available. Krueger, therefore, ordered Swift to dispatch Hoffman's second echelon, establish control over all the Admiralty Islands, and develop the airfield and naval facilities. Despite being in a situation that contradicted MacArthur's optimistic appraisal of Japanese strength in the islands, Chase's men continued their attack over the next few days. After some hard fighting, the troopers secured Momote airdrome by 2 March. Chase feared, however, that his men could not hold it, as he had received intelligence indicating that the Japanese possessed formidable reserves of approximately 3,000 men.[22]

Chase was concerned that he would not have enough men to complete his mission. He radioed Krueger on 2 March, telling the Sixth Army commander that he would need more than the 5th Cavalry Regiment now on Los Negros. "Fully appreciating his plight," Krueger responded by accelerating the timetable for reinforcing BREWER TF by dispatching the 2d Squadron/7th Cavalry Regiment on 4 March, the 12th Cavalry Regiment on 6 March, and the 2d Cavalry Brigade on 9 March.[23]

Krueger sent his chief of staff, Brig. Gen. Edwin D. Patrick, to Barbey's headquarters at Cape Sudest, New Guinea, to make the arrangements for sending the 2d/7th. Specifically, Krueger needed the three APDs, which had just returned from Hyane Harbor, but Barbey would not release these ships for Alamo Force use. Krueger recalled that "there was some difficulty in arranging this so I flew there myself on 3 March and succeeded in convincing the Admiral of the imperative necessity for furnishing the vessels to permit reinforcements to reach Hyane Harbor by early 4 March."[24]

Krueger wanted the APDs unloaded at Seeadler Harbor, since Hyane Harbor would be congested from three previous landings. Barbey, however, thought that Seeadler Harbor posed too many dangers to his ships. He knew that the Japanese had placed heavy guns along the coast to protect the entrance to the harbor, making any attempt to enter a dangerous proposition. In addition, American mines in the harbor, dropped there by Kenney's air force, might now pose a threat to Barbey's own transports. In the end, however, Krueger's arguments prevailed, and Barbey agreed to use Salami Beach inside Seeadler Harbor.[25]

During these deliberations, Barbey described Krueger as "worried" over the situation on Los Negros. The VII Amphibious Force commander believed that Krueger was concerned, "as were all of us," about getting enough reinforcements to Los Negros as quickly as possible. While this is no doubt true, Krueger also had other reasons to fret, specifically the way in which Chase was reacting to the repeated Japanese assaults on his position. Beginning about 2100 on 3 March, after a day in which BREWER TF shored up its defensive position, the Japanese initiated another assault. This time, Ezaki pushed his offensive at a single point on the Americans' northern flank. Wave after wave of uncoordinated and undisciplined infantry hurled themselves at the 2d Squadron/5th Cavalry's positions. The troopers' firepower was just too much, and they stemmed the tide, as the Americans mowed down hundreds of Japanese by artillery, mortar, and machine-gun fire.[26]

Unbeknownst to Chase, Ezaki and the Japanese army had shot their last bolt on Los Negros and were destined from this point onward to remain only on the defensive. Chase reasoned, however, based on his own intelligence estimates that the Japanese could go on the attack, which his forces might not be able to withstand. Consequently, during the morning hours of 4 March, Chase sent Krueger several more radio messages, demanding additional troops besides the 2d Squadron/7th Cavalry Regiment within—unrealistically—twenty-four hours. Alarmed by the tone and substance of Chase's communications, Krueger wanted Swift, who was preparing to take command at Los Negros, to gain information on Chase's situation. When he arrived back at Cape Cretin on 4 March, Krueger wrote a letter to inform Swift,

> As you are proceeding to take command at Manus, I want to acquaint you with my impressions of General Chase. His task was undoubtedly a difficult one, but did not, in my judgment, warrant the nervousness apparent in some of his dispatches. This, and his failure to obey repeated positive orders to furnish detailed information of his situation and his losses, his closing his radio station during long periods, and his evident ignorance that reinforcements could not possibly reach him by the times he demanded, were not calculated to inspire confidence.

Krueger, in light of his concerns, requested that Swift "look into the matter and give me the facts."[27]

In the meantime, Chase and his men spent the morning of 4 March cleaning up after the nighttime Japanese attack. It was a bloody and gory scene, with dead Japanese soldiers "piled up three and four deep in front of the cavalry position." After such grim work, the soldiers of BREWER TF got a morale boost as they greeted their reinforcements: the 2d Squadron of the 7th Cavalry Regiment at Hyane Harbor on 4 March, and the 12th Cavalry Regiment at Seeadler Harbor on 6 March. Chase postponed final operations to secure the entire island until the latter regiment was ashore.[28]

Swift, for his part, made it to Los Negros on 5 March. After meeting Chase, Swift was disturbed by his demeanor: "He was quite nervous and distraught. He gave definite evidence of being rather unsettled by talking in a very loud tone of voice … for the benefit of all present." Chase particularly criticized GHQ SWPA for underestimating the strength of the Japanese garrison on the Admiralties. While warning Chase to keep his opinions of higher commanders to himself, Swift nevertheless sympathized with his subordinate's plight. "Upon coming ashore," he reported to Krueger,

> I found Gen. Chase's staff had been sleepless since arrival and had personally fought and killed a number of Japanese in addition to doing the necessary staff work to defend the small beach-head against a vastly superior force. ... I cannot have anything but sincere praise for the tactical disposition of the troops and the personal bravery of Gen. Chase and his staff, for the courageous manner in which they held Momote against a numerically superior force.[29]

With Krueger demanding results, Swift insisted that Chase continue offensive action to seize the entire island. While under close supervision from Swift, Chase renewed his offensive on 5 March. Utilizing combined artillery-tank-infantry teams, the offensive made progress throughout the next few days, securing such valuable positions as Native Skidway, Salami Plantation, and Lombrum. Krueger's prodding paid off. The Japanese could offer only token resistance after the first week of March, and Krueger and the 1st Cavalry secured Seeadler Harbor—except for a few well-hidden Japanese gun batteries—and allowed the safe landing of the 2d Brigade/1st Cavalry Division on 9 March. In short, Swift's division had secured Los Negros despite a harrowing first few days, in which BREWER TF defended it against a numerically superior Japanese garrison. Krueger, his staff, Swift, and Chase all helped to lower the odds for MacArthur's bold gamble.[30]

Swift had successfully led the 1st Cavalry Division into its first-ever test in battle. Swift was a forceful commander in whom Krueger held great faith, labeling his 1st Cavalry Division commander as "competent, dependable, and qualified for corps command." Swift held similar feelings for Krueger. He once said, "If Krueger told me to cut my left arm off up to the elbow, I cut it off. He got me out here. I am sixty-two years of age and General Krueger got the 1st Cav Division and got me out here." Having this type of division commander in his command comforted Krueger. With a trusted subordinate at the helm on Los Negros, Krueger could confidently turn his attention from Rabaul to MacArthur's long-awaited movement up the New Guinea coast: the assault on Hollandia and Aitape, code-named RECKLESS.[31]

Hollandia and Aitape

Hollandia (now Jayapura), halfway between the eastern and western edges of New Guinea along the northern coast, is characterized by two large bays, creating a large peninsula approximately thirty miles long, twelve miles wide, and dominated by the Cyclops Mountains. At the base of this peninsula is Sentani Lake, which stretches about 15 miles. Between the mountain range and the lake is a relatively flat plain on which the Japanese had built an airdrome.

MacArthur ordered Krueger to seize both of Hollandia's bays—Tanahmerah and Humboldt—take control of the airdrome, and then be "prepared to continue offensive operations to the west." To fulfill this mission, scheduled for 22 April, MacArthur added an assault against Aitape, 125 miles east of Hollandia. Operation RECKLESS was different from other SWPA missions. Hollandia was out of range of Kenney's land-based aircraft, so MacArthur had to rely on Admiral Nimitz's aircraft carriers. Nimitz, however, agreed to support Krueger's assault for only three days, which would leave a crucial gap until Alamo Force could get Hollandia's runways in operation. Consequently, MacArthur chose Aitape village and its airdrome to support RECKLESS, primarily because it was lightly defended. The Aitape region is known for its lack of geographical features, except for a small hill near the town. The coastal plain is covered in the typical New Guinea jungle, and several rivers and streams—including the Driniumor, Higia, Raihu, and Esim Rivers—run through the region and empty into the Pacific Ocean.[32]

Krueger had known for some time of the impending Hollandia operation, although the official GHQ SWPA notice came on 5 March 1944, instructing him once more to coordinate planning. In fact, the RECKLESS TF commander, Lt. Gen. Robert L. Eichelberger, had traveled to Alamo headquarters on 2 March to commence planning. The two talked long into the night, hammering out much of the preparatory work.[33]

From 2 March until 14 March, Krueger met with a stream of naval, AAF, and GHQ SWPA representatives as well as members of units under his command. The vast distances separating the various officers of SWPA complicated these meetings. Barbey later explained,

> General MacArthur was in Brisbane, Australia. Admiral Nimitz was in Pearl Harbor. General Krueger ... was at Finschhafen. General Eichelberger ... was at Goodenough Island, three hundred miles to the eastward. My flagship was anchored at Buna, about midway between the two places. Air Force headquarters was at Brisbane, and the headquarters of those bits of the Australian Navy that would operate under my command was at Melbourne. The various units of the Central Pacific Force that were involved were scattered from the Hawaiian Islands to the Solomons.

The situation was such that Krueger talked with Vice Adm. Thomas C. Kinkaid about the possibility of moving Barbey's flagship, the *Blue Ridge*, along with its photographic laboratories, to Cape Cretin.[34]

The major planning conference for the Hollandia operation included all the representatives of the services plus members of RECKLESS TF. Held between 1335 and 1510 on 11 March, the meeting displayed just how far the planning process had evolved since 1943. Gaining experience from previous battles, Krueger and his staff had, by this time, developed a routine and standard pattern of planning operations, which included the discussion and selection of objectives, D-day and H-hour, naval and air forces fire, air cover for the landing and subsequent phase of the assault, supply and reinforcement schedules, possible enemy countermeasures, command arrangements, and logistical support.[35]

As in previous operations, intelligence was in many instances sketchy at best. GHQ SWPA determined that facing Alamo Force would be the Japanese Eighteenth Army. MacArthur's G-2 calculated from ULTRA in April that 8,647 ground troops and 7,650 air troops defended Hollandia and Aitape. Of these, he predicted, 12,000 alone waited at Hollandia. Alamo Force's own intelligence estimated that about 14,000 Japanese were located at Hollandia, the bulk of which were base and service troops, and 500 more were at Aitape. Krueger believed the importance of Hollandia "warranted the assumption that a vigorous and sustained reaction to the landings should be expected from all enemy forces in the area," although he did not expect any enemy naval response.[36]

But eavesdropping on enemy communications did not provide other vital pieces of information. As late as the planning conference of 11 March, Krueger and his staff knew little of the topography around Hollandia. Information on the beaches, for instance, was described by Eddleman in the conference report as "very vague." Consequently, he and the other planners had to wait for further details until the Fifth Air Force supplied them with aerial photos. Analysis of the photos suggested that the landing beaches were excellent but narrow, providing little space for unloading supplies and reinforcements. The photos also demonstrated that the most feasible approach to the airfields was the road from Tanahmerah Bay, so Krueger decided to place the majority of combat personnel and equipment there. Shortly before D-day, however, new aerial reconnaissance from the navy indicated that heavy and dense jungle lay between the beaches and the airdrome. Barbey and Krueger ostensibly wanted to change the plan accordingly, but Eichelberger stuck to his own intelligence, which showed a main landing at Tanahmerah Bay was possible. Because the planning phase was already completed and D-day was quickly approaching, Krueger decided to allow Eichelberger to stick with the original plan.[37]

The plan divided Eichelberger's Hollandia task force into two separate forces. The first, under Maj. Gen. Horace H. Fuller, was composed of the reinforced 41st Infantry Division (less the 163d Regimental Combat Team) and was to land in Humboldt Bay. Fuller's division, veterans of the Papuan campaign called the Jungleers, was staging at Cape Cretin after a six-month stay in Australia. At the same time, Maj. Gen. Frederick A. Irving's reinforced 24th Infantry Division, at the time training on Goodenough Island, was to land in Tanahmerah Bay. Both divisions would establish control over their respective areas and then "exploit vigorously and promptly the success of both landings by seizing and occupying the Hollandia airdromes and adjacent areas."[38]

The Aitape task force consisted of the 163d Regimental Combat Team. Commanded by Brig. Gen. Jens A. Doe, the 163d RCT was ordered to land in the Aitape area and take control of the Tadji airdrome. Krueger also ordered Doe—as he had directed Eichelberger to do—to prepare the airstrips for use in later operations. Although ULTRA identified approximately 500 enemy soldiers around Aitape, Krueger increasingly believed that the Japanese Eighteenth Army, led by Lt. Gen. Hatazo Adachi, could launch a powerful counterattack. MacArthur's own G-2 section reported that Adachi was amassing 50,000 to 60,000 men at Wewak, only ninety-four miles and a two-week march from Aitape. Consequently, Krueger planned to land the Alamo Force reserve—the 127th RCT/32d Infantry Division—at Aitape on D+1. In addition, Krueger told Doe that, if necessary, paratroopers would be deployed if the Aitape task force encountered heavy enemy resistance.[39]

At first MacArthur did not approve of Krueger's plan to reinforce the Aitape task force, code-named PERSECUTION TF. In fact, he had other plans for the 32d Infantry Division. On 10 April, MacArthur issued formal orders to Alamo Force to prepare for operations against the Wakde-Sarmi area, using the 32d Infantry Division. MacArthur wanted Krueger to develop the air and naval facilities of Wakde-Sarmi, located approximately 145 air-miles west of Hollandia, as part of the overall advance up the New Guinea coast. MacArthur, however, eventually allowed Krueger to keep the 127th RCT as PERSECUTION reserve, for he too believed that Aitape might have to be reinforced. A shortage of shipping, moreover, prevented the employment of the remainder of the 32d Division, which was at Saidor, for Wakde-Sarmi. In its place, the 41st Infantry Division was selected because, as it was scheduled to assault Humboldt Bay, it would be closer to the objective area.[40]

Thus, Krueger completed the planning for the Hollandia-Aitape operation by mid-April. In all, approximately 73,000 troops were ready to strike targets 400 miles up the coast from Saidor. It was an operation involving more men and greater distances than any previous Alamo Force mission. As Krueger finished up with RECKLESS and PERSECUTION planning, he had to turn immediately to develop plans for Wakde-Sarmi, which MacArthur expected on his desk by 22 April, D-day for Hollandia-Aitape. But the Sixth Army commander could not devote his complete attention to planning, because the 1st Cavalry Division was still attempting to wrestle control of the Admiralties from the Japanese. Although Swift had taken Los Negros by early March, the larger island of Manus still awaited American attention. Two more months of grueling and exhausting fighting awaited Krueger's trusted subordinate on the Admiralties.

The efforts of Swift's troopers allowed the first of four airstrips to become operational on 1 April and furthermore allowed Krueger to officially terminate the BREWER TF on 18 May.[41] Krueger played a critical role in securing the Admiralties. Because MacArthur was always looking for ways to speed up his offensive—sometimes ignoring tactical and intelligence realities in the process—Krueger orchestrated the operational planning and execution that kept up with MacArthur's strategic wishes. The time table of operations in the face of resource limitations placed constraints on Krueger's generalship. In the Admiralty operation, for instance, Krueger had faced a shortage of suitable transport ships. Consequently, he had to rely on only three APDs, which could carry only the first echelon of the reconnaissance force. With over 500 miles or forty-eight hours separating Chase's task force from reinforcements, the only option available to Krueger in case strong and possibly overwhelming enemy forces awaited on Los Negros was withdrawal, a difficult and risky insurance policy. Since he wisely did not accept Kenney's optimistic intelligence estimates, Krueger had good reason to worry about the Admiralties mission. In short, Krueger demonstrated a deft touch in leading the operation. He cautioned MacArthur when he believed his boss was too optimistic, but prodded Chase when he knew Chase was too timid in the attack. All the while, the Alamo Force commander successfully managed the complex logistical and support echelons. It was a difficult balancing act for Krueger, but he designed, coordinated, and guided an outstanding operation.

As Swift's division mopped up Los Negros and Manus, a task that involved, as the 1st Cavalry Division report pointed out, "the story of many an unsung hero and unheralded engagement," the VII Amphibious Force assembled the invasion force for its next assault against Hollandia and Aitape. The fleet began its movement on 17 April, when the slowest ships and those farthest away set sail. Three days later the first echelon gathered to the northwest of the Admiralties, as the second and third prepared to follow. With the fleet rode all of the top SWPA ground commanders. Eichelberger traveled with Barbey in his flagship, the destroyer *Swanson*. MacArthur, who first visited Krueger at Cape Cretin on 19 April, witnessed the invasion aboard the cruiser *Nashville*, while Krueger was on the destroyer *Wilkes*.[42]

The men of RECKLESS and PERSECUTION TFs executed the landings with great precision. Doe's assault at Aitape took the few Japanese in the vicinity completely by surprise. The soldiers of the 163d Infantry Regiment quickly moved beyond the beachhead and secured Tadji airstrip by 1100. As engineers began construction on the neglected and rundown airdrome, Doe sent patrols into the interior to gather information on the Japanese, specifically the Eighteenth Army, whose three divisions were marching west from eastern New Guinea. By the end of April, GIs ran into enemy activity around the Driniumor River, which "confirmed our belief that the Japanese were bringing up troops from Wewak." Throughout the next month, more and more of Adachi's troops arrived in the Aitape area, and American patrols "began to meet constantly increasing enemy resistance in the coastal area east of the Driniumor River." As a result of such activity, Krueger believed that it would be unwise to leave the 127th Regiment at Aitape after the 163d Regiment left for its role in the Wakde-Sarmi campaign and therefore decided to reinforce PERSECUTION TF with the rest of the 32d Infantry Division from Saidor.[43]

At Humboldt Bay, Fuller's soldiers went ashore at 0700 without any sign of a Japanese presence. The 41st Infantry Division (less the 163d Regiment) therefore moved quickly inland and captured the village of Pim, while the 186th Infantry Regiment, commanded by Col. Oliver P. Newman, advanced to a point approximately halfway between Sentani Lake and Humboldt Bay. The following day, the town of Hollandia fell to the 162d Infantry Regiment, and over the next several days, the unit cleared the northeastern coastal region. The 186th, however, could advance only one mile on 23 April because of the presence of about 200 Japanese soldiers on a nearby hill. But the following morning, Newman's troops made it to the shore of the lake and then executed a shore-to-shore movement to the village of Nefaar, located just to the west of the airdrome. On 26 April, Newman's regiment advanced on the airfields and awaited the 24th Infantry Division, which was pushing inland from the west.[44]

Under the supervision of Krueger and Eichelberger, Irving's division landed at Tanahmerah Bay without opposition, except for one lone machine gun positioned on a small island close to the beach. After these few Japanese defenders were silenced, the 24th Division landed without further delay.

Once ashore and in command of his division, Irving discovered that, for the immediate future, the terrain rather than the Japanese would stand in his way of achieving his objectives. The Americans found that lying behind the narrow beach was a dense and deep swamp that impeded all vehicular traffic. In other words, with little opportunity for the 24th Division to move inland, and with treacherous and uncharted coral reefs offshore, the plan designating Tanahmerah Bay as the base for the primary assault on the airdrome was a mistake. Eichelberger therefore decided to transfer part of the following echelon to Humboldt Bay instead.[45]

On 23 April, the 24th Division attempted to move inland, but the swamps and hilly terrain blunted its progress. Engineers attempted to cut a road through a small hill, but a landslide not only ruined a day's work but almost caused the loss of a tank. Despite the difficulties, the infantry managed to march ten miles. The drive to the Hollandia airdrome continued on D+3. On this day, however, increased Japanese resistance in the form of mortar fire added to the Americans' misery, and it was not until 1530 of 26 April that the 24th Division met up with the 41st Division at Hollandia airdrome. By 28 April, elements from both divisions finished mopping up the scattered Japanese resistance around the airfield, and no further organized enemy resistance was encountered.[46]

Krueger visited Tanahmerah Bay beachhead twice, once on D-day and again on D+1. The first visit involved not only Krueger but MacArthur and Eichelberger as well. Walking along the beach, the three generals inspected the American positions. Afterwards, MacArthur invited Krueger and Eichelberger aboard the *Nashville* for chocolate ice-cream sodas. At one point during the otherwise celebratory meeting MacArthur dropped a bombshell. He suggested that since Operation RECKLESS had unfolded without any serious hitches, the follow-up echelons should be diverted for the immediate seizure of Wakde-Sarmi. When asked for their opinions, MacArthur's lieutenants gave mixed views. Barbey believed his navy could accommodate the accelerated timetable, but the ground commanders had other thoughts. Eichelberger was "vehemently opposed to the idea," while Krueger was "noncommittal." In the end, MacArthur decided to stick to the original plan. "His decision," Barbey theorized, "may have been influenced by the near disaster that had almost overtaken the Admiralty campaign owing to hasty planning and faulty intelligence."[47]

Planning for Future Operations

The next day, after MacArthur started back for Australia, Krueger and Eichelberger went ashore again. According to the I Corps commander,

Krueger "was fine—very happy and very appreciative," although the day before, according to MacArthur's physician, Roger O. Egeberg, Eichelberger had complained to MacArthur about Krueger. Eichelberger, he remembered, "said, with great annoyance, that he felt that General Krueger was breathing down his neck. (And Krueger probably *was* breathing down his neck.)" Krueger left the Hollandia area that night and arrived at Aitape the next day to inspect the progress there, where he was pleased to see that Doe "had the situation well in hand."[48]

Following the capture of the Hollandia and Aitape airdromes, both task forces patrolled the outlying areas to hunt remnants of the Japanese garrisons, which in the case of Hollandia produced more Japanese casualties than the invasion itself. By 6 June, the official termination of the operation, U.S. forces had killed 3,332 and captured 611 Japanese. RECKLESS TF recorded 124 U.S. forces killed, 1,057 wounded, and 28 missing, a sacrifice that paid for a 4,500-foot runway and a 6,000-foot airstrip. Unfortunately, Kenney determined that the Hollandia airdrome was insufficient for future missions because of its limited space. The only air bases that then supported the Fifth Air Force were on the Admiralties; those on Kiriwina, Woodlark, and Goodenough Islands were now out of range. Consequently, Kenney urgently supported the Wakde-Sarmi plan as well as a further mission toward the Japanese-held island of Biak, 350 miles west of Hollandia and the site of three airstrips.[49]

When Krueger arrived back at his headquarters at Cape Cretin, he returned to planning for the Wakde-Sarmi operation.[50] The area targeted by Alamo Force was limited to a stretch of coast that extended approximately thirty-five miles from the village of Sarmi to the village of Masi-Masi. A single road, or coastal track, ran about 100 yards inland, punctuated by numerous creeks, streams, and rivers. Approximately halfway between Sarmi and Arare was Lone Tree Hill, an elevation composed of rugged hills and mountains that created a formidable obstacle to any force attempting to advance toward the Sawar airfield. Because thick vegetation starts to grow about 1,000 yards inland from the ocean, operations were necessarily confined to the coastal region. Located just three miles offshore, Wakde Island actually refers to two islands: Insoemoar and Insoemanai. The latter island is the smaller of the two, measuring just 750 yards across, while the larger is about 1,500 yards across. An airstrip covered much of Insoemoar, which made the island strategically significant for MacArthur's push to the Philippines.

While SWPA officers were familiar with the geographical features of the Wakde-Sarmi region, they had far less knowledge of the Japanese defenses there. MacArthur's intelligence section calculated that approximately 6,050 to 6,750 enemy soldiers (of which 3,950 to 6,650 were combat troops) of the

223d and 224th Infantry Regiments were in the vicinity. These estimates fell short of the actual total of about 11,000, including some 6,000 combat troops under the command of Lt. Gen. Fusataro Teshima's Second Army. In fact, Willoughby failed to determine accurately the strength of the Japanese garrison at Wakde-Sarmi largely because of sketchy intelligence reports.[51]

According to the Alamo Force report on the Wakde operation, planners, unable to get firm and definitive information, "depended solely upon the reports of air power observers and the interpretation of aerial photographs for the timely information of the terrain and the enemy installations in the objectives." Based on his Admiralty Islands experience, Krueger most likely treated these estimates from aerial reconnaissance with a certain degree of suspicion. In fact, in a letter to Krueger just three days after the Wakde landing, Eichelberger noted the problems of this type of intelligence: "Colonel [Donald R.] Hutchinson [who commanded the air cover for the operation] was over Wakde for three hours on D day in a [Curtiss] P-40 [Warhawk]. During a large part of the time he was flying very low and he said he would have been willing to land on Wakde on D day because he knew there were no Japs there. Again one is forced to the conclusion that an observer in a fast plane cannot get a true picture of well camouflaged defensive positions." Eichelberger's chief of staff, Brig. Gen. Clovis E. Byers, who was with Hutchinson on the flight, came to the same conclusion. After finding out that over 800 Japanese soldiers of the 9th Company of the 3d Battalion/224th Infantry Regiment along with various naval units held the island, Eichelberger remembered, "I've never ceased to remind them of it."[52]

With faulty intelligence on enemy strength in hand, Krueger and his staff set out to devise a plan for Wakde-Sarmi. In Field Order No. 16 of 30 April 1944, Krueger assigned one regimental combat team to land near the Sawar-Maffin airdromes, about eight miles to the west of Sarmi on 15 May, while a second was to establish positions on the mainland opposite Wakde Island in order to prepare an assault on the island the next day. The third RCT, meanwhile, was the divisional reserve. In short, Krueger gave the 41st Division the objective to "clear the Wakde-Sarmi area of the enemy, consolidate and defend the area, and prepare facilities for aircraft on Wakde Island and in the Sarmi-Sawar area."[53]

By early May, Krueger had designed another operation, disseminated his orders to his subordinates, and prepared to oversee its execution (while also overseeing other ongoing operations), when MacArthur—as he had done in the Admiralty operation—decided to change the Wakde-Sarmi mission. On 6 May—a week after Krueger had sent out his orders to Alamo Force—MacArthur ordered Krueger to limit the operation to just one landing. After reviewing aerial photographs of the Sarmi area, MacArthur concluded that the two airdromes located in this area were not suitable for heavy bomber use. Consequently, he ordered only one landing, at the village of Arare across from Wakde Island. With Sarmi no longer figuring in Alamo plans, GHQ SWPA informed Krueger that an invasion of Biak Island would follow the Wakde landings by eight to ten days. MacArthur considered Biak, situated about 150 miles west of Wakde, strategically important for its three airstrips, which he had promised to support the navy's drive to capture the Marianas in mid-June.[54]

Coming just eleven days before D-day for Wakde and twenty-one days before Biak, MacArthur's change in plans, Krueger remembered, "naturally upset things materially." In the planning that followed, Krueger and his staff decided to keep the basic Wakde plan as outlined in Field Order No. 16. They had to find the resources, however, to mount the Biak operation as well as synchronize it with the Wakde Island mission.[55] In two conferences, both held on 9 May and attended by Krueger; MacArthur's chief of staff, Lt. Gen. Richard K. Sutherland; the GHQ SWPA operations officer, Maj. Gen. Stephen J. Chamberlin; Alamo Force staff; and various SWPA officials, the participants worked on the details of the next jump in the drive up the New Guinea coast. Krueger's opening comments betrayed the stress of MacArthur's strategy of engaging multiple targets near the same time of one another. Krueger confidently noted that the overall emphasis on speed was sound. However, his remarks emphasized the need for prudence as well. He remained confident that his Alamo Force could successfully accomplish the Wakde-Sarmi operation, but it was the Biak mission that bothered the Sixth Army commander.[56]

After Krueger's introductory remarks, he turned to his intelligence officer, Col. White, to brief the conference on what was then known about Biak and its Japanese garrison. This time, Krueger did not want to employ his Alamo Scouts. With the Japanese obviously reeling as a result of the assault on Hollandia, he did not want to risk giving away American intentions. Therefore, Alamo Force would again have to rely on aerial reconnaissance, in addition to first-hand information from two natives of the island.[57]

Biak Island measures about fifty miles long and about twenty-five miles wide. Like most other areas in the Southwest Pacific, Biak was covered by swamps and thick jungle. What distinguished Biak, however, were the sheer cliffs that punctuated most of the island. At the southern edge of the island, the site of Biak's airdromes and Alamo Force's objective, the cliffs were especially menacing as they rose several hundred feet into the air. What Krueger did not know—again demonstrating the limitations of aerial photography—

was that caves dotted the cliffs that overlook the airdromes. In these depressions, the Japanese had concentrated their guns. Obviously, Biak provided the Japanese with excellent defensive terrain from which they hoped to repel the American invaders. Making Alamo Force's mission even more problematic was that the island had little fresh water. The task force, therefore, would have to bring equipment to drill wells. In short, as Eichelberger remarked after arriving at Biak, "It was a hell of a place in my estimation!"[58]

White also outlined the intelligence estimates of enemy strength. The Alamo Force G-2 believed that between 2,500 and 5,000 Japanese soldiers occupied Biak. Later, Willoughby raised the figure significantly, from 5,000 to 7,000, of which 2,300 were combat troops. Once again, MacArthur's G-2 section failed to determine enemy strength accurately. In fact, Biak held 12,350 enemy troops. Instead of a ground threat, Willoughby feared that the Japanese navy would attempt to attack the American invasion force at sea.[59]

With the geography and intelligence estimates out of the way, the conference turned to the many problems of launching two nearly simultaneous amphibious assaults. From Krueger's perspective, one of the most troubling aspects was whether Kenney would have the Hollandia airfields up and running in time to support the Wakde-Biak operation. The air force "gave a rather pessimistic report" that approximately six inches of mud remained on top of Hollandia's runway. The poor roads leading from the coast inland could not handle the heavy equipment needed to repair the runways. The engineering equipment that did make it to Hollandia so far was transported by air. Despite such problems, Kenney believed the Hollandia airdrome would be operational on 17 May. Krueger suggested that it needed to be completed by 15 May.[60]

The navy, likewise, had obstacles of its own to overcome. There were not enough ships to conduct the Wakde and Biak assaults. Kinkaid's ships, therefore, would have to transport the army to Wakde, travel back to the staging area at Hollandia, then move back to Biak. The limited number of destroyer escorts available particularly bothered both Krueger and Kinkaid. It was a situation, Kinkaid asserted, that "will have to be studied out carefully."[61]

Despite these difficulties, Krueger insisted that MacArthur's reasons for wanting to mount the two assaults at the earliest possible dates were not only "natural, but perfectly sound." In compliance with the SWPA chief's directives and reflecting the conference's discussion, Krueger issued Field Order No. 17 on 12 May, which redefined the mission of the Wakde-Sarmi task force. Commanded by Brig. Gen. Jens A. Doe—commander of the Aitape task force—the invasion force was named the TORNADO TF and was ordered to prepare for a 17 May D-day. Krueger instructed Doe to land in the vicinity of Arare at 0715 with the 163d RCT of the 41st Division. The 3d Battalion had the task of hitting the beaches first and quickly securing the western flank of the planned perimeter at the Tor River, while the 2d Battalion would follow and swing left to Tementoe Creek. The 1st Battalion was to unload and prepare for its assault on Wakde Island the next day. Although MacArthur had scratched Sarmi as an objective, Eddleman had warned Doe at the 9 May conference that the area as far west as Sarmi should be secured, because if TORNADO TF did not do so, the "2000 or 3000 Jap troops in that area will be continually in our hair."[62]

Meanwhile, the Biak force—the 41st Division (less the 163d RCT), known as HURRICANE TF—was to stage in the Hollandia area. Commanded by Maj. Gen. Horace H. Fuller, HURRICANE TF was to land at 0715 on 27 May near the village of Bosnek and quickly seize and occupy Mokmer, Borokoe, and Sorido airfields.[63]

Staging with HURRICANE TF at Hollandia was the Alamo Force reserve, composed of the 128th RCT/32d Division and an independent unit originally from Arizona, the 158th RCT, known as the Bushmasters. The untested 128th had just arrived in SWPA from Hawaii and was assembling at Aitape. Although Krueger designated the 128th and the 158th RCTs as Alamo reserves, he actually considered the 163d RCT as the best candidate to reinforce the Biak operation, since it would be closer than the official reserves, and since the Biak force contained the 163d RCT's parent organization, the 41st Division.[64]

On the eve of the Wakde battle, TORNADO TF consisted of 4,500 combat troops of the 163d RCT and 3,747 combat troops of various other units, for a total of 8,247. Doe's frontline forces were supported by 2,434 service troops from twenty-seven separate units. Alamo Force, then, was sending 10,681 troops to face not the 6,000 or so Japanese it expected on Wakde, but approximately 11,000 soldiers. For Biak, Krueger amassed 15,677 combat troops along with 5,082 service troops for a total of 20,759 to face not the expected 5,000 to 7,000 troops but 12,350. These miscalculations would prove costly, especially on the latter island, whose defenders wisely and tenaciously used the caves overlooking the airdromes to great advantage.[65]

With the planning and execution of the Admiralty operation, Krueger's honeymoon in SWPA was over. Many of the contextual factors that limit all military commanders began to influence operations beginning in February 1944. Among the most significant were the shoestring shipping capacity that hindered amphibious operations, inadequate intelligence, and—the most important—Gen. Douglas MacArthur's desire for speedy operations.

Fortunately, the Admiralty operation had proceeded smoothly and the planning process for Wakde-Sarmi and Biak, while harried at times, also went well. Nevertheless, beginning with the landings on and near Wakde, these forces—up until this point manageable nuisances—now became harsh military realities that stretched not only Alamo Force but its commanding general as well.

Chapter 7

The Fight for New Guinea, Part II: May–October 1944

The pace of military operations increased dramatically for Lt. Gen. Walter Krueger. The Admiralty Islands operation provided a good lesson in operating in Gen. Douglas MacArthur's Southwest Pacific Area—fast-paced, often without adequate resources, and with sketchy intelligence at best. In addition, Krueger had quickly learned to manage multiple operations simultaneously. At one point, he had commitments in eight locations from the Admiralties to Noemfoor, separated by some 800 miles of ocean and jungle-covered terrain. All of these factors forced Krueger to carefully monitor the tactical details of the various operations much more than he would have liked. Despite these obstacles, Krueger was instrumental in making MacArthur's return to the Philippines possible.

Wakde and Biak: Initial Operations

As the 17 May D-day for the Wakde-Sarmi operation drew near, the Fifth Air Force bombed Japanese positions throughout western New Guinea, concentrating its efforts on the Wakde area on D-1. Just before H-hour, heavy air strikes along with intense naval fire saturated Japanese targets on both Wakde Island and the New Guinea mainland. The Japanese—perhaps as a result of the preinvasion bombardment—offered no resistance to the soldiers of the 163d RCT. The three assault battalions soon established defensive positions near the village of Arare and on the Tor River, thereby accomplishing the first-day objectives. TORNADO Task Force next turned its attention toward Wakde Island itself, which required three days of close, hard fighting.[1]

While the battle raged on Wakde, the two battalions of the 163d RCT held their positions, conducting only limited patrols beyond the Tor River. Vigorous offensive action to clear the Sarmi area was postponed until the arrival of the 158th RCT, commanded by Krueger's old chief of staff, Brig. Gen. Edwin D. Patrick. Until the arrival of the Bushmasters, the 163d conducted ground reconnaissance missions that confirmed that the Japanese intended to defend strongly the ground west of the Tor River.[2]

As Patrick's RCT disembarked on 21 May, Krueger learned through a decrypted Japanese naval message and captured documents of a Japanese plan to send two regimental combat teams against American positions around Arare and Toem. With the specter of a large contingent of Japanese forces advancing toward Toem and Arare, U.S. forces still engaged at Aitape, and D-day for Biak only six days away, Krueger did not want a festering problem around Wakde-Sarmi. Consequently, on 22 May he decided to expand the mission of TORNADO TF (TTF) along the lines he had suggested at the 9 May conference. "My decision to enlarge the mission of the TTF," he recalled, "was due to my desire to prevent the Japs from endangering our hold on Wakde, which could not be considered secure without our having more than a toe hold on the adjacent mainland of New Guinea." Instead of employing elements of Alamo Force just to protect the area between the Tor River and Tementoe Creek, he wanted to send the 158th RCT west to conduct a preemptive strike against the Japanese forces on the west side of the Tor.[3] Krueger therefore ordered Patrick "to reconnoiter the area west of the Tor to a distance of 1500 yards." As Krueger directed, the Bushmasters moved out in the early morning hours of 22 May. Throughout the day, the men of the 158th RCT made limited contact with the enemy. Just as preinvasion intelligence failed to discern Japanese strength accurately, so too did the efforts of the 158th Regiment. It estimated that the Japanese could muster only 3,500 combat troops of various units of the 36th Division. Similarly, Willoughby at G-2 GHQ SWPA still indicated that TORNADO TF faced two battalions of the 224th Regiment/36th Division. In reality, enemy forces, poised on the west side of the Tor River, then totaled about 8,000. With this new and misleading information from both SWPA's G-2 and his own sources, Krueger ordered the 3,077 enlisted men and 136 officers to move westward toward Lone Tree Hill. Their mission was to bring the Japanese to battle and eliminate any long-term threat they might pose to American positions around Wakde once and for all. By the end of 23 May, the Americans had forced the Japanese to pull back from their positions along the Tor, and the men of the 158th RCT prepared to resume their westward offensive.[4] Ever since the Admiralty Islands operation, Krueger had to act with little confidence in the intelligence he received. Nevertheless, in this instance, he acted aggressively to preempt any Japanese offensive against his own forces. To his way of thinking, he did not want to leave the Japanese with the opportunity to strike his forces at their leisure.

To make matters worse for Krueger's overall situation, on 24 May, three days before the landing of HURRICANE TF, Alamo Force headquarters received information that the Japanese army was reinforcing its garrison on Biak. Consequently, Krueger ordered the 163d Regiment (less the 2d Battalion) to prepare to move from Toem to Biak on 3 June, seven days after the planned landing. Since Doe was originally the assistant division commander of the 163d's parent division, Krueger directed him also to rejoin the 41st Division; Patrick, then, would take command of TORNADO TF on 25 May. Because MacArthur insisted on this new landing before existing operations were completed, Krueger had to create task forces continually as well as find replacement units, including the 163d. The Alamo Force reserve was a logical choice but not the best. Believing that the Alamo reserve at Aitape, the 123d Regiment, might be needed for the Biak campaign and therefore unwilling to place it under TORNADO TF command, Krueger recommended to MacArthur's headquarters that the 20th Regiment/6th Infantry Division be moved to the Wakde-Sarmi area. The 20th was stationed at Milne Bay, some 1,000 miles to the southeast. The planned move would take about fifteen days, after which the regiment would land at Toem on 10 June. MacArthur approved the transfer while agreeing to move the rest of the division to Toem by 15 July.[5] Sometimes the tasks facing Krueger were mind-boggling.

Even as Krueger struggled with apportioning forces for ongoing and future missions, he found that he was forced to pay more and more attention to the tactical situation unfolding at Wakde-Sarmi. The Japanese defenders were giving Patrick's men all they could handle. By 30 May, TORNADO TF's offensive bogged down before Lone Tree Hill, which the Japanese had reinforced once the American plan became apparent. The tactical situation devolved to such a point that Patrick fired one of his subordinates, Col. J. Prugh Herndon, commander of the 158th Regiment. In a letter dated 3 June 1944, Patrick defended his action to Krueger. He felt justified in relieving Herndon "because of his 'jittery' attitude." "I had to push him from the beginning and as his casualties were counted," Patrick reasoned, "he became increasingly pessimistic and hesitant in his prosecution of the advance. … His withdrawal to the Tirfoam on the 29th of May was not in violation of orders. Under the circumstances, however, I considered it unnecessary and dangerous at that time." Herndon's ostensible failure to push forward his attack because of a fear of sustaining casualties particularly angered Patrick. "He appeared bewildered from the beginning," Patrick concluded. "He was worried and pessimistic. His staff reflected his attitude."[6]

The timing of Herndon's release and the tactical indecision could not have been worse for Krueger, because while Patrick ran into trouble that forced him to regroup his task force, Fuller landed his HURRICANE TF at Biak on 27 May. The 186th Infantry Regiment of the 41st Infantry Division landed in a column of battalions after an intense naval and air bombardment of Bosnek at 0715 and quickly seized a 2-mile-wide beachhead. As planned, the 41st's other regiment, the 162d Infantry, under the command of Col. Harold Haney, followed the 186th and started its assault on Mokmer airfield. Encountering little resistance, the regiment advanced about 3 miles from the beachhead. Haney continued the advance the next day and reached Mokmer village. Although he had pushed his regiment about 5 miles in two days, Haney found himself in a precarious position. Not only was Mokmer village heavily defended, but the Japanese had descended from the north and set up a roadblock on the coastal road, separating the lead battalion—the 3d—from the rest of the regiment. Facing fire from enemy positions in the steep cliffs to the north, possessing no communication with headquarters, and suffering heavy casualties, the 3d Battalion was forced to fight its way back. By nightfall, the battalion reached the main line of the 162d Regiment, incurring sixteen KIA and eighty-seven WIA.[7]

The day's events shook Fuller, who radioed Krueger to announce that the situation on Biak was "grave" and to request reinforcements. In response, Krueger ordered the 163d Regiment/41st Infantry Division (less the 2d Battalion)—already scheduled to move to Biak from its participation in the Wakde operation on 3 June—to relocate instead to Biak on 31 May. Krueger also had the 503d Parachute Infantry Regiment transfer to Hollandia in case it was needed for Biak. Finally, in light of Fuller's radio message, Krueger sent his operations officer, Col. Clyde D. Eddleman, to Biak to observe and report on the situation.[8]

During the last few days of May, Krueger witnessed the unraveling of the battles for Wakde-Sarmi and Biak. When the two battalions of the 163d Regiment left Wakde on 29 May for Biak, Krueger reassessed his situation. He ordered Patrick and the 158th Regiment to consolidate their positions and await the arrival of the 20th Regiment in mid-June to initiate further offensive action. The Biak task force, in comparison, did not have the luxury of resting and refitting. Fuller and his men had advanced into a hornet's nest, and their position was in peril. On 29 May, for instance, the Japanese launched a fierce counterattack, which the Americans beat back with their superior firepower.[9]

Recognizing the inability of his forces to capture the Biak airdromes on schedule, Krueger ordered Fuller to execute an assault on Owi Island. Located several miles offshore between Mokmer and Bosnek, Owi Island's flat interior would, Krueger hoped, provide his engineers the perfect location on which to construct an airfield. So good was its terrain that Krueger would have liked to have made a landing on Owi on the same day as the Biak assault, but there simply were not enough landing craft. On 3 June, Fuller's task force moved onto Owi. Working on the island for more than a week, however, Alamo Force engineers could not get the Owi airstrip ready on time.[10]

Meanwhile, Krueger gave careful attention to the events unfolding on the mainland, specifically the future plans of the HURRICANE TF commander. Fuller realized that he would require not only additional troops but also a new plan to secure the airfields. He recognized that he would require additional forces to clear the way to the airfields and the high grounds surrounding them. With his reinforcements, Fuller planned a simultaneous assault against the airfield itself as well as the caves embedded in the cliffs above the airstrip. The same day the reinforcements arrived, on 1 June, Krueger ordered Fuller to execute his plan boldly, which, Eddleman informed Krueger after his return to HQ Alamo Force, would be successful "if carried out with aggressiveness and force."[11]

After hearing about the lack of progress as a result of Fuller's first offensive, Krueger greeted the news of the impending offensive with optimism. "My initial dissatisfaction with the conduct of operations of the HTF [HURRICANE TF] arose from the drive of the 162d Infantry Regiment through the narrow coastal corridor without adequate reconnaissance," Krueger recalled. "While I ascribed this drive to General Fuller's desire to gain the airdromes quickly, I considered it as imprudent, to say the least. It might well have had much more serious consequences than it did have, the forced retirement of the regiment being at any rate unfortunate and contributing in part at least to delay in accomplishing the mission assigned to the HTF."[12] Whatever confidence Krueger might have had for Fuller or his new plan, however, would be short lived.

Throughout the next several days, Fuller's 162d and 186th Regiments advanced through both Japanese defenses and Biak's inhospitable terrain. A hard day's fight produced negligible results on 4 June, but the following two days saw Col. Oliver P. Newman's 186th Regiment fight its way to a point just north of the Mokmer airfields. While the 162d was still engaged in bitter fighting along the coast, the 186th was in a good position from which its men could clear the important ridges overlooking the airstrip. But just as his men were in a position to finally achieve their objectives, Fuller decided to alter the mission of Newman's regiment. Instead of taking the high ground from which the Japanese were continually thwarting the American attempt to secure the airdrome, Fuller decided to send the 186th down to capture the airfield itself. The plan faced immediate opposition from Newman and the division's assistant commander, Brig. Gen. Jens A. Doe, both of whom "objected very strenuously." They knew that their soldiers would be subjected to murderous Japanese fire from the high ground. Nevertheless, Fuller would not hear any of his subordinates' objections, and he ordered Newman to march on the airdrome. But in one concession to Newman, Fuller allowed his regimental commander to conduct a reconnaissance of the ridges surrounding the airfield on 6 June and replenish his regiment's supplies.[13]

These difficulties prompted Krueger to again send a representative to learn about the situation on Biak, this time his chief of staff, Col. George H. Decker. Krueger, however, was not the only one disturbed by Fuller's troubles. On 5 June MacArthur radioed Krueger that he was "becoming concerned at the failure to secure the Biak airfields." The lack of progress on Biak particularly bothered MacArthur, who had on 28 May (D+1) declared the operation practically over in a GHQ SWPA communiqué![14]

Krueger responded to MacArthur by stating that he had, in fact, been pressing Fuller to end the operation but that the terrain had been one of HURRICANE TF's biggest obstacles, as was noted in Fuller's first plan. Complicating the situation, Krueger continued, was that Fuller was not providing him with enough information concerning the battle's progress. Nevertheless, he reported that Fuller finally seemed to have the situation in hand. It appeared to Krueger that he had abandoned his faulty single thrust along the coastal plain and substituted for it a two-pronged attack. Victory seemed to be at hand:

> Fuller has been directed repeatedly to push his attack with the utmost vigor. Since it appeared to me some time ago that his operation was not progressing as satisfactorily as I desired, I seriously considered relieving him. Before taking that action I awaited reports from my G-3 Colonel Eddleman and other senior staff officers whom I sent at various times to observe the action. Their reports did not warrant such action. … A radio that is not entirely clear indicated that patrols of the 3d Bn 186th Inf reached the ridge north of Mokmer drome … and "the Third on moving on to drome. … No resistance encountered, no enemy observed on airdrome." Clarification has been requested. I am awaiting a full report on the situation from my Chief of Staff before taking any further action. Shall advise you promptly.[15]

Meanwhile, Decker appeared at HURRICANE TF headquarters shortly after the dispute over Fuller's sudden change in the 186th Regiment's mission and listened to both sides, including the plan for the 6 June reconnaissance. Decker reported to Krueger that "although the terrain was exceedingly difficult and hostile resistance was stubborn in the coastal corridor west of Bosnek, the attack could be successfully concluded by strong aggressive action."[16]

With the opportunity to reconnoiter the cliffs fully before descending upon the airdrome on 6 June, Newman dispatched his 1st and 3d Battalions for reconnaissance duty while the 2d Battalion hand-carried supplies to the regiment from the beachhead. The 1st and 3d Battalions reported nothing except the presence of three enemy soldiers. With this report in hand, Newman confidently sent his regiment onto Mokmer the next day and then began to set up a defensive perimeter.[17]

Unfortunately, there were more than three soldiers in those cliffs. Newman's men had, in fact, been on the left and rear of the strongest Japanese defenses on the entire island. The regiment, then, was in a perfect position to destroy them but failed to do so. Instead, as the army's official historian writes, "the 186th Infantry had lost a grand opportunity to outflank the Japanese.... As fate would have it, [by moving on the airfield] the attacker had placed himself where the defender most wanted him to be."[18]

But as of yet, the Americans did not know what had happened. Fuller believed that he had captured the airfield and told Krueger that the only major task left was to mop up the Japanese in the cliffs above Mokmer who were placing harassing fire on the 186th Regiment. Based on the reports of Eddleman, Decker, and most recently Fuller, Krueger was cautiously optimistic. "The latest information from Biak indicates that Mokmer [air]drome is in our possession and that the strip can be made serviceable within twenty-four hours after arrival of Engineer equipment on the drome," he wrote MacArthur on 8 June. "While the strip is still under enemy fire from Japs located to the north and west, it is expected that this resistance will be reduced without difficulty. General Fuller is fully aware of the necessity of rapid completion of a fighter strip on Mokmer drome and of the seizure of the other dromes and is exerting every effort to that end."[19]

At this point, Krueger concluded that Fuller had made several mistakes in his first offensive. First, he did not make a full and complete reconnaissance of the area before advancing the 162d (a mistake he had just made with the 186th Regiment). Second, his faulty first plan had called for a single axis of advance, one that a Japanese flank and rear attack from the cliffs exploited. "It would have been better," Krueger wrote, "had the main attack been made over the very difficult terrain west of the surveyed drome, coupled with an advance along the littoral—a plan that was finally adopted and carried out." To Fuller's credit, he conceded, Fuller did not have the men to complete the double envelopment until the 163d arrived.[20]

Planning for Further Advances: Noemfoor

Believing that his task force commanders were well on their way to securing both Biak and Wakde, Krueger prepared for his next mission in MacArthur's advance up the northern coast of New Guinea: Noemfoor Island (also spelled Numfoor). This next stop in the road to the Philippines lies about 75 miles west of Biak on the western side of the entrance to Geelvink Bay. Shaped like a mitten, Noemfoor is about 15 miles long and 12 miles wide. Possessing Noemfoor in addition to Biak would not only bring Geelvink Bay into U.S. hands but would allow the AAF to extend its reach to the far western edges of New Guinea. On 5 June, MacArthur informed Krueger that Noemfoor might be Alamo Force's next objective; he confirmed it in a 14 June radio message. The SWPA commander ordered Krueger to seize, occupy, and defend the island; establish an airdrome capable of handling fighter and bomber squadrons; and, last of all, develop a minor naval facility.[21]

The G-2 section of GHQ SWPA determined by late May that about 1,750 Japanese—from the 219th Infantry Regiment/35th Infantry Division and the 222d Infantry Regiment/36th Division—occupied the island. An Alamo Scout team that landed on 21 June, however, mistakenly put the total at 5,000 Japanese. Ground and aerial photographic reconnaissance did report that the enemy had heavily fortified one of the island's three airfields—Kamiri; but the other airfields possessed few defenses. Namber airstrip was occupied by a small number of troops, and only Japanese construction troops worked at Kornasoren. Overall, the island was an attacker's dream, with three-fourths of the northwestern coastal area, where the three airstrips were located, "suitable for tanks and mechanized vehicles."[22]

With a designated D-day of 30 June, Krueger had little time to prepare for the invasion of Noemfoor, code-named TABLETENNIS. In addition to MacArthur's orders, Krueger had his own reasons to get the operation moving. Since the Japanese could logically infer that Noemfoor would be the next target of U.S. forces, it would be reasonable to assume that they would try to reinforce it. Alamo Force planners estimated that 3,250 more Japanese soldiers could be shipped to the island, making their task of seizing it much more difficult. Krueger therefore immediately began to plan for Operation TABLETENNIS even while observing ongoing operations from his—as of 24 May—new advance command post at Hollekang in Humboldt Bay, some 600 miles ahead of his old headquarters at Cape Cretin. The rest of his staff joined him the following month.[23]

Despite the hopes of MacArthur and Krueger, the 30 June D-day proved to be just too optimistic. The all-important naval escorts were en route to the Admiralty Islands for refueling and were not, in the words of Barbey, "immediately available." Furthermore, "there was the usual acute shortage of amphibious shipping." Kenney also had a reason for postponement as the Biak airfields would not be ready to support the scheduled landing. Therefore, and with the approval of MacArthur, Krueger changed the landing date to 2 July so that the navy and AAF would have more time to prepare.[24]

Krueger early in the planning process selected Patrick's 158th RCT, which was still at Wakde, for the Noemfoor landing. For Patrick's reserve, Krueger chose the 34th Infantry Regiment and, because of the lack of adequate shipping, the 503d Parachute Regiment. This force, code-named CYCLONE TF, totaled 8,069 combat troops and 5,495 service troops. Geography largely determined the way in which these troops were deployed. Although Kamiri was the most heavily defended part of the island, Krueger decided to land near it. Not only would Patrick's troops be near the main objective, but the beaches there provided the best landing site.[25]

Along with the landing procedures, Krueger altered the preparatory bombardment as well, since the landing was to take place in the teeth of the Japanese defenses. He decided to have naval and air units subject the island to a more intensive bombardment than was the case in other operations. His plans included an eighty-minute barrage by cruisers and destroyers followed by an aerial assault conducted by thirty-three B-24s, six B-25s, and fifteen Douglas A-10 Havocs, all of which would bomb and strafe defensive emplacements. "Considering the presumably weak enemy forces on Noemfoor," Krueger wrote, "this preliminary bombardment may seem unduly heavy. But I felt it was better to use gunfire and bombing liberally than expose my ground troops, in particular my infantry, to unnecessary losses."[26]

The day after notifying Krueger about the possibility of the Noemfoor invasion, MacArthur also warned his Alamo Force commander about follow-up missions, specifically the completion of the New Guinea journey—the Vogelkop Peninsula. GHQ SWPA radioed Krueger on 6 June that after the Noemfoor operation, Alamo Force would execute a landing against a point somewhere in the Vogelkop–Waigeo Island area. MacArthur's plans originally envisioned an assault on the Halmahera Islands, and Krueger had already worked on preliminary plans in this direction. After several weeks of further study that showed the Japanese Second Army had about 30,000 troops on Halmahera, MacArthur and his staff instead selected Cape Sansapor, located on the northern coast of the Vogelkop Peninsula and about 180 miles west of Noemfoor. Intelligence estimates placed between fifty and one hundred troops there, making it a better and more obvious choice than the two villages on either side of Sansapor. Manokwari—about 120 miles to the east—held approximately 12,000 troops, while 60 miles to the west, 12,500 Japanese occupied Sarong.[27]

The Vogelkop Peninsula presented particular problems for SWPA planners. The Tamrau Mountains dominate the area and extend almost to the beaches, providing little room for the construction of an airdrome, which would support the jump to the Philippines. Nevertheless, engineers identified a triangular-shaped area large enough to support a runway. With the objective set, Krueger began immediately to work on plans, since the 30 July D-date gave him little time for delay.[28]

Wakde and Biak Redux: Japanese Opposition

But even as Krueger was preparing the 158th RCT for its next mission at Noemfoor and was drawing up a tentative outline for an invasion at Sansapor as well as monitoring the troubles of HURRICANE TF, he still had to pay attention to Patrick's stalled offensive in the Wakde-Sarmi area. Ever since losing the services of the 163d Regiment, Patrick stayed within his defensive perimeter, awaiting the arrival of the 20th Regiment/6th Division. Unfortunately for Patrick's men, the Japanese garrison did not allow TORNADO TF to rest. On the night of 30 May, the enemy launched three attacks, which were "fanatically carried out." Thanks to Patrick's sound defensive preparations, the Japanese assaults failed. Frustrated by being on the defensive and being an aggressive ground commander, Patrick wanted to go on the offensive, despite not yet having the 20th Regiment.[29]

Krueger had other plans, however. The Alamo Force commander informed Patrick of MacArthur's new directive to take Noemfoor Island and ordered him "to avoid involving the 158th RCT so seriously that its withdrawal for a new impending operation … might be jeopardized." Krueger planned on replacing the Bushmasters with the 20th Regiment from the 6th Infantry Division on 14 June. One regiment of the 6th Division, the 1st, had already preceded the 20th, arriving in the Wakde-Sarmi area on 6 June. Its mission, however, was confined to protecting the mainland across from Wakde Island. Consequently, it did not join the 158th RCT in battle to the west of the Tor.[30]

While the circumstances at Wakde-Sarmi were relatively quiet for a time, the situation at Biak deteriorated rapidly, despite Fuller's and Krueger's optimism. After watching the 186th Regiment settle on Mokmer airdrome, the Japanese began pouring mortar, artillery, and machine-gun fire down on the Americans, making any attempt to recondition the airfield dangerous if not impossible. As the 186th defended the airfield and established a defensive position, the 162d Regiment continued to fight its way westward along the coastal plain. By 9 June, it had set up a tenuous supply line from Bosnek to the 186th Regiment, although pockets of Japanese defenses remained along the route.[31]

Despite the arrival of the 2d Battalion of the 163d Infantry Regiment on 11 June, Fuller requested from Krueger additional manpower, as his men were exhausted from what essentially became a battle of attrition through mid-June. Krueger instructed the 34th Infantry Regiment/24th Infantry Division to move from Hollandia to Biak. Lacking the proper vessels, the navy used supply ships and transported the regiment on 18 June.[32]

Just as Krueger found himself having to monitor Fuller's actions on Biak, so to did the SWPA commander. MacArthur had promised the U.S. Navy that the Biak airfields would be operational by 15 June, in time to support the Marianas campaign. Based on the inability to secure Biak, he feared he could not keep his commitment to the navy. Consequently, he put increasing pressure on Krueger for results. On 14 June, for instance, he radioed his Sixth Army commander that "the situation at Biak is unsatisfactory. The strategic purpose of the operation is being jeopardized by the failure to establish without delay an operating field for aircraft."[33]

Well aware of not only MacArthur's desire to gain control over Biak but also the strategic importance of the island, Krueger became troubled by Fuller's offensive. From his inspection tour a few days before, Decker had reported to Krueger that the key to Fuller's plan was aggressive action. Now, however, Krueger received reports "indicating that there was evidence of a lack of coordination, determination and supervision" in the HURRICANE TF. In fact, in postwar statements, both Newman and Haney asserted that Fuller never told them that there were deadlines for the capture of the Biak airdromes or of the pressure Krueger was placing on their commander for a rapid conclusion to the battle. In fact, had Newman been aware of the situation, he claimed that he might have conducted his operations differently.[34]

Krueger finally determined that Fuller was in over his head:

> Although I appreciated General Fuller's difficulties, I gradually came to the conclusion that he was overburdened by his dual duties as Task Force and Division Commander. Moreover, reports, which I had no reason to doubt, that he was not making full use of his Assistant Division Commander, Brigadier General Doe, disturbed me. General Doe was an experienced, outstanding combat commander, whose services, if fully utilized, would in my opinion undoubtedly have served to ease General Fuller's burden and to speed up the operation.

Consequently, Krueger relieved Fuller of his position as commanding general of HURRICANE TF but left him in charge of the 41st Infantry Division. To take over, Krueger brought in Lt. Gen. Robert L. Eichelberger, who at the time was supervising army operations at Hollandia.[35]

Krueger instructed Eichelberger to proceed at once to his advanced command post at Humboldt Bay on 14 June. By now, Eichelberger had grown to dislike his superior officer thoroughly. After sitting on the sidelines in Australia for a full year between March 1943 and March 1944, Eichelberger became bitter not only toward what he saw as his rival but toward MacArthur as well for bringing Krueger to SWPA in the first place. Nevertheless, Eichelberger temporarily set aside his differences when he went to see Krueger, who told him that army operations on Biak were not progressing as planned and that the infantry were nearing the brink of exhaustion. Krueger then told Eichelberger to take over command of HURRICANE TF and quickly end the battle.[36]

Upon arriving at Biak on 15 June, Eichelberger and his staff were greeted by an angry Fuller, who felt that Krueger had been unnecessarily badgering him throughout the campaign. It surely must have been an awkward moment for Eichelberger, who had graduated from West Point with Fuller. "The dignity of man stands for something," Fuller complained to Eichelberger's chief of staff, Brig. Gen. Clovis E. Byers. "I'll take no more insulting messages." Fuller went on to inform Byers that, in fact, he had sent a letter to Krueger, notifying him that he was stepping down as head of the 41st Division. Stunned, Byers attempted to explain to Fuller exactly what was happening to him. "Horace, you're not being relieved. This is to become a corps operation. Bob [Eichelberger] is coming in, additional troops are coming in, and it's a corps operation. You're not being relieved.... George Decker is a dear personal friend. Let me send a signal for him, so that when he gets the letter from you he will return it to you unopened."[37]

Byers's pleas went unheeded; Fuller had already made up his mind. By this time, the stress of war had broken the 41st Infantry Division commander. Eichelberger recorded that after Fuller informed the I Corps staff of his intention to resign, "He cried when he recalled that it was thirty-nine years ago yesterday since we entered the military academy together."[38]

After dealing with Fuller, Eichelberger spent the rest of the day (and the following day as well) inspecting the situation on Biak. He concluded that Krueger was right in his description concerning the state of the GIs. He decided, therefore, to spend the next few days resting his division while formulating a new plan.[39]

With MacArthur breathing down his neck, Krueger wanted immediate results from Eichelberger and encouraged him to initiate offensive operations immediately. Two days after arriving at Biak, Krueger sent a message to his I Corps commander, prompting him to reduce the Japanese defenses near Mokmer airdrome and capture the other two airfields.[40]

Frustrated with Fuller's performance, Krueger was too hasty in his orders to Eichelberger. It was too much to expect for a new commander to initiate immediate action before assessing the situation and first repairing what had been broken. After Fuller's poor plan of attack that led to an attritional stalemate, Eichelberger was right to rest his troops. The men of the 41st Division had not fully recovered from their recent struggles. Furthermore, he did not want to throw his men into action when he believed that he had not properly surveyed the situation. He sent a short message to Krueger outlining his plan and concerns. Following several days of rest and reorganization, he first planned to employ the 162d Regiment on 19 June to hold the Japanese garrison in its positions overlooking Mokmer airdrome, while sending the 186th Regiment around the enemy's position from the south and northeast to attack from the rear. Meanwhile, he was going to prepare the newly arrived 34th Infantry Regiment of the 24th Infantry Division to strike west to capture Borokoe and Sorido airfields on 20 June. Satisfied with Eichelberger's proposal, Krueger allowed him to execute it.[41]

Eichelberger's decision to rest the division, along with his new plan, in the end secured Biak, but not until after several weeks of hard fighting in the caves overlooking the Biak airfields. By the end of June, HURRICANE TF secured its objectives. Krueger, therefore, transferred Eichelberger and his I Corps staff back to Hollandia, and he then turned over operations on Biak to Fuller's successor, Brig. Gen. Jens A. Doe. By 22 July, all major pockets of Japanese soldiers were destroyed, and between 22 July and 20 August, HURRICANE TF patrolled the entire eastern portion of the island for stragglers and snipers in addition to capturing several small islands near Biak. On 20 August, Krueger officially terminated the operation.[42]

SWPA engineers established four airstrips: two on Owi Island, one at Mokmer, and one at Borokoe. Ready on 22 June, these strips eventually supported both bomber and fighter operations. The enlisted men and officers of HURRICANE TF, however, had paid dearly for these runways on Biak. Krueger's troops lost 432 men and incurred 2,799 wounded. The Japanese suffered even more, with 4,824 KIA.[43]

Although it was one of the most controversial aspects of Krueger's command, Fuller's relief as commanding general of HURRICANE TF was, under the circumstances, justified. Fuller's decisions and actions during the first few days of the campaign cast considerable doubt on his ability to handle both jobs competently. First, even though it was clear to all involved prior to D-day that little was known about the geography and disposition of enemy troops, Fuller failed to send out reconnaissance parties to gain much-needed information. As a result, he sent his troops down the coastal plain and right into the sights of enemy guns. Second, Fuller's scheme of advance contributed significantly to the early setbacks. The attack on Mokmer involved a single thrust—there was minimal attempt at maneuver and no attempt at conducting a flanking attack. To be sure, Biak's landscape hardly favored any type of maneuver, but American experience thus far in the jungles of the SWPA had demonstrated the necessity of attacks against the enemy's rear or flanks despite the odds. Third, Krueger had legitimate concerns about the way in which Fuller utilized his command and delegated his authority. Specifically, he thought that Fuller underutilized the services of Doe, who Krueger believed to be an exceptional combat commander. Relying on Doe and others would have relieved Fuller of divisional duties and freed him to look after the affairs of his task force. In addition, although Krueger emphasized the need for speed, Fuller, on the basis of the recollections of his regimental commanders, did not relay this vital information to his subordinates. Finally, based on his mind-set on 15 June, it is clear that Fuller could not handle the tempo of SWPA operations and the pressure it imposed on commanders.[44]

For his part, Krueger was pleased with Eichelberger's performance. The I Corps commander recalled that during a meeting with Krueger on a 30 June boat ride, Krueger told Eichelberger's chief of staff, "'I congratulate you on the fine job you have done.' Then as he got in the jeep to leave, he again made the same statement.... His chief of staff, George Decker, told Clovis [Byers] this morning that they are all proud of the wonderful job we have done." Indeed, Krueger recognized Eichelberger's accomplishment and passed on his evaluation of Eichelberger to MacArthur by writing, "I am very much pleased with Eichelberger's performance at Biak."[45]

Krueger did not have time to relax or rest on his own laurels, however. Around the same time that Eichelberger initiated his offensive on Biak, TORNADO TF prepared to resume its offensive beyond its small beachhead opposite of Wakde Island. By this time, the entire 6th Infantry Division had arrived. Maj. Gen. Franklin C. Sibert, who commanded both TORNADO TF and 6th Infantry Division, told Krueger—on 14 June—that he would require several more weeks to prepare his attack on the Japanese. This timetable, however, was completely unacceptable to the Alamo Force commander. Krueger believed the offensive should begin immediately. "Although the relief of the 158th Infantry by the 20th had been completed on 14 June," Krueger wrote in *From Down Under to Nippon*, "the advance toward the west was so slow in starting that on the 17th I sent General Sibert a radiogram directing prompt aggressive action." The radio message was then followed by a letter on 19 June, which again pressed Sibert: "While the situation in your area appears most favorable, the enemy is still in considerable force west of the Tor River where he constitutes an ever present threat to the security of your position.

Consequently, early action to eliminate all enemy forces in the Toem-Sarmi area is urgently necessary. Time is a most important factor, and your mission must be aggressively and expeditiously consummated."[46]

Accordingly, Sibert revised his schedule and prepared an offensive to begin on 20 June, the second day of Eichelberger's offensive on Biak. With several weeks' relative rest for Sibert's men—and reinforcements—Krueger believed that the time was right for TORNADO TF to go on the offensive. Krueger was right, and the additional manpower proved to be decisive. After a month of hard and costly fighting, American troops finally captured Lone Tree Hill. TORNADO TF, however, needed four more days devoted solely to mopping-up operations.[47]

Aitape Redux: Trouble Brewing along the Driniumor River

With the end of June and the conclusion of the Wakde-Sarmi and Biak battles, Krueger turned to the upcoming Noemfoor and Sansapor operations. However, Krueger had other worries as well. GHQ SWPA intelligence determined that the Japanese were planning an attack against Aitape. MacArthur's and Krueger's campaign along the New Guinea coast had isolated many Japanese soldiers, including those who belonged to the Eighteenth Army under the command of Lt. Gen. Hatazo Adachi. Adachi's army had been protecting Wewak in anticipation of an American landing, but thanks to ULTRA, the Americans landed far to the west at Hollandia and Aitape, thereby by-passing the strength of Japanese defenses in eastern New Guinea. As Krueger pushed his men farther west to Wakde-Sarmi and Biak, Imperial Japanese Headquarters also ordered Adachi to move west, to link up to Japanese forces in western New Guinea and help those units slow the American advance. For his part, Adachi believed that part of his mission included an attack against Alamo Force positions at Aitape. After an arduous trek through the dense jungle, exhausted, and short of food and ammunition, Eighteenth Army arrived in the Aitape region by the end of July.[48]

GHQ SWPA started to discern Adachi's intentions in late May through intercepted and decrypted radio messages. Maj. Gen. Charles A. Willoughby, MacArthur's G-2, determined that despite the condition of his men, Adachi was planning an attack. He would, GHQ SWPA theorized, engage the American main line on the Driniumor River while sending another force around the right or southern flank to attack Aitape. Willoughby and his analysts, however, could not determine exactly when the Japanese were going to strike. At first, Willoughby predicted late June, but June came and went with no attack. He then predicted that the date would be between 1 and 10 July.[49]

Krueger met the news of the impending Japanese attack by reorganizing the defenses of PERSECUTION TF. He had already dispatched the 43d Infantry Division—a New England National Guard Division commanded by Maj. Gen. Leonard F. Wing—from New Zealand. Since the 43d was due to arrive after the expected Japanese attack, Krueger sent the 112th Cavalry Regiment and the 124th Infantry Regiment of the 31st Infantry Division to join at Aitape the 32d Infantry Division, whose commander—Maj. Gen. William H. Gill—commanded PERSECUTION TF after Doe's 163d RCT left for Wakde.[50]

With two divisions making up the bulk of the Aitape defenses, Krueger established a corps headquarters to take charge of PERSECUTION TF and selected for the task Maj. Gen. Charles P. Hall and his XI Corps. Hall, in turn, organized two defensive zones. The Eastern Defense Area was under Gill's charge and was composed of elements of his 32d Infantry Division. Hall also set up the Eastern Defense Command under Brig. Gen. Clarence A. Martin. Made up of units from both the 32d Division and the 112th Cavalry Regiment, Martin's force was designated as a covering force deployed along the western bank of the Driniumor River.[51] While ULTRA provided Krueger with projections of an imminent Japanese attack, his frontline commanders provided additional information on the enemy. Gill's G-2 had informed him that units of the Japanese Eighteenth Army that faced his forces across the Driniumor River were in bad shape. Responding to some Japanese attacks on his right flank against the 112th Cavalry Regiment, Gill sent his G-2 down to inspect the situation since the regiment's commander, Brig. Gen. Julian W. Cunningham, had requested reinforcements. Gill recalled,

> There were some minor attacks down there on the right of the line, but my G-2, Col. Bond, was right in telling me that he was sure that these were connected with the fact that the Japs were starving to death. He had been down there looking things over and he found that their provisions were giving out and that many of them were half sick with malaria. They had no medicine and were in bad shape. A lot of activity that was reported as Japanese attacks were simply attempts on the part of the disorganized elements of the Japanese army to raid our supply lines and get food for themselves, and ammunition to do some more fighting with. So it wasn't serious, but it was interesting.[52]

Intelligence reports from both units on the Driniumor River and GHQ SWPA indicated to Krueger that about 20,000 Japanese soldiers were across the Driniumor, that they were prepared to attack in the near future, and that they were short of food and suffered from disease and exhaustion. This situation unsettled Krueger, who was monitoring the operations at Wakde-Sarmi and Biak while planning the Noemfoor campaign. The last situation he wanted was to have his rapidly advancing army attacked 600 miles behind his forward units. He decided, therefore, to act by meeting the Japanese offensive with an offensive of his own.

On 24 June, Krueger informed GHQ SWPA of his intention to meet the anticipated Japanese attack with "vigorous action," and, not wanting anything to impair his return to the Philippines, MacArthur readily agreed. Krueger traveled to Aitape on 27 June to talk over his ideas with Hall and Gill. After Krueger outlined his planned offensive, Gill offered his objections, citing the difficulties of mounting such an operation in a harsh jungle environment. Gill, in short, preferred to withdraw his men from the Driniumor River to the Aitape defensive perimeter. Krueger, however, was not about to sit passively on the defensive while Adachi executed a flanking attack. The XI Corps's counteroffensive would be executed, difficulties or not. "I strongly disapproved of that [Gill's plan]," Krueger recalled, "and directed instead that the Driniumor line be reinforced and held and that as soon as practicable a vigorous counteroffensive be launched by the PTF [PERSECUTION TF] against the Japs." However, Hall failed to carry out Krueger's orders fully, for he deployed six battalions far behind near the Aitape airdrome and placed only five along the Driniumor River, with the remaining three battalions as reserve near Tadji.[53]

Noemfoor

While Krueger was discussing the situation at Aitape with Hall, Patrick made last-minute preparations for his CYCLONE TF's assault on Noemfoor Island. On 28 June, CYCLONE TF loaded its supplies and equipment on to the available LSTs after completing a dress rehearsal of the amphibious assault. With everything loaded, including the task force's 13,564 soldiers, the armada set sail in two echelons, one on 29 June and the other on 30 June.[54]

After meeting only ineffective Japanese defenses, Patrick's men landed safely and attained all of their first day's objectives. Despite the relative ease of the first day, Patrick received some disheartening news. A captured Japanese soldier told his American captors that the garrison consisted of about 3,500 to 4,500 troops. On the basis of this sole piece of information, which turned out to be false, Patrick requested the services of the 503d Parachute Regiment. Krueger "immediately" ordered the regiment to be air-dropped on Kamiri airdrome at 1010 on 3 July. Unfortunately, the discretion that Krueger earlier demonstrated at Cape Gloucester against employing parachute infantry in battle was not evident at Noemfoor, because the operation was a disaster. Patrick wanted the paratroopers on the runway to keep them clear of the remains of destroyed enemy aircraft and American engineering equipment. He therefore requested that the pilots make their runs in single file directly over the runways. Communications broke down between CYCLONE TF and the airplanes, and the air crews never received the message. Flying two abreast, the airplanes dropped the paratroopers over a wide area. To make matters even worse, some pilots flew at the astonishing altitude of just 175 feet. On the first day of the planned two-day operation, 72 men of the 739 who jumped were injured, and approximately 10 percent of the injured received severe fractures. Twenty-four hours between the two drops allowed the air force to correct its mistakes, and almost all of the paratroopers in the second echelon landed safely on the airstrip.[55]

With the added strength, Patrick resumed his operation. CYCLONE TF brushed aside light enemy opposition to capture Kornasoren airdrome on 4 July. Two days later, Patrick executed a shore-to-shore movement to seize Namber airstrip. The only major Japanese resistance came on the night of 4 July, when a Japanese force attacked one American defensive position. The successful defense all but eliminated further organized resistance on Noemfoor. Patrick and his men then devoted themselves to mopping-up operations. Throughout the rest of July and August, Patrick's men scoured the island for remnants of the Japanese garrison, and on 31 August, Krueger terminated the operation.[56]

Despite the costs of the 503d's drop, Noemfoor provided the SWPA and the Fifth Air Force with two valuable airstrips. Engineers built airdrome facilities for a fighter group at Kamiri by 9 September and established two 7,000-foot runways at Kornasoren by 2 September. When completed, the Noemfoor airstrips became the location of the 5th and 307th Heavy-Bombardment Groups as well as the headquarters of Maj. Gen. St. Clair Streett's Thirteenth Air Force.[57]

Aitape Redux: The Driniumor River Campaign

With Noemfoor in Patrick's capable hands, Krueger grew increasingly impatient with the situation back at Aitape. Hall's men waited and waited for an attack that SWPA intelligence confidently predicted was coming. As noted earlier, the dates on which Willoughby had expected the attacks would occur came and went without any sign of enemy activity. Nevertheless, reliable intelligence did indicate that the enemy was about to attack. Krueger—who was monitoring the situation closely—finally decided to act and ordered his men to attack for several reasons. First, MacArthur—who also was scrutinizing Alamo Force tactical operations—did not want anything to disrupt his advance toward the Philippines. Consequently, just as he had at Biak, he put pressure on Krueger to smash the Japanese around Aitape. Second, not only was the enemy supposedly about to attack his army far in the rear, but PERSECUTION TF was tying down two and two-thirds divisions, formations that Krueger desperately needed elsewhere. In order to fulfill MacArthur's ambitious strategy in SWPA, Krueger needed all of the forces he could muster. Third, SWPA GHQ intelligence might have not have gotten the start date right on the Japanese attack, but signs of an impending assault were undeniable. Unlike in previous operations in the Admiralties and Wakde-Sarmi, where the intelligence picture was incomplete at best and dead wrong at worst, here the intelligence picture was fairly accurate, especially in light of enemy intentions. By the first week of July, Krueger's own intelligence picture suggested that the Japanese would by-pass the American forces stationed along the Driniumor River and descend upon Aitape. As the G-3 of the 32d Division, Millard G. Gray, stated, Krueger "apparently wanted the task force to attack [to] the east and drive the advancing Japanese back or destroy them." On 8 July, Krueger ordered Hall to execute a strong reconnaissance in force across the Driniumor River.[58]

The responsibility for the reconnaissance in force fell to the commander of the Driniumor covering force, Clarence A. Martin. To carry out Krueger's reconnaissance in force, Hall curiously did not materially alter the disposition of his task force. Unfortunately for the covering force commander, Hall provided no reinforcements. From his original allotment of five battalions, Martin would not only have to man his covering force but also find the troops for the reconnaissance in force. Instead of providing Martin with extra manpower, Hall kept his other nine battalions well behind the front lines.[59]

After hearing of the plan, Martin was "amazed." On one hand, he reasoned, GHQ SWPA had been warning of an impending enemy attack, and on the other hand, he was being ordered to send out a reconnaissance in force without adequate reinforcements. Hall's instructions required that Martin send one reinforced infantry battalion (1st Battalion/128th Infantry) and a reinforced cavalry squadron (2d Squadron/112th Cavalry) east of the Driniumor River, leaving only two battalions and one cavalry squadron to protect the 9,000-yard Driniumor River line. This was not a particularly satisfactory situation, but Martin realized that Krueger and Hall were under pressure to finish the Aitape operation. In fact, Martin concluded that Hall was motivated by "some factor" that impelled him to retain the nine battalions around Aitape. He therefore prepared his meager force despite his concerns.[60]

Early on 10 July, Hall wrote to Krueger about the forthcoming reconnaissance. He tried to assure the Alamo Force commander that he was pursuing an aggressive strategy by stating, "It has never been my intention to sit tight in the perimeter and let the enemy come to me if I could avoid it." Instead, his priority was strengthening his defensive positions first, and once that was accomplished, sending out the reconnaissance in force, which "I had planned … before the receipt of your radio." But as the days wore on at Aitape, and as he saw GHQ SWPA G-2's failed predictions come and go, he concluded, "I am beginning to believe that the forces which confront Aitape are not of the strength indicated by the reports either numerically or physically." In fact, he was so confident in the upcoming operation that he was planning to execute a shore-to-shore maneuver to establish blocking positions behind the Japanese forces so that his task force could destroy Adachi's army once and for all.[61]

Although Martin believed Hall was aware of intelligence that compelled him to hold such a large force around Tadji airdrome, the reality was far different. In fact, Hall reassured Krueger that in the near future he was going to reinforce the Driniumor covering force. "I am prepared to further reinforce both Martin's force and the 124th CT [combat team] by troops from the perimeter defense provided it appears safe to do so at that time," Hall wrote. "These plans are predicated on my belief, backed up by what I consider reliable information that there is no large number of enemy south and southeast of Aitape either north or south of the Torricelli Mountains; all the information leads to this conclusion, and I am willing to gamble on it." Regrettably, Hall did not reinforce Martin's force as Krueger had hoped. Hall, it seems, believed Adachi's army—starving and near death—posed no threat and, as Gill recalled, "that there was no likelihood of an attack and that the reconnaissance force would not be interfered with." Hall therefore saw no urgency in reinforcing Martin's forces.[62]

Confident and lacking the urgency that Krueger wanted, Hall started his reconnaissance in force on 10 July. Hall no doubt believed that he was on the verge of finishing off the last of the Japanese army. Any such confidence was shattered that midnight, when Adachi's long-awaited attack began. In "screaming, maniacal waves," Japanese forces—considered by Krueger, Hall, Gill, and Martin to be largely devoid of offensive capabilities—attacked the thin Driniumor River covering force.[63]

Although the Americans put up a heroic defense, they were simply spread too thin to cover the entire front, and the Japanese broke through. By morning, the Japanese had ripped a 2,000-yard gap in the American lines. In two telephone conversations with Hall on 11 July, Martin described the grim situation and requested permission to recall the two battalions of the reconnaissance force to the Driniumor River line. Hall reluctantly gave his consent but gave no indication to the hard-pressed Martin that any of the six battalions around the airdrome would provide extra manpower to halt the Japanese offensive. Indeed, Martin was not at all sure what Hall planned to do next.[64]

As Martin saw it, his mission was to *delay* any enemy force before it got to the main American defenses around Tadji. Thanks in large part to the men of the 2d Battalion/128th Infantry Regiment, his covering force had, in fact, done just that. In other words, Martin believed his job was done. With his forces outnumbered, therefore, Martin decided to withdraw his entire force to a more tenable position.[65]

As the covering force moved into its new positions, Hall decided to reorganize the command of PERSECUTION TF on 12 July. Martin—a brigadier general—was not prepared to take on such a large operation as was necessary to defeat the Japanese Eighteenth Army. Consequently, Hall replaced Martin with Gill. As a division commander, Gill had a staff large enough to orchestrate the final offensive. Martin, Gill succinctly concluded, "was a very brilliant man but he was fairly delicate; he had been up and fighting all of five or six nights and he was just about played out."[66]

Not surprisingly, Krueger was displeased with the situation at Aitape. He did not approve of Martin's withdrawal from the Driniumor line. Nor did he like the way in which Hall used his forces. With nine battalions of infantry around Tadji airdrome, Krueger believed that the XI Corps commander had more than enough forces to stop the Japanese without falling back. On 11 July, Krueger traveled to PERSECUTION TF to survey the situation and get Hall on the offensive. Hall—having prepared his plans for his counterattack before Krueger's arrival—briefed the Alamo Force commander on the situation. Hall intended to destroy the Japanese units that had broken through the Driniumor River covering force through a double envelopment, scheduled for a 13 July start date. After listening, Krueger "fully approved" of the plan.[67]

In the early morning hours of 13 July, PERSECUTION TF—including the heretofore unused reserves—was in position to start its offensive. Throughout the next several weeks the GIs reclaimed their territory, and by the last day of July they crossed the Driniumor River. By this time, Adachi realized his army was finished and began to retreat to Wewak. Japanese opposition consisted of scattered and uncoordinated resistance, which the Americans eliminated piecemeal. Adachi's army was all but disintegrating into the surrounding jungle, and organized enemy resistance ended by 10 August. Krueger officially terminated Operation RECKLESS two weeks later.[68]

The Aitape operation had indeed wrecked Adachi's army. From 22 April to 25 August, the Japanese losses totaled 8,821 KIA, with 118 captured. American losses, in comparison, were 441 KIA, 2,552 WIA, and 16 MIA. "The most obvious result of the Aitape operation was that two and one-third reinforced divisions of the Eighteenth Army had been shattered in vain attempts to recapture the Aitape area and delay the Allied drive toward the Philippines—neither of which objectives had been achieved," the army's official historian writes. "Instead, the 18th Army had suffered a decisive and costly defeat; it could no longer be a serious threat to Allied forces anywhere in New Guinea."[69]

The Driniumor River Campaign in Retrospect

The Driniumor River campaign demonstrated the continuing influence of MacArthur's military strategy on Krueger's operations. The urgency and haste that MacArthur demanded from Krueger was evident to those throughout the chain of command. While trying to come to terms with the Aitape operation, Martin later concluded that

> it appears that General Kreuger [*sic*] was more influenced by his knowledge of coming operations, and the troop requirements for these operations and to meet the time table of these operations, than he was by the tactical situation at Aitape. His impatience to fight the action to a decision at Aitape and to free the bulk of the troops there for future operations probally [*sic*] weighed more heavily on him than did the tactical situation.[70]

From Krueger's perspective, he needed to act decisively and aggressively. He could not afford to have precious American manpower tied down to garrison duty hundreds of miles behind the leading edge of his army. Furthermore, his interpretation of early American operations in the Pacific demonstrated the need for aggressive tactics that relied on movement. While not ignoring the many problems the jungle posed for maneuver, Krueger nevertheless believed that his units had to move lest they turn into stationary targets for an attacking Japanese force. The best defense therefore was the offensive, and Aitape was no exception. Even without MacArthur's insistence on the prompt resolution of the Aitape operation, Krueger's answer to the lingering specter of Adachi's army would have been an aggressive defense.

Many of the problems at Aitape arose from Hall's execution (or lack thereof) of his superior's orders. Specifically and most important, Hall's decision to hold nine infantry battalions near the airstrip while leaving only five along the Driniumor River contributed more than any other factor to shaping the course of the Aitape battle. Even before the reconnaissance in force order of 8 July, Hall failed to commit more troops to forward positions. Two weeks later, after telling Krueger he was going to send more battalions forward, Hall continued to hold approximately 8,000 men about 9 miles behind the battlefield, while Martin's meager reconnaissance force and defensive line faced 10,000 Japanese soldiers along the Driniumor. The deployment of the nine battalions could have provided a decisive advantage to Martin and perhaps brought an end of the campaign a month earlier.

When asked in a postwar interview exactly why he left nine battalions around the Aitape perimeter while not strengthening Martin's force, Hall, in an answer that belied a grasp of the situation, replied, "It would not have helped to bring any such forces forward. You cannot hit something you can't see and that you can't find. We knew the Japs were there and we had sent out numerous patrols day and night and we could not find the Japs east of the Driniumor. We were satisfied they were there, however, so we sent out the reconnaissance in force to locate them."[71] Hall, it appears, did not understand what the reconnaissance in force was all about even though his subordinates apparently did. Gill, for instance, recalled that in early July, Krueger anxiously wanted to get a "large reconnaissance force which would go out through our defense system, find the enemy, defeat and drive him off, thus eliminating the enemy pressure on our defensive position." Furthermore, PERSECUTION TF's after-action report noted that in the first week of July "all signs pointed to an imminent attack," particularly to an assault on the American southern flank. Therefore, the report concluded, "It was desirable to develop the situation and bring matters to a head."[72]

In short, Hall did not reinforce the Driniumor River line in the face of Krueger's clear orders to do so as a prelude to the reconnaissance in force, which was to locate and destroy Adachi's army. Perhaps Krueger could have provided closer supervision to Hall's execution. But Krueger was not inclined to look over a subordinate's shoulder to such a degree. Nor did he have the time at the end of June, as he was supervising the closing campaigns at Wakde-Sarmi and Biak while managing the newly initiated operation at Noemfoor. The geography of SWPA and the nature of MacArthur's strategy did not permit the type of personal direction that would have been possible under different circumstances.

Cape Sansapor

Turning from action well behind the advanced elements of his army to operations farther west, Krueger's next task was to prepare for the invasion of Sansapor, code-named Operation GLOBETROTTER. In fact, two days before Krueger anticipated the Japanese Eighteenth Army would come storming across the Driniumor River, the Sixth U.S. Army commander hosted the Sansapor planning conference at his headquarters. Since the Sansapor area held only fifty to 100 enemy soldiers, this would be one of Krueger's easier missions. Nevertheless, because large Japanese garrisons—consisting of approximately 127,000 soldiers—defended the area, Krueger decided to send 20,549 troops from the 6th Infantry Division and various other units. Under the command of Maj. Gen. Franklin C. Sibert and named TYPHOON TF, it was to land on 30 July, around the very time as XI Corps activities wound down at Aitape. Once ashore, Krueger instructed Sibert to move ashore as quickly as possible and build an airdrome.[73] Because few Japanese were stationed at Sansapor, Krueger dispensed with the customary naval and air bombardment, and at 0700 on 30 July Sibert's force stormed ashore. Upon seeing the invasion force, the few enemy soldiers scattered into the interior. TYPHOON TF seized its objective by 1055, and immediately thereafter engineers began construction on the airstrip. Subsequent patrolling found only small groups of Japanese, apparently marching to other locations. Krueger terminated the operation on 31 August.[74]

Engineers found it difficult to cut an airdrome out of the tough Vogelkop terrain. The Sansapor area had a high water table as well as poor soil. But through hard work, the engineers by 18 September built a 10,820-foot runway that was home to the 13th Fighter Command.[75]

The newly completed airstrip was not the only valuable part of Operation GLOBETROTTER. By landing at Cape Sansapor, Krueger had separated the two Japanese garrisons of Manokwari and Sorong, which, with the aid of Allied air strikes, were left to wither on the proverbial vine. "Insofar as Japanese ground forces were concerned," Robert Ross Smith writes,

> the Allied development at Sansapor-Mar completed a circle of air bases around 2d Army units in western Dutch New Guinea. That army's troops on the Vogelkop Peninsula—most of the 35th Division, the bulk of the 2d Amphibious Brigade, two provisional infantry brigades formed from miscellaneous combat and service units, and various service organizations—were cut off, their effectiveness destroyed. They could not mount an offensive; they could only "sweat it out" to the end of the war.[76]

Morotai

Although Sansapor provided U.S. forces with firm control over the Vogelkop Peninsula, the 40,000 troops on nearby Halmahera Island posed a significant obstacle between New Guinea and the Philippines. MacArthur decided not to land on Halmahera, but he recognized the need for the enemy forces there to be neutralized. He therefore looked for a nearby island on which he could build an airfield. From this base, he hoped to launch air raids against Halmahera and its Japanese inhabitants. In addition, this base would provide air support and flank protection to the Sixth Army's leap to the Philippines.[77]

MacArthur's attention turned toward the island of Morotai. Located just 10 miles to the northeast of Halmahera, it was only lightly defended and would provide one more excellent air base in MacArthur's continual crawl up New Guinea. GHQ SWPA radioed Krueger on 21 July and ordered him to begin preparations for an attack on the island, scheduled for 15 September.[78]

Krueger selected for the mission Maj. Gen. Charles P. Hall's XI Corps, which had just finished its Aitape campaign. In a 9 August planning conference, Krueger told the attendants what he expected. He first warned that the enemy may react "violently" to the landing. Therefore, he ordered Hall to strike "swiftly and energetically" in order to accomplish the mission's objectives. Before leaving the conference and perhaps hoping to avoid another situation like the one at Aitape, Krueger reminded his commanders of the importance of keeping him carefully and completely informed of the tactical situation, noting that much of the information sent in the past had been "pitiful."[79]

After consultation with the naval representatives on his staff, Krueger ordered the MOROTAI TF to make two simultaneous landings on the west side of the island. MOROTAI TF consisted of the 31st Infantry Division, 126th RCT (32d Division), and various other supporting units for a total of 40,105 men.[80]

Following a thirty-minute barrage on one beach and a fifteen-minute bombardment on another, the MOROTAI TF made an unopposed and successful landing at 0830 on 15 September. Although the landing beaches were the "worst we had ever seen in our operations," Hall—demonstrating more aggressiveness than at Aitape—pushed his men quickly inland, seizing control of Morotai's airstrip by early afternoon. The following day, elements of the task force secured the entire southwestern portion of the island and set up a defensive perimeter against any enemy formations that remained in the north. Patrols that went beyond the perimeter between 18 and 20 September encountered no opposition. Throughout the next few days, Hall assaulted several smaller offshore islands on which the Japanese had placed air-warning facilities. With these landings, the Morotai operation wound down, and Krueger officially ended it on 4 October, the same date its airdrome became operational.[81]

With the capture of Morotai, MacArthur was at long last in arm's reach of the Philippine Islands. As Edward J. Drea points out, the SWPA commander, in his race with the navy, employed two different strategies with two different armies to move up the New Guinea road. The first strategy saw Australian troops push up eastern New Guinea from Buna to Saidor in a war of attrition from January 1943 until January 1944, during which the Allies suffered 24,000 casualties. Following the isolation of Rabaul, MacArthur switched gears to a war of maneuver. Led by Krueger, MacArthur's forces raced 1,200 miles from Finschhafen to Morotai from April to August 1944, isolating about 30,000 Japanese soldiers.[82]

Krueger's Challenges during the New Guinea Campaign

MacArthur's maneuver strategy pushed Krueger and his army to their limits. Although Alamo Force consisted of two corps with ten divisions and other combat units, in May 1944, for instance, Krueger's forces were participating in three operations (Aitape, Hollandia, and Wakde), preparing for several more, and garrisoning points in eastern New Guinea and New Britain, an area approximately 1,400 miles long and 300 miles wide.[83]

Besides stretching Krueger's manpower resources, the strain of MacArthur's fast-paced operations also affected Krueger's logistical system. SWPA operations had to compete with the navy's offensive in the Central Pacific, specifically its Palau operation in September. Complicating this already difficult situation was that it took longer and longer for transport ships to travel from the United States to SWPA and then back as both SWPA and the Pacific Ocean Area stretched farther and farther west.[84]

After the cargo ships arrived in the Southwest Pacific, further challenges arose concerning the distribution of supplies on the battlefield. The Sixth Army experienced a chronic shortage of personnel in its quartermaster units. "This difficulty arose because no assault troops could be spared from tactical operations and all service troops were turned over to the beachmaster unloading cargo in the limited time available for this essential task," writes Alvin P. Stauffer. "Normally, landing craft were discharged only between 0900 and 1700, when naval safety regulations required such vessels to pull away from shore. Under these circumstances, supplies of all sorts were jumbled together and hastily shoved on DUKW's [amphibious trucks] or roller conveyors. This meant that Quartermaster dumps received large quantities of non Quartermaster cargo that held up the issue of rations and other items." Furthermore, a lack of trucks and poor roads made it even more difficult to move the material from the beachheads to the soldiers on the front lines.[85] These problems and others translated into shortages of supplies in combat units. In early 1944, for example, the supply base at Lae lacked such basic items as socks and other articles of clothing.[86]

While Krueger's influence or control did not extend to many aspects of the supply system, he did what he could to make sure the living conditions of his soldiers were as pleasant as possible under less-than-ideal conditions. "Sometimes," Krueger observed, "things that seemed comparatively unimportant viewed from the top level, loomed large indeed to the GI." Consequently, he made sure that the mail was delivered on time and that his men had a varied diet. In one instance, Krueger complained to the commanding general of the U.S. Army Services of Supply in SWPA, Maj. Gen. James L. Frink, that he had discovered that there was a lack of variety in food rations. Most of the ships carried "a preponderance of corned beef, corned beef hash, carrots, cabbage, silver beets, and beet root. In one shipment of 600,000 rations to Biak, two-thirds of the meat component consisted of corned beef hash." At a 18 July 1944 conference, in what must have been considered as a Pyrrhic victory, members of the U.S. Army Services of Supply assured Alamo Force personnel they would replace the cabbage with sauerkraut.[87]

The situation was aggravated by the fact that the army often worked alongside navy personnel. The "Navy in the same localities are, for the most part," Krueger complained, "supplied with the finest rations obtainable, including generous portions of the more desired items seldom seen on our menus." Often, tensions would rise between soldiers and sailors as a result of this inequitable distribution of goods. In one instance, cavalrymen from the 112th Cavalry RCT had to unload beer for their naval counterparts but received none of the prized beverage. "Fortunately, it was not too long before representations made by me resulted in a change of policy, and my men thereafter received their proper ration of beer."[88]

Further undermining morale was the faulty replacement and rotation system. There were never enough replacements for frontline units. Throughout the New Guinea campaign, the Sixth Army lost more men than it received, and not one Sixth Army task force went into battle at full strength. To make matters even worse, the overworked men in frontline units were rarely given a chance for relaxation or rest because of an almost complete lack of a rotation system. Although the GIs had been promised furloughs back in the United States, the lack of shipping prevented it. For a time, the dearth of vessels even prevented Krueger from sending units to Australia.[89]

There was much work yet to be done to improve the Sixth Army, but Krueger would have little time to correct many of the acute problems that hindered the performance of his Sixth Army. In little more than two weeks after the termination of the Morotai operation, Krueger would face his biggest task yet: the invasion of Leyte.

Krueger's offensive up the New Guinea road faced many obstacles. Besides the formidable Japanese army, Alamo Force had to deal with manpower shortages as a result of deficiencies in the replacement and rotation systems and supply shortages, both of which were amplified by the vast expanse of SWPA.

The issue of gathering and interpreting accurate intelligence also proved to be a reoccurring source of trouble. Reaffirming the doubts he had as a result of the Cape Gloucester operation, when a joint army-navy bid to collect information failed, the seven amphibious assaults on New Guinea gave Krueger little confidence about the intelligence apparatus in the Southwest Pacific Area. GHQ SWPA gave faulty estimates on enemy strength and intentions in the Admiralties and Wakde. In the latter, the lack of information proved to hamper severely (and almost endanger) its outcome.

What influenced the SWPA operations above all else was MacArthur's desire to liberate the Philippines as quickly as possible. Krueger noted in his memoirs, *From Down Under to Nippon*:

> The tempo of operations had been materially stepped up with the Admiralty Islands operation. Operations now followed one another with little intermission, and Headquarters Alamo Force had to prepare plans for a number of impending ones while two and even three were actually in progress. Thus Headquarters Alamo Force worked out the plans for the Hollandia-Aitape operations when the fight for the Admiralties was in a critical stage, and the plans for the Wakde-Biak operations before the Admiralty Islands operation was concluded, before the Hollandia-Aitape operations had started and while they were in progress. It formed the plans for the Noemfoor and Sansapor operations while those at Aitape, Wakde and Biak were in full swing, and the plan for the Morotai operation before the operations at the other three places were finished.
>
> The Wakde operation had started on 17 May and the one against Biak was to begin on the 27th, while the Aitape operation was still far from completed. I had terminated the Admiralty Islands operation on 18 May and the Hollandia operation was nearly concluded, but we still had three serious operations on our hands: those at Aitape, Wakde and Biak.
>
> While Headquarters Sixth Army supervised operations and made plans for impending ones in its capacity as Headquarters Alamo Force, it also had to look after and handle the administration, supply, training and inspection of Sixth Army troops, whether these happened to be allotted to Alamo Force

or not. They were scattered all the way from Milne Bay to Biak, some 1,400 air-miles, as well as on New Britain and the Admiralties.[90]

The fast-paced tempo not only made planning, inspection, and supervision of operations difficult but actually influenced the operational and tactical dimensions of individual battles. This was particularly true of TORNADO TF's experience at Wakde. Because HURRICANE TF ran into trouble at Biak, Krueger needed to reinforce it with the only forces readily available, the 163rd Regiment of TORNADO TF. With half of his force gone, the Wakde TF commander, Brig. Gen. Edwin D. Patrick, had to wait until reinforcements arrived to continue his offensive, a delay of about two weeks. Furthermore, the multiple amphibious operations of SWPA created a severe shortage of landing craft, which prevented Patrick from executing a planned shore-to-shore movement that he hoped would shorten the battle.

For Krueger, the fast-paced and concurrent operations meant that he could not personally devote his full attention to one particular fight. Because he had units engaged at Wakde, Biak, and Noemfoor, Krueger could not closely monitor the situation at Aitape. Consequently, Hall—believing that the Japanese Eighteenth Army posed no real threat—did not comply with Krueger's order to reinforce the Driniumor River line before executing the reconnaissance in force.

Krueger, his army, the navy, and the AAF were able to overcome these limiting factors to carry out MacArthur's directives successfully. As MacArthur's point man, Krueger spearheaded SWPA's interservice effort. Through much labor, the three services worked together despite differences of opinion, illustrated by Vice Adm. Daniel E. Barbey's objections to the type and employment of VII Amphibious Force ships that Krueger had suggested for transporting reinforcements to the Admiralty Islands.

Krueger also demonstrated his keen and lucid military mind during this period. With hardly any experience in jungle warfare, the army lacked a mature doctrine for fighting in this type of terrain. Nevertheless, Krueger built upon the knowledge he had gained by studying the army's experience at Buna with his own experience during Operation CARTWHEEL. The notion that jungle warfare was an infantryman's domain was shattered. Instead, jungle warfare needed the combination of all arms working in concert. Krueger therefore made sure, if possible, to equip his task forces with artillery, mortars, engineers, tanks, and, of course, air power.

Overall, Krueger—like most other commanders—found the army's operational doctrine essentially correct and applicable to jungle warfare. Despite the jungle's ability to limit mobility, Krueger insisted that his army utilize maneuver. The necessity for GIs to descend on the flanks and rear of Japanese fixed positions manifested itself in Maj. Gen. Horace Fuller's performance on Biak. He ran into difficulties as he advanced along a single axis, but Lt. Gen. Robert L. Eichelberger's double envelopment placed elements of HURRICANE TF behind the formidable Japanese defenses, making its capture possible.

The best and worst aspects of SWPA operations can be depicted in the landing on the Admiralty Islands. MacArthur's desire to move ever closer to the Philippines ahead of the navy forced him to overlook important evidence that suggested that the islands were heavily defended. Instead, he sent a numerically inferior force to secure the islands' airstrip. Thrown into this situation, MacArthur's lieutenants, led by Krueger, were able to prevail through careful planning, adapting to changing circumstances, combined-arms operations, and interservice coordination. The operational and tactical execution of MacArthur's directives made SWPA's risky strategy a success. Krueger had become a master of industrial-age warfare.

Chapter 8

Leyte, October–December 1944

Lt. Gen. Walter Krueger had made tremendous progress in the five months from April to September 1944. He had driven his army hundreds of miles into Japanese controlled territory, bypassing thousands of enemy soldiers in the process. He placed Southwest Pacific Area forces in a position where they could now enter the Philippine Islands.

While pleased with Krueger's progress, Gen. Douglas MacArthur spent much of the year worried about decisions made above his level of authority. Despite all of Krueger's success, he still feared that the Joint Chiefs of Staff would cast their lot with the U.S. Navy's Central Pacific offensive. With the specter of being pushed aside, MacArthur needed to demonstrate as much progress as possible. On one hand, he did all he could to make sure Krueger moved with as much determination and speed as possible. On the other hand, MacArthur also came up with ambitious plans for retaking the Philippines, created in the hopes of convincing the JCS of the importance of liberating the islands. Named RENO V, the operation called for the attack on Morotai (8 September), along with the Philippine islands of Mindanao (25 October), Leyte (20 December), and Luzon (1 April 1945).[1]

In the fall of 1944, the JCS finally settled the issue by abandoning the Formosa plan (discussed in Chapter 7) in lieu of MacArthur's Philippine strategy. Krueger's progress and MacArthur's RENO V are only two of many reasons that went into the JCS's decision. One of the most important factors was Adm. Chester A. Nimitz's intelligence estimate of Japanese forces on Leyte. He had mistakenly reported to the JCS that the Japanese had virtually abandoned the island and suggested that Leyte could be occupied ahead of scheduled, without several of the planned preliminary operations, such as the one against Mindanao. Although MacArthur knew that Nimitz was wrong, he leaped at the opportunity to accelerate the RENO V time table for operations in his area and prepared for 20 October. With the gateway to the Philippine Islands seemingly undefended, Luzon—and not Formosa—became the next logical Allied objective after Leyte, and on 3 October the JCS authorized MacArthur to prepare for an invasion of Luzon to take place on 20 December.[2]

Although MacArthur had finally succeeded in making his pledge to return to the Philippine Islands official Allied strategy, he continued to pressure Krueger to speed up military operations at the operational and tactical levels. In fact, the closer MacArthur got to Luzon, specifically Manila, the more he pushed Krueger. Throughout the fall of 1944, the SWPA commander sensed victory and became increasingly impatient. From October 1944 until March 1945, MacArthur stressed the necessity of speed in Krueger's military operations more than at any other time during the war.

In addition to the pace of operations, Krueger would face many of the same contextual factors as those he dealt with in the New Guinea campaign. At first glance, Leyte seems to be a perfect place to employ an army with two corps and multiple divisions. The island has rolling plains in the west that appear to be suitable for large-unit combat. A closer examination, however, reveals a much different reality. The climate and geography actually restrict the nature and character of military operations. Rugged mountains characterize many of the Philippine Islands, including large portions of Leyte. Furthermore, descending on the Philippines in autumn meant that Krueger and his men would be campaigning at the height of the typhoon season. In addition, intelligence lapses still remained a constant feature in SWPA. Sixth Army estimates often did not correlate with MacArthur's own, creating confusion and a general air of uncertainty concerning enemy strength, capability, and intentions. Finally, the U.S. Army had not yet overcome its acute shortages of men and equipment. Throughout the Philippine campaign, Sixth Army units would continually enter combat under strength and exhausted.

Planning for K-2

Krueger first received official notification to begin preparations for an invasion of the Philippines on 6 June 1944. This order came as Krueger was monitoring operations at Wakde-Sarmi and Biak. Moreover, Krueger had just begun planning the assault on Noemfoor and the Vogelkop Peninsula.[3] MacArthur followed this plan with the formal Leyte operation (code-named K-2) in GHQ Operations Instructions Number 70. Dated 21 September 1944, the directive ordered Krueger and his Sixth Army—composed of two corps, seven divisions, and various other combat units—to make an amphibious assault on Leyte on 20 October 1944 (A-day); "seize, and secure, simultaneously, objectives in the Tacloban, Dulag and Panaon Strait area"; and then establish air facilities by A+5.[4]

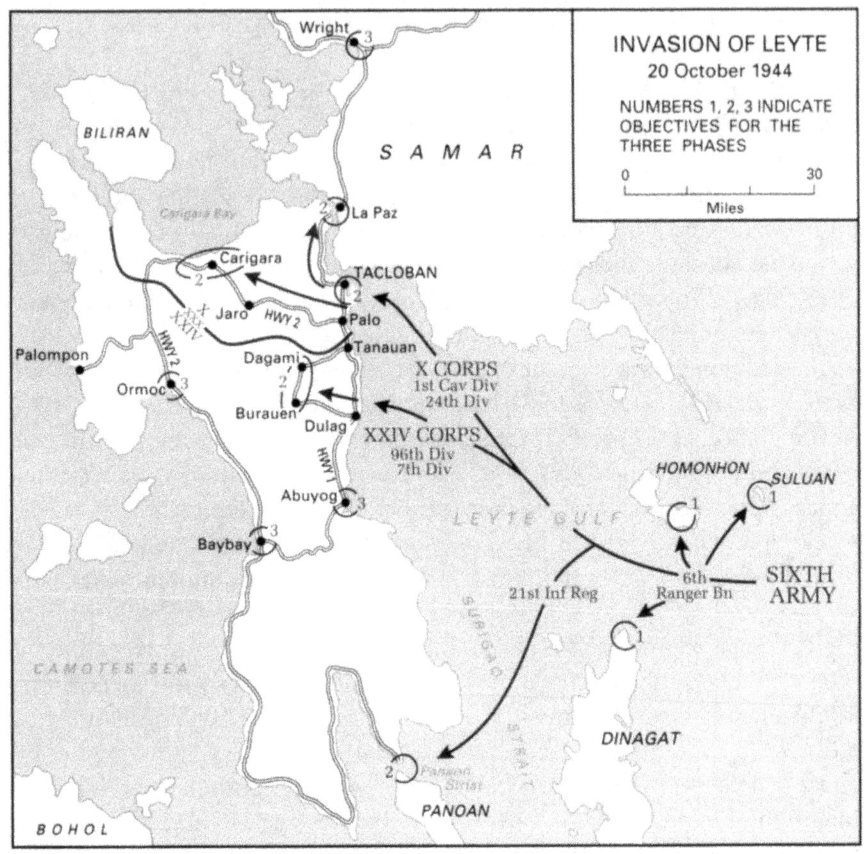

Map 7. The Leyte Campaign
Source: Charles R. Anderson, *Leyte* (Washington, D.C.: U.S. Army Center of Military History, n.d.), 11.

MacArthur also determined that an additional landing would be made on Mindoro, located just to the south of Luzon. He reasoned that SWPA forces needed a base from which he could launch his attack on Luzon, one closer than Leyte. Since Mindoro "met these requirements," MacArthur's staff drew up plans and issued them on 28 September. They ordered Sixth Army to land on the island to establish air and naval facilities. D-day was set for 5 December.[5]

Krueger possessed a fairly accurate picture of Japanese defenses on Leyte. Japan's Imperial General Headquarters (IGHQ) held most of the troops in the Philippine Islands on Luzon, believing that it would fight a decisive battle on this island against the Americans. On Leyte, IGHQ placed only 21,700 soldiers of Lt. Gen. Shiro Makino's 16th Infantry Division. As opposed to previous missions, SWPA intelligence not only had an accurate picture of Japanese strength but uncovered where Makino had deployed his forces as well.[6]

In addition to the Japanese garrison, Krueger paid close attention to Leyte's unusual geography. The island stretches roughly 115 miles from north to south and varies in width from 15 to 43 miles. It is dominated by a chain of rugged mountains that run down its center. Soaring to 4,000 feet, the mountains divide the island into two large valleys—Ormoc and Leyte. Leyte Valley lies in the northeastern portion of the island and is largely a broad, flat plain, which possesses poor drainage with water often just inches under the surface. The marshy conditions only get worse during the fall and winter, when torrential rains make the valley all but impassable. Nevertheless, the beaches along both Leyte Gulf and San Pedro Bay provided the Sixth Army with the best landing on the entire island. On the western section of the island, Ormoc Valley begins just to the north of the city of Ormoc and extends approximately 15 miles to the north.[7]

Faced with the worst campaigning weather of the year and harsh terrain, members of Sixth Army, Allied Air Forces, Allied Naval Forces, U.S. Army Services of Supply, and other branches began planning for the Leyte operation at a series of conferences at GHQ SWPA in Brisbane, Australia, that began on 20 July and lasted until 6 August. For seventeen days, the staff of the various SWPA organizations determined the number of forces needed as well as the shipping necessary to transport them, all based on a tentative Sixth Army tactical plan.[8]

Upon returning to HQ Sixth Army, Krueger's staff continued to work out the details of K–2. In addition to the terrain, the weather, and the Japanese defenders, the Sixth Army plan had to take into account the formidable distances between MacArthur's multiple objectives throughout Leyte, as well as determine which of the five operational airfields to seize in order to establish a forward base for the Fifth U.S. Air Force. After careful study and lengthy deliberations, Krueger decided to land in Leyte Gulf between Dulag and Tacloban. This would place SWPA forces near—in Krueger's view—the two most important airfields on the island, those near Dulag and Tacloban. As an added bonus, since the landing beaches were at the end of Leyte Valley, Krueger's two corps would have plenty of maneuver room. Finally, a landing at Leyte Gulf would place U.S. forces near the heart of the Japanese defense of Leyte—Tacloban.[9] Directly confronting the main Japanese defensive formation on Leyte, the 16th Infantry Division would fulfill one of the basic tenets of U.S. military doctrine: a direct strike on the enemy with the intention of destroying his ability to conduct further operations.

Because MacArthur's objectives were scattered throughout the island and were defended by garrisons of various strengths, Krueger's final plan, issued as Sixth Army Field Order No. 25 on 23 September 1944, envisioned a four-stage operation. Soldiers from the 6th Ranger Infantry Battalion were to initiate phase one of K–2 by securing the entrance to Leyte Gulf by seizing Suluan, Homonhon, and Dinagat Islands. These preliminary actions were to take place on 17 October.[10]

The main landing on Leyte took up phase two. On 20 October, the 21st Infantry Regiment of the 24th Infantry Division was to land, establish positions, and then guard Panaon Strait at 0930. Thirty minutes later, XXIV Corps, composed of the 96th and 7th Infantry Divisions and commanded by Maj. Gen. John R. Hodge, was to make its assault 60 miles north near Dulag. After landing, Hodge's orders were to push inland and seize the Dagami-Burauen area, "destroying the hostile forces in that locality."[11]

The X Corps was to make its landing in phase two as well. Commanded by Maj. Gen. Franklin C. Sibert, the newly arrived corps possessed the 1st Cavalry and the 24th Infantry Divisions (minus the 21st Infantry of the 24th Division, which was to seize Panaon Strait). Krueger considered Sibert, veteran of the Wakde-Sarmi and Sansapor campaigns with the 6th Infantry Division, one of his most capable commanders. "I regard," Krueger noted, "Sibert as the one best fitted for command of a corps by reason of the fact that he is aggressive and has the punch to be expected of a corps commander who may at any time be required to command a large, independent task force in action." In the heat of combat at Wakde-Sarmi, Krueger was particularly impressed with "Sibert's skillful handling of his troops. He is cool and very aggressive and his troops reflect that spirit."[12]

Because Krueger held such a high opinion of his subordinate, he gave Sibert and his corps what he considered the toughest assignment: landing near the Japanese 16th Division. Even though he held Sibert in high regard, Krueger did not want to overburden him. Consequently, Krueger gave Sibert only limited objectives for the first few days. After landing just to the south of the village of Tacloban, the X Corps was to immediately seize the most important objective of A-day, the Tacloban airfield, as well as the town of Palo. Then, Sibert was to move north with the 24th Division to take control over San Juanico Strait and, using the 1st Cavalry Division, push into Leyte Valley toward Carigara. Like Hodge, Sibert was ordered to destroy all hostile forces.[13]

Phase three sought to expand American control to the western half of Leyte by means of a pincer movement. The X Corps was to continue its movement along the coast of Carigara Bay on Highway 2 and then swing south toward Ormoc. Meanwhile, Hodge's XXIV Corps was to push down from Dulag on Highway 1 to Abuyog and then east to Baybay. Upon arriving at Baybay, Hodge was to drive north and link up with Sibert's corps at Ormoc.[14]

Krueger expected phases two and three largely to break the back of the Japanese defenses. Nevertheless, the Japanese most likely were going to offer continuing defense from the northwest mountain range. Phase four was thus designed to eliminate the remnants of the Japanese garrison on Leyte as well as other enemy positions throughout the Visayas Islands. Once the Sixth Army had destroyed the Japanese force, Krueger could complete the mission by initiating the construction program, which included building airfields and naval facilities as the basis for offensive action against Luzon.[15]

In all, Krueger would be committing 202,000 men against the 21,700 men of Makino's 16th Division. From a numerical standpoint, the Americans would enjoy an overwhelming superiority. Nevertheless, Krueger felt he could not be overconfident. Because of the nature of his objectives, Krueger had to land his corps along a wide front. The "objectives for the X Corps and for the XXIV Corps were so widely separated and the directions of attack thereto were so divergent," the Sixth Army report noted, "that the two Corps could not be mutually supporting—20 miles separated the Tacloban airstrip, an important objective of the X Corps, from the Burauen airfield area, the major objective of the XXIV Corps. Even within the corps zone of action the mission vital to each division would limit the capability of the divisions to be mutually supporting." This situation caused Krueger some concern. He knew too well from his experiences with testing the triangular division in 1939 that it had limited independent offensive capability. Instead, to function properly, it had to operate alongside other divisions as well as be reinforced to supplement its fighting ability. In fact, as the Leyte and Luzon campaigns unfolded, the Sixth Army had to add medium tanks, tank destroyers, and Howitzer Motor Carriage M-7s to the division's organic artillery units so that its units could effectively reduce Japanese field fortifications. Krueger feared, therefore, that the Japanese would exploit their interior lines and concentrate their forces for a coordinated attack at a single point against the scattered and underequipped American forces.[16]

To prevent such an event from occurring, Krueger asked MacArthur for additional forces. He first wanted to use the veteran 158th Infantry Regiment (the Bushmasters) or the 112th Cavalry Regiment to seize Panaon Strait so that the 21st Infantry could rejoin its parent organization as part of X Corps. Furthermore, he wanted more troops to supply his corps as they conducted their wide envelopment of the Japanese defense of Ormoc during phase three. MacArthur did not grant Krueger's request for either the 158th or 112th Regiments but did allow him to use the Sixth Army's reserves—the 32d and 77th Infantry Divisions—for phase three. However, the additional manpower would not be available until mid-November because of the unavailability of shipping. Krueger designated the 381st Infantry Regiment of the 96th Division as floating reserve for the initial attack.[17]

The responsibility to move Krueger's force and protect it until Lt. Gen. George C. Kenney could establish his air force on Leyte fell to Vice Adm. Thomas C. Kinkaid and his Seventh U.S. Fleet. Six hundred sixty-eight ships were divided into three task forces: one to transport the assault force of four divisions, and two to protect it. This great convoy began its movement to Leyte on 11 October from points in the Admiralty Islands and Hollandia, New Guinea. Krueger witnessed the vast armada from Kinkaid's flagship, the USS *Wasatch*. Truly, this was the height of Krueger's career. He was far removed from his days at the head of what was essentially a training formation, the Third Army. Up until this point, the New Guinea campaign had involved mostly small units, characterized by mostly regimental combat teams operating on geography that hindered movement and maneuver. The upcoming battle for Leyte marked a dramatic break from previous operations.[18]

The Landings

Phase one—the 6th Ranger Battalion's mission to occupy the three islands protecting the entrance to Leyte Gulf—went off as scheduled on 17 October, rough surf and high winds proving to be more dangerous than the few Japanese defenders. By the following day, the battalion accomplished all of its objectives. Naval bombardment of Leyte began on 18 October when ships supporting minesweeping operations opened up on the landing beaches. On A-day, an unusually clear day in the midst of the rainy season, six battleships along with various cruisers and destroyers shelled targets throughout the landing area and destroyed many Japanese supply depots and other military targets. Joining these ships were approximately 140 airplanes from Kinkaid's aircraft carriers. At 0945, fifteen minutes before H-hour, the navy directed its fire to the flanks of the landing beaches and inland as the first wave of landing craft prepared to go ashore.[19] "From our position on the command ship *Wasatch*, which followed the two Naval Task Forces to the transport area," Krueger recalled, "Vice Admiral Kinkaid and I could observe the stirring spectacle of the bombardment and the shoreward movement of the swarm of landing craft filled with troops."[20] Fortunately, Krueger's soldiers found that the naval and air attacks had forced the Japanese 16th Division away from the beaches and into the interior mountains. In addition, and unbeknownst to the invaders, Makino was in the midst of moving his divisional headquarters from Tacloban to Dagami, which meant he was unable to communicate with his troops for two days. Taking advantage of this situation, the X and XXIV Corps came ashore at approximately 1000, while the 21st Regiment took control over the northern end of Panaon Island. After landing, the 1st Cavalry Division, under the leadership of Maj. Gen. Verne D. Mudge, quickly swung north and captured the vital Tacloban airstrip and then drove inland. The 24th Division, with its two regiments, targeted Hill 522, a key defensive point in the Palo village area. By dusk, elements of the 19th Infantry Regiment had fought through a Japanese defensive screen and seized its heights.[21]

Since the Japanese expected an American assault near Dulag, Hodge's XXIV Corps encountered only mixed resistance. The 96th Division, commanded by Maj. Gen. James L. Bradley, negotiated difficult and swampy terrain to finally reach most of its A-day objectives. Maj. Gen. Archibald V. Arnold's 7th Division met the most severe Japanese response of the day. Though Arnold's men took the village of Dulag, they fell short of seizing its airfield because of Japanese defensive fire from a string of mutually supporting positions.[22]

Krueger had on the first day successfully landed his army with minimal casualties: 49 KIA, 192 WIA, and 6 MIA. Although most Japanese soldiers fled after witnessing the American assault, they did offer sporadic resistance, specifically in the XXIV Corps's zone. There was also a 10-mile gap between the two corps, hardly an ideal situation.[23]

Krueger went ashore on 22 October to see for himself the progress of his army. His first stop was an inspection of the 7th Infantry Division near Dulag. There, MacArthur congratulated him on the success of the first two days of the operation. Before returning to his ship, Krueger called on Philippines president Sergio Osmeña on the amphibious command ship *Blue Ridge* and then went to the *Nashville* for another meeting with MacArthur. On the following day, Osmeña, MacArthur, and Krueger traveled to Tacloban for a ceremony in which MacArthur turned over the civil government to Osmeña.[24]

After the ceremony, Krueger turned his attention back to supervising the operations as well as trying to locate a suitable location for his command post. The congestion of the invasion beaches along with the soggy terrain made finding the ideal site difficult. Eventually, his staff chose the village of San José near the southern tip of the Tacloban airfield. Until the site was operational at 1600 on 24 October, Krueger kept in contact with his army via the communication equipment on board the *Wasatch*.[25]

From his vantage point of San José, Krueger worried over the events taking shape just off shore. While the Sixth Army was invading Leyte, the Japanese navy launched a major effort to regain the initiative. A force of aircraft carriers appeared northeast of the Philippines in a successful effort to decoy Adm. William F. Halsey's Third Fleet away from its positions covering the invasion. While Halsey pursued this decoy in the early hours of 24 October, Vice Adm. Jisabur Ozawa led a force of Japanese battleships and cruisers into Leyte Gulf from the west. Only a few escort carriers and destroyers were available to defend the invasion fleet. Although the Sixth Army operations suffered no ill effects of Nimitz's decision—thanks in large part to the inexplicable decision of Vice Adm. Takeo Kurita to break off his attack against Kinkaid—Krueger viewed Nimitz's actions with dismay. Not only had Halsey's action left the army without much-needed air support, since Kenney had not yet had the opportunity to establish his air force on Leyte, but the Sixth Army's supplies on the beachhead were vulnerable to Japanese naval and air attacks. "Had the plan succeeded, the effect on the Allied troops on Leyte in all likelihood would have been calamitous, for these troops would have been isolated and their situation would have been precarious indeed," he wrote. "If it had been victorious in the naval battle, the Japanese Fleet could have leisurely and effectively carried out the destruction of shipping, aircraft, and supplies that were so vital to Allied operations on Leyte."[26]

The Sixth Army Moves Inland

While Halsey pursued the destruction of Ozawa's fleet, Hodge and Swift expanded their beachheads over the two weeks following A-day. In northern Leyte, the X Corps captured the village of Tacloban and then moved on to secure both sides of San Juanico Strait and simultaneously pushed into Leyte Valley. By the first week of November, Sibert's men occupied the port city of Carigara. To the surprise and delight of X Corps, the Japanese chose not to muster a strong defense of it. Over the next several days, Sibert's forces moved beyond Carigara and in range of both Capoocan and Pinamopoan, two cities vital to their drive southward. Meanwhile, Hodge's XXIV Corps cleared the Japanese from the southern region of Leyte Valley.[27]

Hodge, meanwhile, directed his two divisions to clear the Japanese from the southern region of Leyte Valley. XXIV Corps had the difficult work of facing the bulk of Makino's division and rooting it out of its defensive position around the airfields near Buri and Burauen. Through its two weeks of campaigning, the soldiers of the XXIV Corps secured the eastern central region of Leyte and began to ready themselves to push beyond the central mountain range and into western Leyte toward Ormoc.[28]

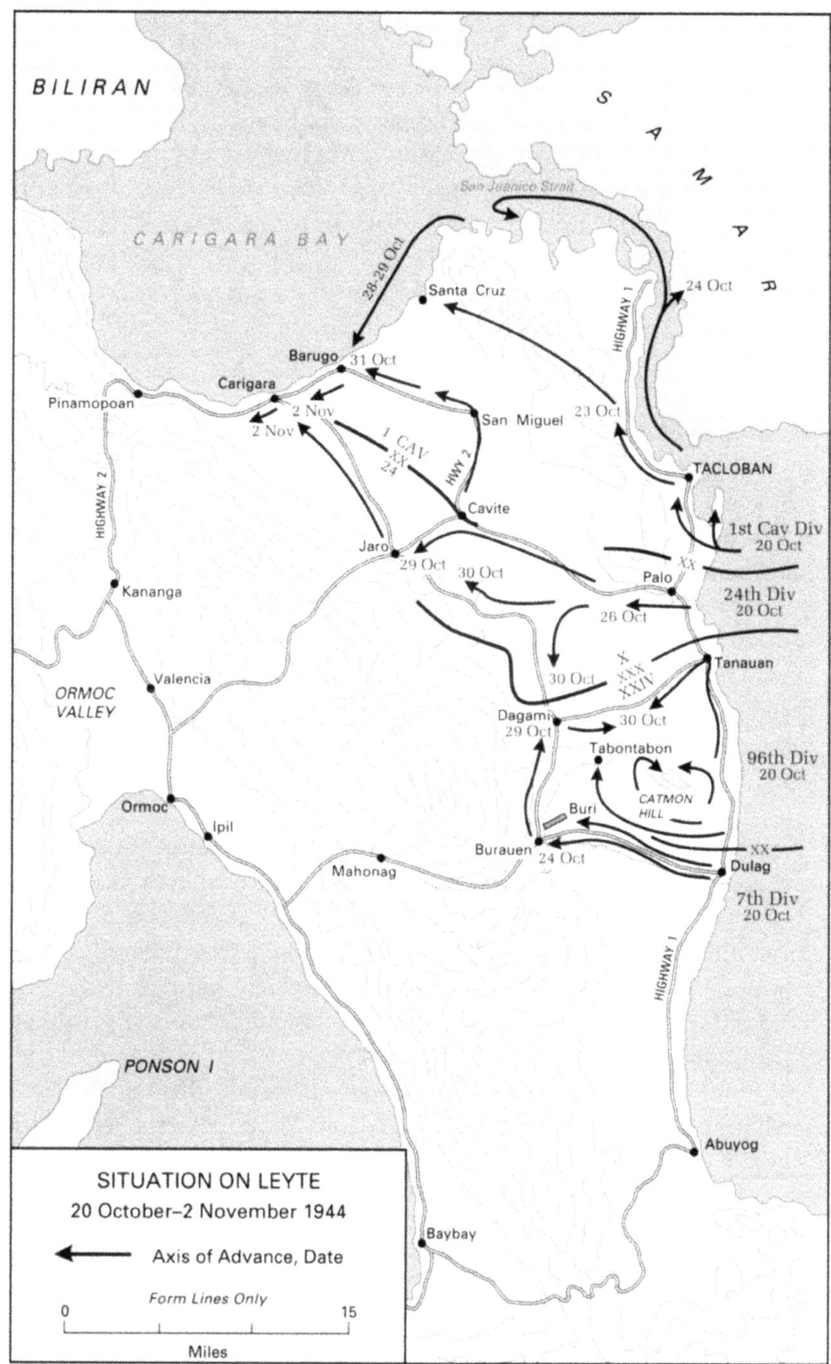

Map 8. The Situation on Leyte, 20 October–2 November 1944
Source: Charles R. Anderson, *Leyte* (Washington, D.C.: U.S. Army Center of Military History, n.d.), 18.

By 2 November, the GIs of the Sixth Army had accomplished phase two—the seizure of Leyte Valley and its airfields. Krueger, therefore, turned his attention to rehabilitating the roads and airfields. Heavy rains throughout the period, however, severely hampered such efforts. Hodge later recalled that because it rained between twenty-five and thirty inches a month, his men were never dry from A-day until the day the battle was won. Such rain—including three typhoons—made road and airfield construction nearly impossible and offensive operations extremely difficult. The Sixth Army report of the K–2 campaign noted:

> Terrain and adverse climatic conditions exercised upon the Leyte Operation an obstructive effect that cannot be minimized, predestining neither a sensational nor rapid offensive but rather a slow and fatiguing advance. Roads that had been rated as the all-weather type rapidly deteriorated into impassable quagmires as a result of the torrential rains and the weight of military traffic. These rains also hindered greatly the construction of the badly-needed airfields. Supply, especially of the units operating in the central mountain range, resolved itself into a pattern of air-droppings and of long hand-carries over tortuous trails. The terrain, much of which was inaccurately mapped, offered every defensive advantage to the Japanese, who fully exploited their opportunities.[29]

Because army engineers could not build and maintain runways in the marshy conditions of Leyte Valley, few Fifth Air Force warplanes could operate from the island until about ten days after A-day. Engineers did not have Tacloban airfield ready until 30 October, Bayug until 3 November, Buri until 5 November, Dulag until 19 November, and Tanauan until 16 December. Even after Tacloban was ready, the Sixth Army could count on only "sporadic" air support.[30]

The lack of useable runways on Leyte had a profound effect on the battle for the island. Without adequate means to deploy its air power, SWPA could not stop the Japanese from reinforcing Leyte. Two days before the American invasion, IGHQ came to the conclusion that it should modify it original defensive plans for the Philippines. Inspired by its mistaken belief that its navy had scored a major victory over Halsey's Third Fleet in mid-October and had inflicted great harm on the American invasion fleet in the Battle of Leyte Gulf, IGHQ determined that the decisive battle of the war should not take place on Luzon as originally planned but instead on Leyte. Over time, the 1st, 8th, 26th, 30th, and 102d Infantry Divisions as well as troops from the 55th and 57th Independent Mixed Brigades were sent to Leyte.[31]

SWPA air power could no more stop the Japanese from reinforcing Leyte than it could detect that the five-plus divisions were on their way. Unfortunately for Krueger and his army, the torrential downpours that shut down Kenney's aircraft coincided with an almost total blackout in the ability to decrypt Allied intercepts of Japanese army communication. Instead of determining that Gen. Tomoyuki Yamashita—commander of the Fourteenth Area Army and responsible for defending the Philippines—was reinforcing Leyte, MacArthur assumed that the Japanese were evacuating the island and considered the battle for Leyte over. So confident was MacArthur that he sent—unbeknownst to Krueger—the 77th Infantry Division of Sixth Army reserve to join Adm. Chester W. Nimitz's command only a week after A-day.[32]

Rain, Mud, and Japanese Reinforcements

With GHQ SWPA telling Krueger that the Japanese were all but finished and that they were evacuating the island, the Sixth Army commander initiated phase three in Field Order No. 28, dated 3 November 1944, the day after X Corps captured Carigara. This order directed X Corps to proceed west and overrun the enemy defenses in Capoocan and then Pinamopoan. After arriving in Pinamopoan, Swift was then to swing south along Highway 2 toward Ormoc. At the same time, Hodge was to push west through the central mountain range to the Camotes Sea, via Highway 1, and then destroy all enemy forces within his zone of control. At the same time, Krueger ordered XXIV Corps to continue its advance westward, destroying any hostile forces in its way. Together, both corps would form the two jaws of a pincer, descending on the city of Ormoc.[33]

As the X Corps readied itself for the final push to Ormoc, Krueger was faced with a troubling situation that quickly came to a head the day after issuing Field Order No. 28. The constant rain had turned Highway 2, connecting the leading elements of X Corps from its logistical base in Leyte Bay, into a nearly impassable muddy path. Soldiers of the 24th Infantry Division, therefore, were supplied by LCMs, which unloaded their supplies near Pinamopoan. The stores were then moved by trucks "with great difficulty to the forward troops." Krueger noted that "three typhoons had flooded the entire Leyte Valley and our heavy vehicles had chewed up the roads to such an extent that so-called all weather roads became a series of quagmires."[34]

Far more troubling, in Krueger's opinion, were indications that the Japanese might attempt an amphibious assault from Carigara Bay along the Sixth Army's right flank, thereby severing the X Corps's tenuous supply line. As early as 26 October, X Corps's intelligence officer (G-2) warned that the

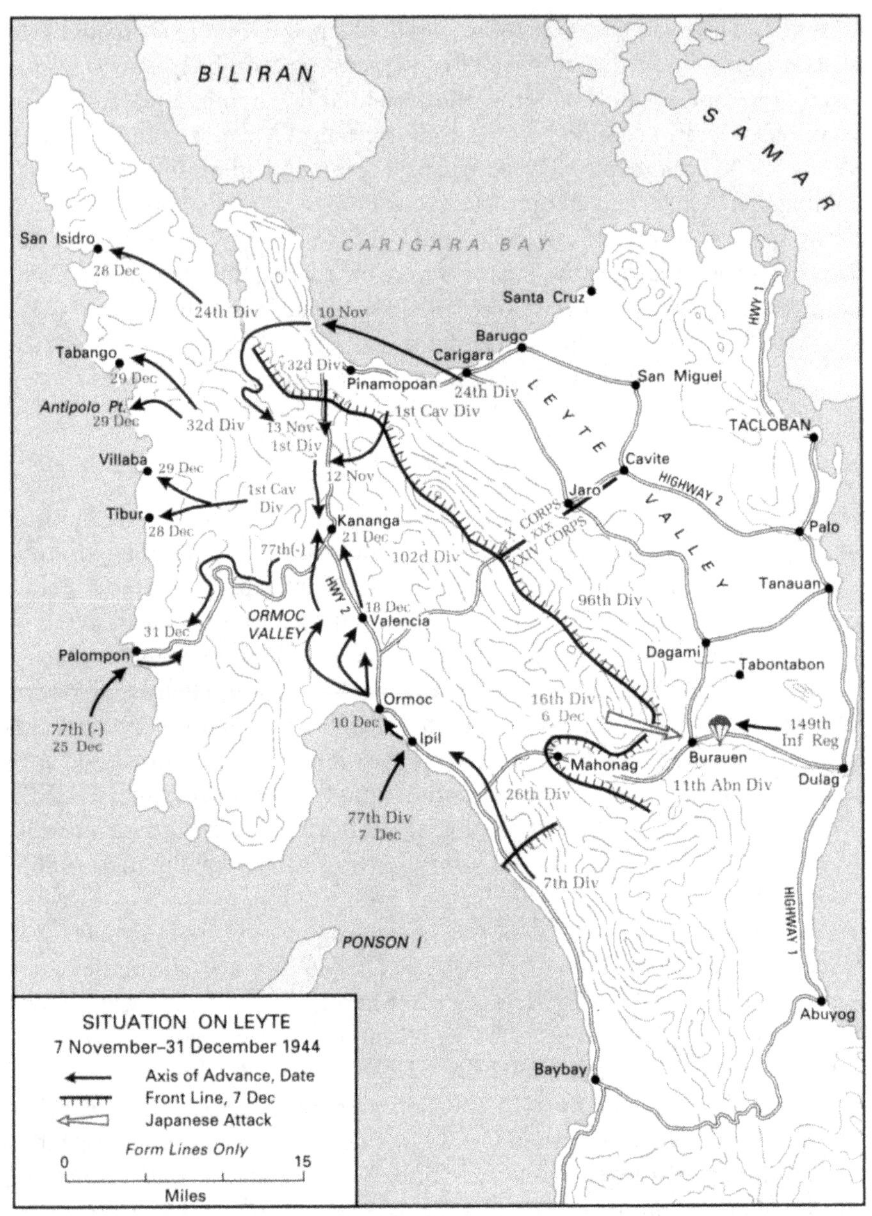

Map 9. The Situation on Leyte, 7 November–31 December 1944
Source: Charles R. Anderson, *Leyte* (Washington, D.C.: U.S. Army Center of Military History, n.d.), 22.

Japanese "can land reinforcements on Leyte from adjacent islands at Carigara and Ormoc Bays."[35]

To further examine the possibility of a Japanese amphibious operation in Carigara Bay, Krueger dispatched the assistant operations officer (G-3) to meet with Rear Adm. William M. Fechteler for his views on the subject. As he was deputy commander of VII Amphibious Force, Fechteler's views would carry quite a bit of weight with Krueger. Fechteler informed the Sixth Army representative that Carigara Bay offered suitable landing beaches. Furthermore, the admiral reasoned, the Japanese had the "suicidal attitude" necessary to conduct such an operation despite the recent losses at the Battle of Leyte Gulf. Although Fechteler believed that the Japanese would not launch an attack, he nevertheless had to admit not only that was he in the dark concerning the disposition of the enemy fleet but also that "if the Japanese want to bring heavy naval units into Carigara Bay, he will be able to provide these naval units with land-based air cover, and that our naval surface or air forces or Army air forces cannot stop him."[36]

While Fechteler did not believe that the Japanese would strike from Carigara Bay despite their capability, the possibility of such an attack weighed heavily on Krueger, particularly in light of the condition of his army. To begin with, Krueger faced a personnel shortage. Not only had MacArthur taken away half of Krueger's reserve, but he had also denied his army commander's request that his combat units be 10 percent over strength prior to A-day. This situation was only made worse by the way in which U.S. Army Forces, Far East (USAFFE), the administrative units of SWPA forces, determined the rates of replacement. The USAFFE considered, for example, injured soldiers in the hospital as part of a unit's "effective strength" until the army's paperwork was completed. "Since evacuations were effected by planes and ships to distant medical installations," Krueger complained, "disposition reports were delayed for long periods." This practice inflated the strength of Krueger's combat units. On 12 November 1944, the USAFFE considered the Sixth Army to be 289 officers and 1,874 enlisted men short of its authorized strength when it was, in actuality, 1,050 officers and 11,754 enlisted men short. The situation grew worse as the campaign dragged on. By 20 December 1944, Krueger was short 1,167 officers and 19,872 enlisted men, but USAFFE calculated that he was only deficient 442 officers and 8,440 enlisted men. In all, Krueger's army received only 5,289 replacements during the Leyte campaign. "The lack of replacements to compensate for this actual shortage of about 21,000 officers and men, the equivalent of much more than an infantry division," Krueger concluded, "naturally caused me serious concern, especially since the shortage was not evenly distributed over the entire command, but affected primarily the infantry, which suffered 79.14 per cent of the casualties in the operation."[37]

Thus, with an undermanned army, overextended supply line, inadequate intelligence, and GHQ SWPA calling the campaign for Leyte all but over, Krueger reassessed his situation. The X Corps was stretched to its limit: "Missions assigned to the X Corps at this time included responsibility for the initial beachhead area in the vicinity of Palo and Tacloban, the security of San Juanico Strait, defense of a 6-mile beach against a possible large-scale amphibious attack, the prevention of any advance from Ormoc Valley over a 15-mile front, and the incidental defense of occupied areas," he wrote. Given its situation, Krueger believed that the X Corps was a prime target for a counterattack, one that would cut off all or part of the 24th Infantry Division, to be destroyed piecemeal on the high ground south of Carigara Bay. Consequently, Krueger decided on 4 November to halt the X Corps's advance to the south and establish positions along Carigara Bay to prevent a possible Japanese attack. In accordance with Krueger's new orders, Sibert—whose own intelligence indicated a possibility of an enemy landing on his right—reoriented his corps to cover a 6-mile stretch of Carigara Bay. As it turned out, Krueger's suspicions had a basis in fact. On two separate occasions, Yamashita considered executing a landing at Carigara Bay on the X Corps's flank. Neither was attempted, however, because in the first instance, the Americans had advanced too far before Yamashita could execute the attack, and in the second, the Sixth Army had landed at Mindoro.[38]

Upon taking up its new positions, X Corps met unexpected and increasingly heavy Japanese resistance on its left flank as units attempted to move to the high ground south of Pinamopoan. Without American airpower to worry about and completely unbeknownst to MacArthur, Willoughby, Krueger and his staff, or anyone else, the Japanese had landed their crack 1st Infantry Division at Ormoc on 1 November and sent it north to the hills surrounding Highway 2, just to the south of the American positions, on 4 and 5 November. As the 21st Regiment tried to move into these hills, appropriately called Breakneck Ridge by the Americans, the enemy launched a series of attacks on 5 and 6 November that pushed the 21st Regiment back to the shores of Carigara Bay. By this time, Krueger had come to realize that the 1st Division had occupied a 9-mile-long defensive line that blocked his advance south to Ormoc. This division, Krueger noted, was "one of the four best divisions in the Japanese Army and it did more than any other enemy unit to prolong the Leyte operation."[39]

Despite the 1st Division's position in the tactically important Breakneck Ridge, Krueger was eager to "maintain the initiative by constantly pressing the offensive," especially after his troops found on a dead Japanese soldier a 1st Division order that called for an offensive designed to recapture the Carigara Bay area. After halting the X Corps on 4 November, Krueger ordered that Sibert resume his offensive on 6 November. In an operation that lasted sixteen days, Maj. Gen. Frederick A. Irving's 24th Division engaged in brutal fighting along some of the most difficult terrain yet encountered in SWPA. By 11 November, the 21st Infantry had gained a toehold on Breakneck Ridge, but the Japanese were able to infiltrate the American lines. X Corps slowly pushed the Japanese out of the mountains in a battle that raged until 23 November.[40]

The battle for Breakneck Ridge was a grueling duel for both sides. Sibert's men counted 2,000 dead Japanese soldiers. The X Corps's casualties soared to 1,498, and the survivors of the battle were exhausted. With virtually no replacements forthcoming from USAFFE, for example, the 24th Division could no longer function and was replaced by the 32d Infantry Division, under the command of Maj. Gen. William H. Gill, on 14 November. Interestingly, Gill would have personnel problems of his own in only three weeks. On 6 December, Gill told Krueger that he was about 2,075 men short. "I cannot," Gill concluded, "fight with the troops available. ... I am too short now to do the job that I have to do. They must get me replacements. ... It is a very serious proposition." Much blood and sweat was shed for only little gain: approximately one mile over a two-week period.[41]

Throughout the battle of Breakneck Ridge, Krueger—now that he had determined that the Japanese were going to make their stand in the western hills—grew increasingly impatient with the pace of X Corps's offensive. Although he admitted that the terrain and weather made a rapid advance difficult, Krueger believed that Gill was not pushing his regimental commanders hard enough. "Don't let them be too cautious," Krueger advised Sibert. "Pep that up a little so we'll get some results." Furthermore, he was concerned about Sibert's plans and actions for taking Breakneck Ridge, labeling them as too "defensive." He instead told Sibert to adopt a plan that was "more offensive in tone."[42]

As the X Corps faced difficulty in the north while pushing down on Ormoc Valley, XXIV Corps continued its own operations in southern Leyte. After piercing Japanese defenses in the central mountain region, Hodge's two divisions reached the west coast of Leyte at the town of Damulaan and planned to head north to their next objective: Ormoc.[43]

Breaking the Stalemate

Faced with opposition in the north and poor campaigning terrain in the central mountain region that slowed the pace of the offensive—and, most important, always looking for ways to achieve his objectives as quickly as possible—Krueger proposed to make an amphibious assault of his own near Ormoc. "Such an operation," he reasoned, "offered the advantage of cutting the Japanese lines of communication through Ormoc and placing the enemy forces in the Ormoc Valley in a vise which could shortly squeeze them into extermination." Unfortunately, the Seventh Fleet could not mount such an operation. Not only did it lack enough landing craft, but it could not ensure the safety of the convoy. Furthermore, the Fifth Air Force still lacked runways, so the amphibious force could not rely on air support. Finally, Krueger simply did not have enough forces to mount the shore-to-shore movement, since MacArthur had transferred the 77th Infantry Division to the navy. As a result of all these factors, Krueger had to postpone the operation.[44]

Forced to abandon his shore-to-shore maneuver, Krueger instead concentrated on his previous plan and attempted to destroy the Japanese within Ormoc Valley. To this end, Krueger attached the 11th Airborne Division, which arrived in mid-November, to the XXIV Corps. Hodge positioned the airborne troopers in the central mountain region along with the 96th Division. The 7th Division—located near Baybay—was to spearhead his corps's efforts toward Ormoc. Meanwhile, the X Corps was to continue its move south and establish itself in the hills north of Ormoc Valley by overrunning Japanese defenses in such places as Limon, Kilay Ridge, and Mt. Cabungaan.[45]

Krueger, however, never abandoned his amphibious assault against Ormoc. When he discovered that the 77th Infantry Division had been released by MacArthur for use by the navy, Krueger "complained" and got the division back. (Once it became apparent that the Japanese were not giving up as MacArthur had hoped, he decided to ask that Nimitz return the division, which was en route to New Caledonia at the time.) Upon arriving at Leyte on 23 November, Krueger placed the division with the XXIV Corps as its reserve, for the time being.[46]

Although he now possessed enough manpower with the 77th Infantry Division, Krueger next had to muster the requisite naval transport. This was a bit more difficult challenge, because in early December, MacArthur was already husbanding Kinkaid's navy for his next operation—the invasion of Mindoro on 5 December. Throughout the first week of December, both Kenney and Kinkaid voiced their opposition to the operation, arguing that their forces were just too involved on Leyte. Furthermore, the lack of airfields on Leyte prevented the Fifth Air Force from protecting the invasion fleet. Kinkaid eventually convinced MacArthur to postpone the Mindoro operation until 15 December. Krueger learned of the postponement on 1 December, and soon thereafter was able to enlist enough ships from Kinkaid to support transporting the 77th Division to Ormoc.[47]

Not only would the capture of Ormoc block any more Japanese from landing in defense of Leyte, but it would also prevent the sizeable numbers of Japanese already there from leaving if IGHQ decided that the United States had won the battle. ULTRA didn't detect the arrival of Japan's 1st Division on the island but did detect, for example, the 26th Division, which arrived on 9 November. Krueger's own G-2 suggested that these forces would be part of a major attack to capture the Pinamopoan-Carigara corridor in northern Leyte. Finally on the move again after personnel shortages, Krueger saw this planned Japanese assault as an opportunity: "These indications that the enemy would launch an attack and probably make his main effort in the north did not disturb me. No matter what he did, I was determined to retain the initiative by constantly pressing my own offensive." On 4 December, then, he issued his orders to Sibert and Hodge. Krueger wanted his two corps commanders to begin the land portion of the offensive. Along with the recently arrived 11th Airborne Division, the XXIV Corps would continue its drive along the coastal road from Damulaan, while the X Corps would drive south on Highway 2 from Limon, drawing Japanese troops north and south from Ormoc. After the Japanese attention had been fixed by the overland movement of his two corps, Krueger then would land the 77th Infantry Division near a—in theory—lightly defended Ormoc.[48]

Right from the start of the operation, the X Corps ran into heavy resistance. Hodge's corps faced little resistance but found the going slow due to the mountainous geography. Nevertheless, Krueger's plan of diverting Japanese attention toward the overland attacks worked. When the 77th Infantry Division landed near Ipil (just to the south of Ormoc), the Americans found little to stop their inland advance. In fact, within two and one-half hours, the Americans had landed and achieved all of their initial objectives, including the capture of Ipil. The division commander, Maj. Gen. Andrew D. Bruce, aggressively exploited the situation by expanding the beachhead and decided upon a "relentless drive northward." Only a ragtag unit of service troops and rear echelon soldiers and two battalions of the Imabori Detachment stood between the Sixth Army and Ormoc.[49]

In a well-executed maneuver, Bruce's division pushed the confused Japanese defenders back into Ormoc. By 9 December, Bruce had developed his plan to take the city, which included a heavy application of artillery, mortars, and landing craft. "The town of Ormoc itself," the 77th Division report described, "was a blazing inferno of bursting white phosphorous shells, burning houses, and exploding ammunition dumps, and over it all hung a pall of heavy smoke from burning fuel dumps mixed with the grey dust of destroyed concrete buildings, blasted by our artillery, mortar, and rocket fire."[50]

In the face of this overwhelming display of American firepower, the Japanese commander decided to retreat northward. With only a weak rear guard action in front of him, Bruce quickly entered the city on 11 December and started mopping-up operations by 1400. "The coordinated use of every available weapon on the main objective, plus the envelopment action on the enemy's northeast flank," Bruce observed, "paid off in the capture of the objective [Ormoc] with light casualties."[51]

After stopping for a short time to resupply, Bruce pursued the retreating Japanese northward. In an attempt to have Hodge aggressively follow up his success, Bruce radioed his boss: "Have rolled two sevens in Ormoc. Come seven come eleven." In fact, the 7th, 11th, and 96th Divisions were indeed closing around the western portion of Leyte, as the three divisions of the X Corps were marching south. The two jaws of Krueger's trap were finally closing around the remnants of the Japanese garrison. Krueger aggressively took advantage of the Japanese willingness to reinforce the island. With one of the most important seaports on Leyte in Krueger's hands, two Japanese divisions—the 26th and 16th—were left to die on Leyte.[52]

Consolidating

After the capture of Ormoc, Krueger turned his attention toward consolidating his hold on Leyte. The 77th Division continued its drive north of Ormoc by capturing the village of Valencia on 18 December. The rest of the XXIV Corps proceeded to clear the mountains east of Ormoc as the X Corps advanced down Highway 2. The two corps—representing the two wings of Krueger's pincer movement—met near the village of Libungao on 21 December.[53]

On 25 December, Krueger directed his army to move into the northwest peninsula and ordered the 77th Division to conduct a shore-to-shore movement against the village of Palompon. MacArthur, however, did not want Krueger to spend the next several months hunting down the last vestiges of organized resistance. Instead, he wanted the Sixth Army to lead the assault against Luzon. Therefore, at midnight on 25 December, Lt. Gen. Robert L. Eichelberger and his Eighth Army took over responsibility for operations on Leyte.[54]

With the change, MacArthur erroneously considered the Leyte campaign over. He informed Eichelberger and the world that the only task remaining was rounding up a few Japanese stragglers. In a congratulatory message sent to Krueger, MacArthur remarked, "This closes a campaign that has few counterparts in the utter destruction of the enemy's forces with a maximum conservation of our own. It has been a magnificent performance on the part of all concerned."[55]

Krueger estimated that only 8,000 enemy soldiers remained throughout Leyte and that his troops had killed about 56,000. Unfortunately for Eichelberger and his troops, Krueger's numbers missed the mark by a considerable margin. Approximately 15,000 still held out and put up stiff but strategically insignificant resistance. It would take another three weeks of hard work before Eichelberger could call the island secure.[56]

Despite faulty intelligence, poor campaigning weather, little air power, and few personnel replacements, Sixth Army's exploits were impressive. IGHQ invested heavily in what it considered the climactic battle of the war but was ruined. "After Leyte, Japan had no army," Stanley L. Falk writes. "There were millions of men under arms. But the best Japanese troops—65,000 of them dead on Leyte, a third of a million more doomed throughout the rest of the Philippines—were already committed, cut off, isolated, and equally unable to mount a major offensive."[57]

Geographical gains and enemy casualties, however, were only part of the criteria by which MacArthur judged military operations, and consequently, he at times became impatient with the pace of the Sixth Army, especially in light of the fact that he called the operation over shortly after the Sixth Army landed on Leyte. Given this mindset in GHQ SWPA, MacArthur could not understand why Krueger did not just finish the mopping-up operations—Japanese reinforcements, typhoons, and a lack of air support not withstanding. By mid-December, the separation between MacArthur's conception of the way things ought to be and reality had become so great that the SWPA commander grew frustrated and attempted to pressure Krueger. Being close to Luzon and Manila made MacArthur restless. On 12 December, near the end of the Sixth Army's phase of operations, MacArthur's G-3, Maj. Gen. Stephen J. Chamberlin, phoned Krueger to relay his commander's concern about the slow progress of both the 7th and 77th Divisions. Krueger defended the record of his army:

> In my opinion, both the 7th and 77th Divisions have done extremely well. I am not sure that the difficulties of the terrain in that area are fully appreciated at GHQ. It is the terrain to a greater extent than the enemy that

> is holding back our advance. … Both of my corps commanders were here today and I again impressed upon them the importance of pushing their attacks with the utmost vigor. I am confident that they are both doing so. … I am doing everything that I can personally to push our advance.

Yet, MacArthur never lost faith in Krueger. After MacArthur set up his headquarters in Tacloban, he visited Krueger and his staff two times, while Krueger conferred with MacArthur six times. Overall, Chamberlain's phone call is an anomaly, not the norm.[58]

Lessons Learned from Leyte

Throughout the struggle for Leyte, Krueger spent most of his time supervising operations, planning for the Luzon campaign, dealing with administrative details, managing construction projects, inspecting supply depots, and visiting troops in the field and in hospitals. Because the Americans lacked air power, Krueger often faced many of the same dangers as the riflemen in the 7th Infantry Division or the cavalrymen in the 1st Cavalry Division. In mid-November, for instance, the ordinary routine of a typical day was suddenly and unexpectedly broken by a Japanese Mitsubishi A6M Zero-Sen. Making a strafing attack, the plane put three bullets though Krueger's tent, allegedly hitting the spot he had been occupying only a short time earlier. Fortunately for Krueger, he had left the tent for breakfast. "During most of the operation," Krueger simply stated, "enemy air raids seriously interfered with work at Headquarters Sixth Army."[59]

Through his inspection trips—despite the frequent air attacks—Krueger was able to gain much firsthand information on the way in which his army fought. "My own experience during the Philippines Campaign, forty-five years before when we also faced difficult conditions," he later explained, "gave me a sympathetic understanding of the problems confronting my troops, and together with the information gained during my visits enabled me to correct many shortcomings, some of them on the spot."[60]

On 25 November 1944, Krueger issued a memorandum entitled "Mistakes Made and Lessons Learned in K-2 Operation," which alerted his army to many of the shortcomings he had witnessed. Included in his report was the observation that there was a tendency for tanks to conduct attacks unaccompanied by infantry or engineers. "Successful employment of tanks requires close infantry and engineer support," the memorandum pointed out. "Instances were noted where tanks were employed in taking an objective, infantry however was not present to consolidate and hold these gains. Similarly, tanks were disabled due to lack of engineer support in the removal of mines and in the crossing of streams."[61]

He also noticed that many units were road-bound and did not take advantage of the power of maneuver. "There were cases where resistance along the road delayed the advance of the bulk of the division. This resistance could have been quickly reduced and the advance of the division expedited by employment of simple envelopments and flanking attacks." Fortunately, the Americans did not face a "smart enemy," who could have taken advantage of this "American trait."[62]

A general lack of aggressiveness on the infantry's part also troubled the Sixth Army commander. On several occasions, units would quickly abandon their missions after encountering the slightest bit of opposition. Although an outspoken advocate of combined-arms operations, Krueger realized that the mountainous terrain, dense forests, and defensive tactics of the Japanese placed particular emphasis on the infantryman. Krueger reminded his troops that "infantry is the arm of *close combat*. It is the arm of *final* combat. The Jap is usually most tenacious particularly when in entrenched and concealed positions. Individual enemy soldiers will remain in their holes until eliminated. Although the supporting arms are of great assistance, it ultimately becomes the task of the small infantry units to dig them out."[63]

Equally disturbing was the poor care of the enlisted men. As Krueger noticed, "There was a pronounced attitude of indifference of the part of commanders in provisions made for the care and comfort of their men." He observed poor sanitation, meals that were "poorly planned and monotonous," and a general lack of adequate shelter. "It must never be forgotten," the memorandum continued, "that the individual soldier is the most important single factor in this war. As discussed in previous paragraphs he is expected to do a lot including risking his life. But to get the most out of him he must have the feeling that everything possible under existing circumstances is being done for his well being and comfort. This is a prime responsibility of command. Attention to it will improve the combat efficiency of any unit."[64]

Krueger had good reason to pay such close attention to lessons learned and training issues in light of future campaigns. Of the six infantry divisions that fought on Leyte under Krueger, only three had spent considerable time under his command before October 1944. The 24th and 32d Infantry Divisions both fought previously under Krueger. The 11th Airborne Division had arrived in SWPA between 25 May and 11 June 1944. Although it had not seen combat before Leyte, it had acted as reserve on several occasions as well as taking part in a tough training program. After arriving in New Guinea, the division's first order of business was acclimating itself to the intense jungle climate, a process that took about a month. The "Angels" of the 11th Division then received training in jungle combat tactics, combined airborne-troop carrier operations, and amphibious assaults. In addition, they took part in various SWPA schools, such as Krueger's Alamo Scout School and the Australian Training Center in Jungle Warfare, which taught the basics of jungle survival as well as small-unit tactics. Besides participating in these specialized schools, Sixth Army training also included realistic combat instruction, including live-fire exercises with mortars, artillery, and machine guns. The other divisions—the 7th, 77th, and 96th Divisions—served little time with the Sixth Army and had various degrees of training and experience.[65] Without the opportunity to devote any time to these divisions, Krueger could only hope that they had received adequate training, especially the 96th, which had yet to stand the test of combat.[66] After all, the Leyte experience was only a foreshadowing of what his men could expect on Luzon, their next stop.

Almost from the start of the struggle for Leyte, several contextual elements came to the front that influenced Krueger's exercise of command. The first was the weather. All of the typhoons and all of the rain turned much of Leyte into a swamp. Logistics and air power became the first and most prominent causalities of the inclement weather. The storms prevented the early and planned development of airfields, from which Allied Air Forces planes would support army operations. Consequently, Krueger never had the air power he needed. He also had a difficult logistical system. Mud bogged down supply trucks, and the forward elements of his units—by the end of October—were wearing out.

In addition to the weather, Krueger had to lead his army during critical periods without intelligence. In combination with inadequate air support, GHQ SWPA intelligence did not know that Japanese forces landed on Leyte to reinforce the 16th Division. Last, Krueger—as he had throughout the New Guinea campaign—had to deal with MacArthur's pressure to get results as quickly as possible so that the next mission could be initiated and his penchant for calling an operation essentially over when, in fact, it was just beginning.

Despite the weather, lack of intelligence, and MacArthur's constant pressure, Krueger's leadership on Leyte is consistent with his earlier leadership at the helm of the Third Army. He always demonstrated care and concern for his soldiers. He did not like the way in which officers had treated their men on Leyte, and he was determined to make sure the pattern was not repeated on Luzon.

Furthermore, Krueger demonstrated a continued devotion to aggressive military action. From the early planning phases for the Leyte operation, he committed himself to the twin objectives of securing the island as a base for future operations while destroying the Japanese occupiers. His double envelopment strategy to capture Ormoc not only fit in with contemporary U.S. Army doctrine but is reminiscent of the way he led his Third Army during the maneuvers of 1941.

Above all, Krueger's generalship provides an excellent example of the successful application of operational art. As the ground commander on Leyte, Krueger had to orchestrate a series of battles to achieve MacArthur's strategic mission. Part of this art was mitigating the oftentimes contradictory tactical realities with the strategic vision. MacArthur's ambitious timetable had little room for inclement weather, logistical breakdowns, shipping shortages, lack of reserves, or uncertainties in intelligence. Krueger successfully balanced the tactical and strategic factors, pushing corps and divisional commanders when necessary and confronting the SWPA commander with limitations of military action at other times.

Finally, Krueger also insisted on constant improvement and training. The lessons-learned memorandum from the Leyte operation was a testament to this. Krueger took personal interest in the task of improving his army, documenting every mistake he or his staff observed. He had to make sure his army was ready for the future, because, in his view, the next two SWPA operations—the invasions of Luzon and Japan—were only going to get tougher. Justifying his report after the war, he explained that it was "extremely valuable, since Sixth Army was shortly to invade Luzon. ... It was thus essential to analyze our shortcomings in order to enable us to profit by them. I admit that the critique was unorthodox, but warfare in the Southwest Pacific was also unorthodox."[67] Krueger was correct in looking forward toward the Luzon campaign; it would be his toughest challenge.

Chapter 9

Luzon and Japan, January 1945–January 1946

The struggle for Leyte was Lt. Gen. Walter Krueger's first introduction to large-unit combat. While he ultimately proved his worth in combat and his abilities as an army commander, the Leyte campaign offered many challenges. The battle for Luzon would follow the patterns of previous ones: Krueger would face the same obstacles, the same problems, the same hurdles, and, like the other times, he would excel. His education, his experience, his philosophy of command, and his personality provided the edge in carrying out his mission of securing the biggest prize in the Southwest Pacific Area: Manila.

Planning for Luzon

Krueger would have preferred to have enough time to distill and disseminate the lessons learned from Leyte, specifically those from the 25 November 1944 memorandum entitled "Mistakes Made and Lessons Learned in K-2 Operation." Yet, he had little time to do so. Early versions of MacArthur's plans set the date for the invasion (S-day) at 20 December, but because of a lack of naval and air units, he postponed it to 9 January 1945. General Headquarters of SWPA ordered Krueger, who was once again charged with coordinating all air, ground, and naval forces, to gain control of the Central Plains–Manila region, establish naval facilities in Lingayen Gulf, build airfields, and prepare for future army operations in the Philippine Islands and beyond.[1]

From the beginning, the Sixth Army and GHQ SWPA came to different estimates concerning enemy strength on Luzon. Maj. Gen. Charles A. Willoughby, the intelligence officer for GHQ SWPA, believed that between 115,000 and 140,000 Japanese soldiers of Gen. Tomoyuki Yamashita's Fourteenth Area Army occupied the island. Other intelligence sources placed the total at 158,500, including four infantry divisions and one armored division. Krueger's own intelligence officer, Col. Horton V. White, came to a much different conclusion. He calculated that Imperial General Headquarters had poured about 234,500 soldiers into Luzon, a figure that was much closer to the actual size of the Japanese garrison of 267,000, under the command of the "Tiger of Malaya," General Yamashita. The differences between the two assessments came from GHQ SWPA's reliance on ULTRA, which did not identify many of the Japanese armored and mobile units that were en route to Luzon from the outer reaches of the crumbling Japanese empire. White, however, did know about the reinforcements, since he used a wider variety of sources, including the testimony of Filipino guerillas.[2]

While Yamashita had large numbers of troops, he faced a whole host of problems in trying to defend Luzon. His army lacked adequate supplies, equipment, and fuel. To complicate matters, the Japanese had lost the contest for control over the Philippine skies and lacked the mobility of the Americans. Unable to conduct a major counteroffensive, Yamashita decided to employ a delaying strategy, designed to bleed the U.S. Army as it drove toward the Japanese home islands.[3]

To execute his defense, Yamashita decided not to make his stand on the Central Plain region, where American firepower and mobility would surely overwhelm his army. Instead, he withdrew his troops into the mountainous interior. There were three specific regions of Luzon with terrain favorable to the defensive, and he divided his army accordingly. The largest part was the Shobu Group, personally commanded by him and composed of four infantry divisions and one armored division. Yamashita positioned the Shobu Group in the mountains to the northeast of the Central Plains. The 152,000-man garrison was to vigorously hold the high ground and threaten the flank of the U.S. Army, which was expected to land in either Lingayen Gulf or to the north in the San Fernando–Damortis area.[4]

The second-largest detachment was the Shimbu Group, located in the southern region of Luzon and composed of about 50,000 men. Although it included Manila, Yamashita instructed the Shimbu Group's commander, Lt. Gen. Shizuo Yokoyama, not to defend the capital. Yokoyama's mission was to delay the American advance into the city by destroying bridges and controlling the dams and reservoirs that provided Manila's drinking water. The third and smallest of the Japanese groups was the Kembu Group. Led by Rear Adm. Ushie Sugimoto, this 30,000-strong element guarded Clark Field and Bataan.[5]

Having an approximate idea of Japanese strength and dispositions, Krueger and his staff turned to planning. MacArthur allocated to the Sixth Army two corps: I and XIV Corps. Under the command of Maj. Gen. Innis P. Swift, the ex-commander of the 1st Cavalry Division, I Corps consisted of the 6th and 43d Infantry Divisions. The XIV Corps, led by Maj. Gen. Oscar W. Griswold, had the 37th and 40th Infantry Divisions. Krueger could also count on the 158th Regimental Combat Team and the 13th Armored Group (composed of various units and equal to an armored division), with the 25th Infantry Division in floating reserve and the 11th Airborne Division in reserve on Leyte. From S+18 to S+32 (27 January to 10 February), additional formations and units were scheduled to arrive in Luzon, including the 1st Cavalry Division, 112th Cavalry RCT, 32d Infantry Division, 33d Infantry Division, and 41st Infantry Division. This impressive force totaled 203,608 soldiers.[6]

Terrain studies indicated that Luzon offered two possible landing sites. The area near San Fernando–Damortis offered the best beaches but was strongly defended and possessed hardly any maneuver room. A landing there would force the Sixth Army to make a sharp right turn immediately after getting ashore in order to reach the important Central Plains. The area eventually selected was the Lingayen Gulf area. Not only was it close to the plains area, but it was weakly defended and had suitable ground for airdrome construction. However, the region immediately behind the beaches was poor. It was dissected by a number of streams and rivers, many of which were between 250 and 300 feet wide. Both corps would require additional engineering units to overcome these formidable water obstacles.[7]

For the landing phase, Krueger emphasized two concepts: firepower and maneuver. Faced with an army that was bigger than his, Krueger wanted to ensure that his men would go in with all the support at his disposal. He believed that "the basic tactical principle of American offensive operations on Luzon was the use of overwhelming material strength to crush the enemy with a minimum loss of American manpower." To do this, he envisioned using the "maximum utilization of America's material and industrial superiority" to "prepare the way for the assaulting infantrymen."[8]

Krueger, however, knew that he could not rely on firepower and overwhelming force alone. He arranged for his army to execute not an envelopment but a breakthrough maneuver. While one corps fixed and held the main Japanese contingent, the other would punch through and rapidly capture Manila. Krueger gave I Corps the job of holding or containing the Shobu Group, and the task of capturing the capital fell to XIV Corps.[9]

Attempting to translate these operational principles into concrete plans, Krueger necessarily had to focus on two factors: the marshy terrain, specifically the Agno River; and the Shobu Group, particularly its four infantry divisions, an independent mixed brigade, and an armored division in the Central Plains area. Part of the Agno River was crescent-shaped and ran parallel to Lingayen Gulf, 20 to 25 miles inland with a width of about 600 feet. Faced with this formidable water obstacle, Krueger determined that the initial ob-

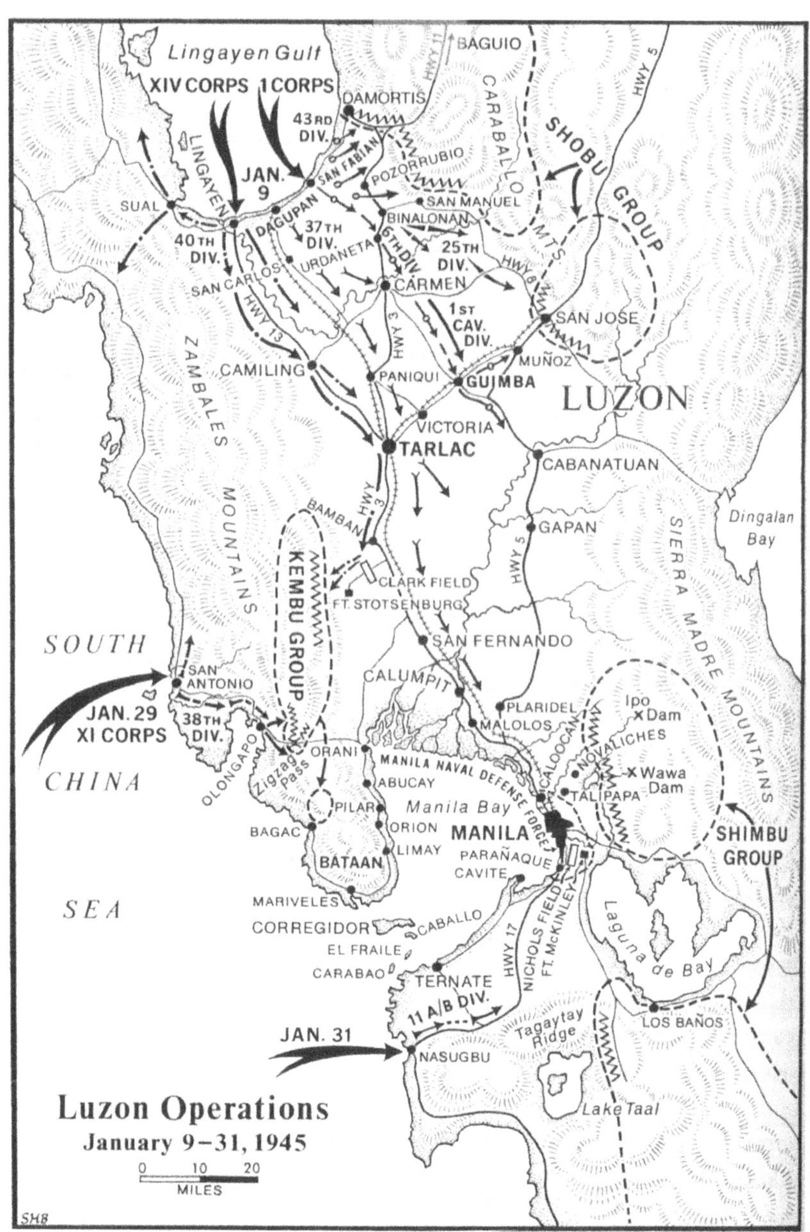

Map 10. Sixth U.S. Army Operations on Luzon, 9–31 January 1945
Source: D. Clayton James. *The Years of MacArthur*, 3 vols. (Boston: Houghton Mifflin, 1970–1985), vol. 2, *1941–1945*, 624. Map by Samuel H. Bryant. Reprinted with permission.

jective of his army was just to get ashore, establish positions across the Agno River, and then determine Yamashita's countermeasures, specifically whether he would attack with his five-plus divisions. After accomplishing these three objectives, Krueger would then formalize his plans to seize Manila. "It would have been manifestly unwise," Krueger concluded, "for my initial orders to go beyond this [establishing a beachhead]." As it turned out, the lack of planning would have both strengths and weaknesses.[10]

According to Krueger's plans, I Corps would land to the left, between the cities of San Fabian and Dagupan. The XIV Corps would come ashore on the right, between Sual and Dagupan. Both corps would enjoy additional armored support equaling two tank battalions, one tank company, and two tank destroyer battalions. In addition, the 13th Armored Group was due to arrive on S+2. Composed of an HQ company, the 44th Tank Battalion (less Company C), 775th Tank Battalion, the 632d Tank Destroyer Battalion, and the 186th Engineer Battalion, the armored group was to stage on the American left and, according to Sixth Army Field Order No. 34 (20 November 1944), be prepared to operate in either corps's zone of action on the orders of HQ Sixth Army.[11]

Krueger specified several different missions that he might assign to the 13th Armored Group. He first suggested that it could be reinforced with infantry and artillery to form "an independent mobile armored task force, operating directly under Sixth Army, and spearhead the drive down the Central Plains to Manila." He also considered attaching the group to either corps to act as "an armored spearhead" for the drive to the capital; alternatively, it could be attached to the 25th Infantry Division—of Sixth Army reserve—to lead the advance on Manila. Later, with his eyes on the Shobu Group, Krueger added protecting his army's left flank as it moved south to the list of the 13th's possible assignments. Whatever its mission, the 13th Armored Group's after-action report stated, the "pending operation afforded the first opportunity for the employment of armor in mass in the SWPA campaign, and morale of Group and attached units was at a high level."[12] Finally, after three years, Krueger imagined the possibility of employing his army as he had done in the GHQ Maneuvers of 1941, and his orders to the armored group demonstrated his demand for flexibility in planning.

In a 15 November 1944 planning conference, Krueger's operations officer, Col. Clyde D. Eddleman, looked forward to the Luzon campaign with confidence. Although several problems loomed large, including a shortage of bridging material, several under-strength units, and a continued personnel replacement shortage, the Sixth Army overall was in better shape than it had been during the battle for Leyte. Krueger's troops had more artillery, tanks, and other tactical equipment. His army could also rely on an improved shipping situation. Vice Adm. Thomas C. Kinkaid's Seventh Fleet could transport 72 percent of the corps's vehicles, whereas in some previous operations the figure had dropped as low as 25 percent.[13]

Krueger completed the basic tactical plan by 14 October but needed another month to coordinate the plans and requirements of the corps, air force, navy, and engineers. Throughout the months of October and November, then, Krueger split his time between supervising operations on Leyte and planning for Luzon. When it was time to present the finished plan to MacArthur, Krueger decided to send Eddleman, who met the SWPA commander and his G-2 at the Palmer House in Tacloban. In front of the imposing "American Caesar," Eddleman began his briefing with White's intelligence estimate of the enemy. Believing that Krueger had overestimated Yamashita's strength, MacArthur immediately objected to White's numbers, shouting: "Bunk! Bunk!"[14]

Knowing he could not convince MacArthur, Eddleman decided to move onto the operational plans. After listening, MacArthur wanted to know why Krueger's plan did not include the capture of Manila. Eddleman explained that Krueger proposed to establish a beachhead and appraise the situation before deciding on the best way to move south. With this explanation, MacArthur approved the plan, although he clearly thought that the Japanese would offer little opposition to a quick drive to Manila.[15]

By this time, the planning process—involving as it did army, navy, and air force units—had achieved a high level of maturity. It did not, however, take place overnight. Instead, it had evolved. "This duty," Krueger explained, "difficult at first, became easier as time went on. ... The joint planning work proved to be very successful, especially after the various officers engaged in it had become sufficiently acquainted to recognize each other's ability." Although he had for many years advocated unified command—a situation that would have made this job "very much easier"—Krueger nevertheless admitted that "since our joint planning was so successful, it would seem as if better results could not have been attained even if I had been designated as joint commander and provided with a joint staff."[16]

The Landings

Prior to unleashing its powerful force on Yamashita's army, SWPA had to execute its preliminary operation against the neighboring island of Mindoro. On 15 December, 17,800 troops of the 19th RCT of the 24th Infantry Division, the 503d Parachute RCT, one battalion of the 21st Infantry

Regiment (also of the 24th Division), and various support units landed on the island. The 1,000 or so Japanese defenders offered slight resistance, and the engineers immediately began construction on the runways, the first of which engineers actually completed seven days ahead of schedule. Twenty-two Americans lost their lives on Mindoro, and 180 were wounded. More damage came as a result of a kamikaze attack against the Mindoro task force two days before the landings than as a result of fighting on the ground. One plane crashed into the light cruiser *Nashville,* causing 275 casualties. Among those killed was Col. Bruce C. Hill, the chief of staff of the task force. Sixteen days after landing on Mindoro, the Sixth Army relinquished control of all troops on the island to the Eighth Army. The Mindoro attack was extremely successful. "It gave us," Krueger noted, "a base from which Fifth Air Force could launch strong air strikes in support of the Luzon operation and in protecting the sea lanes leading to Luzon from the south."[17]

Krueger could only hope that the amphibious assault against Luzon would go as well as the one against Mindoro, and he had good reason to be optimistic. From the deck of Kinkaid's command ship, the *Wasatch*, Krueger traveled to Lingayen Gulf with the Seventh Fleet. The Japanese navy did not seriously challenge the assault force as it made its approach. Only several destroyers and submarines attacked the U.S. Navy, but none hit their targets. Japanese aircraft, in contrast, inflicted severe damage, sinking three ships and inflicting damage on twenty-seven others. "It was … apparent," observed Krueger, "that enemy air power had not been as fully neutralized on Luzon as we had assumed." In response, Halsey's planes pounded the enemy air fleet on Luzon, destroying seventy-five planes.[18]

Upon landing at 0930 on 9 January 1945, both corps encountered no initial opposition along the shores of Lingayen Gulf. Shortly thereafter, however, the 43d Infantry Division—on I Corps's left—came under heavy artillery fire and then met organized resistance that originated from the hills and ridges from the northeast. Nevertheless, the division fought forward, advancing approximately 8,000 yards, while the others advanced about 6,000 yards.[19]

As had happened on many previous occasions, the weather and terrain proved more difficult than the Japanese army. In I Corps's zone, for example, the landing craft could come only within 100 yards of the beach because of high surf and shallow water. Heavy equipment, such as badly needed bridging materials, could not be unloaded in a timely fashion.[20]

The situation at XIV Corps's beaches was even worse. An eight-foot surf and high winds "made it almost impossible" to discharge equipment and supplies from the landing craft, several of which were tossed onto the shore. Krueger made the decision to shift the corps's unloading operations to the south in I Corps's zone. This "transfer placed an additional burden upon the already overtaxed I Corps beaches and the roads leading inland from them," Krueger remembered. "The transfer also necessitated moving supplies by the flank to XIV Corps, thus creating difficult traffic conditions and materially hampering the flow of supplies and equipment to both corps. But all this was unavoidable."[21]

Krueger visited both landing beaches on 10 and 11 January, perhaps believing that the unloading operation lacked proper direction and leadership. Instead, he "found that the progress being made was as good as could be expected." In addition to the weather, his troops lacked a sufficient number of adequate railroad locomotives and quartermaster trucks. The locomotives in Luzon were coal-burning, but the Americans lacked adequate fuel resources. Until diesel locomotives were shipped from the United States, troops used any fuel they could find, including coconut husks and driftwood.[22]

Quartermaster companies found their work complicated by a severe shortage of trucks. At several times during the campaign when shortages of motor vehicles were so acute, Krueger had to pull trucks from his divisions—which were themselves already short of motor transports—to fill the need. The deficient number of trucks translated into severe shortages of ammunition for units on the front lines. From January to March, for instance, Krueger had to limit the units of fire for 155mm howitzers and 81mm mortars. The supply problems continued well into the campaign. Even after reaching Manila in February, XIV Corps received its ammunition via only six truck companies from Lingayen Gulf, 110 miles to the north.[23] Enlisted men and officers alike had to improvise as best they could to overcome the burden of a faulty supply system.

Manila: MacArthur versus Krueger

Despite the Sixth Army's troubles, MacArthur grew impatient with the pace of Sixth Army operations and called Eddleman and Krueger aboard the cruiser *Boise* for a conference on 12 January. According to Krueger, MacArthur "discussed Sixth Army's offensive toward Manila and seemed extremely anxious to have that advance made rapidly. He emphasized repeatedly that our losses so far had been small. He expressed the view that the advance would encounter little opposition and that the Japanese would not attempt to defend Manila but would evacuate it."[24]

Krueger responded to his chief's arguments by pointing out that the terrain, weather, and Yamashita's Shobu Group on his left flank prevented him from unleashing XIV Corps. I Corps did not possess enough strength to tie down the Japanese army and protect Griswold's offensive. Instead, Krueger explained that he needed to keep Swift's formation to defend the beachhead and await the arrival of the 1st Cavalry Division and 32d Infantry Division. If he were to send XIV Corps toward Manila while I Corps guarded the beachhead, as MacArthur suggested, Griswold's troops would be 120 miles south, alone, and with unprotected flanks and rear areas. Indeed, only five days later, his army held a line some 75 miles long, more than enough to keep his five divisions and one RCT occupied without the ambitious drive south. It seems—in this respect—that Krueger's desire to land and assess the tactical situation before launching the Manila offensive was a wise decision. Krueger later remarked, "It was fortunate indeed, ... for our eastern beaches were under severe Japanese artillery fire for some days after we landed—a contingency that compelled me to push my left forward vigorously to drive the Japs back from the general line Damortis-Pozorrubio-Binalonan [before moving south]." If he would have sent both corps south toward Manila—as would be necessary—the Japanese would have seriously threatened the Sixth Army beachhead.[25]

According to Eddleman, the 12 January conference contained much tension between Krueger and MacArthur. It was, he explained, "the only time I ever saw the two of them when they had cross words." This close to Manila after two and one-half years, MacArthur badgered Krueger in the hope of getting him to capture Manila ahead of schedule: "Where are your casualties? Why are you holding the I Corps back? It ought to be moving south." Ever the "Prussian," Krueger was not about to be steamrolled into taking action that he did not deem prudent. He responded, "And abandon my base here? What other base do I have?" In the end, MacArthur did not order Krueger to change his course of action. "The old man stuck to his guns," Eddleman noted, "but he didn't feel to[o] good going back across Lingayen Gulf to our flag ship."[26]

MacArthur employed every tactic he could to get the Sixth Army to Manila. For starters, he sent Krueger numerous messages urging him to keep his troops moving throughout the month of January. On 30 January, after inspecting the 37th Infantry Division, MacArthur radioed Krueger that "there was a noticeable lack of drive and aggressive initiative today" in its offensive. In addition to the occasional notes, MacArthur attempted to prod him along in person. Following the 12 January conference on the *Boise*, MacArthur met several other times with Krueger throughout January 1945. During one such meeting, Krueger again stood up to his boss and defended the pace of his advances. After the discussion, MacArthur remarked to a friend, "Walter's pretty stubborn. Maybe I'll have to try something else."[27]

The "something else" MacArthur had in mind was to use actions instead of words to pressure Krueger. He first moved his headquarters in front of

Krueger's in an obvious attempt to embarrass the Sixth Army commander. He also attempted to exploit the rivalry between the leaders of his two armies by allowing the Eighth Army's Robert L. Eichelberger to land the 11th Airborne Division in Nasugbu Bay, about 55 miles south of Manila, and make a push for the capital. Initially, MacArthur had other objectives for the Nasugbu Bay landing. He hoped that the 11th would divert Japanese attention from the Sixth Army's drive toward Manila. If possible, MacArthur also wanted the airborne division to pin down Japanese forces in the entire southwestern region of Luzon. After landing, however, MacArthur gave Eichelberger the authority to make a drive toward Manila.

Krueger did not fall for MacArthur's manipulative games. Krueger knew that MacArthur was trying to play Eichelberger against him, and vice versa. The two army commanders did not like each other, and MacArthur tried to exploit the situation by suggesting to Krueger that Eichelberger might take the lead in future SWPA operations. MacArthur "was not above playing one commander against another," Eddleman recalled, "and used radio intercept units for both friendly and enemy activities." Krueger concluded that what mattered was not who would be the most favored MacArthur lieutenant, but to do what he thought was right, despite the cost, even if it meant being labeled "stubborn."[28]

Based on the information available to him and the doctrine to which he subscribed, Krueger was not about to be bullied into speeding the pace of his army or participating in MacArthur's thinly veiled attempts at promoting a "race" between the Sixth and Eighth Armies. Throughout January, he had to weigh several factors as his forces proceeded down the Central Plains from Lingayen Gulf to Manila. The first was the complex problem of supplies. As soon as his army came ashore on Luzon, Krueger had to contend with everything from poor weather to natural obstacles, all of which hindered logistical operations. Furthermore, Griswold's supply line grew increasingly tenuous as it crossed many rivers and moved ever southward. Under these conditions, Krueger did not want to push his troops into a tough city fight without adequate provisions. "Our advance toward the south was slower than desirable," Krueger admitted, "but its pace depended upon reconstruction of the many destroyed bridges, some very large ones, rehabilitation of the roads and the Manila-Dagupan Railroad. Shortage of vital bridge material, lack of locomotive[s,] and limited rolling stock complicated matters."[29]

Furthermore, what MacArthur wanted Krueger to do violated many of the basic precepts of U.S. operational doctrine. One of the fundamental prerequisites of offensive action—whether a breakthrough or envelopment—is the division of troops into two or more groupings. The first is the main force, designed specifically "to secure the objective and to destroy the hostile force." The second, called the secondary attack group, is "designed to *hold the enemy* in position, *to force him to commit his reserves* prematurely and to an indecisive location, and *to prevent him from reinforcing* the front of the main attack"[emphasis in the original].[30] In the amphibious operation against Luzon, Krueger had only two sets: one to protect the beachhead area, and another for offensive purposes. There was no group to hold and fix the enemy. Krueger had made clear during the GHQ Maneuvers of 1941 that fixing the enemy position before striking was absolutely necessary, and he was loath to do so at a time when the stakes were much greater. In addition, MacArthur's orders to capture Manila rapidly before his reinforcements came ashore forced him to scatter his troops to protect the beachhead as well as guard the rear and flanks of XIV Corps as he moved south. His handling of the I Armored Corps during 1941 now a distant memory, Krueger had to fritter away the advantages that the 13th Armored Group afforded just to protect his army. MacArthur's strategy forced Krueger to abandon some of the key offensive concepts (concentration, fixing the enemy, and envelopment) that he had helped to develop four years before. Under these circumstances any force committed to a "dash" to Manila would be too weak to take the city. Krueger only had the 37th Division (less one Regimental Combat Team).[31]

Krueger also had to be wary of Yamashita's defensive preparations. On the day of the invasion, the commander of the Japanese garrison planned to employ his 2d Armored Division to strike the American flank if the enemy advanced too far too quickly. By the second day of the operation, because of the way in which Krueger handled the beginning phases, it became clear to Yamashita that there would be no opportunity to use his tanks in an offensive role.[32] Furthermore, in a situation that had played itself out many times before, there were considerable differences in the intelligence picture between GHQ SWPA and Sixth Army G-2. Willoughby suggested that approximately 130,000 Japanese remained on Luzon and that they would not put up much of a defense. Krueger's intelligence painted a much different picture. Col. White, the Sixth Army's intelligence officer, estimated that the Japanese positioned 50,000 more troops on Krueger's left than Willoughby had suggested.[33]

Moreover, White estimated that the Japanese not only had substantial numbers but also had an offensive capability. In his intelligence estimate of a Sixth Army movement toward Clark Field, White maintained that any movement south would expose XIV Corps to a flanking attack. To be sure, Lt. Gen. George C. Kenney's planes had inflicted great losses on the enemy's ability to maneuver, but White predicted that Yamashita's 2d Armored Division would have a window of opportunity to strike Griswold's left while his corps moved from Tarlac to Clark Field from its positions around Cabanatuan. "Therefore, the enemy's strongest armored capability, and the soundest tactically, is to strike at our left flank during the advance of our columns from Tarlac to Clark Field, with the objective of dividing our forces and defeating them in detail." If such an operation was not in the realm of possibility—indeed, in the move toward Clark Airfield, a delaying defense and defense of Clark Airfield itself were more likely Japanese countermoves—White warned Krueger that the Japanese army "also has the unquestioned capability of making piece meal attacks with his armored elements from the front or from the flank at times and places of his own choosing."[34]

To Krueger, this was an all-too-familiar pattern. In the Admiralties, Wakde-Sarmi, and Leyte, MacArthur and his staff had underestimated the numbers and capabilities of the Japanese. Now on Luzon, the SWPA commander and his staff were doing the same thing, claiming the Japanese defenders were defeated and would offer little resistance. It is therefore understandable if Krueger did not believe what his superior told him. Krueger expected the Japanese to offer fanatical resistance on Luzon, just as they had in all other locations. Krueger rightly surmised that if he pushed out of the beachhead, Yamashita's armored force would threaten his extended left flank. Such an advance might be justified if the reason for doing so were of critical importance. However, there was no compelling cause.

Krueger had worked for MacArthur for almost two years and knew of his intense desire to return to the Philippines as quickly as possible. After their 12 January meeting, Krueger concluded that merely "returning" was not enough. MacArthur, Krueger surmised, wanted to enter Manila on his birthday, January 26.[35] Understandably, Krueger concluded that this was hardly a sound reason to risk an entire corps and the future of U.S. Army operations in SWPA.

Krueger Moves toward Manila

Though Krueger lacked the power to take Manila, he could initiate limited offensive action until the 32d Division and 1st Cavalry reached Luzon. On 17 January, when Krueger returned to his command post (established at Bonuan Boquig on 13 January) after his meeting with MacArthur, he found a message from GHQ SWPA that urged him to capture Clark Field, an important objective since its runways were far superior to those hastily built near Lingayen Gulf. As it was, Krueger had already ordered his staff to draw up such plans, and on 18 January, Krueger issued Field Order No. 43, which instructed I Corps to continue its operations near the beachhead and XIV Corps to advance to the line Tarlac–Victoria by 21 January, after which it was to prepare for a march on Clark Field. The 43d Division was to continue its advance beyond Binday into the mountains as the 6th Division and 37th Divisions (of I Corps and XIV Corps respectively) moved forward to protect the left and rear of the 40th Division, which was to make the main effort southward. In addition, Krueger placed the 44th Tank Battalion (less Company C) of the 13th Armored Group in army reserve near Rosales. This placed his tanks south of the Agno River near the roadnet (i.e., network of roads) and would give them access to points east and south, presumably to counteract any possible Japanese flanking attack against XIV Corps. After completing these orders and discerning Japanese countermoves, Krueger would determine his next course of action.[36]

Moving out on 19 January, the XIV Corps encountered little opposition. The 40th Division captured Tarlac on 21 January as scheduled. Even with Krueger's precautions in protecting the XIV Corps's flanks, Griswold's force was vulnerable. By the time it reached its final objective on 21 January, Griswold would have an exposed left of 25,000 yards. Five days later, the left flank grew to 124 miles, with the 40th Division occupying 77 miles and the 37th Division controlling a line of 47 miles. To help protect his flanks, Griswold relied on Marine Air Groups 24 and 32 and the 308th Bombardment Wing. Airplanes from these units helped to ensure that no Japanese units moved against XIV Corps's flanks. In addition, the corps had to work with a long and increasingly tenuous supply route. Griswold doubted that he could move any farther.[37]

After conferring with Griswold and Maj. Gen. Edwin D. Patrick, commander of the 6th Division, on 21 January, Krueger decided to limit further movement south so that the XIV Corps could send the 37th Division on a reconnaissance mission in the Cabanatuan region, reportedly where the enemy had concentrated his troops. "This reconnaissance," the XIV Corps after-action report explained, "was to prevent any surprise on an already overextended and vulnerable flank." As it turned out, the Japanese were not massing in the Cabanatuan area, and Krueger decided to resume the offensive.[38]

By 23 January, the 40th Division reached the northeastern runway of Clark Field. Griswold knew that though no Japanese forces were behind him, the Kembu Group strongly held the air complex and the high ground behind it. Consequently, he decided to commit his entire corps and spent 24 January bringing the 37th Division south to positions north of Clark, around Bamban, and then swung his corps 90 degrees to face west toward the airfield. Over the next week, the GIs met tough and resilient Japanese defenses that took carefully planned tank–infantry attacks to overcome. The whole area fell to the Americans by 29 January.[39]

Around the same time, Maj. Gen. Charles P. Hall's XI Corps (composed of the 38th Infantry Division, the 34th RCT of the 24th Infantry Division, and other units) landed under the command of the Eighth Army on the west coast of Luzon. Upon hitting the beaches, the new corps came under Krueger's command on 30 January. Anticipating the corps's arrival, along with the 1st Cavalry Division, the 112th Cavalry RCT, and the 32d Infantry, Krueger issued two new field orders—No. 46 on 30 January, and No. 47 on 2 February—that took into account the additional forces. Krueger attached the 32d Division to I Corps, which, along with the 6th, 25th, and 43d Infantry Divisions, made it a four-division corps. In reserve, Krueger held the 13th Armored Group to support XIV Corps operations. Because of manpower shortages, he was forced to employ his armored forces not as part of combined-arms force in offensive operations but rather as part of a defensive screen to protect the enormous left flank of XIV Corps, where its mobility could be used to advantage to stop the Japanese 2d Armored Division. As for I Corps, Krueger wanted Swift's troops to advance along the Verde Villa Trail in order to gain control over the northeast section of Luzon and also to move south to support the impending offensive against Manila. This action included blocking enemy units from moving down from their mountain stronghold. The XI Corps, meanwhile, was to proceed along Highway 7 toward Dinalupihan, where it would meet up with XIV Corps.[40]

The work of I and XI Corps would allow the Sixth Army's other corps to concentrate on the Manila assault. For the task, Krueger assigned the veteran 1st Cavalry Division to Griswold's corps. Field Order No. 46 (30 January) called for XIV Corps to attach the 44th Tank Battalion (less Company C) to the 1st Cavalry. These two would act as a "fast, flying column for the main effort" of a two-pronged drive to Manila. The Sixth Army commander also made provisions for nine Douglas SBD Dauntless dive-bombers from Marine Corps Aviation to be on call for close air support missions. Moving in concert and in a supporting role was the 37th Infantry Division. Because Krueger still had to take into account the possibility of Japanese flanking attacks, the drive to Manila would be accomplished in successive bounds. For the first phase, beginning on 1 February, Krueger directed Griswold to move across the Pampanga River and establish contact between the two divisions. He then instructed the corps's third division, the 40th, along with the 745th Tank Battalion, to clear the enemy from positions in the mountains surrounding Clark Field.[41]

To monitor his army's operations, Krueger kept his command post near the front. He left his first post near Lingayen Gulf on 23 January to open a new one at Calasiao. He then moved to Gerona on 3 February and finally to San Fernando on 12 February. San Fernando, located just to the north of Manila Bay, brought back many memories for Krueger. It was there that he had taken his examination for commission as a second lieutenant in 1901. His office and living quarters, moreover, were the same as those occupied by Maj. Gen. Arthur MacArthur (father of Douglas) almost fifty years earlier. This would be his last headquarters before moving to Kyoto, Japan, on 28 September.[42]

During the morning hours, Krueger usually conducted tours of the front line. In fact, Krueger made more inspections throughout the Luzon campaign than at any other time. Not only did he find it physically easier to make these tours (the field of battle was much smaller than it had been during the New Guinea campaign), but the increased number of them was most likely in response to the shortcomings he had witnessed on Leyte. Similarly, he produced more evaluation reports that chronicled the problems he had observed and the corrections he wanted made. He discussed his inspection tours with his chief of staff and closest aides after returning to his headquarters in late morning or early afternoon.[43]

With Krueger closely monitoring his army's action, XIV Corps moved out on 1 February on its mission of liberating Manila. The 1st Cavalry Division—divided by the division commander, Maj. Gen. Verne D. Mudge, into its own "flying columns," each built on a cavalry squadron, a tank company, a 105mm howitzer battery, and other supporting elements—quickly captured Cabanatuan along Highway 5, while other units bypassed the town to take hold of another, Gapan. The following day, Mudge's flying columns crossed the Angat River near Baliuag and then executed a pincer movement to seize the city of Santa Maria.[44]

Meanwhile, the 37th Division crossed the Pampanga River on Highway 3, after which it overran minor Japanese resistance in Malolos. During the next twenty-four hours, it captured Marilao, about 10 miles south, and made contact with elements of the 1st Cavalry around Plaridel. In two days, Griswold's troops had encountered minor opposition and were on the verge of taking Manila, just over 10 miles away.[45]

After establishing contact with one another, the two divisions made a concerted effort to take Manila on 3 February. Upon entering Grace Park in north Manila and liberating 3,521 civilian internees from a makeshift prison in Santo Tomás University, the Sixth Army began rooting out the approximate 17,000 Japanese from Manila.

MacArthur's belief that the Japanese would not defend Manila was unfounded. The battle evolved into a slugging match that raged until 3 March 1945, due in part to the decision of Rear Adm. Sanji Iwabuchi, commander of the Manila Naval Defense Force, to defend the city instead of carrying out Yamashita's orders to evacuate the city. The contest involved savage house-to-house fighting, complicated by MacArthur's initial refusal to allow Krueger to employ air power and artillery in the hopes of keeping civilian casualties to a minimum. Even after MacArthur allowed the use of artillery, he did not permit Kenney's planes to aid Griswold's men. More than 100,000 Philippine citizens were killed in the fight for Manila, along with 1,000 Americans, and the Japanese lost almost their entire garrison. The physical destruction matched the human toll. Large parts of the city were burned out or destroyed by the fighting. The Japanese army contributed much to the misery by deliberately starting fires, wrecking bridges, and raping and killing citizens. As one historian has observed, only Warsaw, Poland, experienced more damage during the war up to that time.[46]

The Race for Manila in Retrospect

In light of all the energy MacArthur placed in capturing the Philippine capital, and of all the death and destruction that resulted from wrestling it out of Japanese hands, one must wonder if it was worth it. From the vantage point of military necessity, it was definitely not. MacArthur had employed a bypassing strategy to get to the Philippines, then promptly discarded it upon arriving in the archipelago. He sent his forces—primarily the newly activated Eighth U.S. Army—in a long and difficult campaign to liberate the "Pearl of the Orient" largely because of its symbolic value. As three historians who have recently examined the battle for Manila argue,

> Such a single-minded aim was manifested in a number of ways, all of which virtually guaranteed a battle for control of Manila. When the Sixth Army advanced south from Lingayen, MacArthur insisted on speed despite Krueger's understandable worries about Japanese counterattacks against his exposed flanks. The fact that no similar orders were given to those elements of the same army which faced Yamashita's main force to the northeast, implies that Manila was the only objective in MacArthur's mind. This is reinforced when it is realized that he was actively planning his victory parade before the city had been secured … and by his insistence on touring Manila while the fighting was going on.[47]

By his words and actions, in comparison, Krueger demonstrated that he had first wanted to deal with Yamashita's army. MacArthur's own plans for the capture of the Philippine cite the enemy army as the primary objective, along with clearing central Luzon. The underlying tension between the SWPA commander and the Sixth Army commander was thus based on the former's concern with geographical objectives versus the latter's focus on destroying the enemy's army.[48]

This divergence of views over the military significance of Manila helps explain the controversy surrounding Krueger's drive toward Manila. However much he might have disagreed with MacArthur's desire to make Manila the primary objective, Krueger had to do what MacArthur ordered. Consequently, he executed a campaign that took into consideration MacArthur's geographical objectives while minimizing the threat that the enemy's military forces posed. Krueger knew that he had to move at a more prudent pace, one aggressive and quick but that took into account the obvious pitfalls. Consequently, he executed a campaign at the operational level by balancing strategic demands with tactical realities. "In these circumstances, any precipitate southward advance with insufficient forces would have played directly into the enemy's hands and probably would have led to an unnecessary reverse," he reflected. "Accordingly, although I was anxious to push south quickly in order to secure Manila—if possible by 26 January, General MacArthur's birthday—I did not consider this feasible and instead decided to await the arrival of the reinforcements due on 27 January, then to launch an all-out drive against Manila. Subsequent events proved the soundness of that decision."[49]

On some level, MacArthur might have agreed with Krueger. Krueger's keen military mind acted as a counterbalance to MacArthur's own personal reasons for taking Manila. Maybe this explains why, during January 1945, he kept Krueger as the commander of Sixth Army even as his chief of staff, Lt. Gen. Richard K. Sutherland, wanted him sent home. But MacArthur more than just decided to keep him. In the middle of February, when MacArthur's pressure on Krueger was intense, he recommended Krueger for promotion to full general along with Kenney. The U.S. War Department accepted MacArthur's recommendation, and Krueger was promoted on 5 March 1945. In his evaluation report, MacArthur compared his Sixth Army commander to other better-known generals: "I know both Krueger and [Lt. Gen. George S.] Patton [Jr.] intimately and I believe his contribution is more outstanding than that of Patton." Comparing Krueger to Lt. Gen. Omar N. Bradley, MacArthur wrote, "Bradley is junior to Krueger and the latter in my opinion is not only the more competent officer of the two but is entirely familiar with this theater." Paul P. Rogers—MacArthur's military secretary—had seen MacArthur at the height of impatience over Krueger's drive toward the central Luzon region and observed that "MacArthur's aggravation was not all that deep.... Krueger ... was exactly MacArthur's age and between them there was a certain bond of understanding."[50]

While Krueger's lack of planning beyond getting ashore allowed him flexibility in terms of executing MacArthur's obsessive Manila strategy, Krueger's decision not to look beyond the beachhead also had some unfortunate side effects. Planning for the massive effort of removing the Japanese defenders of Manila did not take place until the last minute, when XIV Corps encountered the main enemy defenses. Why Krueger failed to do so is a mystery. By the middle of January, he discarded MacArthur's rosy estimate that the Japanese would walk away from the city. In fact, Krueger came to the conclusion that they would put up quite a strong fight, but still he did not address the problem of urban warfare nor did he offer much support once XIV Corps entered Manila. On 15 February, for instance, Griswold contacted Sixth Army HQ for directions concerning his assault against the Intramuros, the old part of Manila built by the Spanish. "I am going to have to breach walls at several places," Griswold explained to Krueger's G-3. "It is an all-historic thing. I think it is a military necessity. You know how these things are, and I am just wondering if General Krueger or yourself have any advice." "General Krueger's advice is to take Manila" is the only response Decker could muster. "I think, insofar as he is concerned, you can use such means as necessary."[51] Such inattention to an impending major battle could only complicate the already delicate task of urban warfare and lead directly to the destruction of the Philippine capital. In the absence of forethought, preparation, and training, Griswold and the 37th Infantry Division commander—Maj. Gen. Robert S. Beightler—did what they had to do to claim the city without incurring unacceptable American causalities. They relied on direct and indirect fire to blast the Japanese defenders out of their strongholds; 155mm and even 240mm howitzers became favorites for GIs after they discovered that the 105mm tubes did not pack enough punch. These tactics came at a high price that undermined the strategic and operational rationale for taking the city in the first place. The city's largest pier was damaged and could not be used, and the airfields required much work before they could be used. Furthermore, the city's lone power plant, its major hospital, and the water distribution system were nearly or completely destroyed. The extensive damage delayed MacArthur's intent of using the central Luzon region for a staging base for future operations.[52]

Although he neglected to plan for the battle of Manila, Krueger did formulate a strategy for rehabilitating the city. He prioritized the work in store for him and his army: preservation of law and order, rehabilitation of essential utilities, relief of the civilian population, and administration. For this task, Krueger assigned Beightler's 37th Division, an Ohio National Guard unit. Krueger ordered Beightler to report directly to him, bypassing Griswold. After receiving additional personnel, Beightler organized cells to fulfill Krueger's mandate. By early February Beightler's staff had already come up with detailed plans for the coming weeks and months. Along with the essential aid provide by the inhabitants of Manila, Beightler's troops began to produce promising results by mid-March.[53]

Mopping-Up Operations on Luzon

Along with the battle for Manila, Krueger and his Sixth Army began the extremely difficult task of clearing the rest of the Philippines, a formidable task considering that most of the Japanese garrison still remained. Hall's XI Corps, after landing near San Narciso, moved east along Highway 7 just north of Bataan. Approximately 15 miles from the beachhead, it ran into carefully prepared and "desperate" enemy defenses positioned in some of the roughest jungle-covered terrain on all of Luzon, called Zig-Zag Pass. Not until 14 February could the Americans consider the area cleared. Hall's men then continued their offensive toward Dinalupihan, where they met elements of I Corps. The XI Corps next swung south to clear Bataan, after which the 503d Parachute Regimental Combat Team and the 3d Battalion (reinforced)/34th Infantry of the 24th Infantry Division assaulted Corregidor, the small island that protects the entrance to Manila Bay, and secured it by 26 February.[54]

Krueger's next order of business was to push about 30,000 men of the Shimbu Group away from the outskirts of Manila and capture the important dams that supply water to the city. He first assigned the 6th Infantry Division the task, but when it ran into the heavily fortified Shimbu Group, assembled along Mount Pacawagan, Mount Mataba, and Antipolo, it became apparent that more troops would be needed. Consequently, Krueger attached the 1st Cavalry Division to the 6th Division's right flank. Together, the two divisions fought an intensive and exhausting battle, which forced Krueger to reorganize the front. On 15 March, the XI Corps relieved the XIV Corps along the Shimbu Group sector. Hall's corps retained the 6th Division and the 112th Cavalry to fight along side the 43d Division (less the 169th RCT).[55]

Despite the hard work of Griswold's men over a two-week period, the Shimbu Group remained largely intact, strongly holding three areas: the Ipo Dam in the north, the Wawa Dam in the center, and Antipolo in the south. Hall determined that continuing the frontal assault would be futile, so he ordered a mechanized 25-mile sweep of the Japanese left flank by the 103d

Infantry Regiment. This envelopment helped to convince the Japanese commander that his left flank was collapsing, and he withdrew on 20 March.[56]

With the 43d Division mopping up the Japanese in the south, Hall instructed the 6th and 38th Divisions to continue the offensive to seize Wawa and Ipo Dams. By the end of May, Hall's troops had captured both dams, restored water supply to Manila, and wrecked the Shimbu Group's ability to continue productive resistance. Having retreated deep into the Sierra Madre Mountains, the once-proud Japanese soldiers were reduced to foraging for food.[57]

Since being relieved by XI Corps, Griswold's XIV Corps faced the mission of clearing the area south of Manila. It quickly secured Balayan and Batangas Bays and approached the Bicol Peninsula. Krueger landed the 158th RCT near Legaspi on the southern edge of Luzon on 1 April and then had it advance to the north as the 1st Cavalry Division spearheaded the XIV Corps's drive southward. The two formations met on 2 May and participated in clearing the rest of Bicol Peninsula. By the end of May, all major enemy opposition had disintegrated in the south.[58]

The XIV Corps, however, still had much to do. On 15 June, Krueger transferred it to the north to aid I Corps's attack against the still formidable Shobu Group. As the XIV and XI Corps conducted their operations in the south, Swift's men had sealed Yamashita's group into the northeast peninsula and had established a line that ran approximately from Dagupan to Rizal. Krueger wanted to strike to the west near Bambang with the 25th and 32d Divisions. But on the left side, Maj. Gen. Percy W. Clarkson's 33d Infantry Division had broken through the more heavily defended area surrounding Baguio and captured the city on 27 April.[59]

Although Clarkson's division met unexpected success, Krueger still wanted to capture Bambang. The city is the gateway to the important Cagayan Valley, which was, in Krueger's words, "the enemy's breadbasket," a fertile farming area. While the 25th Division battered its way north through Balete Pass, which dominated Highway 5 and impeded the Americans' progress along that road, Krueger earmarked the 37th Division to exploit any breakthrough. After the 25th captured Balete Pass by means of an enveloping maneuver in mid-May, the 37th "took up the advance against crumbling Japanese resistance." It bypassed many concentrations of enemy troops and strong points, while the 6th Division followed to eliminate them. As these two divisions pushed through Cagayan Valley, Yamashita concluded that his army was crumbling, so he decided to withdraw his beleaguered army into the rugged Cordillera Mountains.[60]

In the midst of Krueger's battle against Yamashita in the north, MacArthur notified his Sixth Army leader that his army would be replaced by Eichelberger's Eighth Army, effective 30 June 1945. Krueger and his staff were to prepare for their toughest job yet: the invasion of Japan.

Krueger and Luzon in Retrospect

The Luzon campaign—lasting 173 days—cost the Japanese army 173,563 KIA and 7,297 captured. The Sixth Army lost 8,140 KIA, 28,557 WIA, and 157 MIA. Particularly disturbing were the additional 93,400 nonbattle casualties, the great bulk of which were caused by sickness and disease. To put this figure into perspective, the Sixth Army's disease record was the worst since the Seventh U.S. Army's record in Sicily the year before. While the surgical and evacuation services performed well throughout the battle for Luzon, disease-resistance measures slacked off. On New Guinea, Krueger had made sure that malaria-prevention techniques were followed, but such discipline broke down on Luzon. Clearly, with the fight against the Japanese foremost in his mind, Krueger failed to maintain the proper discipline. Further complicating the health conditions of the army was that Manila was the first major city many of Krueger's soldiers had seen in months. Predictably, venereal disease became a problem. Nevertheless, MacArthur refused to crack down, noting that "they've got some pretty good treatment for that disease now, haven't they?" Although Yamashita's force suffered greatly, approximately 65,000 men remained in Luzon, 50,000 of whom still roamed the north until after the war ended in August. Clearly, Eichelberger faced another tough job in rooting out the tenacious Japanese soldiers.[61]

Throughout the combat on Luzon, the Sixth Army continually had to overcome several obstacles that hampered its ability to fight. Besides the aforementioned shortages of bridging material and motor vehicles, the Americans experienced acute shortages of spare parts, tires, recoil mechanisms, gun tubes, 60mm mortars, and .30-caliber machine-gun mounts. Krueger blamed the lack on inadequate storage bases, insufficient shipping, and the fact that he had to use his material not only for his army but for the Philippine Army and guerillas as well.[62]

The largest burden by far was a deficiency of personnel. In the XI Corps's offensive against the Shimbu Group, for example, the 6th and 43d Divisions were almost completely exhausted. The nine rifle companies of the 172d Infantry Regiment/43d Division had only slightly more than 450 men capable of further offensive action. The 1st and 20th Regiments of the 6th Division were in similar shape. Together, they could field only 1,750 men. The four regiments of XIV Corps were losing between fifty-five and sixty men a day through death, sickness, injury, or fatigue. "Such attrition would soon destroy the regiments as effective combat units," the U.S. Army official historian of the Luzon campaign pointedly writes, "and it began to appear that XI Corps would have to halt until the regiments could either be replaced or brought back up to strength. Certainly, a stalemate, jeopardizing the success of the corps' plans, threatened."[63]

I Corps fared no better in the north during its offensive against the Shimbu Group. The Japanese outnumbered Swift's men almost two to one right from the start, but as the campaign wore one, the situation got worse. The 35th Infantry Regiment of the 25th Division came out of the brutal offensive to capture Balete Pass 750 men understrength. The 32d Division's battle with the 2d Armored Division along the infamous Villa Verde Trail was even more costly. Its 126th Regiment was 1,325 men understrength, and the 127th was 1,025 men short. Replacements could not keep up with the losses.[64]

Further complicating the dearth of manpower was MacArthur's curious abandonment of his earlier leapfrogging strategy. Unlike his willingness to bypass the strong Japanese garrisons at Hansa Bay and Wewak, by September 1944 MacArthur had decided to commit the entire Eighth Army to liberate the rest of the Philippine Islands and the East Indies after the Sixth Army had secured Luzon. Called the Victory Plan, it envisioned a series of amphibious assaults to free the islands of Palawan, Panay, Negros, Cebu, Bohol, and Mindanao. To fulfill these missions, MacArthur pulled three divisions from the Sixth Army. For an army that already had manpower shortages, the impact was critical. It prevented, for instance, Swift's I Corps from exploiting a rupture in the Japanese lines along the Old Spanish Trail rather than continue its advance along the Villa Verde Trail. To divert units away from other areas would have left large gaps in the corps's front line and compromised its security. Because MacArthur was taking divisions away from the Sixth Army, Krueger could not supply Swift with the necessary forces to capitalize on his corps's success. Overall, the effort to consolidate Luzon would have been much better served had MacArthur directed Eichelberger to assist Krueger, especially since many of the isolated Japanese garrisons posed little threat.[65]

With shortages of men and certain types of equipment, how did Krueger engineer his successful campaign? The answer may be found in the way in which Krueger deployed his forces. Loath to send his infantry against the well-positioned defenders of Luzon, Krueger orchestrated a combined-arms effort. During its offensive near Antipolo in late February, the 6th Division employed many of the weapons at its disposal, including artillery, 4.2-inch mortars, tanks, and air support (including B-24s, P-47s, P-40s, and SBDs). Particularly useful was the use of napalm. "Napalm firebombs were used," the Sixth Army after-action report noted, "and although their flames did not penetrate the deepest caves, they did succeed in destroying camouflage and vegetation, making enemy positions visible to American front line troops and artillery observers." The division commander, Maj. Gen. Edwin D. Patrick, was impressed with the results of Krueger's coordination of arms, specifically the air support. During his division's operations east of Manila, Patrick observed that "close air support by Army and Marine air forces of operations of this division [during the] past two days has been magnificent.... Enthusiastic cooperation of air force personnel to include visits by pilots to front line troops has materially improved coordination between ground and air forces."[66]

Although the coordination of forces eventually overwhelmed the Japanese, the task was not easy. An incident during XIV Corps's drive toward Manila provides a case in point. As the 6th Division assaulted the village of San José on 4 February, several B-25s from the Fifth Air Force conducted an unscheduled strafing mission, which drifted on to the American lines, killing one GI and wounding seven. The incident prompted a contentious telephone conversation between Kenney and Krueger. The two agreed that Allied Air Force–army cooperation was difficult to achieve under the circumstances in Luzon, and they decided to work together more closely. Some of the difficulties included the varied competency of liaison officers; the distances between army units, AAF headquarters, and navy air planes; and the fast-paced tempo of operations. "Coordination is as nearly perfect as you can get at some places and at other places it isn't; I think it is practically all due to the experience of the liaison people," Krueger told Kenney. "It couldn't be explained in any other way. The liaison officers in some cases are superior and in other cases they are not."[67]

Despite such problems, Krueger forged his men, weapons, and equipment into a powerful combined-arms force. At least the deputy chief of staff of the Japanese Fourteenth Area Army thought so. When asked in a postwar interview what role the various services of the U.S. armed forces played in his army's defeat in the Philippines, Maj. Gen. Haruo Konuma replied, "The most important factor in the Japanese defeat in the Philippines was our relative weakness, but the excellent coordination of the U.S. forces was also important."[68]

The complex nature of warfare on Luzon placed more pressure on Krueger than at any other time during the war. In addition to the type of operations, Krueger had to deal with MacArthur's words and antics, both of which were designed to get him to move more quickly to Manila in late January. But perhaps the most disturbing aspect of the campaign was the burden it placed on his men. From their first day on Luzon, his troops were locked in combat with little hope of replacement or rotating out of the front lines. Besides death or being wounded, there was hardly any way to be released from the fighting. The toll on the infantry was great. The psychological stress of combat contributed to 20 percent of the total Sixth Army casualties.[69]

Furthermore, combat on Luzon took a more personal turn for Krueger when his former chief of staff and current 6th Infantry Division commander, Edwin D. Patrick, was killed. On 14 March 1945, Patrick was visiting a forward battalion observation post with the leader of the 1st Regiment, Col. James E. Rees, when Japanese machine-gun fire raked the position. Rees was killed instantly. A wounded Patrick was sent to a Manila hospital, where he died three days later.[70]

Early in the war, Krueger made it a point to separate work from his personal life so the pressures of the war would not consume him. "Of course I always sleep well, do not worry, and never take my cares and responsibilities to bed with me. Moreover, being able to relax thoroughly helps," he wrote in a letter.[71] Such relaxation took the form of reading and watching movies. During the first two years of the war, he enjoyed reading history, such as volume two of Douglas Southall Freeman's *Lee's Lieutenants* and Carl Van Doren's *Mutiny in January*.[72] As the war dragged on, however, observers noted a change in his reading habits. MacArthur's personal physician recorded, after visiting Sixth Army headquarters, that there was a "large pile of books, paperbacks, fifty or seventy-five of then, not a stack but more like a stack that had been kicked over. All the titles that I could see were mystery and spy stories which, I later gathered from Colonel Hagen [Col. William A. Hagins], the Sixth Army surgeon, General Krueger really needed as an escape from his responsibility for the lives of all the men fighting under him."[73]

Japan

There was, however, little time for any form of relaxation, because immediately upon being relieved of duties on Luzon, Krueger and his staff plunged into planning for the invasion of Japan, code-named Operation DOWNFALL. It was an invasion that called for Krueger's Sixth Army to make the all-important first landing on the island of Kyūshū (Operation OLYMPIC), scheduled for 1 November 1945 (X-day), and then establish sufficient naval and air bases to support the First and Eighth Armies in their mission against the heart of Japan, the island of Honshū. For this massive undertaking, MacArthur provided Krueger four corps, the I Corps, IX Corps, XI Corps, and V Marine Amphibious Corps (VMAC), including thirteen divisions, along with various independent RCTs and supporting units. This force totaled approximately 650,000 men.[74]

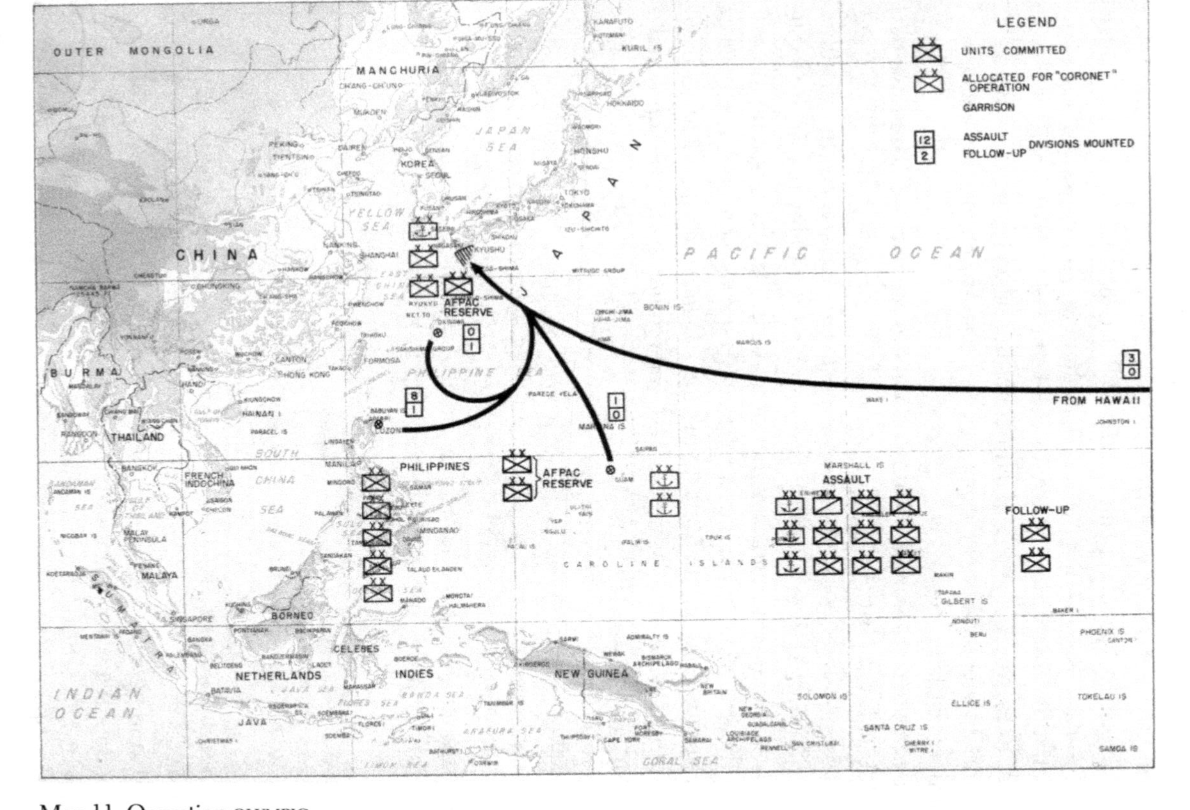

Map 11. Operation OLYMPIC
Source: Charles A. Willoughby, ed., *Reports of General MacArthur*, 2 vols., vol. 1, *The Campaigns of MacArthur in the Pacific* (Washington, D.C.: Government Printing Office, 1966), 413.

Krueger knew that the Japanese were ready and waiting for him. In the northern region of Kyūshū the Japanese deployed the 56th Army, and in the south, the 40th and 57th Armies, totaling approximately 680,000 men and further reinforced by late July. A string of mountains bisected the island into northern and southern sections, creating, in the words of historian John Ray Skates, "two almost self-contained defensive areas." Krueger also suspected that the Japanese might attempt an amphibious assault in the Sixth Army rear areas as IGHQ had stationed at leased one amphibious brigade on the island. Furthermore, the threat of kamikaze attacks weighed heavily on everyone's mind. Although Japan's conventional airpower was destroyed, the Sixth Army G-2 staff took careful note of the recent U.S. invasion of Okinawa, especially Vice Adm. Richmond K. Turner's experience as joint task force commander, wherein Japanese suicide pilots accounted for 90 percent of the damage to the American fleet. With about 800 Japanese combat planes thought to be on Kyūshū, Sixth Army planners feared the worst.[75]

Krueger divided his operations into four phases. The 40th Infantry Division and the 158th RCT were to conduct preliminary operations prior to X-day. These missions included seizing offshore islands and establishing advanced naval anchorages, seaplane bases, and radar sites to control the sea lanes for the approach to Kyūshū. Phase one involved the main amphibious assault. On the east side of Kyūshū, Krueger planned to land the I Corps in the Miyazaki area, while he sent the XI Corps at Ariake Wan. He also wanted VMAC to assault the west coast near Kushikino. Once his Sixth Army established a beachhead, Krueger ordered his forces to immediately block Japanese units in the north from reinforcing the south along the east and west coasts. In addition, Krueger's final plan called for the three corps to begin construction of air and naval facilities as early as possible. Krueger allocated the IX Corps, with the 98th Infantry Division, as the Sixth Army's floating reserve. During this first phase, his plan emphasized the need to "attack vigorously to destroy hostile forces encountered" and to be "prepared to advance aggressively from the corps beachhead."[76]

In Phase two, Krueger's troops were to execute coordinated attacks to seize additional territory for more airfields. The Sixth Army would then destroy the remaining forces in southern Kyūshū in phase three. After these three stages were completed, I Corps, IX Corps, XI Corps, and VMAC were to be prepared to conduct further offensive operations.[77]

Postwar assessments by the army determined that like the army's experiences on Leyte and Luzon, the most difficult part of Operation OLYMPIC would have been moving inland after the amphibious phase of the operation. The most potent defenses faced by I and XI Corps would come from the high ground behind the beaches, where the Japanese had prepared fixed positions.[78]

In the objective area targeted by VMAC, the terrain favored the defenders. A ridge ran parallel to the beach, offering high ground from which the Japanese could rain down considerable firepower upon the marines as they landed. If the marines overcame this initial line and made it to the ridge, they would have found a wide-open area of rice fields, backed by mountains providing another line of defense. The exits from the beaches were dominated by even more hills. The beaches, however, were weakly defended. The Japanese apparently did not expect an attack in this sector and had placed only two battalions along the beaches where the two marine divisions were to land. In short, the Japanese most likely would not have been able to stop the marine onslaught. Because they lacked mobility and their defenses were not mutually supporting because of the rough terrain, the Japanese most likely could have been defeated by the marines, who enjoyed aerial and firepower superiority.[79]

However the battle played out, the Americans would have faced a formidable and difficult task. Since the Japanese had in previous operations executed tactics that sought to defeat the enemy at the beaches as well as tactics that attempted to fight a decisive battle inland to no avail, they felt compelled to devise a new defensive system. In early June 1945, IGHQ published its new tactical manual, outlining how the armed forces would deal with the invasion. Forward units positioned near the beaches would fix the invaders in place while the more mobile formations in the interior would organize within ten days of the invasion and destroy the enemy in their beachhead positions. Exacerbating the situation was a poor road network, which Sixth Army G-2 estimated was "far poorer than it is on Luzon." Although Japan had shortages of raw materials, mobility, and ammunition, its army would have presented a fanatical and potent defense of its homeland.[80]

Assessment of how the battle for Kyūshū might have played out is difficult and involves counterfactual analysis. Nevertheless, some things are clear. The Japanese had the advantages of raw numbers. They planned to mobilize everyone on the island to fight another decisive battle, one that would push the number of American casualties to an unacceptable limit. Indeed, casualties would have been high. Joint Chiefs of Staff statistics, for example, forecasted that 25,741 American men would die on Kyūshū. Ultimately, OLYMPIC would have most likely played out like the campaigns for Leyte and Luzon. Krueger and his Sixth Army would have achieved their objectives, but the Japanese would have offered tenacious defense by utilizing the terrain to their advantage. In his thoughtful analysis of Operation DOWNFALL, Richard B. Frank argues that OLYMPIC's success would have boiled down to two issues: American firepower, and the determination of the American rifleman. These two attributes, as well as effective combined-arms coordination and superior generalship by Krueger, were in abundant supply.[81]

Of course, Krueger never executed OLYMPIC. A complex number of factors—including the two atomic bombs and Soviet entry into the war—pushed the Showa emperor Hirohito to accept surrender, and MacArthur ordered Krueger to execute his part of Operation BLACKLIST, the occupation of Japan, which had been in the planning stages since 2 August 1945. Using the Sixth, Eighth, and Tenth Armies, BLACKLIST had three overall objectives: occupy the most important governmental and military centers of Japan; establish control over the remaining "major political centers and avenues of sea communication"; and maintain those "areas for the establishment of control of food supply and of principal overland and coastwise communications."[82]

Krueger's zone of responsibility included Kyūshū, Shikoku, and western Honshū, an area that extended from the southwest of Japan to a north-south line about 8 miles west of Tokyo. This area had a population of approximately 40 million. After making sure that his three corps—the I and X Corps and VMAC—landed safely and took up their positions, Krueger supervised Japanese demobilization, instituted military government, recovered Allied prisoners of war, and made sure that the Japanese carried out the terms of surrender. The Sixth Army began landing on 23 September 1945 and moved into position by mid-October.[83]

While Krueger prepared for the occupation of Japan, Yamashita surrendered his forces to the newly established U.S. Army Forces, Western Pacific. This was a bittersweet event for Krueger, who later explained, "Since Sixth Army had defeated General Yamashita and his forces on Luzon, it was naturally a matter of keen regret to me to be absent from that ceremony."[84]

Krueger set sail for Japan from Luzon on 14 September. After visiting Sergio Osmeña, president of the Philippines, he set sail for Japan. He made a stop at Nagasaki, where he viewed the results of the recent atomic raid and noted that "the ghastly destruction caused in Nagasaki only six weeks before by the atomic bomb made an indelible impression upon me and every member of my party." But he was equally affected by the devastation caused by conventional and fire-bomb attacks on many other Japanese cities, such as Wakayama, which, he noted, was "thoroughly destroyed."[85]

The results of the U.S. bombing campaign led Krueger to believe that the atom bombs did not bring the war to an end. "No doubt the impression has been widely created that the Jap capitulation was brought about largely by the atomic bombs which were dropped on Hiroshima and Nagasaki," he explained to a friend. "However, I do not share that belief, since the destruction caused by ordinary bombs, in particular by napalm bombs (fire bombs) was so staggering that the Japs would probably have surrendered anyway."[86]

After visiting the bombed-out cities, Krueger finally reached his destination, Kyoto, a city with approximately 1.4 million inhabitants. He took up residence in the Miyako Hotel in Kyoto and made the Daiken Building the site of Sixth Army headquarters. A short time thereafter, Krueger assumed command of his three corps.[87]

Of all of his missions, one of the most important was enforcing the surrender terms. To this end, Krueger spent much of his time traveling throughout his zone via his B-17, *Billy*, and his train, the *Alamo Limited*. "These inspections kept us in close touch with the living conditions, health and state of morale of the troops, and enabled us to check construction work and the progress made in carrying out SCAP [Supreme Commander, Allied Powers]," he explained.[88]

Another vital task confronting Krueger was inactivating his Sixth Army, which on 31 December 1945 was relieved of its duties by the Eighth Army. Over the next month, Krueger devoted most of his time to all the paperwork associated with deactivation as well as preparing his trip home to San Antonio, Texas. The day before the Sixth Army was deactivated on 25 January 1946 and the day before boarding his train to start the long journey home, Krueger addressed the troops assembled to bid him farewell. He told them,

> My association with you will always be the most precious recollection of my military career. I am proud indeed to have been one of you. I part with you with deep regret and with profound gratitude for your loyal devotion to duty and faithful service and bid you farewell with real affection. I am confident that you who remain will continue to perform your tasks with the same high sense of duty and efficiency as in the past, in order that our comrades who made the supreme sacrifice will not have died in vain. And now goodbye and God bless you one and all.[89]

On the long trip home, a journey that would take more than two weeks, Krueger no doubt reflected on the momentous events in which he had participated over the past three years. He took pride in his achievements as well as those of the great number of men who served with him. But he was also excited to see his family and looked forward to retirement, taking pride not only in his accomplishments but also those of his two sons, James and Walter, and his son-in-law, Aubrey D. Smith, all of whom served in the army. The sun had finally set on an excellent military career.

The campaigns of Leyte and Luzon gave Krueger his closest opportunity to executing the operational doctrines that he had forged in 1941. Although neither island provided the wide-open expanses of land that the southern United States or even western Europe offered, their terrain allowed him to utilize at least some of the tactics he had learned in 1941. He fashioned, for instance, a combined-arms force that overwhelmed the Japanese defenders. Although often outnumbered, short on equipment, and often fighting exhausted and fatigued without hope of personnel replacements, the Sixth Army utilized the two advantages it did possess: mobility and firepower generated through the coordination of all branches of the army and all services of the U.S. armed forces. He also used these strengths where they would have the greatest impact. Krueger continually sought to outflank and outmaneuver his opponent whenever possible, as embodied by the 77th Infantry Division's amphibious assault on the west coast of Leyte.

Krueger, however, demonstrated that he was not willing to sacrifice his army for unwarranted objectives. He resisted, for example, MacArthur's desire for a quick drive on Manila so that the capital would be liberated by his birthday. Krueger's tenacity perhaps saved his army and MacArthur's offensive from an attack from Yamashita's army that included the services of an armored division. Krueger's unwillingness to plan for the battle for Manila and the high rate of illness throughout his army marred an otherwise first-rate campaign. Despite these blemishes, Krueger demonstrated in the final phase of World War II that he could apply proven principles of warfare to difficult and less-than-ideal conditions.

Part III

The Postwar Years: 1946–1967

Chapter 10

Retirement and Tragedy, 1946–1967

The end of Gen. Walter Krueger's long military career coincided with the beginning of a dangerous new era, the Cold War. As the nation and its armed forces geared up to fight international and domestic communism, Krueger looked forward to being a civilian for the first time in forty-six years. Even though he was glad to return to his wife, he was not at all happy to leave the military.[1] He told the Sixth Army engineer, Brig. Gen. Samuel D. Sturgis Jr.,

> It will be quite a jolt for me to leave the active list after so many years of active service. But I shall take it philosophically, for I believe that old timers like myself should make way for younger men. After all, I shall have the satisfaction of looking back upon many varied and interesting experiences and last but not least upon my association with you and the other top flight members of the Sixth Army Staff, whose loyal, devoted and outstanding services and friendship I shall always cherish.[2]

Although Krueger was willing to accept retirement "philosophically" as he had all unwelcome events, he was not going to simply fade away. Instead, he believed that the postwar years would allow him "to cogitate about the future" and perhaps contribute to shaping the nuclear-age army through lecturing on his experiences in World War II and his views concerning the shape of future warfare.[3]

Unfortunately, Krueger would have little time to spend on such endeavors. Within several short years, he would experience a series of tragedies that had him wishing he could trade all of his career accomplishments for a better personal life.

Adjusting to Retirement

After returning to the United States in February 1946, Walter and Grace Krueger decided to call Texas their home. While the two had moved all over the country throughout his career, Texas had served as their home base during the important years that he commanded the 2d Infantry Division, VIII Corps, and the Third U.S. Army. In fact, Grace had stayed in the San Antonio area (the site of Third Army headquarters) after Walter left for the Southwest Pacific Area.

The Kruegers bought a stone bungalow at 112 Ridgemont Avenue in San Antonio and occupied it on 29 June 1946. The couple was naturally excited about their purchase, in part because it was the first home that they had ever owned. The house, as Krueger described to a friend, had a large yard, "much fine shrubbery and large trees and an excellent lawn sprinkler system." Inside, Krueger spent much of his time in his study. It was there that he displayed some of his most prized possessions: his books and the pictures of aides, friends, and senior officers of the Sixth Army and SWPA. He wanted these photographs as a constant reminder of all the "fine associations" he had made during the war. He no doubt took great pride in the accomplishments of his former staff. By 1946, several members of the Sixth Army had already earned important positions in the military. Brig. Gen. Clyde D. Eddleman, his old operations officer, was at the time the commandant of the Armed Forces Staff College and eventually became assistant chief of staff for operations in 1952. Krueger's former chief of staff, Maj. Gen. George H. Decker, was eventually promoted to general and in 1959 became the chief of staff.[4]

Unfortunately, the enjoyment of the Kruegers' new home was soon plagued by financial difficulties. When he arrived home, Walter Krueger faced a large income tax bill that included all of what he owed from the war years. Consequently, he and Grace could not afford to purchase their house alone. Some sympathetic friends organized the Krueger Fund Committee, which paid for a large portion of the house. The Kruegers then had to watch their remaining money carefully. Walter even had to refuse an invitation to visit Sturgis, writing him that "I still have a large income tax to pay and that hangs like a veritable sword of Damocles over my head. Moreover, the cost of our new home has just about strapped me. However, we manage."[5]

Krueger's house was not the only thing that occupied his time during the first few years after the war. He first had to deal with the many lingering issues of his Sixth Army, particularly ensuring that certain individuals and units received the proper citations. Furthermore, he participated in many civic organizations, serving as the regional chairman of Southern Texas for the United Service Organization Drive, chairman of the Red Cross Drive, the director of Civil Defense of San Antonio and Bexar County, and cochairman for Texas of the National Foundation for Infantile Paralysis.[6]

His efforts were hampered by—for the first time in many years—a lack of a staff. He therefore had to do all of the burdensome paperwork himself, a task he did not at all enjoy. "No one seems to recall that I am definitely retired and have neither the staff, yea not even a typist nor stenographer, and that, to make matters worse, my one-finger system of typing is neither speedy nor accurate," he explained to a friend. "Quite often, I fail to put the carbon paper in properly and in consequence my reply is recorded on the back of the original and not on the carbon paper. As a result, Mrs. Krueger claims that my language is getting much worse—and no doubt she is right."[7]

The problems he had operating a typewriter did not prevent him, however, from making his own contribution to the growing number of books by high-level participants of World War II in the late 1940s and early 1950s. Shortly after Krueger returned to Texas, the former Sixth Army intelligence officer, Col. Horton V. White, contacted him on behalf of George Brett, the president of the Macmillan Company. Brett was interested in publishing a biography of the Sixth Army commander's exploits and had White approach Krueger with the idea.[8]

While stating that he would not stand in the way of a biography, Krueger responded by explaining that he had many problems with the prospect of a biography or autobiography. Not only was he a private individual who was loath to expose his personal life to the public, but he also was aware of the dangers of how an autobiography would be perceived: "I can only say that I am favorably disposed, but shy at publishing an autobiography. An autobiography is invariably apt to be an apologia, and I do not feel like writing one." He did offer an alternative. "However, I may turn to and write up some of the interesting operations of the Sixth Army."[9]

Macmillan ostensibly was not interested in Krueger's proposal for an operational history of the Sixth Army, and he eventually was enticed by the North American Newspaper Alliance to write a series of articles. But Krueger still insisted on writing about the Sixth Army and not himself: "I am being prodded to write up my war experiences. ... I am loath to do so and have so far side-stepped [the issue]," he explained in June 1947.[10]

Friends and publishers, it appears, were attempting to persuade Krueger to tell a behind-the-scenes book of war in SWPA. Specifically, they were trying to lure him with the bait of Adm. William F. Halsey's deal to write an autobiography. According to published reports, Halsey had received an advance payment of $75,000 from his publisher, but Krueger was unpersuaded and his mind was made up. Halsey's book, Krueger explained, "is of course an autobiography and that's something that I would not care to let myself in for, since I hate to undress in public." He was set to write the story, not of himself, but of the Sixth Army and all the men who fought and died in the islands of SWPA.

"I felt that I owed this," he wrote in the foreword to the completed book, "to all who served under me there—in particular to the many thousands who laid down their lives."[11]

In the summer of 1947, then, Krueger plunged into writing what eventually became *From Down Under to Nippon: The Story of Sixth Army in World War II*. The book relied heavily on Sixth Army after-action reports, and in many respects it suffered because of this dependence. The wartime reports, just like the book, described *what* happened but often did not tell *why* events occurred as they did. In the heat of battle, Krueger naturally did not bother to remember the intricate forces behind the scene that shaped strategy and operations. "I now regret," Krueger wrote to his former aide-de-camp, H. Ben Decherd, "that I did not keep a diary of some kind; the so-called Journal that you and other aides kept is not much help since it merely covers engagements, visitors, and so on and does not describe conversations, agreements and controversies. Of course, this shortcoming is my own fault, because I had directed that a real diary should not be kept."[12]

Krueger found the writing process to be difficult. He explained to Eddleman,

> My difficulty is not entirely lack of material, but its superfluity, so that it is difficult at times to know what to leave out. Another, very great problem is how to manage to omit as far as possible the eternal personal pronoun. On the one hand, it's [*sic*] omission looks like an attempt to shirk responsibility; on the other hand, it savors of self-glorification. However, I manage somehow or other to steer around this fairly satisfactorily.[13]

Writing dragged on for more than five years and was hindered by his own and his wife's poor health. In one instance, Grace's illness delayed the manuscript's completion by six months. Near the end, Krueger regretted even starting the project. "Every day I plug away at my book, but progress is slow," he wrote in January 1949. "I often wish that I had never undertaken the task."[14]

Krueger's decision to write a chronicle of the Sixth Army instead of his own impressions of the war proved to be unfortunate choice, as it provides little of his role in the making of crucial decisions. As one of the army's official historians states, *From Down Under to Nippon* is a "most disappointing volume since it is little more than a paraphrase of the Sixth Army's wartime after action reports."[15]

Others did not like the volume either, but for different reasons. Robert L. Eichelberger, who retired in 1949, believed it painted an inaccurate picture of events in SWPA. *From Down Under to Nippon* brought back a flood of bad memories and rekindled his bad feelings toward not only Krueger but Gen.

of the Army Douglas MacArthur as well. "About all Walter could tell, if he keeps to the truth," Eichelberger remarked, "is what the maps looked like as he stuck pins in them."[16]

With the free time that comes with retirement, Eichelberger's feelings toward Krueger and MacArthur had turned toward hatred. In fact, he wished only the worst for Krueger in his old age and pledged never to speak with him again. He kept his word. Eichelberger never talked to Krueger or Richard K. Sutherland, MacArthur's old chief of staff, and rarely had any dealings with MacArthur. Near the end, Eichelberger even planned a "tell-all" book that would expose MacArthur and Krueger. An important commander in World War II, Eichelberger died in 1961, a bitter, resentful man filled with hate toward many of the officers with whom he served.[17]

Krueger, in comparison, did not have such feelings for his colleagues. Just as he had during World War II, he remained largely above the petty personal squabbles. Even though he and MacArthur had exchanged heated words on Luzon, for instance, Krueger held no animosity toward his former taskmaster. In fact, when asked by Gen. Albert C. Wedemeyer (Ret.) to support Robert A. Taft's 1952 campaign for the presidency, Krueger replied, "I appreciate your invitation to have me join your Military Committee for Taft, but regret that I can not accept, as I am for MacArthur." Whenever he could, he made the annual trip to New York to celebrate MacArthur's birthday with many of the men who had served in the Pacific.[18]

Krueger also did not have any ill feelings toward Eichelberger. To be sure, he never felt close to the former Eighth Army commander, but, as Walter Krueger Jr. remembered, Krueger never said "anything critical of Eichelberger."[19]

Despite the book, the reunion with Grace, and his new home, Krueger was soon restless with civilian life. Surely it must have been frustrating for him to be literally shaping the course of history one moment and then having little responsibility the next. "We love San Antonio and our home and I am kept rather busy with matters pertaining to my old command, the Sixth Army, and with diverse civic affairs," he explained to his old friend Fay W. Brabson. "But I sometimes wish that my experience could be utilized in an executive capacity in connection with the training of our young men, a field of usefulness that strongly appeals to me."[20]

The Public Krueger

Regrettably, he received no such opportunity. However, he did the next best thing by giving many lectures at the various army schools and to many civic organizations. Throughout these lectures, Krueger advanced several themes, which he hoped would provide the United States an army for the nuclear age based on the proven concepts he had been advocating throughout his professional life. The first issue was one that he had been concerned with almost since the beginning of his military career: national preparedness. He first made his views known about the issue, it will be recalled, in 1917, with the publication of his article entitled "Preparedness." Basing the American military system on "military amateurs," he argued, harmed rather than helped the national defense. Instead, he urged the nation to adopt a system of universal military training that would continually supply a well-trained manpower reserve. His views changed, however, in favor of the American system with the passage of the National Defense Acts of 1916 and 1920, which featured federal supervision of the National Guard (see Chapters 2 and 3).

His views evolved again after being in the front lines of training the U.S. Army for combat in World War II. He came to believe that the two National Defense Acts had done little to prepare the nation for modern war. The National Guard divisions he had trained and supervised from 1941 to the end of 1942 were in shambles and even needed instruction in the basic art of soldiering. This led him to be an outspoken critic of the Guardsmen; in fact, Krueger wrote to the War Department during the war requesting that he receive no National Guard divisions.[21]

Fortunately, the United States, through a unique combination of circumstances, was able to rebound and fight successfully. Krueger told an audience at Trinity University in San Antonio:

> The outbreak of every war in which our country has been engaged found us woefully lacking in militarily trained manpower. During my own forty-eight years' service in the Army, I had ample opportunity to know this from personal observation. … In both World Wars, we were fortunate again, since the time we needed to prepare for the conflicts, in particular that required to enable us to remedy our shortcomings in the matter of trained manpower, was bought by the valiant efforts and blood of our Allies.[22]

But the atomic age, he believed, had changed the dynamics of warfare dramatically by making it more technologically based and giving the enemies of the United States the ability to project their power more easily. The United States therefore could no longer assume that the navy and air force alone could protect the nation's interests. He claimed, "While in the past we have thus been fortunate, it would be dangerous, indeed, to assume that we shall be equally lucky in the future. Oceans no longer constitute barriers to assault under the conditions created by present day three-dimensional warfare, and time, which has always been a potent factor in war, is at present more vitally important than ever before."[23]

To prepare properly for this new environment, Krueger once again stressed the necessity of universal military training. The best way to train an army for the nuclear age, he argued, is through "universal military training, not after an emergency occurs, but *before we have to face it*" (Krueger's emphasis).[24] Service along these lines would not only ensure a strong nation but build strong character in the young men who received the training. He argued:

> Universal Military Training is a fair and democratic system that falls equally on all our people. To ask a young American to give a year of his time to permit his being trained to be able effectively to do his share in defending his country is not asking too much. It would benefit him personally, would enormously increase our defensive readiness, and would eradicate many shortcomings that developed in our Armed Forces during the last war and in previous wars.[25]

The second theme Krueger developed also had long been an important issue to him: unity of command. He believed that the National Security Act of 1947 was a positive first step in this direction but did not go far enough. It unified the armed forces by establishing the Department of Defense and the Joint Chiefs of Staff but kept separate the agencies that formed national policy (the National Security Council), allocated national resources (the National Security Resources Board), and executed national policy (Department of Defense). He believed that the three organizations needed to be unified to operate effectively.[26]

Similarly, while the National Security Act of 1947 and the National Security Act Amendments of 1949 unified the armed forces at the highest levels through the Joint Chief of Staff, they did not assure such unity at the operational level. Krueger admitted that cooperation existed during World War II, but it could not be taken for granted: "We can not safely afford to depend upon the voluntary efforts of the three services to assure such teamwork, since in a future conflict the stakes will be far too high and the time available far too short to run the risk of delay and failure."[27]

Krueger was such an advocate of unity of command and universal military training because, in his view, they were essential for combined-arms operations. Both were necessary to build the teamwork between the various branches of the army and the three services. In 1947 Krueger told an audience, "The wonderful fighting teams that vanquished our enemies in the late war, were developed by intensive training that extended over a period of over a year, before they entered combat." A few years later, he lamented their quick dismemberment following World War II and pointed to their absence as a cause of the Korean War. "If we had retained a sizeable part of the magnificent fighting team which we had at the close of World War II, we would have had no difficulty in dealing with the Korean situation," he reasoned. "In fact, that situation would probably never have arisen, since no one would have dared challenged us directly or indirectly."[28]

Equally as important in combined-arms warfare was unity of command. "To make our National Defense effective," Krueger advised, "we must be prepared to wage war offensively from the start in order to carry it to the enemy. ... But, in order to be effective, such an offensive must be launched and conducted by a highly skilled ground-naval-air team under one commander."[29]

Krueger also carefully watched the post–World War II deliberations concerning the organization of the new infantry division. While it was obvious to most involved that the triangular division lacked sufficient combat power, there was considerable debate concerning the size of the proposed division. Krueger feared that sentiment would swing toward making the formation too large, which would then curtail mobility. Krueger wrote to the commanding general of the Infantry School, Maj. Gen. John D. O'Daniel:

> As I am a strong advocate of flexibility and mobility, I am somewhat disappointed that these two factors did not carry as much weight as size in the division organization recommended and that, in consequence, we shall probably have a rather large instead of a medium sized division. However, the division organization recommended gives us a good division, though in my opinion, it is not as well adapted as a smaller, more mobile division would be to great amphibious operations, such as are likely to be needed in a future war.[30]

Instead of fielding a division that "is practically self-sustaining—in a word, a small field army," Krueger suggested that the U.S. Army employ a division that could adapt to any circumstances. "Any foreseeable war, whether it be large or small and whether or not it involve[s] the use of nuclear weapons," he believed, "will require ground forces of maximum flexibility and mobility, in my opinion."[31]

Family Tragedies

Despite his passion for the future of the military, Krueger's attention increasingly focused on personal and family issues. Even before he returned from Japan, Krueger had been notified of Grace's poor health. She suffered from many ailments, including high blood pressure and coronary artery disease. These conditions led to periodic and symptomatic illnesses. She had, for instance, a hemorrhage in her left eye, for which she was hospitalized for one month.[32]

No sooner had Grace recovered from her eye hemorrhage than the Kruegers heard that the military career of their oldest son, James, prematurely came to an end. In the early spring of 1947, Jimmie, as he was called, was dismissed from the army for behavior unbecoming an officer (stemming from an incident of drunkenness). Although his military career was over, he soon landed on his feet and eventually became an engineer at Aero Corporation.[33]

As difficult as Jimmie's dismissal was, it was only the beginning of bad news for Krueger. His personal life was shattered on 3 October 1952, when Walter and Grace's daughter, Dorothy, killed her husband. Col. Aubrey D. Smith's job as the chief of the U.S. Army's Far East Command's plans and operations supply section had taken him and his family to Tokyo. Ostensibly, Dorothy had been suffering from mental illness and displayed signs of an impending breakdown. On 2 October 1952 a neighbor took Dorothy to the army dispensary. "She seemed upset," Mrs. Joseph Hardin later testified. "She said she felt like killing herself but didn't know how to do it." The next day, according to Shigeko Tani, the Smiths' maid and main prosecution witness, Dorothy stabbed her husband in the chest with a ten-inch hunting knife. Aubrey was taken to the hospital and died the next day.[34]

Army officials in Japan decided to try her before a court martial, which ruled in favor of prosecution psychiatrists. They argued that she suffered from a type of psychopathic state that should be considered a character disorder rather than a mental one. Maj. Gen. Joseph Sullivan read the decision of the court and, according to the reporter for the *New York Times*, "in a voice quivering with emotion and barely audible in the bleak Army barrack courtroom," pronounced Dorothy Krueger Smith guilty and sentenced her to life imprisonment with hard labor.[35]

Naturally, Walter and Grace were devastated by the news, a situation complicated by Grace's failing health and the fact that the two now apparently had to take care of Dorothy's two children. In the late 1940s, the emotional strain and general poor health started to take their toll not only on Grace but Walter as well. Beginning in 1948, Grace was plagued with pains that radiated throughout her chest and arms. The high blood pressure, furthermore, did not allow sufficient blood flow to her internal organs, producing continual nausea. "I've been under a terrific strain ever since last October," Krueger explained to Brabson. "Dorothy's situation has involved us in endless correspondence and, besides, Grace has been severely ill and I am getting discouraged about her recovery. Fortunately, I'm bearing up somehow under it all, but feel that I am not far from reaching the end of my rope." Walter doubted that his wife—described by him as "literally crushed" by her daughter's actions—would ever fully recover.[36]

She never did. In late 1955, doctors discovered she had developed cancer. Walter wrote to George H. Decker in early 1956, "The doctors are doing everything they can for her and she is constantly attended by a special nurse, but there is little hope for her recovery as an operation is impossible because of her heart condition and arteriosclerosis. She is in constant pain, but bears her suffering like a brave soldier." Within months her condition worsened, and she died on Mother's Day, 13 May 1956.[37]

Grace's long-term illness and death, the murder of Aubrey Smith, and Jimmie's dismissal from the army finally took their toll on the retired general. "Walter Krueger has broken terribly," Brabson observed while at Grace's burial at Arlington National Cemetery. Krueger was "crying openly much of the time. Said he would join Grace soon. He is ... shaken with what he has to undergo."[38]

For the next two years, Krueger was in an obvious state of depression. In letters to friends, his handwriting was closer to unintelligible scrawl than script and betrayed a man who harbored great psychological and emotional pain. Without his wife, he sadly began to reminisce in these letters about happier times. One such message ended in a particularly fatalistic note: "As you can imagine, I miss my precious Grace every moment and am very lonely. However, it won't be very long, I suppose, until I can join her."[39]

Eventually, Krueger worked through his despondent state of mind and returned to lecturing and other activities, although on a limited basis. A source of joy came when the U.S. Supreme Court ruled on 10 June 1957 that the trial against Dorothy had been unconstitutional. In a 6-to-2 decision (with one justice absent), it found that a military court did not have jurisdiction over a civilian. The court's ruling freed Dorothy, who returned to Texas to live with her father.[40]

For a time, Dorothy seemed to be adjusting to her new life. She not only took care of her father but even enrolled in secretarial courses at a local business college. However, she soon was struggling with mental illness, and in August 1958 she had an emotional and nervous breakdown, which required a long stint in the psychiatric ward of John Seealy Hospital in Galveston, Texas. After her release, Dorothy took a job as a medical secretary. Krueger observed in 1961 that she "works hard and enjoys it."[41]

Although he took pride in the accomplishments of Jimmie's rebuilt career, Walter Jr.'s army career, and his many grandchildren and great grandchildren, as he grew older and the memories of World War II faded, Krueger increasingly felt unproductive as he made appearances at various ceremonies. He complained, "I totter about as usual, attend to my voluminous correspondence, appear as one of the potted plants at official civic and military functions and feel more or less useless with every passing day."[42]

In the late 1950s and early to mid-1960s, Krueger's own health started to fail. He developed glaucoma that restricted the vision in his right eye. Arthritis in his lower back became so painful that he could "scarcely stand it." Sciatica caused severe pain in his left hip that made it difficult for him to sit down for more than a few minutes at a time. He underwent a hernia operation in 1960 and kidney surgery in 1963.[43]

His failing health did not prevent him from traveling and visiting friends and family. In late 1960 he traveled to the Philippines with the American Battle Monuments Commission to dedicate a memorial to those Americans who died in the Pacific. In 1963 he attended MacArthur's birthday and a SWPA reunion in New York. But during a visit to Valley Forge, Pennsylvania, he succumbed to pneumonia due to generalized arteriosclerosis, on 20 August 1967.

Throughout his years of retirement, Walter Krueger persisted in telling anyone who would listen about issues close to his heart. Increasingly, however, he found such pursuits hollow as the walls of his personal life began to crumble. Although he had been instrumental in creating the U.S. Army's operational doctrine, was vital in training a large number of the men who fought in World War II, and labored as Gen. Douglas MacArthur's principal lieutenant in the war against Japan, Krueger considered his life unfulfilled and incomplete. When Fay W. Brabson complained that he had not been promoted before retirement, Krueger explained to him in 1960,

> I wish you would compare your situation with mine for a moment. You are fortunate in having a loving wife by your side and three wonderful children. I, on the other hand, have lost my precious wife, my son Jimmie's career ended in disgrace and my only daughter's tragic action broke my heart. All the promotions and honors that have come to me cannot possibly outweigh these heartaches and disappointments. If true happiness is the aim of life—and I believe it is—then you are more fortunate than I and I would gladly trade with you.[44]

Chapter 11

Conclusion

Although Walter Krueger may have considered his life a disappointment because of the tragedies in his final years, he played a significant and pivotal role in World War II. He coordinated a vast army-navy-air joint force that conducted twenty-one operations across 4,500 miles in the span of two years.[1] Having honed his skills while assisting the U.S. Army in developing its interwar doctrine, he became its operational leader—in the process translating Gen. Douglas MacArthur's strategy into reality.

Yet in the years since World War II's end, Krueger has been criticized as an overly cautious and methodical commander who impeded MacArthur's fast-paced strategy. This image has been based largely on the perceptions of two individuals rather than on what Krueger actually accomplished and provides an interesting case study on the way in which history is written.

MacArthur on several occasions criticized Krueger for leading his army too slowly and conservatively. Since he wanted to return to the Philippine Islands as soon as possible, MacArthur would accept nothing less than a rapid and uninterrupted crusade back to the islands that provided him with his sense of well-being. Frustrated by the fact that the offensive toward the Philippines was not proceeding as fast as he would have liked, MacArthur on several occasions in late 1944 and early 1945 reproached Krueger in a vain attempt to motivate the commander of the Sixth U.S. Army. MacArthur also used and exaggerated his criticism of Krueger to manipulate his other ground commander, Lt. Gen. Robert L. Eichelberger.

MacArthur knew that Eichelberger and Krueger did not particularly like one another, and he tried to use this animosity to his own advantage. He threatened Krueger with giving Eichelberger the lead in the Southwest Pacific Area, particularly when he set up a "race" to free Manila between Sixth and Eighth Army units. MacArthur also knew that Eichelberger wanted and needed praise, which Krueger's presence in SWPA threatened. To Eichelberger's face, MacArthur would make disparaging remarks concerning

Krueger and promise the Eighth Army commander promotions and prominent positions in future operations. Eichelberger carefully recorded these conversations with the SWPA chief and chronicled MacArthur's supposed displeasure with Krueger to his wife. With Krueger unwilling to tell his own story through his memoirs or an authorized biography, Eichelberger's letters, as well as his postwar dictations, eventually became the basis for the historical portrait of Krueger.

However, anyone utilizing Eichelberger's version of what MacArthur told him concerning Krueger must proceed with extreme caution. A more accurate picture of MacArthur's views of Krueger and Eichelberger can be derived from examining his actions, not his words. While he disapproved of Krueger's delay near Carigara Bay on Leyte, MacArthur wanted the Sixth Army, not the Eighth, to lead the invasion of Luzon. Even though MacArthur grew impatient with the drive toward Manila, he chose Krueger for promotion to full general and selected him, not Eichelberger, to lead the invasion of Japan. Despite what MacArthur may have told Eichelberger, and despite what many historians have assumed, MacArthur still had the utmost confidence in Krueger. In light of these actions, one therefore must reassess Krueger's contributions as well as his motivations.

If intense personal and psychological factors drove MacArthur and Eichelberger during the war (a desire for a rapid return to the Philippines and a desire for approval and praise, respectively), what drove and inspired Krueger? The question, important as it is, is a difficult one to answer. Krueger protected his private side, and even his son Walter Jr. failed to comprehend this aspect of his father fully.[2] Of the many characteristics he exhibited throughout his life, an intense determination to succeed was one of the most prominent. Everything he had achieved in life came through hard work and tenacity. "He had the strongest character of any man I ever knew," Walter Krueger Jr. observed while reflecting on his father's personality. "His integrity, loyalty, and iron will were fundamental."[3] Krueger applied these same principles to his efforts in World War II. He was not driven by publicity, recognition, or the acceptance of his superiors but instead focused his considerable energy and talents to succeed in his profession. In this sense, his motivations are akin to what sociologist Morris Janowitz has termed the "missionary zeal of the military profession":

> While for many persons, and perhaps even a majority, the military career represented the pursuit of a relatively secure, safe, and promising prospect, more or less similar to other professionals, for a substantial minority, at least, the choice of a military career was a strong decision. To speak of

> strong career choice means that a person feels that a particular occupation is singularly important to him, since he believes that it will give him the rewards and gratification he wants.
>
> For such persons, the military career had overtones of a "calling," with a sense of mission. It represented a deliberate rejection of what was believed to be the prosaic and limited horizons of the business world.[4]

Krueger most likely considered the military not merely a career but rather a calling. His first choice was to join the most aristocratic of American services—the navy—but he was prevented from pursuing his dream by his mother. Instead, the Spanish-American War and the Philippine Insurrection provided him the opportunity to experience life in the army. After a few years, he knew that this was the life for him and threw himself into it. The profession of arms became not only his career but occupied much of his free time as well, evolving into, in fact, almost a hobby.[5] This is not to suggest that Eichelberger and MacArthur did not possess this missionary zeal, but rather to submit that it seems to have been particularly strong and perhaps the sole motivating factor in Walter Krueger. Colleagues and comrades alike took note of his ambitions, which, combined with his work ethic—and his aggressive, forceful, and defensive personality—won him few friends.

His personal motivation, powerful as it was, led to directly to the first component of his philosophy of command: thorough preparation. No doubt a result of the aforementioned missionary zeal, Krueger studied the art of war passionately. He was not, however, a military intellectual, an individual who engaged in the world of ideas creatively not only for practical purposes but for the sake of the ideas themselves. Krueger was not a creative and original thinker. Rather, he kept up to date with current military thought and at times expanded on it. In the main, he was a conventional thinker when it came to such matters as military history, military theory, and national policy.

A second component of his philosophy of command concerned the particular characteristics of a great captain. These attributes included being the guiding spirit and force of one's unit, remaining cool in the face of danger and great responsibility, and possessing the ability to be flexible. There was little doubt among those in Krueger's Sixth Army staff who commanded the formation: Krueger clearly was the dominating figure. Furthermore, he cherished flexibility almost too much. He disliked, for instance, any war plan against Japan that provided the president with only one option, that of a naval thrust through the Central Pacific. He even refused to develop a plan for the assault on Manila. For Krueger, command was more of an art than a science that required not only thorough preparation but flexibility in execution.

The third part of Krueger's philosophy of command consisted of how a commander should exercise command itself. Here, Krueger remained consistent throughout his career. From his earliest writing on the matter, he continually emphasized both unity of command and a decentralized command arrangement. After receiving the authority to command (and not coordinate) the forces allotted to him to accomplish the mission, he must accept input from subordinates and allow them the latitude to execute orders. In practical terms, this meant that once the commander had issued the orders, he should step back and allow his subordinates to execute these orders without undue interference from above. During his time as commander of the Sixth Army, Krueger consistently adhered to this form of command.

A fourth component of his philosophy of command was his devotion to the welfare of his soldiers, an attitude that had developed during his years as an enlisted man in Cuba and the Philippines around the turn of the century. He experienced firsthand the neglect of the army that occupied Cuba and fought insurgents on Luzon. From the day he became an officer, Krueger committed himself to provide the best care he could for the men under him. In return, his soldiers gave him their loyalty and respect and, more important, fought hard for him.

A fifth element of Krueger's philosophy of command was his approach to the art of warfare itself, embodied in the tactical and operational doctrines he helped to develop. With the publication of his translation of Wilhelm Balck's *Tactics* and his work at Fort Leavenworth, Kansas, he helped to steer the U.S. Army toward extended order tactics to break the dominance of the defense on the modern battlefield. He understood in the early years of the twentieth century, when many did not, that warfare was in a state of change, necessitating flexible and extended-order tactics. Ultimately, Krueger both advocated aggressive offensive action and valued the heart of operational art—balance and prudence in creating a military strategy that attains national goals.

This last component of his conception of command translated directly to the development of U.S. Army operational doctrine. Unlike his contributions to national policy and military strategy, Krueger's contribution here was original and innovative considering the context. In the fall of 1941, he and his Third U.S. Army produced a de facto operational doctrine, the premise of which was aggressive offensive operations that used envelopments and breakthroughs to strike far into the enemy's rear. At the heart of the offensive doctrine were combined-arms teams, composed of all branches of the army and, if possible, all three services.

Upon his arrival in SWPA, Krueger organized his new army into combined-arms teams to execute the operational doctrine he had developed in

1941. If the situation permitted, he broke his forces into at least two groups: one to hold the enemy's main body, and another to break through the defensive line or preferably to maneuver around it. For an amphibious assault, he needed an additional task force to protect the beachhead. The objective was then to strike at the enemy force and wreck his ability to wage war. Krueger would not participate in an action that violated any tenet of U.S. military doctrine. Partly for this reason, he astutely declined to make his dash to Manila immediately after landing on Luzon, since his army lacked the adequate forces for the requisite three task forces of an amphibious assault force: one to fix the Japanese on his left and right flanks, one to act as the breakthrough force, and a third to protect the beachhead. Had Krueger followed MacArthur's directive, Gen. Tomoyuki Yamashita would have had the opportunity to attack the left flank of the Sixth Army.[6]

In most of the battles throughout the Southwest Pacific, however, Krueger faced many mitigating circumstances that prevented him from applying this doctrine exactly as he had practiced it in Louisiana. The first, and probably the most important, was the pressure MacArthur placed on Krueger and his army to conduct one operation after another, sometimes even ordering up to five simultaneous battles. This placed enormous strain on Krueger's ability to command, control, and communicate with his scattered forces. During the particularly hectic summer months of 1944, for example, Krueger had troops distributed across 1,400 miles from the New Guinea mainland and its surrounding islands to New Britain and the Admiralties. His army was engaged at Hollandia, Aitape, Wakde-Sarmi, and Biak and was preparing for further operations on Noemfoor. Placed in this situation by MacArthur, Krueger gave high priority to the security of his far-flung army. When he was presented with evidence that Japanese forces were preparing an attack in the Wakde-Sarmi region, Krueger launched a preemptive strike against what turned out to be heavier-than-expected resistance. Although Krueger has been criticized for his actions, MacArthur's fast-paced strategy often forced him—not to be methodical or cautious—but rather to take risks, not only at Wakde-Sarmi but at Aitape as well, lest his army be attacked far in the rear, some 400 miles behind his forward units. The difficulties were also acute for other commanders, including the commander of the VII Amphibious Force, Vice Adm. Daniel E. Barbey. Throughout several periods during Operation CARTWHEEL and the New Guinea campaign, his ships were in almost constant duty, taxing both men and equipment.

Multiple operations like those conducted in SWPA would have been difficult under the best of circumstances, but as it turned out, they were complicated by a shortage of manpower, equipment, and ammunition. During the fight for Luzon, Krueger and his men had to overcome deficiencies in 155mm howitzer and 81mm mortar ammunition, motor vehicles, and bridging equipment. Furthermore, the personnel replacement system effectively and inadvertently kept many formations and units understrength. Those sent into combat quickly became exhausted, especially since the basic building block of an army—the division—was not sufficient in terms of firepower to make up for the lack of riflemen. In fact, Krueger, as he knew all too well, had to reinforce the infantry division to make it capable of sustained offensive action.

Besides the time factor, a lack of supplies, manpower shortages, and a dearth of organic firepower at the division level, Krueger had to deal with the complex world of gathering, interpreting, and utilizing intelligence. Although the Allies had access to intercepted and decrypted messages (ULTRA), this intelligence did not provide a clear-cut blueprint for military action. Individuals still had to collate the information gained from a variety of different sources, analyze, interpret, and then make use of this information. Consequently, GHQ SWPA and Sixth Army headquarters in many instances came to different conclusions. One of the first and most dramatic examples was in the case of the Admiralty Islands. MacArthur disregarded ULTRA intelligence in favor of aerial reconnaissance, which conveniently gave him the evidence he wanted to try to capture the islands ahead of schedule. Because of such incidents, over time Krueger became extremely skeptical of intelligence estimates from GHQ SWPA, because it became clear that the SWPA commander used whatever intelligence sources supported his own preconceived ideas.[7] Without consistently reliable appraisals of enemy strength from higher echelons, Krueger either had to use GHQ SWPA intelligence with great care or rely on his own. When MacArthur told of clear sailing through Leyte, Krueger had strong reasons to guard his flanks. When GHQ SWPA insisted that Yamashita would not oppose a march into Manila, Krueger wisely determined that his army was vulnerable and that the enemy had the capacity for executing a counterattack. In short, Krueger learned the hard way that he could not accept at face value the intelligence he received from GHQ SWPA, because all such data was filtered through MacArthur's well-known desire to liberate the Philippines quickly.

Ultimately, Krueger's willingness to question and stand up to MacArthur points to one of the Sixth Army commander's strongest attributes. In many circumstances, Krueger acted as a counterweight to MacArthur. Because he knew all too well that speed motivated MacArthur's strategy—often over other considerations—Krueger had to accept with skepticism not only the intelligence from GHQ SWPA but the pressure he received from MacArthur and his staff to keep Sixth Army offensives moving at a brisk tempo. Speed, to be sure, had an important role to play, and Krueger knew it. There were, for instance, legitimate reasons to bring operations to a close at Wakde-Sarmi and Biak. At the former, Krueger needed to complete the campaign to secure the area as a base for further operations, while during the latter speed was necessary to support the navy's Central Pacific drive. Nevertheless, there were times when speed was not a legitimate basis on which to conduct military operations, such as the early phase of the Manila offensive. Arriving in the capital for the SWPA commander's birthday was simply not a good reason to expose one of his corps to possible destruction. Krueger proved to be an expert at weighing MacArthur's strategy with tactical reality. Alluding to Krueger's flexibility, Gordon Walker, who wrote an article for the *Christian Science Monitor* weekly magazine section in mid-1945, stated, "He [Krueger] can either gamble on an operation or hold back his forces with a conservatism which is justified only in the final analysis." George H. Decker—Krueger's chief of staff of Sixth Army—noted a special symbiotic relationship between MacArthur and Krueger, one that MacArthur himself relied on when conducting his military campaigns:

> By the time of Leyte, MacArthur's pattern of intervention in Krueger's exercise of command [was] clear. MacArthur made his presence known at the beginning of an operation by setting clear restrictions on forces involved in an operation, the objectives, and the followed operations. These were restrictive enough, and the time-line of MacArthur's strategy was the most problematic issue that Krueger faced. Along with his own natural inclinations, the schedule forced Krueger to be aggressive, to make sure one operation was finished before the next one began. Above and beyond this, MacArthur never intervened to any great extent. To be sure, MacArthur tried to pressure Krueger (Biak, Leyte, Luzon), but the record demonstrates that MacArthur never threatened Krueger with dismissal. In fact, the pattern suggests that MacArthur trusted Krueger's operational and tactical judgments, if not deferred to them.

In addition, Decker later observed that

> They [MacArthur and Krueger] complimented each other real well. MacArthur was primarily the strategist and a fine one. General Krueger was, although a fine strategist also, more knowledgeable in the tactical field, I think.... I sometimes feel that our situation in Korea would have been a bit different had General Krueger been the ground force commander. I think General MacArthur pressed his commanders to go north to the Yalu, and

> they tried to go without too much concern for the tactical situation that they faced. I don't think General Krueger would have ever put himself in the position that the Eighth Army got into in Korea. He was a master tactician.[8]

The study of Krueger's role in World War II confirms the existence of the so-called schoolhouse of war. According to Michael D. Doubler in his book *Closing with the Enemy: How GIs Fought the War in Europe, 1944–1945*, the American soldier fought in Europe with a healthy dose of common sense. "When unique problems arose," Doubler writes, "successful commanders applied doctrine with flexibility, combined it with their own training and judgment, and produced effective solutions."[9] Doubler, however, applies this notion primarily to tactics. Krueger's effort demonstrates that the "schoolhouse of war" extended to the operational level as well. He successfully modified and then applied an operational doctrine designed for Central Europe to the mountainous and jungle-covered islands of the Southwest Pacific.

Krueger's background, his training, his part in the evolution of pre–World War II army doctrine, and his contribution to the war against Japan all call for a reevaluation of his military career, one that moves beyond the one-dimensional and inaccurate characterization of him as conservative and methodical. A good starting point for this reassessment is Janowitz's description of Krueger as a military manager, who, he explains, is "concerned with the scientific and rational conduct of war" and who reflects "the scientific and pragmatic dimensions of war-making."[10] This characterization, while largely correct, nevertheless overlooks the innovative and creative side of Krueger's career. He not only was instrumental in developing an operational doctrine prior to the entrance of the United States in World War II but also successfully adapted and applied it to operations in SWPA.

Krueger's contributions to the success of Allied forces in SPWA were significant. While MacArthur—the "American Caesar"—has overshadowed every other personality in SWPA, he could not have implemented his strategy without the enormous involvement of his lieutenants.[11] Gen. Walter Krueger not only led MacArthur's ground forces but also coordinated the ground, air, and naval team. Ironically, MacArthur may have summed up Krueger's career best when he wrote,

> History has not given him due credit for his greatness. I do not believe that the annals of American history have shown his superior as an Army commander. Swift and sure in attack, tenacious and determined in defense, modest and restrained in victory—I do not know what he would have been in defeat, because he was never defeated.[12]

NOTES

Abbreviations

CMH	Center of Military History (Washington, DC)
GCMRL	George C. Marshall Research Library (Lexington, VA)
MJCPL	Madison–Jefferson County Public Library (Indiana)
MM	MacArthur Memorial (Norfolk, VA)
NARA	National Archives and Records Administration (College Park, MD, and Washington, DC)
RG	Record Group
UMI	University Microfilms International
USAMHI	United States Army Military History Institute (Carlisle Barracks, PA)
USMA	United States Military Academy (West Point, NY)
WK	Walter Krueger
WPD	War Plans Division

Introduction

1. Walter Krueger, *From Down Under to Nippon: The Story of Sixth Army in World War II* (Washington, DC: Combat Forces Press, 1953; reprint, Nashville: Battery Classics, n.d.), 369–371.

2. Krueger, *From Down Under to Nippon*, 369–371; Letter, WK to Grace Krueger, 27 January 1946, as quoted in letter, Walter Krueger Jr. to William M. Leary, 20 May 1985, Box 40, Walter Krueger Papers, USMA; General Krueger's Diary, 1–13 February 1945, Box 10, ibid.

3. Krueger's Diary, 1–13 February 1945.

4. "Throngs Greet Krueger 6th Army Head Home," *San Antonio Express*, 14 February 1946.

5. Three examples of the wartime publicity Krueger received are Frank L. Kluckhohn, "Master of Amphibious Warfare," *New York Times Magazine*, 31 December 1944, 11 and 32; Gordon Walker, "General Krueger: Mystery Man of Pacific," *Christian Science Monitor*, 9 June 1945, 3; and the cover story, "Old Soldier," *Time*, 29 January 1945, 29–33.

6. The discussion of critical works on Krueger in this paragraph was, in part, drawn from William Leary, "Walter Krueger: MacArthur's Fighting General," in William M. Leary, ed., *We Shall Return! MacArthur's Commanders and the Defeat of Japan* (Lexington: University Press of Kentucky, 1988), 86–87. See, for example, John Francis Shortal, *Forged by Fire: Robert L. Eichelberger and the Pacific War* (Columbia: University of South Carolina Press, 1987), 113, 114, and passim; John F. Shortal, "MacArthur's Fireman: Robert L. Eichelberger," *Parameters, Journal of the US Army War College* 16, 3 (Autumn 1986): 58–67; Jay Luvaas and John F. Shortal, "Robert L. Eichelberger: MacArthur's Fireman," in Leary, *We Shall Return!*,

155–177; Ronald H. Spector, *Eagle against the Sun: The American War with Japan* (New York: Free Press, 1985), 513–514 and passim; Geoffrey Perret, *There's a War to be Won: The United States Army in World War II* (New York: Random House, 1991), 241; Geoffrey Perret, *Old Soldiers Never Die: The Life of Douglas MacArthur* (New York: Random House, 1996), 336–337; Louis Morton, *Strategy and Command: The First Two Years* (Washington, DC: Office of the Chief of Military History, Department of the Army, 1962), 581–582; Edward J. Drea, *Defending the Driniumor: Covering Force Operations in New Guinea, 1944*, Leavenworth Paper No. 9 (Fort Leavenworth, KS: Combat Studies Institute, U.S. Army Command and General Staff College, 1984), 138; D. Clayton James, *The Years of MacArthur*, 3 vols. (Boston: Houghton Mifflin, 1970–1985), Vol. 2, *1941–1945*, 346. See also Russell F. Weigley's review of *We Shall Return!* in *Parameters* 19, 3 (September 1989): 114–117.

7. For examples, see Nathan Prefer, *MacArthur's New Guinea Campaign, March–April 1944*, (Conshohocken, PA: Combined Books, 1995); Basil Liddell Hart, *History of the Second World War* (New York: G. P. Putnam's Sons, 1970); James L. Stokesbury, *A Short History of World War II* (New York: William Morrow, 1980); John Costello, *The Pacific War* (New York: Rawson, Wade, 1981); Harry A. Gailey, *The War in the Pacific: From Pearl Harbor to Tokyo Bay* (Novato, CA: Presidio Press, 1995).

8. Leary, "Walter Krueger," 60–87; George B. Eaton, "General Walter Krueger and Joint War Planning, 1922–1938," *Naval War College Review* 48, 2 (Spring 1995): 91–113; George B. Eaton, "From Luzon to Luzon: Walter Krueger and the Luzon Campaign," *Valley Forge Journal: A Record of Patriotism and American Culture* 6, 11 (June 1992): 17–36; Kevin C. Holzimmer, "Walter Krueger, Douglas MacArthur, and the Pacific War: The Wakde-Sarmi Campaign as a Case Study," *Journal of Military History* 59, 4 (October 1995): 661–686; and Arthur S. Collins Jr., "Walter Krueger," *Infantry* 73, 1 (January–February 1983): 15–19. In addition to examining the U.S. Army's theory and practice of covering force operations, Edward J. Drea examines Krueger's generalship in one particular battle in *Defending the Driniumor* and in *MacArthur's ULTRA: Codebreaking and the War against Japan, 1942–1945* (Lawrence: University Press of Kansas, 1992).

9. Letter, Krueger Jr. to Leary, 20 May 1985, Box 40, Krueger Papers, USMA.

10. Letter, WK to H. Ben Decherd, 27 June 1947, Box 11, Krueger Papers, USMA; Robert Ross Smith, *Triumph in the Philippines* (Washington, DC: Office of the Chief of Military History, Department of the Army, 1963), 711.

11. Harold R. Winton, "Toward an American Philosophy of Command," *Journal of Military History* 64, 4 (October 2000): 1035.

12. There are many critical works of the interwar U.S. Army; for the most recent and significant, see David E. Johnson, *Fast Tanks and Heavy Bombers: Innovation in the U.S. Army, 1917–1945* (Ithaca, NY: Cornell University Press, 1998); William O. Odom, *After the Trenches: Transformation of U.S. Army Doctrine, 1918–1939* (College Station: Texas A&M University Press, 1999); and George F. Hofmann, "Combatant Arms vs. Combined Arms: The U.S. Army's Quest for Deep Offensive Operations and an Operational Level of Warfare," *Armor* 106, 1 (January–February 1997): 6–13, 51–52. The second school is composed primarily of one major contributor: Michael R. Matheny. See his "The Roots of Modern American Operational Art," Department of Military Strategy, Planning and Operations Home Page, n.d., Army War College, 1 April 2003, carlisle-www.army.mil/usawc/dmspo/Staff%20Publications/modern_operations.pdf.

13. Leary, *We Shall Return!* was vital in this regard.

14. One of the most exciting current historiographical discussions is the nature of the Allied victory during World War II. Several recent books and articles seek to understand exactly *how* and *why* the Allies won. Much of the debate began with Russell F. Weigley's *Eisenhower's Lieutenants: The Campaigns of France and Germany, 1944–1945* (Bloomington: Indiana University Press, 1981). A number of books were sparked, in part, by Weigley's arguments. See, for example: John Ellis, *Brute Force: Allied Strategy and Tactics in the Second World War* (New York: Viking, 1990); Keith E. Bonn, *When the Odds Were Even: Vosges Mountains Campaign, October 1944–January 1945* (Novato, CA: Presidio Press, 1994); Michael D. Doubler, *Closing with the Enemy: How GIs Fought the War in Europe, 1944–1945* (Lawrence: University Press of Kansas, 1994); and Richard Overy, *Why the Allies Won* (New York: W.W. Norton, 1995). The debate has largely centered on the European theater of operation and unfortunately was not extended to the Pacific theater until the publication of John Ellis's *Brute Force* and, more important, Eric Bergerud's *Touched with Fire: The Land War in the South Pacific* (New York: Viking, 1996). Bergerud effectively explores *how* the Allied war was waged through a detailed examination of actual combat conditions. It is hoped that this study will then extend the discussion to include *why* the conditions of success came about. In other words, who was responsible for planning the war at the operational and tactical level?

Chapter 1. From Germany to the Philippines, 1881–1903

1. Edward M. Coffman and Peter F. Herrly, "The American Regular Army Officer Corps between the World Wars: A Collective Biography," *Armed Forces and Society* 4, 1 (November 1977): 55–73.

2. Ibid., 62.

3. Letter, Walter Krueger Jr. to William M. Leary, 20 May 1985, Box 40, Walter Krueger Papers, USMA; "General Walter Krueger" (Biographical Sketch), Walter Krueger Papers, USAMHI.

4. Letter, Krueger Jr. to Leary, 20 May 1985; "Madison Not the Same Town General Knew as a Boy," *Madison Courier*, 5 April 1946, Newspaper Clipping, Local History Department, MJCPL.

5. "Madison Is Home," [no source], and "Mrs. Sam Hill Recalls General as Schoolboy," *Madison Courier*, 5 April 1946, Newspaper Clipping, MJCPL; the quote is from Letter, Walter Krueger Jr. to Walter Nardini, 29 November 1976, Krueger Papers, USAMHI; Letter, Krueger Jr. to Leary, 20 May 1985; Letter, WK to Col. John M. Virden, 26 July 1953, Box 12, Krueger Papers, USMA. For a detailed description of Krueger's early reading habits, see Letter, Maj. Ike S. Kampmann to Hayden Nichols, 28 August 1945, Box 9, Krueger Papers, USMA.

6. *Cincinnati Times Star*, 23 August 1945, Newspaper Clipping, Box 28, Krueger Papers; the quote is from "Old Soldier," *Time*, 29 January 1945, 29.

7. *Cincinnati Times Star*, 23 August 1945.

8. Russell F. Weigley, *History of the United States Army*, enlarged ed. (Bloomington: Indiana University Press, 1984), 297–298; Graham A. Cosmas, *An Army for Empire: The United States Army in the Spanish-American War* (Columbia: University of Missouri Press, 1971; reprint, Shippensburg, PA: White Mane Publishing, 1994), 127; "Old Soldier," 29.

9. Eric F. Goldman, *Rendezvous with Destiny: A History of Modern American Reform*, rev. ed. (New York: Vintage Books, 1955), 54–55; see also Perry D. Jamieson, *Crossing the Deadly Ground: United States Army Tactics, 1865–1899* (Tuscaloosa: University of Alabama Press, 1994), 141.

10. Cosmas, *An Army for Empire*, 206–208 and 247; Allan R. Millett and Peter Maslowski, *For the Common Defense: A Military History of the United States of America* (New York: Free Press, 1984), 279.

11. Graham A. Cosmas, "Securing the Fruits of Victory: The U.S. Army Occupies Cuba, 1898–1899," *Military Affairs* 38, 3 (October 1974): 85 and 88; Weigley, *History of the United States Army*, 296–297; Cosmas, *An Army for Empire*, 255 and 259–260; Indiana World War Records, Meritorious Service Record, Box 40, Krueger Papers, USMA; William M. Leary, "Walter Krueger: MacArthur's Fighting General," in William M. Leary, ed., *We Shall Return! MacArthur's Commanders and the Defeat of Japan* (Lexington: University Press of Kentucky, 1988), 60.

12. Indiana World War Records, Meritorious Service Record; Leary, "Walter Krueger," in Leary, *We Shall Return!* 60–61; "Old Soldier," *Time*, 29.

13. Kenneth Ray Young, *The General's General: The Life and Times of Arthur MacArthur*; (Boulder, CO: Westview Press, 1994), 214–290.

14. Ibid., 247.

15.Ibid., 238; Daniel F. Anglum, "Journal of Company K, 1899–1901," passim, USMA; the Krueger quote comes from a letter he wrote to his local newspaper, the *Madison Courier*. The letter is dated 18 October 1899 and appeared in a December 1899 edition. See his lifetime scrapbook from 1898–1930s in Box 41, Krueger Papers, USMA.

16. The first Krueger quotation is taken from "Biographical Sketch," 1 June 1945, 6th Army 106–1.19, RG 407, Box 2415, NARA. The second is from "Critique—D-2, 2d Division—May 16, 1941," 12, Box 19, Krueger Papers, USMA. Letter, General Clyde D. Eddleman to William M. Leary, n.d., Box 40, Krueger Papers, USMA; Dan H. Ralls interview with Gen. George Henry Decker, 32, 9 November 1972, George H. Decker Papers, USAMHI; and Robert S. Allen, *Lucky Forward: The History of Patton's Third U.S. Army* (New York: Vanguard Press, 1947), 10.

17. The encounter with Krueger at Hollandia is from Letter, Walter Krueger Jr. to Walter Nardini, 12 October 1976, Krueger Papers, USMA. There are many examples of Krueger's care for the welfare of his troops besides the one mentioned here. For additional accounts, see Letter, Roy L. Miller to William M. Leary, 20 May 1989, Box 40, Krueger Papers, USMA; and Arthur S. Collins Jr., "Walter Krueger: An Infantry Great," *Infantry* 73, 1 (January–February 1983): 15–19.

18. William C. Chase, *Front Line General: The Commands of Maj. Gen. William C. Chase* (Houston: Pacesetter Press, 1975), 27.

19. Krueger quoted in "Old Soldier," *Time*, 29–30; Orders, Headquarters, Department of Southern Luzon, 6 July 1901, Box 1, Krueger Papers, USMA.

20. Special Order No. 9, Marinduque, Philippine Islands, 14 July 1901; Special Order No. 30, Headquarters, 30th Infantry, 1 November 1901; Special Order No. 43, Headquarters, 30th Infantry, 1 December 1901; Special Order No. 32, Station at Boac, 10 May 1902; Special Order No. 2, Headquarters, Department of Luzon, 7 January 1903; and Special Order No. 70, Malahi Island Military Prison and Post, 18 May 1903; all in Box 1, Krueger Papers, USMA. For the army's anti-intellectual element see Carol Reardon, *Soldiers and Scholars: The U.S. Army and the Uses of Military History, 1865–1920* (Lawrence: University Press of Kansas, 1990), 23–26.

21. Forrest C. Pogue, *George C. Marshall*, 4 vols. (New York: Viking, 1963–1987), Vol. 1, *Education of a General*, 82–83; George C. Marshall, *George C. Marshall: Interviews and Reminiscences for Forrest C. Pogue*, rev. ed. (Lexington, VA: George C. Marshall Research Foundation, 1991), 132–133.

22. Forrest C. Pogue interview with WK, 7 November 1957, GCMRL; Memo, George C. Marshall to the Secretary of War, 22 May 1940, cited in Larry I. Bland, ed., *The Papers of George Catlett Marshall*, 4 vols. (Baltimore: Johns Hopkins University Press, 1981–1996), Vol. 2, *"We Cannot Delay," July 1, 1939–December 6, 1941*, 219–220.

23. Letter, Krueger Jr. to Leary, 20 May 1985.

24. Krueger was widely known as a "soldier's soldier." See the *New York Times*, 21 August 1967, 31; and Letter, Krueger Jr. to Nardini, 12 October 1976.

Chapter 2. Education of a Tactician, 1903–1920

1. Walter and Grace Krueger eventually had three children: James Norvell (born 29 July 1905), Walter Jr. (born 25 April 1910), and Dorothy Jane (born 24 January 1913). Both James and Walter attended the U.S. Military Academy at West Point, New York, and Dorothy married an army officer, Aubrey D. Smith. Special Order No. 82, Fort Crook, Nebraska, 6 June 1904, Box 1; Special Order No. 90, Fort Crook, Nebraska, 2 August 1904, Box 1; Special Order No. 92, Fort Crook, Nebraska, 5 August 1904, Box 1; Special Order No. 143, Headquarters, Department of the Missouri, 2 August 1904, Box 1; Letter, Walter Krueger Jr. to William M. Leary, 20 May 1985, Box 40; all in Krueger Papers, USMA.

2. Special Order No. 24, Headquarters, Department of the Missouri, 6 February 1905; and Special Order No. 172, War Department, 27 July 1905; both in Box 1, Krueger Papers, USMA; Timothy K. Nenninger, *The Leavenworth Schools and the Old Army: Education, Professionalism, and the Officer Corps of the United States Army, 1881–1918* (Westport, CT: Greenwood Press, 1978), 24–25 and 74–75; Special Order No. 105, Fort Crook, Nebraska, 10 August 1905, Box 1, Krueger Papers, USMA; Timothy K. Nenninger, "The Army Enters the Twentieth Century, 1904–1917," in Kenneth J. Hagan and William R. Roberts, eds., *Against All Enemies: Interpretations of American Military History from Colonial Times to the Present* (Westport, CT: Greenwood Press, 1986), 229.

3. Pogue interview with WK, 7 November 1957, GCMRL; Special Order No. 166, War Department, 17 July 1907, Box 1, Krueger Papers, USMA.

4. Nenninger, *Leavenworth Schools*, 84 and 107; Edward M. Coffman, "The American Military Generation Gap in World War I: The Leavenworth Clique in the AEF," in Military History Symposium, Second, U.S. Air Force Academy, *Command and Commanders in Modern Warfare: Proceedings of the Second Military History Symposium, U.S. Air Force Academy, 2–3 May 1968*, ed., William Geffen (Washington, DC: Government Printing Office, 1969), 39–48.

5. Nenninger, *Leavenworth Schools*, 92–93.

6. Indiana World War Records, Meritorious Service Record, Box 40; Special Order No. 166, War Department, 17 July 1907; Special Order No. 232, Headquarters, Department of the East, 7 October 1907, Box 1; Special Order No. 77, Headquarters, 23d Infantry, Norfolk, Virginia, 14 October 1907, Box 1; Special Order No. 130, Fort Ontario, New York, 4 December 1907, Box 1; Letter, Colonel Philip Reade to the Adjutant General, Division of the Philippines, 6 March 1908, Box 1; all in Krueger Papers, USMA.

7. The two quotes are from Fay W. Brabson Diary, 17 March 1908 and 13 August 1908, Fay W. Brabson Papers, USAMHI; for other descriptions of Krueger, see Brabson Diary, 6 February–21 August 1908; Special Order No. 226, Headquarters, Philippine Division, 9 October 1908, Box 1, Krueger Papers, USMA; and Letter, WK to the Secretary, Army Service Schools, 24 November 1911, Box 1, Krueger Papers, USMA. See also Letter, Fay W. Brabson to the Editor, *Time*, 5 February 1945, Brabson Papers, USAMHI. Edward J. Drea alludes to

Krueger's impatience as the head of the Sixth U.S. Army during World War II in *Defending the Driniumor: Covering Force Operations in New Guinea, 1944*, Leavenworth Paper No. 9 (Fort Leavenworth, KS: Combat Studies Institute, U.S. Army Command and General Staff College, 1984), 136.

8. Report of the Commandant (Fredrick Funston), *Annual Report of the Commandant*, 1908–1909 (Fort Leavenworth, KS: Army Service Schools Press, 1909), 9; the quotation is from Report of the Department of Languages, Army School of the Line (Arthur Thayer), *Annual Report of the Commandant*, 1909–1910 (Fort Leavenworth, KS: Army Service Schools Press, 1910), 39–40; Report of Department of Languages, Army School of the Line (Thomas. G. Hanson), *Annual Report of the Commandant*, 1910–1911 (Fort Leavenworth, KS: Army Service Schools Press, 1911), 33–34.

9. The quotation is from Report of the Department of Languages, Army Staff College (Thomas. G. Hanson), *Annual Report of the Commandant*, 1910–1911, 36; Report of the Department of Languages, Army Staff College (Arthur Thayer), *Annual Report of the Commandant*, 1909–1910, 55–59; Report of the Department of Languages, Army Staff College (Thomas G. Hanson), *Annual Report of the Commandant*, 1911–1912 (Fort Leavenworth, KS: Army Service Schools, 1912), 52–54.

10. Marshall, *Interviews*, 157; William O. Odom, "The Rise and Fall of U.S. Army Doctrine, 1918–1939" (PhD diss., Ohio State University, 1995, UMI Order Number DA9534040), 156; Special Order No. 120, War Department, 23 May 1910, and Special Order No. 126, War Department, 31 May 1910, both in Box 1, Krueger Papers, USMA.

11. H. Rohne, "The French and German Field-Artillery: A Comparison," trans. by Walter Krueger, *The Journal of the Military Service Institution of the United States* 40, 136 (March–April 1907): 204–215 and ibid., 40, 137 (May–June 1907): 377–384; Walter Krueger, "Desertions and the Enlistment Oath," *Cavalry Journal* 18, 65 (July 1907): 44–47.

12. Krueger, "Desertions and Enlistment Oath," 45 and 47.

13. Wilhelm Balck, *Taktik*, 6 vols. (Berlin: R. Eisenschmidt, 1903–1907).

14. William Balck, *Tactics*, 2 vols., 4th rev. ed., trans. by Walter Krueger (Fort Leavenworth, KS: U.S. Cavalry Association, 1911), Vol. 1, *Introduction and Formal Tactics of Infantry*, 14, 16, and 102–105. Balck quoted Goltz's *Zur Gefechtsausbildung: Versuche und Vorschlage* (Berlin: E. S. Mittler, 1903), 26. Balck's work then fits within the much-needed reinterpretation of military doctrine prior to World War I, thanks to the work of Antulio J. Echevarria, specifically his *After Clausewitz: German Military Thinkers before the Great War* (Lawrence: University Press of Kansas, 2000).

15. Balck, *Tactics*, Vol. 1, *Introduction and Formal Tactics of Infantry*, 104–106.

16. For the essentials as well as the significance of the *Infantry Drill Regulations, 1911*, see Henry Jerry Osterhoudt, "Evolution of U.S. Army Assault Tactics, 1778–1919: The Search for Sound Doctrine" (PhD diss., Duke University, 1986, UMI Order Number DA 8710809), 157–158; and Douglas Valentine Johnson, "A Few 'Squads Left' and Off to France: Training the American Army in the United States for World War I" (PhD diss., Temple University, 1992, UMI Order Number DA 9227482), 78–79.

17. Letter, WK to Fay W. Brabson, 19 July 1914, Brabson Papers, USAMHI.

18. Special Order No. 230, War Department, 2 October 1911; Special Order No. 49, War Department, 28 February 1912; Special Order No. 52, Headquarters, Eastern Division, 7 March 1912; Special Order No. 179, Headquarters, Eastern Division, 5 August 1912; Special Order No. 28, Madison Barracks, NY, 17 March 1913; Special Order No. 241, War Department, 13 October 1914; all in Box 1, Krueger Papers, USMA.

19. Letter, Krueger Jr. to Leary, 20 May 1985.

20. Indiana World War Records; Clarence C. Clendenen, *Blood on the Border: The United States Army and the Mexican Irregulars* (New York: Macmillan, 1969), 285–298; Russell F. Weigley, *Towards an American Army: Military Thought from Washington to Marshall* (New York: Columbia University Press, 1962), 199–222; Letter, WK to Fay W. Brabson, 2 April 1917, Brabson Papers, USAMHI.

21. Walter Krueger, "Preparedness," *Infantry Journal* 13, 6 (March 1917): 553. For context on the issue of preparedness on the eve of World War I, see Weigley, *Towards an American Army*, 199–222; and John Patrick Finnegan, *Against the Specter of a Dragon: The Campaign for American Military Preparedness, 1914–1917* (Westport, CT: Greenwood Press, 1974).

22. Krueger, "Preparedness," 554–555.

23. Ibid., 555–556.

24. See Weigley, *Towards an American Army*, 199–222; and Krueger, "Preparedness," 553.

25. Walter Krueger, "The German Army," lecture, Army Service Schools, n.d., Box 21, Krueger Papers, USMA; Krueger, "Preparedness," 551.

26. For an excellent analysis on Emory Upton and his influence, see Weigley, *Towards an American Army*, 100–161.

27. Letter, Krueger to Brabson, 2 April 1917.

28. Indiana World War Records; Brabson Diary, 20 July–12 August 1918.

29. Letter, WK to Fay W. Brabson, 4 June 1917, Brabson Papers, USAMHI; Special Order No. 193, War Department, 20 August 1917, Box 1, Krueger Papers, USMA; Special Order No. 207, 6 September 1917, Box 1, Krueger Papers, USMA; Theodore Draper, *The 84th Infantry Division in the Battle of Germany, November 1944–May 1945* (New York: Viking Press, 1946), 1.

30. Julius K. L. Mertens, *Taktik and Technik der Flussubergange* (Berlin: R. Eisenschmidt, 1913); Julius K. L. Mertens, *Tactics and Technique of River Crossings*, trans. by Walter Krueger (New York: D. Van Nostrand, 1918), v.

31. Draper, *The 84th Infantry Division*, 1; Indiana World War Records, Box 40, Krueger Papers, USMA; The quotation is from Nenninger, *Leavenworth Schools*, 138; see also Timothy K. Nenninger, "American Military Effectiveness in the First World War," in Allan R. Millett and Williamson Murray, eds., *Military Effectiveness*, 3 vols.(Boston: Unwin Hyman, 1988), Vol. 1, *The First World War*, 134–136.

32. Brabson Diary, 21 May 1918; Indiana World War Records; Edward M. Coffman, *The War to End All Wars: The American Military Experience in World War I* (New York: Oxford University Press, 1968; reprint, Madison: University of Wisconsin Press, 1986), 147–149 and 250–261. The daily routine of the G-3 is portrayed in Emerson Gifford Taylor, *New England in France, 1917–1919: A History of the Twenty-Sixth Division, U.S.A.* (Boston: Houghton Mifflin, 1920), 142.

33. Reunited with the 84th, Krueger was once again its G-3. Brabson Diary, 30 June 1918; Memorandum, Gen. George C. Marshall to the Secretary of War, 22 May 1940, in Larry I. Bland, ed., *The Papers of George Catlett Marshall*, 4 vols. (Baltimore: Johns Hopkins University Press, 1981–1996), Vol. 2, *"We Cannot Delay," July 1, 1939–December 6, 1941*, 219–220; Letter, WK to Fay W. Brabson, 10 August 1918, Brabson Papers, USAMHI.

34. Draper, *The 84th Infantry Division*, 1–2; Letter, WK to Fay W. Brabson, 14 October 1918, Brabson Papers, USAMHI; Memorandum, Marshall to Secretary of War, 22 May 1940, 219–220.

35. Special Order No. 264, Headquarters, 84th Division, 18 October 1918, Box 1, Krueger Papers, USMA; Letter, WK to Fay W. Brabson, 4 November 1918, Brabson Papers, USAMHI.

36. Special Order No. 314, General Headquarters, AEF, 10 November 1918, Box 1, Krueger Papers, USMA; Letter, WK to Fay W. Brabson, 1 January 1919, Brabson Papers, USAMHI.

37. "VI Army Corps: Command and Staff," *Order of Battle of the United States Land Forces in the World War*, 5 vols. (Washington, DC: United States Army, Center of Military History, 1988), Vol. 1, *American Expeditionary Forces: General Headquarters, Armies, Army Corps, Services of Supply, Separate Forces*, 316–327; "IV Army Corps: Command and Staff," ibid., 268–289; Special Order No. 106, Headquarters, VI Army Corps, 17 April 1919, Box 1, Krueger Papers, USMA; Letter, WK to Fay W. Brabson, n.d. [May 1919], Brabson Papers, USAMHI.

38. Indiana World War Records; "Walter Krueger," in Maxine Block, ed., *Current Biography: Who's News and Why, 1943* (New York: H. W. Wilson, 1943), 411–412.

39. "Krueger of the Sixth," *Newsweek* (1 March 1943): 22; "Krueger of the Sixth," *Newsweek* (4 February 1946): 58; "Krueger a Learned Strategist," *New York Times*, 19 February 1943; Charles A. Willoughby and John Chamberlain, *MacArthur, 1941–1951* (New York: McGraw-Hill, 1954), 123.

40. Nenninger, *Leavenworth Schools*, 84, 134, and passim.

Chapter 3. Preparation for High Command, 1920–1938

1. William E. Leuchtenburg, *The Perils of Prosperity, 1914–1932* (Chicago: University of Chicago Press, 1958), 84; George F. Hofmann, "Combatant Arms vs. Combined Arms: The U.S. Army's Quest for Deep Offensive Operations and an Operational Level of Warfare," *Armor* 106, 1 (January–February 1997): 8; Russell F. Weigley, *History of the United States Army*, enlarged ed. (Bloomington: Indiana University Press, 1984), 399.

2. Letter, WK to Fay W. Brabson, 28 June 1919, Fay W. Brabson Papers, USAMHI; "Walter Krueger," in Maxine Block, ed., *Current Biography: Who's News and Why, 1943* (New York: H. W. Wilson, 1943), 412.

3. Block, *Current Biography: Who's News and Why, 1943*, 412.

4. Harry P. Ball, *Of Responsible Command: A History of the U.S. Army War College* (Carlisle Barracks, PA: Alumni Association of the United States Army War College, 1983), 162, 148, 171–172, and 488.

5. Ibid., 162 and 174; George B. Eaton, "From Teaching to Practice: General Walter Krueger and the Development of Joint Operations, 1921–1945" (advanced research project, Naval War College, February 1994), 10–11.

6. Letter, WK to Fay W. Brabson, 15 March 1921, Brabson Papers, USAMHI; Indiana World War Records, Meritorious Service Record, Walter Krueger Papers, USMA.

7. Letter, WK to Brabson, 15 March 1921.

8. Krueger delivered at least five lectures: Walter Krueger, "The Evolution of the German War Plan of 1914," lecture delivered in the War Plans Division Course No. 2, Army War College, 8 November 1921, File No. 224–28, U.S. Army War College Curricular Archives, USAMHI; Walter Krueger, "The Basic War Plan," lecture delivered at the War Plans Division Conference, No. 13, Army War College, 12 January 1922, File No. 224–28, U.S. Army War College Curricular Archives, USAMHI; Walter Krueger, "Observations and Reflections on the Situation in Germany," lecture delivered at the Army War College, 28 September 1922, File No. 240–33, U.S. Army War College Curricular Archives, USAMHI; Walter Krueger, "The Military System of the German Empire," lecture delivered in the War Plans Division

Course No. 1, Army War College, 24 October 1922, Box 21, Krueger Papers, USMA; Walter Krueger, "The Conditions of Success in War Illustrated by Hannibal's Campaigns in Italy," lecture delivered in the Command Course No. 20, Army War College, 20 March 1923, Box 21, Krueger Papers, USAMHI. The lecture on Hannibal's campaigns in Italy was published in *Coast Artillery Journal* 60, 2 (February 1924), 98–124. No complete record exists recording the lectures Krueger delivered or the sections he taught. Eaton, "From Teaching to Practice," 12.

9. Krueger, "Observations and Reflections on the Situation in Germany," passim. National unity was also a concept he used to analyze Hannibal's campaign against Rome; see Krueger, "The Conditions of Success in War."

10. Walter Krueger, "Comments on the Essay 'Joint Army and Navy Operations, Part I,'" 14 October 1924, Box 21, Krueger Papers, USMA.

11. Krueger, "The Military System of the German Empire," 1.

12. Krueger, "The Basic War Plan," 2; see also Krueger, "The Evolution of the German War Plan of 1914," 35; and Krueger, "The Military System of the German Empire," 17.

13. Krueger, "The Conditions of Success in War," 21; in his lecture on the Schlieffen Plan of 1914, he emphasized that "you can not win a war by standing still; you can win it only by maneuvering and by annihilating the enemy." Krueger, "The Evolution of the German War Plan of 1914," 36.

14. Krueger, "The Conditions of Success in War," 1 and 13.

15. Ibid., 22. In another lecture, Krueger extends his discussion of the "human factor" to include high-ranking officers and government officials. He specifically condemned Kaiser William II for providing weak leadership: "The very defeat of the once so proud [German] Empire should be an object lesson to us that the human factor can never be disregarded with impunity and that a military system, even if it is a good one, does not suffice to achieve victory, to avert or to stave off defeat." Krueger, "The Military System of the German Empire," 17.

16. Name and Subject Index to the General Correspondence of the War Plans Division, 1921–1942, card #2, Series 1080, reel 10, RG 165, NARA; Eaton, "From Teaching to Practice," 13.

17. I would like to thank my colleague Dr. J. T. LaSaine for assisting me to place Krueger's ideas within the broader intellectual climate of the U.S. Army during this time.

18. Eaton, "From Teaching to Practice," 13; Name and Subject Index to the General Correspondence of the War Plans Division, 1921–1942, card #1; "IV Army Corps: Command and Staff," *Order of Battle of the United States Land Forces in the World War*, 5 vols. (Washington, DC: United States Army, Center of Military History, 1988), Vol. 1, *American Expeditionary Forces: General Headquarters, Armies, Army Corps, Services of Supply, Separate Forces*, 268.

19. Name and Subject Index to the General Correspondence of the War Plans Division, 1921–1942, card #1; Eaton, "From Teaching to Practice," 13–14.

20. Name and Subject Index to the General Correspondence of the War Plans Division, 1921–1942, cards #1–2.

21. Louis Morton, *Strategy and Command: The First Two Years* (Washington, DC: Chief of Military History, Department of the Army, 1962), 22; Eaton, "From Teaching to Practice," 17; Walter Krueger, "The Detailed Working of the War Plans Division, Its Tasks and Their Method of Execution," lecture delivered in the War Plans Division Course No. 9 at the Army War College, 18 October 1924, Box 21, Krueger Papers, USMA.

22. Edward S. Miller, *War Plan Orange: The U.S. Strategy to Defeat Japan, 1897–1945* (Annapolis, MD: Naval Institute Press, 1991), 83–84; Eaton, "From Teaching to Practice," 18.

23. The quotes are from Krueger, "The Basic War Plan," 3; the information in the rest of the paragraph is from Eaton, "From Teaching to Practice," 68–69; Russell F. Weigley, "The

Interwar Army, 1919–1941," in Kenneth J. Hagan and William R. Roberts, eds., *Against All Enemies: Interpretations of American Military History from Colonial Times to the Present* (New York: Greenwood Press, 1986), 265. The following part on Krueger's work on joint projects relies heavily on George B. Eaton's well-researched Naval War College research project, "From Teaching to Practice," although I disagree with portions of his conclusion.

24. Eaton, "From Teaching to Practice," 70–75; Weigley, "The Interwar Army," in Hagan and Roberts, *Against All Enemies*, 265; Miller, *War Plan Orange*, 33–35 and 150; Morton, *Strategy and Command*, 27–28; Ronald H. Spector, *Eagle against the Sun: The American War with Japan* (New York: Free Press, 1985), 56–57. The quotes are from "Joint Army and Navy Basic War Plan," JB 325, Serial No. 228, 1 July 1924, in Steven T. Ross, ed., *American War Plans, 1919–1941*, 5 vols. (New York: Garland Publishing, 1992), Vol. 2, *Plans for War against the British Empire and Japan: The Red, Orange, and Red-Orange Plans, 1923–1938*, 18.

25. "Joint Army and Navy Basic War Plan," JB 325, Serial No. 228, 1 July 1924, in Ross, *American War Plans, 1919–1941*, Vol. 2, *Plans for War against the British Empire and Japan*, 29.

26. Louis Morton, "War Plan ORANGE: Evolution of a Strategy," *World Politics* 11, 2 (January 1959): 231.

27. Spector, *Eagle against the Sun*, 54–57; Morton, "War Plan ORANGE," 229–230.

28. Walter Krueger, Memorandum, Subject: Army War Plan Orange, 23 January 1925, Entry 281, Box 268, File1991, RG 165, NARA; for other views of these two camps in regards to the purpose of war planning, see Fox Connor, Memorandum, Subject: War Department Mobilization Plan to Strategic Plan, Army War Plan Orange, 18 May 1925, Entry 281, Box 268, File 1991, RG 165, NARA.

29. For the views of these two camps in regards to the purpose of war planning, see Fox Connor, Memorandum, Subject: War Department Mobilization Plan to Strategic Plan, Army War Plan Orange, 18 May 1925, Entry 281, Box 268, File 1991, RG 165, NARA.

30. Krueger, "The Detailed Working of the War Plans Division;" Name and Subject Index to the General Correspondence of the War Plans Division, 1921–1942, cards #2–4; Eaton, "From Teaching to Practice," 75.

31. Name and Subject Index to the General Correspondence of the War Plans Division, 1921–1942, cards #3–4; Eaton, "From Teaching to Practice," 19.

32. The general background material for this paragraph as well as the quote is from Eaton, "From Teaching to Practice," 20–21. The material for the tactical problems is from Krueger's solutions: Walter Krueger, "Blue Situation," Tactical Problem II, 2, Naval War College, 22 August 1925, Box 21; Walter Krueger, "Orange Situation," Tactical Problem III, Naval War College, 26 October 1925, Box 21; and Walter Krueger, "Blue Situation," Tactical Problem IV, Naval War College, 18 January 1926, Box 21; all in Krueger Papers, USMA. In a joint exercise conducted between March and May 1926, Krueger expanded his thinking about a war with Japan. The joint war game was a variation of War Plan Orange, with both nations already mobilized after a long period of tension. Krueger believed that the United States could gather its forces in at least ten days, while it would take approximately twenty-three days to move to the Philippines. In order to avoid giving the Japanese adequate time to establish a strong defensive position in the Philippines, Krueger advocated sending an American fleet to the Western Pacific to engage and defeat the Japanese fleet, perhaps even before the Japanese captured Manila. Eaton, "From Teaching to Practice," 78–81.

33. Krueger, "Command," 3–4.

34. Ibid., 4.

35. Ibid.

36. Ibid., 5–6.
37. Ibid., 6–7; Krueger did not identify the source of the quote.
38. Ibid., 7–8.
39. Ibid., 9.
40. Ibid., 10–11. Krueger did not identify the source of the quote.
41. Ibid., 19.
42. U.S. War Department, *War Department Training Regulations No. 10: Doctrines, Principles, and Methods* (Washington, DC: Government Printing Office, 1921).
43. William Felix Atwater, "United States Army and Navy Development of Joint Landing Operations 1898–1942" (PhD diss., Duke University, 1986, UMI Order Number 8718403), 114.
44. Eaton, "From Teaching to Practice," 38; Russell F. Weigley, *The American Way of War: A History of United States Military Strategy and Policy* (New York: Macmillan, 1973), 213–214; Krueger, "Command," 20.
45. Krueger, "Command," 22; Eaton discusses in detail Krueger's role in attempts of the army and navy at forming a joint operating doctrine in "From Teaching to Practice," passim.
46. Krueger, "Command," 26–27 and 29.
47. Ibid., 30–31.
48. Harold R. Winton, "Toward an American Philosophy of Command," *Journal of Military History* 64, 4 (October 2000): 1035–1060.
49. Ibid., 1057–1058.
50. Eaton, "From Teaching to Practice," 20.
51. Walter Krueger, "National Policy: A Study," n.d., 15, Box 21, Krueger Papers, USMA. This study, as well as "Foreign Policy of the United States in the Pacific: A Study" (both of which were written when Krueger was a colonel), is based on his 1925 Naval War College thesis, entitled "Policy," 5 December 1925, Box 21, Krueger Papers, USMA. See also his other thesis written at the Naval War College, "Command," 1, 12 September 1925, Box 21, Krueger Papers, USMA. The concern of national unity was a recurring theme of Naval War College students during the interwar period. See John B. Hattendorf, B. Mitchell Simpson, and John R. Wadleigh, *Sailors and Scholars: The Centennial History of the U.S. Naval War College* (Newport, RI: Naval War College Press, 1984), 125–128; and Michael Vlahos, *The Blue Sword: The Naval War College and the American Mission, 1919–1941* (Newport, RI: Naval War College Press, 1980), 78–81.
52. Krueger, "National Policy," 15.
53. At the Naval War College, Krueger met, for instance, Adm. William V. Pratt and Comm. Husb. E. Kimmel. Eaton, "From Teaching to Practice," 22.
54. Letter, WK to Fay W. Brabson, 27 March 1927, Brabson Papers, USAMHI.
55. Ibid.; Letter, Walter Krueger Jr. to William M. Leary, 20 May 1985, Box 40, Krueger Papers, USMA.
56. Letter, WK to Fay W. Brabson, 7 December 1927, Brabson Papers, USAMHI.
57. Ibid.
58. Eaton, "From Teaching to Practice," 22–23; Letter, WK to Brabson, 30 April 1928.
59. The nine principles of war are objective, superiority, cooperation, simplicity, economy of force, surprise, movement, security, and offensive. Eaton, "From Teaching to Practice," 23; Memorandum, WK to the Chief of Staff of the Naval War College, "The So-Called Nine Principles of War," 9 July 1931, 1–2, Box 21, Krueger Papers, USMA.
60. Memorandum, WK, "The So-Called Nine Principles of War," 7; Walter Krueger, "Command: The Military Command System," outline of lecture, Naval War College, 1930–1931, 23, Box 16, Krueger Papers, USMA. See also Eaton, "From Teaching to Practice," 52.

61. Eaton, "From Teaching to Practice," 83–84; the Eaton quote is from George B. Eaton, "General Walter Krueger and Joint War Planning, 1922–1938," *Naval War College Review* 48, 2 (Spring 1995): 101.

62. Brabson Diary, 27 March 1931.

63. Letter, WK to Fay W. Brabson, 2 September 1928, Brabson Papers, USAMHI.

64. With the Civilian Conservation Corps, Krueger participated in Missouri's Reforestation Movement. Of Krueger's work, Missouri governor Guy B. Park wrote to Maj. Gen. Frank Parker, commander of the Sixth Corps Area, under which Krueger served: "Several weeks ago I visited a portion of your command at Jefferson Barracks, Missouri, in order to get first hand information concerning the Civilian Conservation Corps. At that time, June 13th, there were thousands of men in camp and I was afforded every opportunity to make a thorough inspection. As a result of that visit let me express to you my admiration of the able work of Colonel Walter Krueger and his command. Their efforts have certainly gone far to make the Reforestation Movement a success. The officers in charge are to be commended." Letter, Guy B. Park to Frank Parker, 14 July 1933, Box 1, Krueger Papers, USMA. See also Letter, Frank Parker to WK, 8 July 1933, Box 1; Letter, Frank Parker to WK, 19 October 1933, Box 1; and Letter, Krueger Jr. to Leary, 20 May 1985, Box 40; all in Krueger Papers, USMA.

65. Letter, WK to Fay W. Brabson, 25 August 1932, Brabson Papers, USAMHI.

66. Ibid.

67. The church incident was recounted to Walter Jr. by his wife, Betty, as well as the rest of the information in this paragraph in Letter, Krueger Jr. to Leary, 20 May 1985.

68. In addition to his lecture, he also wrote two related studies on national strategy, both of which are undated. Walter Krueger, "National Policy" and "Foreign Policies of the United States in the Pacific," Box 21, Krueger Papers, USMA.

69. Untitled lecture delivered at St. Louis, Missouri, Walter Krueger, n.d., 1 and 2, Box 21, Krueger Papers, USMA.

70. Ibid., 3. It is worth noting that the Dick Act did not explicitly prohibit the use of the militia beyond the borders of the United States, but Krueger interpreted it as doing so.

71. Ibid., 4–5.

72. Letter, WK to Fay W. Brabson, 20 December 1932, Brabson Papers, USAMHI.

73. Letter, Charles E. Kilbourne to WK, n.d., Box 1, Krueger Papers, USMA.

74. Ibid.

75. Name and Subject Index to the General Correspondence of the War Plans Division, 1921–1942, card #4; Letter, WK to Fay W. Brabson, 7 February 1934, Brabson Papers, USAMHI.

76. Eaton, "General Walter Krueger and Joint War Planning," 102; Weigley, "The Interwar Army," in Hagan and Roberts, *Against All Enemies*, 265; Morton, *Strategy and Command*, 34.

77. Memorandum for the Commanding General, Philippine Department, Stanley D. Embick, Subject: Military Policy of U.S. in Philippine Islands, 19 April 1933, WPD 3251-15, RG 165, NARA; For Embick's career, see Ronald Schaffer, "General Stanley D. Embick: Military Dissenter," *Military Affairs* 37, 3 (October 1973): 89–90.

78. Letter, WK to Wilbur R. Van Auken, 1 May 1934, Box 1, Krueger Papers, USMA.

79. Memorandum, WK, Subject: Our Policy in the Philippines, 28 October 1935, F-573, Entry 284, Box 284, RG 165; Fred Greene, "The Military View of American National Policy, 1904–1940," *American Historical Review* 66, 2 (January 1961): 373. I would once again like to thank my colleague J. T. LaSaine for sharing with me his ideas concerning the place of Krueger within the broader national and army context of the 1930s. His doctoral thesis is

important in this regard, especially for the Navy and War Departments: "The Evolution of United States National Security Policy in Global Crisis, 1935–1940" (PhD diss., Brown University, 1990, UMI Order Number 9101792). He also shared with me some of his extensive research notes used in this section.

80. Schaffer, "General Stanley D. Embick: Military Dissenter," passim.

81. The quote is from Appendix A, The Defense of the Philippine Islands by the United States, to Memorandum initialed by Stanley D. Embick, WPD 3389-29, RG 165. For other information contained in this paragraph see Morton, *Strategy and Command*, 35; and Eaton, "General Walter Krueger and Joint War Planning," 102.

82. Eaton, "General Walter Krueger and Joint War Planning," 102–103; Spector, *Eagle against the Sun*, 57; Miller, *War Plan Orange*, 184; Morton, *Strategy and Command*, 37–38; Steven T. Ross, *American War Plans, 1890–1939* (London: Frank Cass, 2002), 144; Morton, "War Plan ORANGE," 243.

83. Memorandum, WK to the Chief of Staff; the Deputy Chief of Staff; and the Assistant Chief of Staff, WPD, 14 February 1936, Tab 23, Entry 284, Series 573, Box 17, RG 165, NARA.

84. Memorandum, WK to the Chief of Staff, 28 October 1937, file #2720-104, RG 165, NARA, as quoted in Eaton, "General Walter Krueger and Joint War Planning," 107. See also Morton, *Strategy and Command*, 39.

85. It is unclear as to the origin of the call for a "flexible" military policy. Embick—who was at the time deputy chief of staff—advocated the same thing at almost the same time. See for example, Memorandum for the Assistant Secretary of War from Stanley D. Embick, 25 October 1937, filed with Japan Registered Document #225 in records of the Adjutant General's Office, Administrative Services Division, Special Projects—War Plans "Color," 1920–1949, RG 407, NARA.

86. Memorandum, WK, Subject: Some Thoughts on the Joint Basic War Plan Orange, 22 November 1937, WPD File #2720-104, Operations Division, Special Projects—War Plans "Color," RG 165. See also Memorandum, initialed by WPD/WK [Walter Krueger] and OCS/SDE [Stanley D. Embick], Subject: Joint Army and Navy Board, War Plan Orange, 3 November 1937, filed with the Japan Registered Document #225, in records of the Adjutant General's Office, Administrative Services Division, Special Projects—War Plans "Color," 1920–1948, RG 407, NARA.

87. Apparently some of these ideas were making their way to the president himself. See Memorandum, Louis Johnson (Assistant Secretary of War) to Franklin Delano Roosevelt, Subject: Joint Army and Navy Basic War Plan—ORANGE, n.d., Folder: War Department: Louis Johnson, PSF: War Department, Franklin Delano Roosevelt Papers, Franklin Delano Roosevelt Library, Hyde Park, New York.

88. Letter, Harry E. Yarnell to William D. Leahy, 15 October 1937, Leahy File, Harry E. Yarnell Papers, Library of Congress Manuscript Division, Washington, DC. For the differences between the navy and army, see LaSaine, "The Evolution of United States National Security Policy in Global Crisis, 1935–1940," 106–121; Miller, *War Plan Orange*, 224–225; Morton, *Strategy and Command*, 39–42; Spector, *Eagle against the Sun*, 58–59.

89. Eaton, "General Walter Krueger and Joint War Planning," 106–108; Morton, *Strategy and Command*, 41; Miller, *War Plan Orange*, 224–225; Morton, *Strategy and Command*, 39–42; Spector, *Eagle against the Sun*, 58–59.

90. Memorandum, "Report on Fleet Problem No. XVI," WK to Chief of Staff, 7 August 1935, Document 3829, 6, Records of the War Department, War Plans Division, General

Correspondence, 1920–1942, Box 165, RG 165, NARA; for additional comments Krueger made on air-naval operations, see Walter Krueger, "Air Defense as a Factor in National Defense," 6 December 1935, Document 888-93, Records of the War Department, War Plans Division, General Correspondence, 1920–1942, Box 57, RG 165, NARA; for Krueger's views on air operations in conjunction with ground units, see Memorandum, "Report of Observation in Connection with the GHQ Air Force Maneuvers in California, May 10–21, 1937," WK to Chief of Staff, 2 June 1937, Document 3997-1, Records of the War Department, War Plans Division, General Correspondence, 1920–1942, Box 169, RG 165, NARA; Walter Krueger, "Air Power in Our National Defense," n.d., Box 15, Krueger Papers, USMA; Memorandum for the Chairman, War Department Reorganization Committee, through the Assistant Chief of Staff, G-3, Walter Krueger, Subject: Comments on Proposed Organization, Cavalry Division, 8 April 1937, File 3662-2 to 3662-5, War Plan Division General Correspondence, 1920–1942, Box 138, RG 165, NARA.

91. Memorandum, Krueger, Subject: Comments on Proposed Organization, Cavalry Division. See also Robert Grow, "The Ten Lean Years, 1930–1940," in *Armor* 96, 1 (January-February 1987): 22–25 and 28–30; 96, 2 (March-April 1987): 25–33; 96, 3 (May-June 1987): 21–28; and 96, 4 (July-August 1987): 34–42; George F. Hofmann, "Combatant Arms vs. Combined Arms," 10; Brabson Diary, 2 April 1937, Brabson Papers, USAMHI. The connection between Krueger's concern over the mechanized cavalry division and economic considerations is made in George F. Hofmann, "The Tactical and Strategic Use of Attaché Intelligence: The Spanish Civil War and the U.S. Army's Misguided Quest for a Modern Tank Doctrine," *Journal of Military History* 62, 1 (January 1998): 125. Krueger also worked on revising the Joint Board's 1935 edition of *Joint Action of the Army and Navy*, which laid down policies of joint army-navy operations. It incorporated many of Krueger's ideas concerning the importance of combined-arms operations and unity of command. Eaton, "From Teaching to Practice," 55–57.

92. Ray S. Cline suggests that the WPD was the "keystone" of the General Staff since it "had an interest in almost all kinds of Army affairs in which the Chief of Staff's authority had to be exercised, and had primary interest in those issues that most directly affected the Army's ultimate purpose, military operations." Ray S. Cline, *Washington Command Post: The Operations Division (United States Army in World War II: The War Department)* (Washington, DC: Office of the Chief of Military History, Department of the Army, 1951), 37. See also Interview with Gen. Walter Krueger by Harold Dean, 18 March 1948, Army General Staff Interviews, Office of the Center of Military History, USAMHI.

93. Letter, Fay W. Brabson to Editor, *Time*, 5 February 1945, Brabson Papers, USAMHI.

94. Memorandum, Krueger, "The So-Called Nine Principles of War," passim.

Chapter 4. Training with the Third Army, 1938–1943

1. Letter, Adjutant General to All Chiefs of Branches and Bureaus, AG 333 E.P. (7-30-289), 1 August 1929, File 333, Office of the Chief of the Chief of Cavalry, Correspondence, 1921–1942, Box 12, RG 177, NARA, as quoted in David Eugene Johnson, "Fast Tanks and Heavy Bombers: The United States Army and the Development of Armor and Aviation Doctrines and Technologies, 1917–1945" (PhD diss., Duke University, 1990, UMI Order Number DA9106619), 251–252.

2. George F. Hofmann, "Combatant Arms vs. Combined Arms: The U.S. Army's Quest for Deep Offensive Operations and an Operational Level of Warfare," *Armor* 106, 1 (January-

February 1997): 8; see also Arthur A. Ekirch Jr., *The Civilian and the Military: A History of the American Antimilitarist Tradition* (New York: Oxford University Press, 1956; reprint, Colorado Springs: Ralph Myles, 1972), 234–253.

3. Johnson, "Fast Tanks and Heavy Bombers," 255–264.

4. Russell F. Weigley, *The History of the United States Army*, enlarged ed. (Bloomington: Indiana University Press, 1984), 402; William O. Odom, "The Rise and Fall of U.S. Army Doctrine, 1918–1939" (PhD diss., Ohio State University, 1995, UMI Order Number DA9534040), 179–180.

5. Letter, WK to Fay W. Brabson, 21 June 1938, Fay W. Brabson Papers, USAMHI.

6. The 1993 edition of the U.S. Army's FM 100-5, *Operations* provides a suitable and succinct definition of operational doctrine as "the operational level provides the vital link between strategic and tactical employment of forces. At the operational level, military forces attain strategic objectives through the design, organization, and conduct of campaigns and major operations. Tactical battles and engagements are fought to achieve operational results." Headquarters, Department of the Army, FM 100-5, *Operations* (Washington, DC: Government Printing Office, 1993), 1–3. By controlling tactical units through his Sixth Army in order to execute Gen. Douglas MacArthur's strategic directives, Krueger functioned at the operational level during the Pacific War.

7. Russell F. Weigley, "Shaping the American Army of World War II: Mobility Versus Power," *Parameters, Journal of the U.S. Army War College* 11, 3 (September 1981): 13–21; Russell F. Weigley, *Eisenhower's Lieutenants: The Campaign of France and Germany, 1944–1945* (Bloomington: Indiana University Press, 1981), 5. An expanded version of this discussion of the U.S. Army's two traditions during the interwar period may be found in Kevin C. Holzimmer, "A Soldier's Soldier: A Military Biography of General Walter Krueger" (PhD diss., Temple University, 1999, UMI Order Number 9938675), 131–139.

8. John B. Wilson, "Influences on U.S. Army Divisional Organization in the Twentieth Century," *Army History* 39 (Fall 1996): 4; Odom, "The Rise and Fall of U.S. Army Doctrine," 193–195; Christopher R. Gabel, *The U.S. Army GHQ Maneuvers of 1941* (Washington, DC: Center of Military History, United States Army, 1992), 10–11; Weigley, *Eisenhower's Lieutenants*, 22–23; *New York Times*, 20 August 1939, 28.

9. See, for example, Reuben E. Jenkins, "Offensive Doctrines: Opening Phase of Battle," *Military Review* 20, 77 (June 1940): 13–16.

10. The quote is from Memorandum, WK to Commanding General, Eighth Corps Area (Maj. Gen. Herbert J. Brees), 8 June 1939, VIII Corps Area, Adjutant General, General Administrative File, 1920–1942, 320.2, Box 58, RG 231, NARA; Headquarters, 2d Infantry Division, "Historical Summary of the 2d Infantry Division," 16 November 1943, 3, History–2d Infantry Division, 302-0.1, Box 5975, RG 407, NARA; Memorandum, WK to Commanding General, Eighth Corps Area (Maj. Gen. Herbert J. Brees), 12 August 1939, VIII Corps Area, Adjutant General, General Administrative File, 1920–1942, 320.2, Box 59, RG 231, NARA.

11. Letter, WK to Fay W. Brabson, 12 July 1939, Fay W. Brabson Papers, USAMHI.

12. Walter Krueger, "Special Report based on Field Service Test of the Provisional 2d Division conducted by the 2d Division, U.S. Army, 1939," n.d., [26 September 1939], 4–6 and 15, VIII Corps Area, Adjutant General, General Administrative File, 1920–1942, 320.2, Box 59, RG 394, NARA. For the concept of pooling and the problems associated with it, see Gabel, *The U.S. Army GHQ Maneuvers of 1941*, 11; and Cameron, "Americanizing the Tank," Vol. 1, 213.

13. Krueger, "Special Report Based on Field Service Test of the Provisional 2d Division Conducted by the 2d Division, U.S. Army, 1939," 3–4 and 12; for U.S. Army doctrine

concerning auxiliary units, see Weigley, *Eisenhower's Lieutenants*, 23; Cameron, "Americanizing the Tank," Vol. 1, 238–239; Odom, "The Rise and Fall of U.S. Army Doctrine," 246–253.

14. Memorandum, Adjutant General to the Commanding Generals of the 1st, 2d, 3d, 5th, and 6th Divisions, 18 December 1939, 1, VIII Corps Area, General Administrative File, 1940–1941, 320.2, Box 27, RG 394, NARA.

15. "Report: IX Corps, Third Army Maneuvers, 1940," Section I, 1, USAMHIL; Francis G. Smith, *History of the Third Army*, Study No. 17 (Historical Section, Army Ground Forces, 1946), 6.

16. "Report: IX Corps, Third Army Maneuvers, 1940," Section I, 1.

17. Letter, Gen. George C. Marshall to Lt. Gen. Stanley D. Embick, 26 January 1940, in Larry I. Bland, Sharon R. Ritenour, and Clarence E. Wunderlin Jr., eds., *The Papers of George Catlett Marshall*, 4 vols. (Baltimore: Johns Hopkins University Press, 1981–1996), Vol. 2, "*We Cannot Delay," July 1, 1939–December 6, 1941*, 149; "Report: IX Corps, Third Army Maneuvers, 1940," Section I, 1; Walter Krueger, "Reports from Triangular Divisions," 24 June 1940, 1 and 15, VIII Corps Area, General Administrative File, 1940–1941, 320.2, Box 27, RG 394, NARA.

18. Memorandum, Adjutant General to the Commanding Generals of the 1st, 2d, 3d, 5th, and 6th Divisions, 18 December 1939, 1.

19. Krueger, "Reports from Triangular Divisions," 24 June 1940, 19–20.

20. Ibid., 7; see also 8.

21. Ibid., 25; for the theoretical aspects of triangular division and the amount of firepower it could produce, see Cameron, "Americanizing the Tank," Vol. 1, 210.

22. U.S. War Department, "Biennial Report of the Chief of Staff, July 1, 1941," *Annual Report of the Secretary of War*, 60; Gabel, *The U.S. Army GHQ Maneuvers of 1941*, 9; Odom, "The Rise and Fall of U.S. Army Doctrine," 194.

23. Memorandum, Maj. Gen. Herbert J. Brees to the Adjutant General, 30 September 1939, 2, VIII Corps Area, Adjutant General, General Administrative File, 1920–1942, 320.2, Box 59, RG 394, NARA; Cameron, "Americanizing the Tank," Vol. 1, 210.

24. "Report, Third Army Maneuvers, 5–25 May 1940," Section V, Vol. I, Sabine Area as quoted in Smith, *History of the Third Army*, 7; Letter, Gen. George C. Marshall to Lt. Gen. Stanley D. Embick, 1 May 1940, in Bland, *The Papers of George Catlett Marshall*, Vol. 2, "*We Cannot Delay," July 1, 1939–December 6, 1941*, 206.

25. "Report: IX Corps, Third Army Maneuvers, 1940," Section I, 2.

26. The quote is from "Report: IX Corps, Third Army Maneuvers, 1940," Section I, 2; the information for the composition of the two corps as well as the location of the maneuvers is from Smith, *History of the Third Army*, 7; the composition of the Provisional Tank Brigade came from John Leslie S. Daley, "From Theory to Practice: Tanks, Doctrine, and the U.S. Army, 1916–1940," 2 vols. (PhD diss., Kent State University, 1993, UMI Order Number DA 9403192), Vol. 2, 841; the numbers come from the *New York Times*, 12 May 1940, 17; 17 May 1940, 15; 18 May 1940, 8; 19 May 1940, 23; 20 May 1940, 10; 21 May 1940, 19; 23 May 1940, 10; 24 May 1940, 14; and 25 May 1940, 6.

27. *New York Times*, 21 May 1940, 19, and 23 May 1940, 10; the Krueger quote is from "Comments of Major General Walter Krueger, CG IX Corps, at Final Critique," Annex 21, Vol. II, Annex to Report, Third Army Maneuvers, 5–25 May 1940, 354.2 as quoted in Smith, *History of the Third Army*, 8.

28. *New York Times*, 26 May 1940, 2; Daley, "From Theory to Practice," Vol. 2, 861–865. Interestingly, Brees helped to create the situation that forced both Krueger and Short to

stretch their reconnaissance units. He had opposed, for instance, attempts to increase the reconnaissance capabilities of the triangular division. Daley, "From Theory to Practice," Vol. 2, 863.

29. Memorandum, Gen. George C. Marshall to Lt. Gen. Lesley J. McNair, 18 June 1941, in Bland, *The Papers of George Catlett Marshall*, Vol. 2, 538. Unfortunately, Marshall wrote only vaguely of the extent of Krueger's reaction. He merely discusses with Krueger the "situation." Letter, George C. Marshall to WK, 14 May 1941, in Bland, *The Papers of George Catlett Marshall*, Vol. 2, 474.

30. "Report: IX Corps, Third Army Maneuvers, 1940," Section III, 2.

31. Ibid., 3. See also Cameron's analysis of these maneuvers in his "Americanizing the Tank," Vol. 2, 480–492, specifically 491.

32. "Report: IX Corps, Third Army Maneuvers, 1940," Section III, 5; see also Section IV, 2.

33. Ibid., Section III, 2.

34. Allan R. Millett and Peter Maslowski, *For the Common Defense: A Military History of the United States of America* (New York: Free Press, 1984), 396; Walter Krueger, "Report of Third Army Maneuvers, August 1940," VIII Corps, Section III, 1, Box 21, Walter Krueger Papers, USMA.

35. Headquarters, Fourth Corps Area, "Final Report, Third Army Maneuvers, August 1940," Appendix 2: Basic Plan, 1, USAMHIL.

36. Ibid., 2.

37. Krueger, "Report of Third Army Maneuvers, August 1940," Section III, 2.

38. Ibid.

39. "Report of Third Army Maneuvers, August 1940," Appendix 15, as quoted in Smith, *History of the Third Army*, 10.

40. Krueger, "Report of Third Army Maneuvers, August 1940," Section III, 1; Headquarters, Fourth Corps Area, "Final Report, Third Army Maneuvers, August 1940," Appendix 15: Final Critique, 8. Embick, Blanding, and other Third Army personnel shared many of Krueger's criticisms of the readiness of National Guard units. See "Final Report, Third Army Maneuvers, Final Critique," passim. Even Chief of Staff Gen. George C. Marshall was disappointed by the performance of many in the National Guard and regular army as well. Forrest C. Pogue, *George C. Marshall*, 4 vols. (New York: Viking Press, 1963–1987), Vol. 2, *Ordeal and Hope, 1939–1942*, 90. For a complete description of the inadequacies of the troops involved in the August 1940 maneuvers, see Gabel, *The U.S. Army GHQ Maneuvers of 1941*, 13.

41. Smith, *History of the Third Army*, 11 and 13.

42. Ray S. Cline, *Washington Command Post: The Operations Division* (Washington, DC: Office of the Chief of Military History, Department of the Army, 1951), 8; Kent Roberts Greenfield and Robert R. Palmer, "Origins of the Army Ground Forces: General Headquarters United States Army, 1940–1942," in Kent Roberts Greenfield, Robert R. Palmer, and Bell I. Wiley, *The Organization of Ground Combat Troops* (Washington, DC: Office of the Chief of Military History, Department of the Army, 1947), 6–7.

43. Cline, *Washington Command Post*, 8; Greenfield and Palmer, "Origins of the Army Ground Forces," in Greenfield, Palmer, and Wiley, *The Organization of Ground Combat Troops*, 6–7.

44. Letter, George C. Marshall to Charles D. Herron, 13 December 1940, in Bland, *The Papers of George Catlett Marshall*, Vol. 2, 370.

45. In an annotation of Marshall's 13 December letter to Herron, the editors of *The Papers of George Catlett Marshall* suggest—without any direct evidence—that Marshall did not

want Krueger as head of the Hawaiian Department because he "may have been concerned with Krueger's ability to cooperate with his navy counterpart in Hawaii" (ibid., n1, 371). This idea, however, does not fit the evidence. First, as I argued in the previous chapter, Krueger had many fruitful years working with the navy, including stints as a student and instructor at the Naval War College. Second, in his letter, Marshall states, "What I wanted to tell you is this: For reasons on this side of the water, it appears desirable to send Walter Short to Hawaii instead of Krueger, and for the same reason it appears best to make the transfer at an earlier date than originally intended" (ibid., 370). One can only wonder that if Marshall decided not to send Krueger because he could not cooperate with the navy, then why would it have been better to send Short to Hawaii *earlier* than originally planned? Surely the issue of Krueger's inability to work congenially or not with the navy would not be an issue of *when* to send Short. Marshall's biographer Forrest C. Pogue, for his part, maintains that Marshall "had been impressed by his [Short's] excellent record with troops in World War I and his command experience in the years between the two wars. Perhaps most important, he had done an outstanding job as assistant commandant at Fort Benning, the job Marshall had once held." Pogue sees Marshall's decision based on Short's merits rather than Krueger's shortcomings. Indeed, Marshall's decision was probably based on his assessments of both men's strengths. With Krueger's thorough understanding of tactics and operations and his no-nonsense approach to training, Marshall probably believed that Krueger was an excellent choice to head the Third Army after Brees, especially after the poor performance of the army as a whole in the maneuvers of 1940. Pogue, *George C. Marshall*, Vol. 2, *Ordeal and Hope, 1939–1942*, 171.

46. Letter, Herbert J. Brees to WK, 25 March 1941, Krueger Papers, Box 1, USMA.

47. Letter, George C. Marshall to WK, 14 April 1941, in Bland, *The Papers of George Catlett Marshall*, Vol. 2, 473.

48. Ibid., 473–474.

49. Ibid., 474.

50. Letter, WK to George C. Marshall, 20 April 1941, George C. Marshall Papers, GCMRL, as quoted in ibid., n3, 474.

51. Memorandum, George C. Marshall to Henry L. Stimson, 3 May 1941, in Bland, *The Papers of George Catlett Marshall*, Vol. 2, 492–293. As for Marshall's comment about Krueger's being "my senior in rank," Krueger was, in fact, fourth on the list of potential candidates for Chief of Staff after Gen. Malin Craig retired in 1939. On the list were Lt. Gen. Hugh A. Drum, Lt. Gen. John L. Dewitt, Maj. Gen. Frank W. Rowell, Krueger, and Marshall, who was a brigadier general at the time of consideration and became a permanent major general on the same day as becoming a temporary four-star general and Chief of Staff. Krueger's chances of attaining the top post were hurt by his German birth. Eric Larrabee, *Commander in Chief: Franklin Delano Roosevelt, His Lieutenants, and Their War* (New York: Harper and Row, 1987), 106; and Pogue, *George C. Marshall*, Vol. 1, *Education of a General, 1880–1939*, 2 and 329.

52. The first quote is from Letter, George C. Marshall to WK, 5 May 1941, Krueger Papers, Box 1, USMA; the second quote is from "Critique—D-2, 2d Division—May 16, 1941," Box 19, Krueger Papers, USMA; other information in this paragraph is from Smith, *History of the Third Army*, 15.

53. The quote is from Letter, WK to George C. Marshall, 11 June 1941, GCMRL, as quoted in Bland, *The Papers of George Catlett Marshall*, Vol. 2, 534, n1. Smith, *History of the Third Army*, 6; Dwight D. Eisenhower, *At Ease: Stories I Tell to Friends* (Garden City, NJ: Doubleday, 1967), 242; Forrest C. Pogue interview with WK, 7 November 1957, 2, GCMRL.

54. Smith, *History of the Third Army*, 16–19.

55. "Notes for Critique by General Krueger—September 11, 1941," 4–5, Box 19, Krueger Papers, USMA. See also his critiques of other maneuvers: "Critique—D-2, 2d Division—May 16, 1941"; "Notes for Critique, 2d Field Exercise, VIII Army Corps, June 12–13"; "Critique—1st FM—V vs. VIII Army Corps, August 21, 1941"; and "Critique—2d FM—V vs. VIII Army Corps, August 28, 1941"; all in Box 19, Krueger Papers, USMA.

56. "Critique—1st FM—V vs. VIII Army Corps, August 21, 1941," 3; see also Smith, *History of the Third Army*, 15 and 18.

57. "Critique—2d FM—V vs. VIII Army Corps, August 28, 1941," 5; see also "Notes for Critique by General Krueger—September 11, 1941," 2, Box 19, Krueger Papers, USMA.

58. Gabel, *The U.S. Army GHQ Maneuvers of 1941*, 58–59; Smith, *History of the Third Army*, 18–19.

59. Letter, Dwight D. Eisenhower to Leonard T. Gerow, 18 July 1941, cited in Daniel D. Holt, ed., *Eisenhower: The Prewar Diaries and Selected Papers, 1905–1941* (Baltimore: Johns Hopkins University Press, 1998), 530.

60. Letter, Lesley J. McNair to WK, 5 June 1941, GHQ U.S. Army, 1940–1942 General Correspondence, 354.25: GHQ Binder #1, Box 78, RG 337, NARA.

61. Gabel, *The U.S. Army GHQ Maneuvers of 1941*, 59; the quote is from 65.

62. Ibid., 67–68; Smith, *The U.S. Army GHQ Maneuvers of 1941*, 19–20.

63. Gabel, *The U.S. Army GHQ Maneuvers of 1941*, 64.

64. Ibid., 67.

65. Despite the army's experimentation, not all of the infantry divisions were reorganized as triangular divisions. The Third Army only had one such division, the 2d.

66. Gabel, *The U.S. Army GHQ Maneuvers of 1941*, 70–72.

67. Ibid., 72–74; "Notes for General Krueger's Remarks at Critique on September 23, 1941," 3, Box 19, Krueger Papers, USMA.

68. Gabel, *The U.S. Army GHQ Maneuvers of 1941*, 74–77; "Notes for General Krueger's Remarks at Critique on September 23, 1941," 4.

69. Gabel, *The U.S. Army GHQ Maneuvers of 1941*, 79–84.

70. Ibid., 84–87.

71. The quote is from "Notes for General Krueger's Remarks at Critique on September 23, 1941," 6; Gabel, *The U.S. Army GHQ Maneuvers of 1941*, 84–87.

72. Gabel, *The U.S. Army GHQ Maneuvers of 1941*, 73; Smith, *History of the Third Army*, 20.

73. Smith, *History of the Third Army*, 21; Gabel, *The U.S. Army GHQ Maneuvers of 1941*, 96–97.

74. Gabel, *The U.S. Army GHQ Maneuver of 1941*, 97 and 99–100; "Plan of Third Army," 1st and 2d Maneuver's Armored Forces, Louisiana, September 1941, GHQ General Staff, G-3 Section, Box 337, RG 337, NARA.

75. Gabel, *The U.S. Army GHQ Maneuvers of 1941*, 100–103.

76. Telephone Message, Col. Monroe and G-3 Director's Office, 25 September 1941, 1645, 1st and 2d Maneuver's Armored Forces, Louisiana, September 1941, GHQ General Staff, G-3 Section, Box 408, RG 337, NARA; Telephone Message, Col. Blakeney and G-3 Director's Office, 25 September 1941, 2100, 1st and 2d Maneuver's Armored Forces, Louisiana, September 1941, GHQ General Staff, G-3 Section, Box 408, RG 337, NARA; Forrest C. Pogue interview with WK, 7 November 1957, 2, GCMRL; Gabel, *The U.S. Army GHQ Maneuvers of 1941*, 103.

77. Gabel, *The U.S. Army GHQ Maneuvers of 1941*, 103–105.

78. Ibid., 107–109.
79. Ibid., 109–110.
80. "Comments by Lieutenant General Lesley J. McNair," 1st Phase, GHQ-Directed Maneuvers, Camp Polk, Louisiana, 14–19 September 1941, Box 19, Krueger Papers, USMA; "Remarks by Lieutenant General Walter Krueger," Commanding General, Third Army, at the Critique, Army vs. Army Maneuvers (2d Phase), Box 19, Krueger Papers, USMA; Smith, *History of the Third Army*, 22; Gabel, *The U.S. Army GHQ Maneuvers of 1941*, 115–118; Joseph R. Cerami, "Training: The 1941 Louisiana Maneuvers," *Military Review* 57, 10 (October 1987): 34–43.
81. Drew Pearson and Robert S. Allen first made the connection between Eisenhower and Third Army's success in their syndicated column. Stephen E. Ambrose, *Eisenhower*, 2 vols. (New York: Simon and Schuster, 1983–1984), Vol. 1, *Soldier, General of the Army, President-Elect, 1890–1952*, 130; Forrest C. Pogue interview with WK, 7 November 1957, 2; Eisenhower, *At Ease*, 244; for a recent example of a historian crediting Eisenhower, see Geoffrey Perret, *Old Soldiers Never Die: The Life of Douglas MacArthur* (New York: Random House, 1996), 336; Gabel, *The U.S. Army Maneuvers of 1941*, 106.
82. Gabel, *The U.S. Army GHQ Maneuvers of 1941*, 106 and 187–188; E-mail message, Christopher R. Gabel to author, 22 August 1996, in author's possession.
83. "Notes Taken at Conference on Use of Air Force," 14 August 1941, 12, Box 19, Krueger Papers, USMA; see also p. 8.
84. E-mail message, Gabel to author, 22 August 1996.
85. "Notes Taken at Conference on Use of Air Force," 14 August 1941, 8.
86. The first quote is from ibid., 7–8; the second quote is from "Remarks by General Walter Krueger, U.S. Army, Commanding General, Third Army, at the Critique, Army vs. Army Maneuvers (2d Phase)," 7.
87. "Remarks by General Walter Krueger, U.S. Army, Commanding General, Third Army, at the Critique, Army vs. Army Maneuvers (2d Phase)," 4–5.
88. Ibid., 5.
89. Ibid., 1.
90. Gabel, *The U.S. Army GHQ Maneuvers of 1941*, passim.
91. The quote is from Gabel, *The U.S. Army Maneuvers of 1941*, 188; U.S. War Department, FM 100-5, *Field Service Regulations: Larger Units* (Washington: Government Printing Office, 1942), 33–34 and 38.
92. At virtually all levels, integration of the various branches was hampered by inexperienced leadership. Particularly at the small-unit level, commanders did not fully integrate the branches into a coordinated force, and offensives often deteriorated into piecemeal assaults. Cameron, "Americanizing the Tank," Vol. 3, 702–704; Gabel, *The U.S. Army GHQ Maneuvers of 1941*, 121.
93. E-mail message, Gabel to author, 22 August 1996; the Marshall quote is from Forrest C. Pogue interview with George C. Marshall, 14 February 1957, GCMRL, as quoted in Pogue, *Marshall*, Vol. 2, *Ordeal and Hope, 1939–1942*, 89; Letter, WK to Edward F. McGlachlin Jr., 7 November 1941, Box 5, Krueger Papers, USMA.
94. Robert S. Allen, *Lucky Forward: The History of Patton's Third U.S. Army* (New York: Vanguard Press, 1947), 10; Fay W. Brabson Diary, 4 October 1941, Brabson Papers, USAMHI.
95. The Mauldin quote is from Lee Kennett, *G.I: The American Soldier in World War II* (New York: Charles Scribner's Sons, 1987), 34. Kennett does not cite the source of the quotation.

96. The first quote is from Letter, WK to Matthew Forney Steele, 28 July 1942, Matthew F. Steele Papers, USAMHI; the second quote is from Letter, WK to Colonel Frank Kowalski Jr., 27 March 1957, Box 40, Krueger Papers, USMA.

97. The quote is from Radio Interview with Gen. Walter Krueger, 6 November 1942, Box 18, Krueger Papers, USMA; Letter, WK to Kowalski Jr., 27 March 1957; Letter, WK to Maj. Gen. John P. Lucas, 11 March 1942, Box 4, Krueger Papers, USMA.

98. For a more complete discussion of the Third Army's JOTC, on which this summary is based, see Smith, *History of the Third Army*, 29–30; the story of Krueger's inspection of the JOTC is from Dan H. Rall's interview with Gen. George Henry Decker, 6, Session 2, 9 November 1972, George H. Decker Papers, USAMHI; Telephone Conversation, Lesley J. McNair and WK, 30 March 1942, Box 3, Krueger Papers, USMA; Letter, WK to Lucas, 11 March 1942; for examples of the general improvement of basic conduct of the enlisted component of the Third Army, see Letter, George C. Marshall to WK, 23 April 1942, Box 4, Krueger Papers, USMA; Letter, WK to Maj. Gen. Daniel I. Sultan (CG, VIII Corps), 28 April 1942, Box 4, Krueger Papers, USMA.

99. The quote is from Letter, WK to Brig. Gen. Alfred M. Gruenther, 28 October 1942, Box 4, Krueger Papers, USMA; Smith, *History of the Third Army*, 33–37.

100. Letter, WK to Gruenther, 28 October 1942.

101. Telephone conversation, Dwight D. Eisenhower and Brig. Gen. Albert L. Cox, 9 December 1941, as quoted in Smith, *History of the Third Army*, 24.

102. Smith, *History of the Third Army*, 24–25.

103. Greenfield and Palmer, "Origins of the Army Ground Forces," in Greenfield, Palmer, and Wiley, *The Organization of Ground Combat Troops*, 103; Robert R. Palmer, "Mobilization of the Ground Army," in ibid., 221; Robert R. Palmer, "Organization and Training of New Ground Combat Elements," in ibid., 411–412; Smith, *History of the Third Army*, 25–26.

104. The M-4 Medium Tank, the U.S. Army's primary tank in World War II, was conceived in late 1940, and production started in February 1942. R. P. Hunnicutt, *Sherman: A History of the American Medium Tank* (Novato, CA: Presidio Press, 1978), 117–124.

105. Jonathan M. House writes, "Had the war begun in 1942 or later, the British, French, and Americans would all have had time to experiment with and adjust their mechanized organizations and doctrine." Jonathan M. House, *Toward Combined Arms Warfare: A Survey of 20th-Century Tactics, Doctrine, and Organization*, Combat Studies Institute, Research Survey No. 2 (Fort Leavenworth, KS: U.S. Army Command and General Staff College, 1984), 78.

106. Letter, WK to Steele, 28 July 1942.

107. The radiogram is quoted from Walter Krueger, *From Down Under to Nippon: The Story of Sixth Army in World War II* (Washington, DC: Combat Forces Press, 1953; reprint, Nashville: Battery Press, n.d.), 3.

108. Unfortunately for the army, war came to the United States just over two months after the conclusion of the first phase of the GHQ maneuvers. As a result, the army did not have the time to digest many of the lessons of the exercises, and the development of a sound operational doctrine fell in priority to other concerns, such as filling its ranks with soldiers, developing suitable equipment, cultivating competent junior officers, and securing hemispheric defense. Senior army officers, in other words, focused their energy on creating an army out of virtually nothing. This predicament helps to account for the poor showing of many army commanders early in the war, many of whom lacked any operational vision. Nevertheless, as the war progressed, many practiced an operational doctrine that was similar to the one used by Krueger. Lt. Gen. Alexander M. Patch's plans for his Seventh U.S. Army during the Vosges

Mountain campaign, for example, were similar to those used by Krueger. See Bonn, *When the Odds Were Even*, 69–70; see also Weigley, *Eisenhower's Lieutenants*, 634. For the army's poor performance at the operational level during the early years of the war, see Russell F. Weigley, "From the Normandy Beaches to the Falaise-Argentan Pocket," *Military Review* 70, 9 (September 1990): 45–64.

109. Kevin C. Holzimmer, "In Close Country: World War II American Armor Tactics in Jungles of the Southwest Pacific," *Armor* 105, 4 (July–August 1997): 21–22.

Chapter 5. New Britain, May 1943–February 1944

1. Oral Interview with Eddleman, Interview #2, Section 2, 28 January 1975, 23; Walter Krueger, *From Down Under to Nippon: The Story of Sixth Army in World War II* (Washington, DC: Combat Forces Press, 1953; reprint, Nashville: Battery Classics, n.d.), 3.

2. Radio No. 321, Douglas MacArthur to George C. Marshall, 11 January 1943, as quoted in Charles A. Willoughby, ed., *Reports of General MacArthur*, 2 vols. (Washington, DC: Government Printing Office, 1966), Vol. 1, *The Campaigns of MacArthur in the Pacific*, 107.

3. Walter Krueger, "MacArthur," n.d., Krueger Papers, USMA, as quoted in William M. Leary, "Walter Krueger: MacArthur's Fighting General," in William M. Leary, ed. *We Shall Return! MacArthur's Commanders and the Defeat of Japan* (Lexington: University Press of Kentucky, 1988), 66.

4. Paul Chwialkowski, *In Caesar's Shadow: The Life of General Robert Eichelberger* (Westport, CT: Greenwood Press, 1993), 75; the rest of the information came from 72–75; see also Daniel E. Barbey, *MacArthur's Amphibious Navy: Seventh Amphibious Force Operations, 1943–1945* (Annapolis, MD: Naval Institute Press, 1969), 27; Excerpts from Oral Reminiscences of General Clyde D. Eddleman, 29 June 1971, 27, Box 1, RG 49, D. Clayton James Interviews, MM.

5. In fact, MacArthur was barred from commanding "directly any national force" by a 20 March 1942 Joint Chiefs of Staff directive included in George C. Marshall and Ernest J. King, 29 March 1942, RG 4, MM, as quoted in D. Clayton James, *The Years of MacArthur*, 3 vols. (Boston: Houghton Mifflin, 1970–1985), Vol. 2, *1941–1945*, 120.

6. For MacArthur's lack of interference with his commanders, see Letter, Clyde D. Eddleman to William M. Leary, 13 August 1985, Box 40, Krueger Papers, USMA; and Oral Interview with General Clyde D. Eddleman, Interview #2, Section 2, 28 January 1975, 23, Clyde D. Eddleman Papers, USAMHI.

7. Barbey, *MacArthur's Amphibious Navy*, 27.

8. Krueger, *From Down Under to Nippon*, 5–6; Letter, W. W. Jenna to WK, 9 February 1943, Box 7, Krueger Papers, USMA.

9. Krueger, *From Down Under to Nippon*, 6; Paul P. Rogers, *The Bitter Years: MacArthur and Sutherland* (New York: Praeger, 1990), 18; James, *The Years of MacArthur*, Vol. 2, *1941–1945*, 312–313.

10. Krueger, *From Down Under to Nippon*, 6.

11. Ibid., 6–7.

12. Ibid., 12–13.

13. U.S. War Department, FM 100-5, *Field Service Regulations: Operations* (Washington, DC: Government Printing Office, 1941), 235–237; Kevin C. Holzimmer, "In Close Country: World War II American Armor Tactics in the Jungles of the Southwest Pacific," *Armor* 106, 4 (July–August 1997): 21–22.

14. Krueger, *From Down Under to Nippon*, 13–14.

15. The quote is from Letter, WK to Robert L. Eichelberger, 11 June 1943, Box 9, Krueger Papers, USMA; the rest of the information on the Sixth Army is from Office of Chief of Staff, Sixth Army, "Historical Journal," Records of HQ Sixth Army, Box 3, RG 338, NARA.

16. Memorandum, WK to Douglas MacArthur, 20 February 1943, Box 9, Krueger Papers, USMA.

17. Ibid.

18. Information on the JCS 28 March 1943 directive came from "Joint Chiefs of Staff Directive: Offensive Operations in the South and Southwest Pacific Areas during 1943," 28 March 1943, as printed in Appendix K in Louis Morton, *Strategy and Command: The First Two Years* (Washington, DC: Office of the Chief of Military History, Department of the Army, 1962), 641; the background information for the directive came from ibid., 390–395; James, *The Years of MacArthur*, Vol. 2, *1941–1945*, 307–308; John Miller Jr., *CARTWHEEL: The Reduction of Rabaul* (Washington, DC: Office of the Chief of Military History, Department of the Army, 1959), 19 and 26; Krueger, *From Down Under to Nippon*,19.

19. Miller, *CARTWHEEL*, 49; Barbey, *MacArthur's Amphibious Navy*, 58–59; see also Walter Krueger, "History of Chronicle Operation," 1, Sixth Army 106-0.3, Box 2399, RG 407, NARA; Krueger, *From Down Under to Nippon*, 9.

20. Interview with General Clyde D. Eddleman conducted by William M. Leary, 24 August 1985, Box 40, Walter Krueger Papers, USMA; Barbey, *MacArthur's Amphibious Navy*, 58; Miller, *CARTWHEEL*, 50; HQ Sixth Army, "Journal of Events," 28 April 1943–31 May 1945, 1–2, HQ Sixth Army, Office of the Chief of Staff, 314.7, Box 2, RG 338, NARA.

21. "Journal of Events," 1–3; Barbey, *MacArthur's Amphibious Navy*, 55.

22. Krueger, *From Down Under to Nippon*, 21.

23. "The Operations Diary of the Woodlark Task Force from 23 June to 4 August 1943," 1, 98-TF3-0.3, Box 1530, RG 407, NARA; Miller, *CARTWHEEL*, 55–56.

24. Barbey, *MacArthur's Amphibious Navy*, 55–56.

25. "Journal of Events," 5; Krueger, "History of Chronicle Operation," 4; Krueger, *From Down Under to Nippon*, 23. An excellent description of the hostile environment of Milne Bay is provided by Barbey in his *MacArthur's Amphibious Navy*, 61.

26. Letter, WK to Orlando Ward, 12 September 1951, 3, Box 1, Krueger Papers, USMA.

27. Krueger, *From Down Under to Nippon*, 76.

28. "Journal of Events," 5.

29. Ibid., 4; Barbey, *MacArthur's Amphibious Navy*, 57 and 54.

30. Miller, *CARTWHEEL*, 58. Unfortunately, Miller does not cite the source of his information concerning Krueger's visit. For other information used in this paragraph, see "History of the Kiriwina Task Force," 3–5; Krueger, *From Down Under to Nippon*, 21–23.

31. "The Operations Diary of the Woodlark Task Force," 3; Krueger, "History of Chronicle Operation," 8; Miller, *CARTWHEEL*, 56–57; Krueger, *From Down Under to Nippon*, 23.

32. The quote is from Krueger, "History of Chronicle Operation," 15; "History of the Kiriwina Task Force," 5; Krueger, *From Down Under to Nippon*, 24; Miller, *CARTWHEEL*, 50.

33. The quotes are from Krueger, "History of Chronicle Operation," 8 and 12; for Krueger's opposition to the command arrangements during amphibious assaults in SWPA, see Gerald E. Wheeler, "Thomas C. Kinkaid: MacArthur's Master of Naval Warfare," in William M. Leary, ed., *We Shall Return! MacArthur's Commanders and the Defeat of Japan* (Lexington: University Press of Kentucky, 1988), 120; Kinkaid and Krueger met to discuss a doctrine for changing command on 3 December 1943, but the Sixth Army records do not contain the

minutes of this meeting. "Journal of Events," 23. Krueger never did like the command arrangements and throughout the war believed that an army commander should be in charge of the assault phase of an amphibious operation. Walter Krueger, "Command Responsibilities in a Joint Operation," lecture delivered at the Army Forces Staff College, 18 April 1947, Box 12, Krueger Papers, USMA.

34. Krueger, "History of Chronicle Operation," 12.

35. Ibid., 14.

36. "Journal of Events," 10–17; Krueger, *From Down Under to Nippon*, 24; Lida Mayo, *The Ordnance Department: On Beachfront and Battlefront* (Washington, DC: Office of the Chief of Military History, United States Army, 1968), 357–360; Walter Krueger, "The Commander's Appreciation of Logistics," lecture delivered at the Army War Collage, 3 January 1955, 2, Box 12, Krueger Papers, USMA.

37. "Journal of Events," 18–19; Alvin P. Stauffer, *The Quartermaster Corps: Operation in the War against Japan* (Washington, DC: Office of the Chief of Military History, Department of the Army, 1956), 199–200.

38. Actually, Krueger had started to plan "long before" any GHQ SWPA directive came to HQ Sixth Army instructing him to do so. See Krueger, *From Down Under to Nippon*, 27; and "Journal of Events," 16.

39. Miller, CARTWHEEL, 272; Krueger, *From Down Under to Nippon*, 28.

40. For Krueger's familiarity with the U.S. Army and Kiska, see Lance Q. Zedric, *Silent Warriors of World War II: The Alamo Scouts behind Japanese Lines* (Ventura, CA: Pathfinder Publishing, 1995), 41; for the Kiska operation, see Ronald H. Spector, *Eagle against the Sun: The American War with Japan* (New York: Free Press, 1985), 181.

41. For this unusual story, see Zedric, *Silent Warriors of World War II*, 40–41. Apparently Zedric used for the basis of this story an interview or correspondence with the army officer involved, Lt. Milton Beckworth. He does not, however, directly identify the source.

42. Letter, WK to Innis P. Swift, 20 October 1943, Decker Papers, USAMHI.

43. The quote is from ibid. For a complete description of the Alamo Scouts' training, see Zedric, *Silent Warriors of World War II*, 63–89 and 251; see also Letter, Horton V. White to WK, 23 April 1946, Box 10, Krueger Papers, USMA.

44. Krueger, *From Down Under to Nippon*, 27; George C. Kenney, *General Kenney Reports: A Personal History of the Pacific War* (New York: Duel, Sloan, and Pearce, 1949; reprint, Washington, DC: Office of Air Force History, United States Air Force, 1987), 336–337.

45. United States Marine Corps, *History of U.S. Marine Corps in World War II*, 5 vols. (Washington, DC: Historical Branch, G-3 Division, Headquarters, U.S. Marine Corps, 1958–1971), Vol. 2, Henry I. Shaw Jr. and Douglas T. Kane, *Isolation of Rabaul*, 300.

46. 1st Marine Division, "Special Action Report, Cape Gloucester Operation," 1943–1944, Phase I, Annex E: Task Alamo Force (GHQ Directive), 3, GHQ SWPA and USAGF, Pacific, Box T-4168, RG 407, NARA; Shaw and Kane, *Isolation of Rabaul*, 300–301; Miller, CARTWHEEL, 277; Frank O. Hough and John A. Crown, *The Campaign on New Britain* (Washington, DC: Historical Branch, Headquarters, U.S. Marine Corps, 1952), 13.

47. Miller, CARTWHEEL, 276.

48. Shaw and Kane, *Isolation of Rabaul*, 303.

49. Miller, CARTWHEEL, 275.

50. Kenney, *General Kenney Reports*, 326–327; Shaw and Kane, *Isolation of Rabaul*, 303–304.

51. Miller, CARTWHEEL, 274.

52. Ibid., 277; "Historical Report: 112th Cavalry Regiment," 24 November 1943 to 10 February 1944, 2, CAVR—112-0.3, Box 18082, RG 407, NARA.

53. The Rupertus quote is from Letter, William H. Rupertus to Alexander A. Vandegrift, 7 December 1943, Alexander A. Vandegrift Correspondence, Headquarters, United States Marine Corps, as quoted in Shaw and Kane, *Isolation of Rabaul*, 305; Miller, CARTWHEEL, 277–278; 1st Marine Division, "Special Action Report, Cape Gloucester Operation," 1943–1944, Phase I: Planning and Training, Annex D: Alamo Force G-3 Plan, 5, GHQ SWPA and USAGF, Pacific, Box T-4168, RG 407, NARA, College Park, Maryland; see also Shaw and Kane, *Isolation of Rabaul*, 305–306; Hough and Crown, *The Campaign on New Britain*, 18–20.

54. Letter, WK to A. C. Smith, 31 October 1953, 3, Office of the Chief of Military History, 270 19/07/04, File No. 2-3-7 CE4, Box 289, RG 319, NARA; George McMillan, *The Old Breed: The First Marine Division in World War II* (Washington, DC: Infantry Journal Press, 1949), 168–170; D. Clayton James, *The Years of MacArthur*, 3 vols. (Boston: Houghton Mifflin, 1970–1985), Vol. 2, *1941–1945*, 342–343; Miller, CARTWHEEL, 278.

55. Report of Conference, "Paratroops in BACKHANDER," 14 December 1943, 1–2, HQ 6th Army Chief of Staff, 337, Box 3, RG 338, NARA; Letter, WK to Smith, 31 October 1953, 2.

56. Letter, WK to Smith, 31 October 1953, 3; Report of Conference, "Paratroops in BACKHANDER," 2–3; Krueger, *From Down Under to Nippon*, 32; Miller, CARTWHEEL, 278–279.

57. Miller, CARTWHEEL, 295; James, *The Years of MacArthur*, Vol. 2, *1941–1945*, 346; Edward J. Drea, *MacArthur's ULTRA: Codebreaking and the War against Japan, 1942–1945* (Lawrence: University Press of Kansas, 1992), 91.

58. The trip lasted from 13 to 16 December and included the issue of the 503d Parachute drop in the BACKHANDER operation. "Journal of Events," 24–25.

59. Ibid., 24; Miller, CARTWHEEL, 295–296.

60. Ibid.; Miller, CARTWHEEL, 286.

61. J. Sladen Bradley, "Report of Michaelmas Operation," 16 December 1943–10 February 1944, Appendix 5: Diary, i, Michaelmas Task Force, 98-TF5-3, Box 1539, NARA.

62. Miller, CARTWHEEL, 298.

63. Ibid.

64. Krueger, *From Down Under to Nippon*, 36.

65. "Journal of Events," 26; Hough and Crown, *The Campaign on New Britain*, 34; 1st Marine Division, "Special Action Report, Cape Gloucester Operation," 1943–1944, Phase II: Landing & Seizure of Cape Gloucester Airfield, Part I-Yellow Beach Landing, GHQ SWPA and USAGF, Pacific, Box T-4168, RG 407, NARA.

66. Shaw and Kane, *Isolation of Rabaul*, 356 and 360.

67. Ibid., 360.

68. "1st Marine Division D-3 Journal-I," Entry No. 20, 29 December 1943, as quoted in Shaw and Kane, *Isolation of Rabaul*, 361.

69. As quoted ibid., 13.

70. Miller, CARTWHEEL, 293–294; Krueger, *From Down Under to Nippon*, 35; see also 1st Marine Division, "Special Action Report, Cape Gloucester Operation," 1943–1944, Phase IV: Extensive Patrolling of Western New Britain–Borgen Bay–Itini River Area and Occupation of Rooke Island, GHQ SWPA and USAGF, Pacific, Box T-4168, RG 407, NARA.

71. Krueger, *From Down Under to Nippon*, 34.

72. WK to Douglas MacArthur, 28 December 1943, Richard K. Sutherland Papers, RG 30, Reel 1002, MM.

73. Barbey, *MacArthur's Amphibious Navy*, 126.

74. Ibid., 127.

75. Radio, Douglas MacArthur to WK, 28 December 1943, Sutherland Papers, RG 30, Reel 1002, MM.

76. Miller, CARTWHEEL, 299.

77. Barbey, *MacArthur's Amphibious Navy*, 130; Miller, CARTWHEEL, 299.

78. Bradley, "Report of Michaelmas Operation," 16 December 1943–10 February 1944, Appendix 5: Diary, 5; Krueger, *From Down Under to Nippon*, 36–38; Miller, CARTWHEEL, 301–302.

79. Shaw and Kane, *Isolation of Rabaul*, 391–392; "Historical Report: 112th Cavalry Regiment," 9–12.

80. The quote is from Krueger, *From Down Under to Nippon*, 31; "Historical Report: 112th Cavalry Regiment," 11–12; Miller, CARTWHEEL, 289.

81. Miller, CARTWHEEL, 294–295; Kenney, *General Kenney Reports*, 350 and 386.

82. Charles A. Willoughby, ed., *Reports of General MacArthur*, Vol. 2, Part 1, *Japanese Operations in the Southwest Pacific Area*, 240–241; Drea, *MacArthur's ULTRA*, 91–92.

83. Krueger, *From Down Under to Nippon*, 38–39.

84. Walter Krueger, "Command Responsibilities in a Joint Operation," lecture delivered at the Armed Forces Staff College, 18 April 1947, 2–3, Box 12, Krueger Papers, USMA.

85. Ibid., 2; see also Letter, WK to Ward, 12 September 1951, 4; Krueger, *From Down Under to Nippon*, 137.

86. Decker Oral History, Session 2, 9 November 1972, 25; Krueger, *From Down Under to Nippon*, 15 and 136.

87. "Historical Journal," 13 April–21 June 1943, HQ Sixth Army, Box 3, RG 338, NARA; Krueger, *From Down Under to Nippon*, 24; Decker Oral History, Session 2, 9 November 1972, 10. Of Honnen, Krueger wrote, "As you know he is a man of very fine character and personality. Able, loyal and devoted to his work and to me, honest and conscientious and absolutely dependable, he has been an excellent Chief of Staff." Krueger suggested that after Honnen's recovery, he should be given command of troops instead of staff duty. Honnen became the commandant of cadets at the United States Military Academy at West Point, New York. Letter, WK to Lesley J. McNair, 16 June 1943, Box 7, Krueger Papers, USMA.

88. The Decker quote is from Decker Oral History, Session 2, 9 November 1972, 10; other information for this paragraph came from Krueger, *From Down Under to Nippon*, 69 and 99; "Historical Journal," 18 and 21 June 1943; Wilson A. Heefner, *Twentieth Century Warrior: The Life and Service of Major General Edwin D. Patrick* (Shippensburg, PA: White Mane Publishing, 1995), 69–71; Eddleman Interview, 24 August 1985.

89. Eddleman Interview, 24 August 1985; Decker Oral History, Session 2, 9 November 1972, 12; see also page 31.

90. Decker Oral History, Session 2, 9 November 1972, 12.

91. Eddleman Interview, 24 August 1985; the Krueger quote is from Krueger, *From Down Under to Nippon*, 137.

Chapter 6. The Fight for New Guinea, Part I: February–May 1944

1. Edward J. Drea, *MacArthur's ULTRA: Codebreaking and the War against Japan, 1942–1945* (Lawrence: University Press of Kansas, 1990), 94; Walter Krueger, *From Down Under to Nippon: The Story of Sixth Army in World War II* (Washington, DC: Combat Forces Press, 1953; reprint, Nashville: Battery Classics, n.d.), 381.

2. Stanley L. Falk, "Douglas MacArthur and the War against Japan," in William M. Leary, ed., *We Shall Return! MacArthur's Commanders and the Defeat of Japan* (Lexington: University Press of Kentucky, 1988), 15.

3. Louis Morton, *Strategy and Command: The First Two Years* (Washington, DC: Chief of Military History, Department of the Army, 1962), 535; G-3 Historical Division, General Headquarters, United States Army Forces Pacific, "Studies in the History of General Douglas MacArthur's Commands in the Pacific," in 4 parts, "The Philippine Liberation Campaign, 1944–45," Part 3, 11, RG 4, Records from General Headquarters, United States Army Forces Pacific, MM; "Summary of RENO III, Outline Plan for Operations of the Southwest Pacific Area to Reoccupy the Southern Philippines, Prepared by GHQ SWPA," 20 October 1943, as printed in Appendix S in Morton, *Strategy and Command*, 661–667; D. Clayton James, *The Years of MacArthur*, 3 vols. (Boston: Houghton Mifflin, 1970–1985), Vol. 2, *1941–1945*, 366–367; Krueger, *From Down Under to Nippon*, 45; John Miller Jr., *CARTWHEEL: The Reduction of Rabaul* (Washington, DC: Chief of Military History, Department of the Army, 1959), 316.

4. The geographic description of the islands comes from Miller, CARTWHEEL, 317–318; the MacArthur quote comes from George Kenney, *General Kenney Reports: A Personal History of the Pacific War* (New York: Duell, Sloane and Pearce, 1949; reprint, Washington, DC: Office of Air Force History, United States Air Force, 1987), 360.

5. Daniel E. Barbey, *MacArthur's Amphibious Navy: Seventh Amphibious Force Operations, 1943–1945* (Annapolis, MD: United States Naval Institute, 1969), 145–147; Krueger, *From Down Under to Nippon*, 45–47.

6. Kenney, *General Kenney Reports* 359; Wesley Frank Craven and James Lea Cate, eds., *The Army Air Forces in World War II*, 7 vols. (Chicago: University of Chicago Press, 1948–1958), Vol. 4, *The Pacific: Guadalcanal to Saipan, August 1942 to July 1944*, 549–574.

7. Barbey, *MacArthur's Amphibious Navy*, 147–148.

8. Ibid., 151; Stephen R. Taaffe, *MacArthur's Jungle War: The 1944 New Guinea Campaign* (Lawrence: University Press of Kansas, 1998), 59; Krueger, *From Down Under to Nippon*, 48; Drea, *MacArthur's ULTRA*, 102–103.

9. The quote is from (and unidentified in) U.S. War Department, Historical Division, *The Admiralties: Operations of the 1st Cavalry Division, 29 February–18 May 1944* (Washington, DC: Historical Division, War Department, 1946; reprint, Washington, DC: Center of Military History, United States Army, 1990) 15–16; Lance Q. Zedric, *Silent Warriors of World War II: The Alamo Scouts behind Japanese Lines* (Ventura, CA: Pathfinder Publishing, 1995), 97–98.

10. HQ Alamo Force, Conference Report, "Manus Island Operation: Reconnaissance in Force," 25 February 1944, 6, HQ Sixth Army, Office of the Chief of Staff, 311.3, Box 3, RG 338, NARA.

11. Ibid., 4.

12. Walter Krueger, "Report on the Brewer Operation," 3, Alamo Force, Brewer Operation Report, 98-TF1B-0.3, Box 1446, RG 407, NARA.

13. Barbey, *MacArthur's Amphibious Navy*, 148 and 151; Taaffe, *MacArthur's Jungle War*, 61.

14. Conference Report, "Manus Island Operation: Reconnaissance in Force," 1–6.

15. Ibid., 6.

16. Ibid., passim.

17. Wright, *The 1st Cavalry Division in World War II*, 16; Barbey, *MacArthur's Amphibious Navy*, 151–152; U.S. War Department, *The Admiralties*, 19.

18. U.S. War Department, *The Admiralties*, 21–22.

19. Ibid., 23–27.

20. Ibid., 27–31; Krueger, "Report of Brewer Operation," 10.

21. Miller, CARTWHEEL, 330; Krueger, "Report of Brewer Operation," 10.

22. Miller, CARTWHEEL, 328–333; Krueger, *From Down Under to Nippon*, 50; U.S. War Department, *The Admiralties*, 40–41.

23. Krueger, *From Down Under to Nippon*, 51; Miller, CARTWHEEL, 336.

24. None of the men involved explained why Barbey resisted turning over his three APDs to Alamo Force. Krueger, *From Down Under to Nippon*, 51; Barbey, *MacArthur's Amphibious Navy*, 156.

25. Barbey, *MacArthur's Amphibious Navy*, 156; Krueger, *From Down Under to Nippon*, 51; Walter Krueger, "Command Responsibilities in a Joint Operation," lecture delivered at the Armed Forces Staff College, 18 April 1947, 4, Box 12, Walter Krueger Papers, USMA.

26. Barbey, *MacArthur's Amphibious Navy*, 156; U.S. War Department, *The Admiralties*, 45–47; Alamo Force, "Diary of the Admiralty Islands Campaign, 29 February 1944–2 April 1944," 7, Alamo Force, Brewer (Admiralties) Operation, 98-TF1B-0.9, Box 1446, RG 407, NARA.

27. Letter, WK to Innis P. Swift, 4 March 1944, Box 8, Krueger Papers, USMA.

28. Alamo Force, "Diary of the Admiralty Islands Campaign," 10; U.S. War Department, *The Admiralties*, 52.

29. Letter, Innis P. Swift to WK, 8 March 1944, 1–2, Box 8, Krueger Papers, USMA.

30. U.S. War Department, *The Admiralties*, 63; Miller, CARTWHEEL, 338.

31. Letter, WK to Douglas MacArthur, 24 March 1944, George Decker Papers, USAMHI. James F. Collins Interview, Interview 2, 40, James F. Collins Papers, USAMHI, as quoted in Taaffe, *MacArthur's Jungle War*, 68.

32. The quote is from Krueger, *From Down Under to Nippon*, 57, see also 58–59; Robert Ross Smith, *The Approach to the Philippines* (Washington, DC: Office of the Chief of Military History, Department of the Army, 1953), 16 and 20–22; Drea, *MacArthur's ULTRA*, 96–97; for a complete discussion of air requirements for the Hollandia operation, see Craven and Cate, eds., *The Army Air Forces in World War II*, Vol. 4, *The Pacific: Guadalcanal to Saipan*, 575–614.

33. HQ 6th Army, "Journal of Events," 28 April 1943–31 May 1945, 1–2, HQ 6th Army, Office of the Chief of Staff, 314.7, Box 2, RG 338, NARA; Jay Luvaas, ed., *Dear Miss Em: General Eichelberger's War in the Pacific, 1942–1945* (Westport, CT: Greenwood Press, 1972), 94–95.

34. Barbey, *MacArthur's Amphibious Navy*, 159–160; for Krueger itinerary and his attempts to have Barbey's HQ near his own, see HQ 6th Army, "Journal of Events," 29–30 and 32–33.

35. HQ Alamo Force, Report of Conference, "Hollandia Operation," 11 March 1944, HQ 6th Army Chief of Staff, 337, Box 3, RG 338, NARA; for the evolution of the Sixth Army's supply system, see Lida Mayo, *The Ordnance Department: On Beachhead and Battlefront* (Washington, DC: Office of the Chief of Military History, United States Army, 1968), 372.

36. The quote and Sixth Army estimates are from Walter Krueger, "Report on the Reckless Operation," 17–19, Alamo Force, 98-TF1C-0.3, Box 1463, RG 407, NARA; GHQ SWPA estimates are taken from Drea, *MacArthur's ULTRA*, 115. Actual Japanese strength at Hollandia and Aitape reached about 16,000. Drea, *MacArthur's ULTRA*, 115. Other information in this paragraph was derived from Krueger, *From Down Under to Nippon*, 59.

37. HQ Alamo Force, Report of Conference, "Hollandia Operation," 3; Krueger, "Report on the Reckless Operation," 19–20; HQ I Corps, "Report of Enemy Operations in the Hollandia Campaign, 22 April–13 June 1944," 1–2, Reckless Task Force, 98-TF7-2.0, Box 1544,

RG 407, NARA; Paolo E. Coletta, "Daniel E. Barbey: Amphibious Warfare Expert," in Leary, *We Shall Return!* 230.

38. HQ Alamo Force, Field Order No. 12, 23 March 1944 as quoted in Krueger, *From Down Under to Nippon*, 62; Smith, *The Approach to the Philippines*, 29; William F. McCartney, *The Jungleers: A History of the 41st Infantry Division* (Washington, DC: Infantry Journal Press, 1948; reprint, Nashville: Battery Press, 1988), 71–72.

39. Krueger, *From Down Under to Nippon*, 62–63; Smith, *The Approach to the Philippines*, 31; HQ 6th Army, "Journal of Events," 35.

40. Smith, *The Approach to the Philippines*, 32; Krueger, *From Down Under to Nippon*, 53–54; Miller, CARTWHEEL, 348–350; Taaffe, *MacArthur's Jungle War*, 74.

41. Miller, CARTWHEEL, 339–340.

42. "History of the Admiralty Islands Campaign," 56; Barbey, *MacArthur's Amphibious Navy*, 168–169.

43. Krueger, *From Down Under to Nippon*, 69–70.

44. Reckless Task Force, "Historical Report on Hollandia Operation," 6 June 1944, Appendix B, Part A, 98-TF7-0.3, Box 1542, RG 407, NARA.

45. Ibid., Appendix B, Part B.

46. Ibid.; Krueger, *From Down Under to Nippon*, 65–66.

47. The quotes are from Barbey, *MacArthur's Amphibious Navy*, 173; James, *The Years of MacArthur*, Vol. 2, *1941–1945*, 451–452; Robert L. Eichelberger in collaboration with Milton MacKaye, *Our Jungle Road to Tokyo* (New York: Viking Press, 1950; reprint, Washington, DC: Zenger, 1982), 107.

48. The Eichelberger quote is from Luvaas, *Dear Miss Em*, 107; the Egeberg quote is from Roger Olaf Egeberg, *The General: MacArthur and the Man He Called 'Doc'* (New York: Hippocrene Books, 1983), 53; the Krueger quote is from Krueger, *From Down Under to Nippon*, 70; see also Eichelberger, *Our Jungle Road to Tokyo*, 107; Taaffe, *MacArthur's Jungle War*, 88.

49. Krueger, "Report on the Reckless Operation," 42; Kenney, *General Kenney Reports*, 394.

50. This section on the battle for Wakde-Sarmi largely comes from Kevin C. Holzimmer, "Walter Krueger, Douglas MacArthur, and the Pacific War: The Wakde-Sarmi Campaign as a Case Study," *Journal of Military History* 59, 4 (October 1995): 661–686.

51. Drea, *MacArthur's ULTRA*, 123–151.

52. The first quote is from Walter Krueger, "Report on the Wakde-Biak Operation, 17 May 1944 to 2 September 1944," 11, Sixth Army, 106-0.3, Box 2399, RG 407, NARA; the second quote is from Letter, Robert L. Eichelberger to WK, 20 May 1944, George Decker Papers, USAMHI; the third quote is from Eichelberger, *Our Jungle Road to Tokyo*, 137; other information used in this paragraph came from Smith, *The Approach to the Philippines*, 209 and 222; Krueger, *From Down Under to Nippon*, 81; and Drea, *MacArthur's ULTRA*, 132.

53. Smith, *The Approach to the Philippines*, 208–210; Krueger, "Report on the Wakde-Biak Operation," 8–9; the Field Order quote is from Krueger, *From Down Under to Nippon*, 80–81.

54. Smith, *The Approach to the Philippines*, 210–211; Krueger, "Report on the Wakde-Biak Operation," 9–10; Krueger, *From Down Under to Nippon*, 82–85; Taaffe, *MacArthur's Jungle War*, 146–147.

55. Krueger, *From Down Under to Nippon*, 82.

56. HQ Alamo Force, Conference Report, "Wakde-Sarmi and Biak Island Operations," 9 May 1944, Conference 1 (0915–1105), 1, HQ 6th Army Chief of Staff, 337, Box 3, RG 338, NARA.

57. Krueger, *From Down Under to Nippon*, 80, 82, and 83; HQ Alamo Force, Conference Report, "Wakde-Sarmi and Biak Island Operations," Conference 1 (0915–1105), 1.

58. Eichelberger's comments on Biak's terrain can be found in Robert L. Eichelberger, "Background for the Biak Operation," 4 April 1948, Biak Notes, 2–3.7.CE7, Box 305, RG 319, NARA; Krueger, *From Down Under to Nippon*, 83; Smith, *The Approach to the Philippines*, 280–282.

59. HQ Alamo Force, Conference Report, "Wakde-Sarmi and Biak Island Operations," Conference 1 (0915–1105), 1–2; Drea, *MacArthur's ULTRA*, 135.

60. HQ Alamo Force, Conference Report, "Wakde-Sarmi and Biak Island Operations," Conference 1 (0915–1105), 3–4; and Conference 2 (1505–1620), 1.

61. Ibid., Conference 1 (0915–1105), 3; and Conference 2 (1505–1620), 1; Coletta, "Daniel E. Barbey," in Leary, *We Shall Return!* 231.

62. HQ Alamo Force, Conference Report, "Wakde-Sarmi and Biak Island Operations," Conference 1 (0915–1105), 1 and 2; Krueger, "Report on the Wakde-Biak Operation," 11; Krueger, *From Down Under to Nippon*, 83–84.

63. Krueger, *From Down Under to Nippon*, 85.

64. Ibid.; Krueger, "Report on the Wakde-Biak Operation," 12; Shelby L. Stanton, *World War II Order of Battle* (New York: Galahad Books, 1984), 220.

65. Krueger, *From Down Under to Nippon*, 84.

Chapter 7. The Fight for New Guinea, Part II: May–October 1944

1. Walter Krueger, *From Down Under to Nippon: The Story of Sixth Army in World War II* (Washington, DC: Combat Forces Press, 1953; reprint, Nashville: Battery Classics, n.d.), 87; Robert Ross Smith, *The Approach to the Philippines* (Washington, DC: Office of the Chief of Military History, Department of the Army, 1953), 214–215 and 222–231; Walter Krueger, "Report on the Wakde-Biak Operation, 17 May 1944 to 2 September 1944," 19–20, Sixth Army, 106–0.3, Box 2399, RG 407, NARA.

2. Krueger, "Report on the Wakde-Biak Operation," 21; Krueger, *From Down Under to Nippon*, 89; Smith, *The Approach to the Philippines*, 236–237.

3. Edward J. Drea, *MacArthur's ULTRA: Codebreaking and the War against Japan, 1942–1945* (Lawrence: University Press of Kansas, 1990), 133; Smith, *The Approach to the Philippines*, 237–238; Letter, WK to Orlando Ward, 2 January 1951, 4, External Reviews on *Approach to the Philippines*, 2–3.7CE7, Box 306, RG 319, NARA.

4. "158th Regimental Combat Team Operations Report," Sarmi-Wakde Campaign, 11 May–21 June 1944, 2–3, INRG 158-0.3, Box 21182, RG 407, NARA; Field Order #2, 23 May 1944, "Unit Journal–158th Infantry Regiment," INRG 158-0.7, Box 21185, RG 407, NARA; figures of actual Japanese combat troops vary because of the absence of any solid Japanese sources. Drea calculates the Japanese strength at probably 8,000, while Smith estimates that 11,000 were available (6,500 of which were combat ready); see Drea, *MacArthur's ULTRA*, 132–134; Smith, *The Approach to the Philippines*, 235 and 239; Krueger, "Report on the Wakde-Biak Operation," 21.

5. Krueger, *From Down Under to Nippon*, 89–90; Krueger, "Report on the Wakde-Biak Operation," 22.

6. Letter, Edwin D. Patrick to WK, 3 June 1944, Box 1, George Decker Papers, USAMHI.

7. Krueger, "Report on the Wakde-Biak Operation," 39; William F. McCartney, *The Jungleers: A History of the 41st Infantry Division* (Washington, DC: Infantry Journal Press, 1948; reprint, Nashville: Battery Press, 1988), 102–107; Smith, *The Approach to the Philippines*, 307.

8. Krueger, *From Down Under to Nippon*, 95.

9. Letter, Edwin D. Patrick to Earle O. Sandlin, 31 May 1944, "Unit Journal–158th Infantry Regiment;" Krueger, *From Down Under to Nippon*, 89–90; Krueger, "Report on the Wakde-Biak Operation" 39; McCartney, *The Jungleers*, 107.

10. Smith, *The Approach to the Philippines*, 340–341; Stephen R. Taaffe, *MacArthur's Jungle War: The 1944 New Guinea Campaign* (Lawrence: University Press of Kansas, 1998), 158.

11. The quote is from Krueger, "Report on the Wakde-Biak Operation," 40; McCartney, *The Jungleers*, 107–109; Smith, *The Approach to the Philippines*, 315.

12. Letter, WK to Ward, 2 January 1951, 6.

13. Krueger, "Report on the Wakde-Biak Operation," 40–41; "Operations Report, 186th Infantry Regiment/41st Infantry Division, 27 May–19 August 1944," 9, Operations Report-Hurricane (Biak) Task Force, 341-INF(186)-0.3, Box 10641, RG 407, NARA; the Newman quote is from Oliver P. Newman interview notes, as quoted in Smith, *The Approach to the Philippines*, 321; Taaffe, *MacArthur's Jungle War*, 159–160.

14. Radio message, Douglas MacArthur to WK, 5 June 1944, Richard K. Sutherland Papers, RG 30, Reel 1002, MM; Krueger, *From Down Under to Nippon*, 99; Taaffe, *MacArthur's Jungle War*, 145.

15. Letter, WK to Douglas MacArthur, 5 June 1944, Sutherland Papers, RG 30, Reel 1002, MM.

16. Krueger, *From Down Under to Nippon*, 99.

17. "Operations Report, 186th Infantry Regiment/41st Infantry Division, 27 May–19 August 1944," 12.

18. Smith, *The Approach to the Philippines*, 301 and 323.

19. Letter, WK to Douglas MacArthur, 8 June 1944, 3, United States Army Forces, Pacific, RG 3, Reel 593, MM.

20. Ibid.

21. Krueger, *From Down Under to Nippon*, 106; Taaffe, *MacArthur's Jungle War*, 177.

22. The quotes are from Krueger, *From Down Under to Nippon*, 108; for the intelligence estimates, see Drea, *MacArthur's ULTRA*, 141–142; for the Alamo Scouts' findings, see Zedric, *Silent Warriors*, 118.

23. Krueger, *From Down Under to Nippon*, 109; Drea, *MacArthur's ULTRA*, 142; "Date of Arrival at New CPs and Date of Departures," n.d., Box 3, Krueger Papers, USMA.

24. Barbey, *MacArthur's Amphibious Navy*, 205–207; Taaffe, *MacArthur's Jungle War*, 179.

25. Krueger, *From Down Under to Nippon*, 108–109; "Historical Report of the Noemfoor Operation, 22 June 1944 to 31 August 1944," 6–7, Alamo Force, Tabletennis (Noemfoor Island) Operation, 98-TF1E-0.3, Box 1508, RG 407, NARA; Taaffe, *MacArthur's Jungle War*, 179.

26. Krueger, *From Down Under to Nippon*, 109.

27. Ibid., 114–116;Walter Krueger, "Report on the Globetrotter Operation," 28 December 1944, 1–2, 98-TF1F-0.3, Box 1516, RG 407, NARA; D. Clayton James, *The Years of MacArthur*, 3 vols. (Boston: Houghton Mifflin, 1970–1985), Vol. 2, *1941–1945*, 486; Drea, *MacArthur's ULTRA*, 142.

28. Krueger, *From Down Under to Nippon*, 117.

29. "158th Regimental Combat Team Operations Report," Sarmi-Wakde Campaign, 7–8; Operations Report #10, 1 June 1944, "Unit Journal–158th Infantry Regiment."

30. Krueger, *From Down Under to Nippon*, 90; "158th Regimental Combat Team Operations Report," Sarmi-Wakde Campaign, 10; "Tornado Task Force G-3 Operations Report," No. 20–23, 9 June 1944, 98-TF9-3.1, Box 1566, RG 407, NARA (hereafter cited as "Tornado TF G-3 Report").

31. Krueger, *From Down Under to Nippon*, 99; McCartney, *The Jungleers*, 112–113.

32. Krueger, *From Down Under to Nippon*, 101.

33. Radio message, Douglas MacArthur to WK, 14 June 1944, Sutherland Papers, RG 30, Reel 1002, MM; Smith, *The Approach to the Philippines*, 305.

34. For Krueger's views, see Letter, WK to Ward, 2 January 1951, 7; for the views of Newman and Haney, see Smith, *The Approach to the Philippines*, 345.

35. Letter, WK to Ward, 2 January 1951, 8.

36. Paul Chwialkowski, *In Caesar's Shadow: The Life of General Robert Eichelberger* (Westport, CT: Greenwood Press, 1993), 81–91 and 98–99; Robert L. Eichelberger, "Background for the Biak Operation," 4 April 1948, Biak Notes, 1, 2–3.7.CE7, Box 305, RG 319, NARA; Hurricane Task Force, "History of the Biak Operation," 15–27 June 1944, 3, 98-TF10-0.3, Box 1571, RG 407, NARA.

37. Oral reminiscences of Lt. Gen. Clovis E. Byers, 18, 24 June 1971, Box 2, RG 49, D. Clayton James Interviews, MM. Krueger's messages could hardly be classified as being "insulting." See two of his messages ("41st Division Journal," 35 and 56, Box 10528, RG 407, NARA), as quoted in Taaffe's *MacArthur's Jungle War*, 167. On 5 June, Krueger tells Fuller that his progress is "very disturbing" and that it "is imperatively necessary that you push forward with the utmost energy and determination and gain your objective quickly." Then on 11 June, Krueger wrote: "I again must urge you to liquidate hostile resistance with utmost vigor and speed to permit construction on Mokmer and other dromes to be undertaken. Since you have not reported your losses, it is assumed that they were not so heavy as to prohibit advance."

38. Jay Luvaas, ed., *Dear Miss Em: General Eichelberger's War in the Pacific, 1942–1945* (Westport, CT: Greenwood Press,1972), 128.

39. Hurricane Task Force, "History of the Biak Operation," 4; Chwialkowski, *In Caesar's Shadow*, 99.

40. Chwialkowski, *In Caesar's Shadow*, 99–100; John F. Shortal, *Forged by Fire: General Robert L. Eichelberger and the Pacific War* (Columbia: University of South Carolina Press, 1987), 89; Taaffe, *MacArthur's Jungle War*, 169.

41. For Eichelberger's plan of attack, see Hurricane Task Force, "History of the Biak Operation," 6–9; for Eichelberger's message to Krueger, see Shortal, *Forged by Fire*, 89.

42. Krueger, *From Down Under to Nippon*, 101–102.

43. Ibid., 102 and 381.

44. Taaffe, *MacArthur's Jungle War*, 168–169.

45. Luvaas, *Dear Miss Em*, 140; Letter, WK to Douglas MacArthur, 2 July 1944, Sutherland Papers, RG 30, Reel 1002, MM.

46. Krueger, *From Down Under to Nippon*, 90; the second Krueger quote is from Letter, WK to Frank C. Sibert, 19 June 1944, Box 7, Krueger Papers, USMA; "Sixth Army Report," 24–25; for Sibert's plan, see Letter, Frank C. Sibert to WK, 17 June 1944, Box 7, Krueger Papers, USMA.

47. "Tornado TF G-3 Report," No. 40, 26 June 1944.

48. Edward J. Drea, *Defending the Driniumor: Covering Force Operations in New Guinea, 1944* (Fort Leavenworth, KS: Combat Studies Institute, U.S. Army Command and General Staff College, 1984), 24–29.

49. Drea, *MacArthur's ULTRA*, 144–147; Drea, *Defending the Driniumor*, 31–32; Taaffe, *MacArthur's Jungle War*, 191.

50. Krueger, *From Down Under to Nippon*, 70–73.

51. Smith, *The Approach to the Philippines*, 136.

52. William H. Gill, as told to Edward Jaquelin Smith, *Always a Commander: The Reminiscences of Major General William H. Gill* (Colorado Springs: Colorado College, 1974), 59.

53. Letter, WK to Ward, 2 January 1951; and Charles P. Hall Interview with Robert R. Smith, 27 March 1947, 1, Office of the Chief of Military History Interviews, USAMHI; Krueger, *From Down Under to Nippon*, 71–72; Millard G. Gray, "The Aitape Operation," *Military Review* 31, 4 (July 1951): 5. Letter, WK to Ward, 2 January 1951; and Charles P. Hall Interview with Robert R. Smith, 27 March 1947, 1, Office of the Chief of Military History Interviews, USAMHI.

54. Walter Krueger, "Report of the Tabletennis Operation," 7 December 1944, 5, Alamo Force, Tabletennis (Noemfoor) Operation, 98-TF1E-0.2, Box 1508, RG 407, NARA; "Historical Report of the Noemfoor Operation," 7–8.

55. "Historical Report of the Noemfoor Operation," 8–9; Smith, *The Approach to the Philippines*, 415–416.

56. Krueger, *From Down Under to Nippon*, 111–112.

57. Ibid., 112; George C. Kenney, *General Kenney Reports: A Personal History of the Pacific War* (New York: Duel, Sloan, and Pearce, 1949; reprint, Washington, DC: Office of Air Force History, United States Air Force, 1987),427.

58. Gray, "The Aitape Operation," 51; Drea, *Defending the Driniumor*, 39; Drea, *MacArthur's* ULTRA, 148–149; Taaffe, *MacArthur's Jungle War*, 196; Smith, *The Approach to the Philippines*, 133–134.

59. Smith, *The Approach to the Philippines*, 138–139; Letter, Clarence A. Martin to Orlando Ward, 12 November 1950, 8, External Reviews on *Approach to the Philippines*, 2–3.7CE7, Box 306, RG 319, NARA.

60. Letter, Martin to Ward, 12 November 1950, 7–8; Krueger, "Report on the Reckless Operation," 33.

61. Letter, Charles P. Hall to WK, 1, 10 July 1944, Decker Papers, USAMHI.

62. Ibid; the Gill quote is from William H. Gill interview, Tape #6, 13, Box 1, William H. Gill Papers, USAMHI.

63. Persecution Task Force, "Report After Action: Persecution Task Force, Aitape, New Guinea, 28 June to 25 August 1944," 3, Report of G-3 Section, XI Corps, 98-TF8-0.3, Box 1561, RG 407, NARA; for Hall's confidence, see Hall interview, passim.

64. Taaffe, *MacArthur's Jungle War*, 198; Letter, Martin to Ward, 12 November 1950, 12–14.

65. Letter, Martin to Ward, 12 November 1950, 14; Smith, *The Approach to the Philippines*, 155–156.

66. The Gill quote is from Gill, *Always a Commander*, 62; for the reason surrounding Gill assuming command, see Letter, WK to Ward, 2 January 1951, 4; and Smith, *The Approach to the Philippines*, 159.

67. The Krueger quote is from Krueger, *From Down Under to Nippon*, 72; for Hall's plan, see Persecution Task Force, "Report After Action: Persecution Task Force," 5; Smith, *The Approach to the Philippines*, 158–159; Taaffe, *MacArthur's Jungle War*, 200.

68. Krueger, "Report on the Reckless Operation," 35; Smith, *The Approach to the Philippines*, 177–205; Persecution Task Force, "Report After Action: Persecution Task Force," 6; Taaffe, *MacArthur's Jungle War*, 206–207.

69. The quote is from Smith, *The Approach to the Philippines*, 204; the casualty figures are from Krueger, *From Down Under to Nippon*, 381.

70. Letter, Martin to Ward, 12 November 1950, 7.

71. Hall interview, 27 March 1947, 2.

72. Gill, *Always a Commander*, 60; Persecution Task Force, "Report After Action: Persecution Task Force," 2.

73. Walter Krueger, "Report of the Globetrotter Operation," 20 December 1944, 5–7, Globetrotter (Sansapor) Operation, 98-TF1F-0.3, Box 1516, RG 407, NARA.

74. Ibid., 11–12.

75. Ibid., 14; Kenney, *General Kenney Reports*, 418.

76. Smith, *The Approach to the Philippines*, 449; for the Japanese situation on the Vogelkop Peninsula as a result of Sixth Army operations, see Charles A. Willoughby, ed., *Reports of General MacArthur*, 2 vols. (Washington, DC: Government Printing Office, 1966), Vol. 2, Part 1, *Japanese Operations in the Southwest Pacific Area*, 303; Drea, *MacArthur's ULTRA*, 142–143.

77. Drea, *MacArthur's ULTRA*, 152–153; Krueger, *From Down Under to Nippon*, 122.

78. Krueger, *From Down Under to Nippon*, 122–125.

79. HQ Alamo Force, Conference Report, "Morotai Operation," 9 August 1944, 1, HQ Sixth Army, Office of the Chief of Staff, 337, Box 3, RG 338, NARA.

80. Krueger, *From Down Under to Nippon*, 126.

81. Ibid., 128–130.

82. Edward J. Drea, *New Guinea* (Washington, DC: U.S. Army Center of Military History, n.d.), 2–31.

83. Krueger, *From Down Under to Nippon*, 75–76.

84. Robert W. Coakley and Richard M. Leighton, *Global Logistics and Strategy, 1943–1945* (Washington, DC: Office of the Chief of Military History, United States Army, 1968), 468.

85. Alvin P. Stauffer, *The Quartermaster Corps: Operations in the War against Japan* (Washington, DC: Office of the Chief of Military History, Department of the Army, 1956), 270; Krueger, *From Down Under to Nippon*, 133.

86. Stauffer, *The Quartermaster Corps*, 201.

87. The first quote is from Krueger, *From Down Under to Nippon*, 133; the second is from Letter, WK to James L. Frink, 20 August 1944, 1, Decker Papers, USAMHI; other information in the paragraph is from HQ Alamo Force, Conference Report, "Shipping Situation," 18 July 1944, 5, HQ Sixth Army, Office of the Chief of Staff, 337, Box 3, RG 338, NARA; see also Krueger, *From Down Under to Nippon*, 77.

88. The first quote is from Letter, WK to Frink, 20 August 1944, 1; the second is from Krueger, *From Down Under to Nippon*, 133; for problems with mail delivery, see Letter, WK to Douglas MacArthur, 13 March 1944, Decker Papers, USAMHI.

89. Krueger, *From Down Under to Nippon*, 77; for the broader context and implications of the army's failure to institute a satisfactory replacement and rotation system that affected all theaters, see Russell F. Weigley, "The American Military and the Principle of Civilian Control from McClellan to Powell," *Journal of Military History* 57, 5 (October 1993): 53–54.

90. Krueger, *From Down Under to Nippon*, 75.

Chapter 8. Leyte, October–December 1944

1. D. Clayton James, *The Years of MacArthur*, 3 vols. (Boston: Houghton Mifflin, 1970–1985), Vol. 2, *1941–1945*, 521–525; Edward J. Drea, *MacArthur's ULTRA: Codebreaking and the War against Japan, 1942–1945* (Lawrence: University Press of Kansas, 1992), 153.

2. James, *The Years of MacArthur*, Vol. 2, *1941–1945*, 540–542; Robert Ross Smith, "Luzon versus Formosa (1944)," in Kent Robert Greenfield, ed., *Command Decisions* (New York: Harcourt, Brace, 1959), 366–367; M. Hamlin Cannon, *Leyte: The Return to the Philippines* (Washington, DC: Office of the Chief of Military History, Department of the Army, 1954), 8–9.

3. The work of Philip Ridderhof has eased the process of putting together Sixth Army events thanks to his "Sixth Army/Alamo Force Chronology Based on *From Down Under to Nippon* by Gen. Walter Krueger." I would like to thank Lt. Col. Ridderhof for providing me with a copy of his work.

4. The first quote is from Sixth Army, "Report of the Leyte Operation, 20 October 1944–25 December 1944," 17, 106-0.3, Sixth Army, Box 2400, RG 407, NARA; the second quote as well as information concerning GHQ SWPA's directive is from Walter Krueger, *From Down Under to Nippon: The Story of Sixth Army in World War II* (Washington: Combat Forces Press, 1953; reprint, Nashville: Battery Classics, n.d.), 143. The complete operations instructions is reprinted in Cannon, *Leyte*, Appendix A, 371–377.

5. Krueger, *From Down Under to Nippon*, 203.

6. Falk, *Decision at Leyte*, 48 and 70; Cannon, *Leyte*, 22.

7. Krueger, *From Down Under to Nippon*, 145; Falk, *Decision at Leyte*, 11.

8. Sixth Army, "Report of the Leyte Operation," 17.

9. Cannon, *Leyte*, 23.

10. Sixth Army, "Report of the Leyte Operation," 20; Cannon, *Leyte*, 31–32.

11. Sixth Army, "Report of the Leyte Operation," 20.

12. The Krueger quote is from Letter, WK to Douglas MacArthur, 2 July 1944, Richard K. Sutherland Papers, RG 30, Reel 1002, MM.

13. Sixth Army, "Report of the Leyte Operation," 20; Cannon, *Leyte*, 33.

14. Sixth Army, "Report of the Leyte Operation," 20; Cannon, *Leyte*, 33–34.

15. Sixth Army, "Report of the Leyte Operation," 20–23.

16. Ibid.; for the necessity of reinforcing the infantry division's firepower, see Letter, WK to Albert E. Phillips, 6 June 1945, Box 9, Walter Krueger Papers, USMA.

17. Sixth Army, "Report of the Leyte Operation," 20–23; Krueger, *From Down Under to Nippon*, 150–151.

18. Cannon, *Leyte*, 24–26; Krueger, *From Down Under to Nippon*, 154–155.

19. Sixth Army, "Report of the Leyte Operation," 31–32; Krueger, *From Down Under to Nippon*, 156; Cannon, *Leyte*, 60–62.

20. Krueger, *From Down Under to Nippon*, 158.

21. Cannon, *Leyte*, 80; Falk, *Decision at Leyte*, 93–94; Sixth Army, "Report of the Leyte Operation," 32.

22. Sixth Army, "Report of the Leyte Operation," 32; Falk, *Decision at Leyte*, 98–100; Cannon, *Leyte*, 76–77.

23. Cannon, *Leyte*, 78.

24. Krueger, *From Down Under to Nippon*, 162.

25. Ibid., 162–163.

26. Cannon, *Leyte*, 89–92; Falk, *Decision at Leyte*, 125–215; the Krueger quote is from Sixth Army, "Report of the Leyte Operation," 43.

27. Sixth Army, "Report of the Leyte Operation," 34–38.

28. Sixth Army, "Report of the Leyte Operation, 34–40; Cannon, *Leyte*, 103–130.

29. The quote is from Sixth Army, "Report of the Leyte Operation," 84; see also p. 45; for Hodge's comments, see Letter, John R. Hodge to Orlando Ward, 28 June 1951, 2, Exter-

nal Reviews of *Leyte: Return to the Philippines*, 2–3.7CE8, Box 313, RG 319, NARA; for Krueger's remarks, see Letter, WK to Orlando Ward, 13 August 1951, 1–2, External Reviews of *Leyte: Return to the Philippines*, 2–3.7CE8, Box 313, RG 319, NARA; and Walter Krueger, "The Commander's Appreciation of Logistics," lecture delivered at the Army War College, 3 January 1955, 8–9, Box 12, Krueger Papers, USMA.

30. Krueger, *From Down Under to Nippon*, 193; on the "sporadic" capabilities of SWPA air power, see Radio message, Col. Quinn to the 6, 8, and 9 Air Liaison Parties, 31 October 1944, Sixth Army G-3 Journal, as quoted in Cannon, *Leyte*, 187.

31. Falk, *Decision at Leyte*, 57–60, 79–90, and 104–108; Drea, *MacArthur's ULTRA*, 168–169; Cannon, *Leyte*, 103.

32. Edward J. Drea, *In the Service of the Emperor: Essays on the Imperial Japanese Army* (Lincoln: University of Nebraska Press, 1998), 137; Falk, *Decision at Leyte*, 288.

33. Krueger, *From Down Under to Nippon*, 168; Cannon, *Leyte*, 206.

34. Ibid; the final quote may be found in Letter, WK to Ward, 13 August 1951, 3.

35. X Corps, "G-2 Estimate of the Enemy Situation X Corps," 26 October 1944, Thomas F. Hickey Papers, USAMHI; Cannon, *Leyte*, 209.

36. Memorandum, Assistant G-3 to Clyde D. Eddleman, 5 November 1944, 3, Sixth Army, King II Operation, 106-3.2, Box 2460, RG 407, NARA.

37. The quotes and figures are from Krueger, *From Down Under to Nippon*, 190; Telephone call, Thomas F. Hickey (G-2, X Corps) to George H. Decker, 6 November 1944, Hickey Papers, USMHI; Cannon, *Leyte*, 221–222; William M. Leary, "Walter Krueger: MacArthur's Fighting General," in William M. Leary, ed., *We Shall Return! MacArthur's Commanders and the Defeat of Japan* (Lexington: University Press of Kentucky), 76.

38. Krueger, *From Down Under to Nippon*, 169–170; Letter, Clyde D. Eddleman to William M. Leary, 30 April 1985, Box 40, Krueger Papers, USMA; the quote is from X Corps, "A History of X Corps," 26. For Yamashita's proposal to land at Carigara, see George B. Eaton, "From Luzon to Luzon: Walter Krueger and the Luzon Campaign," *Valley Forge Journal: A Record of Patriotism and American Culture* 6, 1 (June 1992): 25; Falk, *Decision at Leyte*, 304; Charles A. Willoughby, ed., *Reports of General MacArthur*, 2 vols. (Washington, DC: Government Printing Office, 1966), Vol. 2, Part 2, *Japanese Operations in the Southwest Pacific Area*, 430–431.

39. Krueger, *From Down Under to Nippon*, 170, the quote concerning the Japanese 1st Infantry Division is from 166; Drea, *MacArthur's ULTRA*, 172 and 264; Falk, *Decision at Leyte*, 246–247.

40. Krueger, *From Down Under to Nippon*, 172–173; X Corps, "A History of the X Corps in the Leyte-Samar Operation, September 1944–January 1945," 28–29, X Corps, 210-0.2, Box 4108, RG 407, NARA; Sixth Army, "Report of the Leyte Operation," 57; Falk, *Decision at Leyte*, 248–251 has an excellent discussion of the battle for Breakneck Ridge.

41. For American casualties, see X Corps, "A History of the X Corps," 29. For the issue of personnel replacements during the battle, see Telephone conversation, Thomas F. Hickey (X Corps G-3) to George C. Decker, 6 November 1944, Hickey Papers, USAMHI; HQ 6th Army, "Journal of Events," 28 April 1943–31 May 1945, 6 December 1944 entry, HQ 6th Army, Office of the Chief of Staff, 314.7, Box 2, RG 338, NARA.

42. Telephone conversation, WK and Frank C. Sibert, 22 November 1944, Hickey Papers, USAMHI; Telephone conversation, George H. Decker and Frank C. Sibert, 13 November 1944, Hickey Papers, USAMHI; see also Telephone conversation, Frank C. Sibert and William H. Gill, 22 November 1944, Hickey Papers, USAMHI; HQ 6th Army, "Journal of Events," 13 November 1944.

43. Sixth Army, "Report of the Leyte Operation," 50, 58, and 59.
44. Ibid., 62.
45. Ibid., 64.
46. Sixth Army, "Report of the Leyte Operation," 64.
47. Falk, *Decision at Leyte*, 288–289; Drea, *MacArthur's* ULTRA, 172; the Krueger quote is from his *From Down Under to Nippon*, 178; for Kinkaid's efforts to postpone the Mindoro operations, see Wheeler, "Thomas C. Kinkaid: MacArthur's Master of Naval Warfare," in Leary, *We Shall Return!* 145–147.
48. HQ 6th Army, "Journal of Events," 1 December 1944; Sixth Army, "Report of the Leyte Operation," 67; Falk, *Decision at Leyte*, 286; Krueger, *From Down Under to Nippon*, 179; Sixth Army, "Report of the Leyte Operation," 71.
49. 77th Infantry Division, "Headquarters 77th Infantry Division G-3 Operation Summary: Liberation of Leyte, 23 November–25 December 1944," 13–14, Miscellaneous Correspondence, *Leyte: Return to the Philippines*, 377-0.3, Box 11549, RG 407, NARA; for the Japanese Army's disposition in eastern Leyte, see Falk, *Decision at Leyte*, 292.
50. 77th Infantry Division, "Liberation of Leyte," 16.
51. Bruce's comments are from Bruce, "The Operations of the 77th Division in Leyte," 12; for the 77th Division's capture of Ormoc, see Cannon, *Leyte*, 291–293; Falk, *Decision at Leyte*, 300–301.
52. Message, Andrew D. Bruce to John R. Hodge, 10 December 1944, 77th Division G-3 Journal, as quoted in Cannon, *Leyte*, 292.
53. Ibid., 309.
54. Ibid., 311.
55. MacArthur's message is quoted from Krueger, *From Down Under to Nippon*, 187.
56. Falk, *Decision at Leyte*, 312; Paul Chwialkowski, *In Caesar's Shadow: The Life of General Robert Eichelberger* (Westport, CT: Greenwood Press, 1993), 114.
57. Falk, *Decision at Leyte*, 319.
58. HQ 6th Army, "Journal of Events," 20 October–25 December 1944; see also James, *The Years of MacArthur*, Vol. 2, *1941–1945*, 591–593, which provides a slightly higher number of meetings between the two.
59. For his routine, see Krueger, *From Down Under to Nippon*, 195; for the attack on his headquarters, see the *Cincinnati Post*, 14 November 1944, Box 28, Krueger Papers, USMA; the Krueger quote is from Krueger, *From Down Under to Nippon*, 195.
60. Krueger, *From Down Under to Nippon*, 195.
61. Memorandum, "Mistakes Made and Lessons Learned in K-2 Operation," 25 November 1944, 3, Box 7, Krueger Papers, USMA.
62. Ibid., 4.
63. Ibid., 7.
64. Ibid., 9.
65. The 7th Division had participated in retaking Attu in the Aleutians and then invaded Kwajalein before traveling to Hawaii for rest and rehabilitation. It left the Hawaiian Islands in mid-September 1944 for its role in the Leyte operation. The 77th Division departed Guam, where it served under the navy, on 3 November 1944 and arrived in SWPA on 15 November. The 96th Division reached SWPA on 3 October 1944, only three months after leaving California and seventeen days before A-day.
66. E. M. Flanagan, *The Angels: A History of the 11th Airborne Division* (Novato, CA: Presidio Press, 1989), 80–96; for information on the Australian Training Center in Jungle

Warfare, see U.S. Army Ground Forces Observer Board, Pacific Ocean Area, *Report of Observer Boards, Pacific Ocean Areas*, 11 vols., USAMHI library, Vol. 1, Report B-9, Fenton G. Epling, "Report on Australian Training Center (Jungle Warfare)," 12 December 1943; Shelby L. Stanton, *World War II Order of Battle* (New York: Galahad Books, 1984), 87–88, 144–145, and 172–173.

67. Letter, WK to Orlando Ward, 12 September 1951, 5, External Reviews on *Triumph in the Philippines*, 2–3.7CE8, Box 313, RG 319, NARA.

Chapter 9. Luzon and Japan, January 1945–January 1946

1. Walter Krueger, *From Down Under to Nippon: The Story of Sixth Army in World War II* (Washington, DC: Combat Forces Press, 1953; reprint, Nashville: Battery Classics, n.d.), 211.

2. Edward J. Drea, *MacArthur's ULTRA: Codebreaking and the War against Japan, 1942–1945* (Lawrence: University Press of Kansas, 1992), 181–183.

3. Interrogation of Lt. Gen. Shuichi Miyazaki (Chief of Operations, Section of the Imperial General Headquarters), 3, Interrogation of Japanese Officials on World War II (English translation), General Headquarters for East Command, Military Intelligence Section, Historical Division, Vol. A–M, U.S. Army CMH; Robert Ross Smith, *Triumph in the Philippines* (Washington, DC: Office of the Chief of Military History, Department of the Army, 1963), 90.

4. Smith, *Triumph in the Philippines*, 94–96.

5. Ibid., 96–97.

6. Krueger, *From Down Under to Nippon*, 212–213.

7. Ibid., 214–215; Conference Report, "Lingayen Operation," 15 November 1944, 3–4, HQ Sixth Army, Office of the Chief of Staff, 337, Box 3, RG 338, NARA.

8. Sixth Army, "Sixth Army on Luzon," Sections I–IV, Section I: "Lingayen to Manila," 5, Sixth Army, 106-0.3, Box 2405, RG 407, NARA.

9. Ibid., 6–7; for the doctrine concerning the breakthrough maneuver, see U.S. War Department, FM 100-15, *Field Service Regulations: Larger Units* (Washington, DC: Government Printing Office, 1942), 33–37; U.S. War Department, FM 100-5, *Field Service Regulations: Operations* (Washington, DC: Government Printing Office, 1941), 188–192.

10. Conference Report, "Lingayen Operation," 5; Krueger, *From Down Under to Nippon*, 215; Smith, *Triumph in the Philippines*, 31. The Krueger quote is from Walter Krueger, "Command Responsibilities in a Joint Operation," lecture delivered at the Armed Forces Staff College, 18 April 1947, 13–14, Box 12, Walter Krueger Papers, USMA.

11. Conference Report, "Lingayen Operation," 5–6; 13th Armored Group, "Report After Action against the Enemy," 10 August 1945, 4–5, 13th Armored Group, ARGP13-0.3, Box 16855, RG 407, NARA.

12. 13th Armored Group, "Report after Action against the Enemy," 4–5.

13. Conference Report, "Lingayen Operation," 5.

14. Excerpts from Oral Reminiscences of General Clyde D. Eddleman, 22, 29 June 1971, Box 1, RG 49, D. Clayton James Interviews, MM.

15. Ibid.; Drea, *MacArthur's ULTRA*, 186–187.

16. Krueger, "Command Responsibilities in a Joint Operation," 17–18.

17. Krueger, *From Down Under to Nippon*, 202–207; the quote is from p. 207.

18. Ibid., 221–222.

19. Ibid., 224–225.

20. Ibid., 225.

21. Ibid; the XIV Corps after-action report has a useful description of the difficult conditions at its beach as well as photographs. XIV Corps, "Operations on Luzon," 62–67, XIV Corps, 214-0.3, Box 4622, RG 407, NARA.

22. Krueger, *From Down Under to Nippon*, 225; H. D. Vogel, "Logistical Support of the Lingayen Operation," lecture delivered at the Army and Navy Staff College, 4 February 1946, 4, Box 25, Krueger Papers, USMA.

23. Vogel, "Logistical Support of the Lingayen Operation," 4. For a much more detailed examination of the problems of transporting supplies to combat units on Luzon, see Alvin P. Stauffer, *Quartermaster Corps: Operations in the War against Japan* (Washington, DC: Office of the Chief of Military History, Department of the Army, 1956), 279–282.

24. Krueger, *From Down Under to Nippon*, 227.

25. Ibid., 227–228; the Krueger quote is from Krueger, "Command Responsibilities in a Joint Operation," 13–14.

26. Oral interview with General Clyde D. Eddleman by Lowell G. Smith and Murray G. Swindler, Interview #2, Section 2, 28 January 1975, 32–33, USAMHI; see also Clyde D. Eddleman, "The Lingayen Operation," lecture delivered at the Army and Navy Staff College, 4 February 1946, 6, Clyde D. Eddleman Papers, USAMHI; Letter, Clyde D. Eddleman to William M. Leary, 13 August 1985, Krueger Papers, USMA; George H. Decker Oral History interviewed by Dan H. Ralls, Session 2, 9 November 1972, 20, The George H. Decker Papers, USAMHI; Walter Krueger, "The Luzon Campaign of 1945," lectured delivered at Command and General Staff College, 6 April 1954, 4, Box 18, Krueger Papers, USMA.

27. The radio message is Message, Douglas MacArthur to WK, 30 January 1945, Reel 1002, RG 30, Richard K. Sutherland Papers, MM; the account of the meeting between MacArthur and Krueger comes from Egeberg, *The General*, 115.

28. Smith, *Triumph in the Philippines*, 221–222 and 229–230; Letter, Clyde D. Eddleman to William M. Leary, n.d., 4, Box 40, Krueger Papers, USMA.

29. Krueger, "The Commander's Appreciation of Logistics," 11.

30. U.S. War Department, FM 100-5, *Field Service Regulations: Operations*, 98.

31. Letter, WK to R. W. Stephens, 18 December 1956, External Reviews of *Triumph in the Philippines*, 2-3.7CE9, Box 325, RG 319, NARA.

32. Charles A. Willoughby, ed., *Reports of General MacArthur*, 2 vols. (Washington, DC: Government Printing Office, 1966), Vol. 2, Part 2, *Japanese Operations in the Southwest Pacific Area*, 469–470; Krueger, *From Down Under to Nippon*, 257.

33. Smith, *Triumph in the Philippines*, 141; Drea, *MacArthur's ULTRA*, 193–194.

34. Sixth Army, G-2 Estimate of the Enemy Situation with Reference to Proposed Seizure of Clark Field, 17 January 1945, 4 and passim, Sixth Army, 106-3.2, Box 2483, RG 407, NARA.

35. Krueger, *From Down Under to Nippon*, 234; Interview with General Clyde D. Eddleman conducted by William M. Leary, 24 August 1985, Box 40, Krueger Papers, USMA; Oral Interview with General Clyde D. Eddleman, Interview #2, Section 2, 28 January 1975, 33.

36. Sixth Army, Field Order No. 43, 18 January 1945, Sixth Army, 106-3.2, Box 2483, RG 407, NARA; Krueger, *From Down Under to Nippon*, 228–229; 13th Armored Group, "Report After Action against the Enemy," 14; XIV Corps, "Operations on Luzon," 86.

37. Sixth Army, "Sixth Army on Luzon," Section I: "Lingayen to Manila," 18–19; XIV Corps, "Operations on Luzon," 86; Telephone Conversation, Oscar W. Griswold and Deputy Chief of Staff, Sixth Army [Col. Kenneth Pierce?], 21 January 1945, HQ Sixth Army, Office of the Chief of Staff, 311.3, Box 1, RG 338, NARA; Smith, *Triumph in the Philippines*, 169

and 235; Wesley Frank Craven and James Lea Cate, eds., *The Army Air Forces in World War II*, 7 vols. (Chicago: University Press of Chicago, 1948–1958), Vol. 5, *The Pacific: Matterhorn to Nagasaki, June 1944 to August 1945*, 419.

38. Krueger, *From Down Under to Nippon*, 230–231; the quote is from XIV Corps, "Operations on Luzon," 89; Letter, Oscar W. Griswold to Office of the Department of Military History, 11 January 1957, 1, Box 13, Krueger Papers, USMA.

39. Sixth Army, "Sixth Army on Luzon," Section I: "Lingayen to Manila," 19; Smith, *Triumph in the Philippines*, 170.

40. Sixth Army, "Sixth Army on Luzon," Section I: "Lingayen to Manila," 23; Krueger, "The Luzon Campaign of 1945," 5; Krueger, *From Down Under to Nippon*, 240.

41. Sixth Army, "Sixth Army on Luzon," Section I: "Lingayen to Manila," 23–24; XIV Corps, "Operations on Luzon," 109–110; Krueger, *From Down Under to Nippon*, 239–241.

42. Sixth Army, "Sixth Army on Luzon," Section I: "Lingayen to Manila," 24; Krueger, *From Down Under to Nippon*, 232 and 243.

43. Eaton, "From Luzon to Luzon," 31; William M. Leary, "Walter Krueger: MacArthur's Fighting General," in William M. Leary, ed., *We Shall Return! MacArthur's Commanders and the Defeat of Japan* (Lexington: University Press of Kentucky), 83.

44. Smith, *Triumph in the Philippines*, 215–216.

45. Krueger, *From Down Under to Nippon*, 242; Smith, *Triumph in the Philippines*, 216–217.

46. Spector, *Eagle against the Sun*, 524; Smith, *Triumph in the Philippines*, 249–308; Krueger, *From Down Under to Nippon*, 246–252; Krueger, "The Luzon Campaign of 1945," 6.

47. Richard Connaughton, John Pimlott, and Duncan Anderson, *The Battle for Manila: The Most Devastating Untold Story of World War II* (Novato, CA: Presidio Press, 1995), 178–180.

48. Ibid., 181; for MacArthur's plans for retaking the Philippines, see Willoughby, *Reports of General MacArthur*, Vol. 1, *The Campaigns of MacArthur in the Pacific*, 172.

49. Krueger, *From Down Under to Nippon*, 234.

50. Jay Luvaas, ed., *Dear Miss Em: General Eichelberger's War in the Pacific, 1942–1945*. (Westport, CT: Greenwood Press, 1972), 225; Rogers's quote is from Paul P. Rogers, *The Bitter Years: MacArthur and Sutherland* (New York: Praeger, 1990), 248–249; see also 235. D. Clayton James writes, "Yet, on February 18, at the height of MacArthur's intense pressure on his Sixth Army commander to be more aggressive in the drive to Manila, the SWPA chief, without telling him, recommended to the War Department that Krueger be promoted to a four-star general. MacArthur's behavior was contradictory"; James, *The Years of MacArthur*, Vol. 2, *1941–1945*, 669. Along with Krueger, Kenney was also promoted to full general in early 1945.

51. Telephone Conversation, Oscar W. Griswold to George H. Decker, 15 February 1945, HQ Sixth Army, Office of the Chief of Staff, 311.3, Box 1, RG 338, NARA.

52. Smith, *Triumph in the Philippines*, 249; Kevin T. McEnery, "The XIV Corps Battle for Manila, February 1945" (MMAS thesis, U.S. Army Command and General Staff College, 1993), 115; Connaughton, Pimlott, and Anderson, *The Battle for Manila*, 196.

53. Memorandum, WK to Douglas MacArthur, 5 February 1945, Subject: Control and Rehabilitation of the City of Manila, HQ Sixth Army, Office of the Chief of Staff, Correspondence and Events Journal, Manila Command Correspondence, 312.3, RG 338, Box 2, NARA.

54. Krueger, "The Luzon Campaign of 1945," 5; Smith, *Triumph in the Philippines*, 315–334.

55. Sixth Army, "Report of Luzon Operation," Section III: "Cave Warfare in the Mountains," 28–42, Sixth Army, 106.0.3, Box 2405, RG 407, NARA.

56. Ibid., 42–45; Smith, *Triumph in the Philippines*, 386–388.

57. Smith, *Triumph in the Philippines*, 391–422.

58. Ibid., 423–445.

59. Ibid., 449–490.

60. The first quote is from Krueger, "The Luzon Campaign of 1945," 10; the second is from Sixth Army, "Report of Operations on Luzon," Section 4: "Surrender in the North, 13 February–30 June 1945," 25, 106-0.3, Box 2405, RG 407, NARA; for more information on Sixth Army operations in the north, see Smith, *Triumph in the Philippines*, 449–579, and Leary, "Walter Krueger," in Leary, *We Shall Return!* 83–85.

61. The casualties figures are from Krueger, *From Down Under to Nippon*, 318, and Smith, *Triumph in the Philippines*, 579 and 652. I would like to thank Dr. Stanley L. Falk for pointing out to me the issue of disease rates in the Sixth Army during the Luzon campaign. For a thorough assessment of this issue—which was used for this paragraph—see Mary Ellen Condon-Rall and Albert E. Cowdrey, *The Medical Department: Medical Service in the War against Japan* (Washington, DC: Center of Military History, United States Army, 1998), 351–352. The MacArthur quote is from D. Clayton James Interview with Roger O. Egeberg, 29–30 June 1971, as quoted in James, *The Years of MacArthur*, Vol. 2, *1941–1945*, 655.

62. Krueger, *From Down Under to Nippon*, 323.

63. The figures and quotes are both from Smith, *Triumph in the Philippines*, 387–388.

64. Ronald H. Spector, *Eagle against the Sun: The American War with Japan* (New York: Free Press, 1985), 528; figures for the three regiments are from Smith, *Triumph in the Philippines*, 532.

65. D. Clayton James, "MacArthur's Lapses from an Envelopment Strategy in 1945," *Parameters, Journal of the US Army War College* 10, 2 (June 1980): 27–28; John Francis Shortal, *Forged by Fire: Robert L. Eichelberger and the Pacific War* (Columbia: University of South Carolina Press, 1987), 114; Smith, *Triumph in the Philippines*, 538–539.

66. Both quotes are from Sixth Army, "Report of Operations on Luzon," Section 3: "Cave Warfare in the Mountains," 34 and 37; for Krueger's specific views on close air, see Letter, WK to Franklin D'Olier (HQ, US Strategic Bombing Survey), 23 November 1945, Box 9, Krueger Papers, USMA.

67. Smith, *Triumph in the Philippines*, 198; Telephone Conversation, George C. Kenney and Walter Krueger, 5 February 1945, HQ Sixth Army, Office of the Chief of Staff, 311.3, Box 1, RG 338, NARA.

68. Interrogation of Maj. Gen. Haruo Konuma, 1, Interrogations of Japanese Officials on World War II (English translation), General Headquarters, Far Eastern Command, Military Intelligence Section, Historical Division, Vol. A–M, U.S. Army CMH.

69. Condon-Rall and Cowdrey, *The Medical Department: Medical Service in the War against Japan*, 351.

70. The Division Public Relations Section, *The 6th Infantry Division in World War II, 1939–1945* (Washington, DC: Infantry Journal Press, 1947; reprint, Nashville: Battery Press, 1983), 114.

71. Letter, WK to George C. Beach, 14 November 1943, Box 8, Krueger Papers, USMA.

72. Douglas Southall Freeman, *Lee's Lieutenants: A Study in Command*, 3 vols. (New York: Charles Scribner's Sons, 1942–1944), Vol. 2, *Cedar Mountain to Chancellorsville*; Carl Van Doren, *Mutiny in January* (Clifton, NJ: A. M. Kelly, 1943).

73. Roger Olaf Egeberg, *The General: MacArthur and the Man He Called 'Doc'* (New York: Hippocrene Books, 1983), 115; other information contained in this paragraph came from Letter, Boylston B. Bass to the *Infantry Journal*, 17 May 1943, Box 7, Krueger Papers, USMA; and Leary, "Walter Krueger," in Leary, *We Shall Return!* 83.

74. Krueger, *From Down Under to Nippon*, 333–335.

75. Ibid., 333; John Ray Skates, *The Invasion of Japan: Alternative to the Bomb* (Columbia: University of South Carolina Press, 1994), 119–124; Conference Report, "OLYMPIC," 3 July 1945, 5, HQ Sixth Army, Office of the Chief of Staff, 311.3, Box 3, RG 338, NARA.

76. The quotes are from Conference Report, "OLYMPIC," 10; Skates, *The Invasion of Japan*, 179.

77. Report of Conference, "OLYMPIC," 10.

78. Skates, *The Invasion of Japan*, 188–191.

79. Ibid., 189.

80. Edward J. Drea, *In the Service of the Emperor: Essays on the Imperial Japanese Army* (Lincoln: University of Nebraska Press, 1998), 145–153; the quote is from Report of Conference, "OLYMPIC," 9.

81. Skates, *The Invasion of Japan*, 255; Richard B. Frank, *Downfall: The End of the Imperial Japanese Empire* (New York: Random House, 1999), 188–213.

82. Willoughby, ed., *Reports of General MacArthur*, Vol. 1 Supplement, *MacArthur in Japan: The Occupation: Military Phase*, 4.

83. Letter, WK to E. F. McGlachlin, 6 December 1945, Box 9, Krueger Papers, USMA; Krueger, *From Down Under to Nippon*, 335–336 and 349–350.

84. Ibid., 339.

85. Ibid., 349–350.

86. Letter, WK to McGlachlin, 6 December 1945.

87. Krueger, *From Down Under to Nippon*, 350.

88. Ibid., 368.

89. Ibid., 370.

Chapter 10. Retirement and Tragedy, 1946–1967

1. Krueger retired after a three-month temporary appointment in late June 1946 as a full general on the retired list due to physical disability. Letter, WK to George H. Decker, 11 October 1946, Box 10, USMA.

2. Letter, WK to Samuel D. Sturgis Jr., 29 May 1946, Box 10, Krueger Papers, USMA.

3. Letter, WK to Oscar W. Griswold, 31 May 1946, Box 10, Krueger Papers, USMA.

4. The first quote is from Letter, WK to Horton V. White, 15 September 1946, Box 10, Krueger Papers, USMA; the second is from Letter, WK to William N. Leaf, 5 August 1946, Box 10, Krueger Papers, USMA; other information in this paragraph comes from Letter, WK to Ben Decherd, 19 September 1946, Box 10, Krueger Papers, USMA; Letter, WK to Sturgis, 29 May 1946.

5. Letter, Franz C. Goos to WK, 24 June 1946, Box 10, Krueger Papers, USMA; the quote is from Letter, WK to Samuel D. Sturgis, 4 September 1946, Box 10, Krueger Papers, USMA.

6. Letter, WK to Luther D. Miller, 14 August 1946, Box 10, Krueger Papers, USMA; Letter, WK to Sturgis, 4 September 1946; Letter, WK to Harry Reichelderfer, 25 November 1946, Box 10, Krueger Papers, USMA; Letter, WK to Fay W. Brabson, 7 October 1950, Fay W. Brabson Papers, USAMHI.

7. Letter, WK to John H. Crichton, 8 September 1946, Box 10, Krueger Papers, USMA.
8. Letter, Horton V. White to WK, 9 August 1946, Box 10, Krueger Papers, USMA.
9. Letter, WK to Horton V. White, 15 September 1946, Box 10, Krueger Papers, USMA.
10. Letter, WK to Clyde D. Eddleman, 7 June 1947, Box 11, Krueger Papers, USMA.
11. The first quote is from Letter, WK to Clyde D. Eddleman, 30 June 1947, Box 11, Krueger Papers, USMA; the second is from Walter Krueger, *From Down Under to Nippon: The Story of the Sixth Army in World War II* (Washington: Combat Forces Press, 1953; reprint, Nashville: Battery Classics, n.d.), vii; other information in the paragraph came from Letter, H. Ben Decherd, Jr. to WK, 1 July 1947, Box 11, Krueger Papers, USMA.
12. Letter, WK to H. Ben Decherd, 27 June 1947, Box 11, Krueger Papers, USMA.
13. Letter, WK to Clyde D. Eddleman, 31 October 1947, Box 11, Krueger Papers, USMA.
14. Letter, WK to John N. Wheeler, 9 July 1948, Box 12, Krueger Papers, USMA; the quote is from Letter, WK to Fay W. Brabson, 22 January 1949, Brabson Papers, USAMHI; Fay W. Brabson Diary, 20 May 1952, Brabson Papers, USAMHI.
15. Robert Ross Smith, *Triumph in the Philippines* (Washington, DC: Office of the Chief of Military History, Department of the Army, 1963), 711.
16. As quoted in Paul Chwialkowski, *In Caesar's Shadow: The Life of General Robert Eichelberger* (Westport, CT: Greenwood Press, 1993), 187. Chwialkowski does not identify the source of the quotation.
17. Ibid., 185–190.
18. Letter, Albert C. Wedemeyer to WK, 19 May 1952, Box 13, Krueger Papers, USMA; Letter, WK to Albert C. Wedemeyer, 28 May 1952, Box 13, Krueger Papers, USMA; see also Krueger's glowing characterization of MacArthur in Walter Krueger, "Remarks by General Walter Krueger on the Korean Situation," unidentified speech [Army War College?], n.d. [3 January 1955?], 6–7, Box 12, Krueger Papers, USMA.
19. Letter, Walter Krueger Jr. to William M. Leary, 26 April 1985, Box 40, Krueger Papers, USMA; William M. Leary, "Walter Krueger: MacArthur's Fighting General," in William M. Leary, ed., *We Shall Return! MacArthur's Commanders and the Defeat of Japan, 1942–1945* (Lexington: University Press of Kentucky, 1988), 67.
20. Letter, WK to Fay W. Brabson, 5 September 1947, Brabson Papers, USAMHI.
21. See Chapter 3. In his notes of one interview with George C. Marshall, Forrest C. Pogue wrote, "Krueger difficult; stubborn. Didn't want any National Guard troops. I told him he would have to take his share. He was difficult unless he got his way." See George C. Marshall, *George C. Marshall Interviews and Reminiscences for Forrest C. Pogue*, rev. ed. (Lexington, VA: George C. Marshall Research Foundation, 1991), 578.
22. Walter Krueger, "The Need for Universal Military Training," lecture delivered at Trinity University, 1 April 1947, 1, Box 18, Krueger Papers, USMA.
23. Ibid., 1–2.
24. Ibid., 3.
25. Walter Krueger, untitled speech delivered at the First Convention of the Amphibian Engineer Association, 7 December 1946, 5, Krueger Papers, Box 18, USMA.
26. Walter Krueger, "National Preparedness," lecture delivered at the 46th Anniversary Banquet of the Scientific Society of San Antonio, 14 June 1950, 6, Box 13, Krueger Papers, USMA. In response to U.S. Congressman Thomas H. Werdel's inquiry about the dangers of unification of the armed forces to democracy, Krueger tried to assure him that the National Security Act of 1947 did not violate the concept of civilian control since the Commander-in-Chief and the Secretary of Defense were both civilians. "In my judgement," Krueger

concluded, "unification of our armed forces is necessary and sound." Letter, WK to Thomas H. Werdel, 28 September 1951, Box 12, Krueger Papers, USMA.

27. Ibid.; see also Krueger, untitled speech delivered at the First Convention of the Amphibian Engineer Association, 4.

28. The first quote is from Krueger, "The Need for Universal Military Training," 4; Krueger, "Remarks by General Walter Krueger on the Korean Situation," 1; see also Letter, WK to Maxwell D. Taylor, 15 February 1956, Box 13, Krueger Papers, USMA.

29. Krueger, untitled speech delivered at the First Convention of the Amphibian Engineer Association, 5.

30. Letter, WK to John D. O'Daniel, 28 January 1947, Box 11, Krueger Papers, USMA.

31. The first quote is from ibid.; the second is from Letter, WK to Taylor, 15 February 1956.

32. Krueger's correspondence to friends includes numerous references to Grace's poor health; see for example Letter, WK to George S. Price, 1 June 1946, Box 10, Krueger Papers, USMA; Letter, WK to John H. Crichton, 3 August 1946, Box 10, Krueger Papers, USMA; Letter, WK to Fay W. Brabson, 4 April 1948, Brabson Papers, USAMHI.

33. Brabson Diary, 23 April 1947 and 17 May 1956; Letter, WK to Fay W. Brabson, 26 April 1958, Brabson Papers, USAMHI. In his personal papers, Krueger did not provide any details concerning Jimmie's dismissal.

34. The incident is reconstructed from the *New York Times*, 2 December 1952, 10; 6 January 1953, 4; 8 January 1953, 3 (for the quote); and 10 January 1953, 2.

35. The quote is from ibid., 10 January 1953, 2; see also *New York Times*, 31 December 1954, 30.

36. The quote is from Letter, WK to Fay W. Brabson, 9 May 1953, Brabson Papers, USAMHI; Krueger made the reference to "having with us the two grandchildren, respectively 18 and 16 years old" in Letter, WK to William S. Dow, 4 July 1953, Local History Department, MJCPL; for Krueger's views on his wife's potential for recovery, see Letter, WK to Fay W. Brabson, 9 May 1953, Brabson Papers, USAMHI, and Letter, WK to George C. Marshall, 6 August 1953, Box 12, Krueger Papers, USMA; for Grace's poor health, see Letter, WK to Brabson, 4 April 1948; Letter, WK to Clyde D. Eddleman, 18 October 1953, Box 12, Krueger Papers, USMA; Letter, WK to George H. Decker, 22 October 1953, Box 12, Krueger Papers, USMA; Letter, WK to Fay W. Brabson, 7 February 1954, Brabson Papers, USAMHI; Letter, WK to Clyde D. Eddleman, 5 December 1954, Box 12, Krueger Papers, USMA; Letter, WK to William S. Dow, 27 March 1955, MJCPL.

37. The quote is from Letter, WK to George H. Decker, n.d., Box 13, Krueger Papers, USMA; see also, Letter, Walter Krueger Jr. to William M. Leary, 20 May 1985, 5, Box 40, Krueger Papers, USMA.

38. Brabson Diary, 17 May 1956.

39. Letter, WK to Fay W. Brabson, 12 September 1956, Brabson Papers, USAMHI.

40. *New York Times*, 11 June 1957, 1 and 14; Letter, WK to Fay W. Brabson, 25 September 1957, Brabson Papers, USAMHI.

41. Letter, WK to Fay W. Brabson, 20 August 1958; Letter, WK to Fay W. Brabson, 9 September 1961, both in Brabson Papers, USAMHI.

42. As of April 1958, he had eight great-grandchildren; Letter, WK to Brabson, 26 April 1958; the quote is from Letter, WK to Brabson, 9 September 1961, in Brabson Papers, USAMHI.

43. The quote is from Letter, WK to Brabson, 9 September 1961; other material in this paragraph came from Letter, WK to Brabson, 26 April 1958; Letter, WK to Fay W. Brabson, 14 May 1961; Letter, WK to Fay W. Brabson, 23 May 1957; Letter, WK to Fay W. Brabson, 24 September 1960; Letter, WK to Fay W. Brabson, 5 May 1963; all in Brabson Papers, USAMHI.

44. Letter, Krueger to Brabson, 24 September 1960.

Conclusion

1. "General Walter Krueger" (Biographical Sketch), 1, Walter Krueger Papers, USAMHI.

2. George B. Eaton, "From Luzon to Luzon: Walter Krueger and the Luzon Campaign," *Valley Forge Journal: A Record of Patriotism and American Culture* 6, 1 (June 1992): 36, n57. One can only speculate that Krueger destroyed the wartime correspondence with Grace, none of which, Walter Krueger Jr. claimed, has survived. Letter, Walter Krueger Jr. to William M. Leary, 20 May 1985, 5–6, Box 40, Walter Krueger Papers, USMA.

3. Letter, Krueger Jr. to Leary, 20 May 1985, 4.

4. Morris Janowitz, *The Professional Soldier: A Social and Political Portrait* (New York: Free Press, 1971), 107.

5. Letter, Walter Krueger Jr. to Walter Nardini, 29 November 1976, Krueger Papers, USAMHI.

6. Allan R. Millett argues that the "best air-ground operational integration occurred" in SWPA, but ironically and mistakenly gives the credit to MacArthur, "a commander who had the least integrated headquarters and who argued that his genius was strategic, not operational." Allan R. Millett, "The United States Armed Forces in the Second World War," in Allan R. Millett and Williamson Murray, eds., *Military Effectiveness*, 3 vols. (Boston: Unwin Hyman, 1988), Vol. 3, *The Second World War*, 68.

7. In a postwar interview with Forrest C. Pogue, Krueger complained about the general state of intelligence in SWPA and concluded that MacArthur was not aware of just how bad it really was. Forrest C. Pogue interview with WK, 7 November 1957, GCMRL.

8. Gordon Walker, "General Krueger: Mystery Man of Pacific," *Christian Science Monitor*, weekly magazine section, 9 June 1945, 3; George H. Decker Oral History interviewed by Dan H. Ralls, Session 2, 9 November 1972, 20–22, George H. Decker Papers, USAMHI.

9. Michael D. Doubler, *Closing with the Enemy: How GIs Fought the War in Europe, 1944–1945* (Lawrence: University Press of Kansas, 1994), 266–267.

10. Janowitz, *The Professional Soldier*, 21 and 161.

11. The titles of two recent books demonstrate the degree to which MacArthur is identified with SWPA: Stephen R. Taaffe, *MacArthur's Jungle War: The 1944 New Guinea Campaign* (Lawrence: University Press of Kansas, 1998), and Thomas E. Griffith Jr., *MacArthur's Airman: General George C. Kenney and the War in the Southwest Pacific* (Lawrence: University Press of Kansas, 1998).

12. Douglas MacArthur, *Reminiscences* (New York: McGraw-Hill, 1964), 170.

BIBLIOGRAPHY

Primary Sources

U.S. Military Academy Library, West Point, New York

Daniel F. Anglum, Journal of Company K, 1899–1901
Walter Krueger Papers

U.S. Military History Institute, Carlisle Barracks, Pennsylvania

Army War College Curricular Archives
Fay W. Brabson Papers
James F. Collins Papers
George H. Decker Papers
Clyde D. Eddleman Papers
Robert L. Eichelberger Papers
William H. Gill Papers
Thomas F. Hickey Papers
Walter Krueger Papers
Matthew Foney Steele Papers
Joseph M. Swing Papers
Russell W. Volckmann Papers
Headquarters, European Theater of Operations, U.S. Army. *Battle Experiences against the Japanese*. 1 May 1945.
Observer Board, Pacific Ocean Area, U.S. Army, Army Ground Forces. *Reports of Observer Boards, Pacific Ocean Areas*. 11 vols. 1944–1945.
Smith, Francis G. *History of the Third Army*. Army Ground Forces. 1946.
U.S. Army, IX Corps. *Report: IX Corps, Third Army Maneuvers, 1941*.
U.S. Army, Sixth Army, Assistant Chief of Staff, G-3. *Combat Notes*. 10 vols.
——. *G-4 Report: Luzon Campaign*.
——. *History of G-4 Section Headquarters, Sixth Army, 25 Jan. 1943–26 Jan. 1946*. 1946 [?].
——. *Notes for Task Force Commands in Pacific Theaters*. 6 February 1943.
——. *Report of the Leyte Operation, 17 October 1944–25 December 1944*.
U.S. Army, Third Army. *Final Report: Third Army Maneuvers, August 1940*.
U.S. Army, XIV Corps. *After Action Report: M-1 Operation*. 1945.

National Archives and Records Administration

Record Group 165. War Department General and Special Staff. Washington, DC.
Record Group 319. Center of Military History. Department of the Army. College Park, MD.
Record Group 337. Records of Army Ground Forces. Washington, DC.
Record Group 338. U.S. Army Commands. College Park, MD.
Record Group 394. U.S. Army Continental Commands, 1920–1942. Washington, DC.

Record Group 407. Office of the Adjutant General. College Park, MD, and Washington, DC.

The MacArthur Memorial and Archives, Norfolk, Virginia

Record Group 4. Records of General Headquarters, U.S. Army Forces Pacific (USAFPAC), 1942–1947.

Record Group 10. General Douglas MacArthur's Private Correspondence, 1848–1964.

Record Group 30. Papers of Lieutenant General Richard K. Sutherland, USA, 1941–1945.

Record Group 32. Oral History Transcripts: Henry Burgess; Norman Carlyon; LeGrande Diller; William Dunn; Roger O. Egeberg; Robert Sherrod; Robert White.

Record Group 49, D. Clayton James Collection; Clovis E. Byers; Clyde D. Eddleman; George C. Kenney.

Local History Department, Madison–Jefferson County Public Library, Madison, Indiana

Biographical Files, Walter Krueger

United States Army Center of Military History, Washington, DC

Archives, Interrogations of Japanese Officials on World War II

United States Army Command and General Staff College, Fort Leavenworth, Kansas

United States Army Command and General Staff College Curriculum Archives (1907)

Columbia University, Oral History Research Office

Alfred Gruenther Oral History

Eisenhower Administration Project

Letters, Diaries, Memoirs, etc.

Balck, William. *Tactics*. 2 vols. 4th rev. ed. Trans. by Walter Krueger. Fort Leavenworth, KS: U.S. Cavalry Association, 1911–1914.

Barbey, Daniel. *MacArthur's Amphibious Navy: Seventh Amphibious Force Operations, 1943–1945*. Annapolis, MD: Naval Institute Press, 1969.

Bland, Larry I., Sharon R. Ritenour, and Clarence E. Wunderling Jr., eds. *The Papers of George Catlett Marshall*. 4 vols. Baltimore: Johns Hopkins University Press, 1981–1996.

Chase, William C. *Front Line General: The Commands of Maj. Gen. William C. Chase*. Houston: Pacesetter Press, 1975.

Coffman, Edward M., and Paul H. Hass, eds. "With MacArthur in the Pacific: A Memoir by Philip F. La Follette." *Wisconsin Magazine of History* 64, 2 (Winter 1980–1981): 83–106.

Davis, Art H. "An Infantry Regiment in the Attack—Jungle Terrain." Military Monograph. Advanced Officers Class No. 1. Armored School, Ft. Knox, KY. 1 May 1948.

Egeberg, Roger Olaf. *The General: MacArthur and the Man He Called 'Doc.'* New York: Hippocrene Books, 1983.

Eichelberger, Robert L., and Milton MacKaye. *Our Jungle Road to Tokyo*. New York: Viking Press, 1949.

Gill, William H, as told to Edward Jaquelin Smith. *Always a Commander: The Reminiscences of Major General William H. Gill*. Colorado Springs: Colorado College, 1974.

Grow, Robert W. "The Ten Lean Years, 1930–1940." *Armor* 96, 1 (January–February 1987): 22–30; 96, 2 (March–April 1987): 25–33; 96, 3 (May–June 1987): 21–28; 96, 4 (July–August 1987): 34–42.

Holt, Daniel D., ed., and James W. Leyerzapf, associate editor. *Eisenhower: The Prewar Diaries and Selected Papers, 1905–1941*. Baltimore: Johns Hopkins University Press, 1998.

Immanuel, F. *The Regimental War Game*. Trans. Walter Krueger. Kansas City: Hudson Press, 1907.

Kenney, George. *General Kenney Reports: A Personal History of the Pacific War*. New York: Duell, Sloane and Pearce, 1949; reprint, Washington, DC: Office of Air Force History, United States Air Force, 1987.

Krueger, Walter. *From Down Under to Nippon: The Story of Sixth Army in World War II*. Washington, DC: Combat Forces Press, 1953; reprint, Nashville: Battery Press, n.d.

Luvaas, Jay. *Dear Miss Em: General Eichelberger's War in the Pacific, 1942–1945*. Westport, CT: Greenwood Press, 1972.

MacArthur, Douglas. *Reminiscences*. New York: McGraw-Hill, 1964.

Marshall, George C. *George C. Marshall: Interviews and Reminiscences for Forrest C. Pogue*. Rev. ed. Edited by Larry I. Bland. Lexington, VA: George C. Marshall Research Foundation, 1991.

Mertens, Julius K. L. *Tactics and Technique of River Crossings*. Trans. by Walter Krueger. New York: D. Van Nostrand, 1918.

Owens, William A. *Eye-Deep in Hell: A Memoir of the Liberation of the Philippines, 1944–45*. Dallas: Southern Methodist University Press, 1989.

Rhoades, Weldon E. (Dusty). *Flying MacArthur to Victory*. College Station: Texas A&M University Press, 1987.

Rogers, Paul P. *The Bitter Years: MacArthur and Sutherland*. New York: Praeger Publishers, 1990.

Ross, Steven T. *American War Plans, 1919–1941*. 5 vols. New York: Garland Publishing, 1992.

Willoughby, Charles, and John Chamberlain. *MacArthur, 1941–1951*. New York: McGraw-Hill, 1954.

United States Government Publications

U.S. Army. *Annual Reports of the Commandant*, 1905/1906–1911/1912. Washington, DC: Government Printing Office, 1907–1912.

U.S. Army Center of Military History. *Order of Battle of the United States Land Forces in the World War*. 5 vols. Washington, DC: United States Army, Center of Military History, 1988.

U.S. Congress. 56th Congress, 2d Session. 1900. House Document No. 2. Serial No. 4074. *Annual Reports of the War Department*. 6 vols. Vol. 9, "Report of General MacArthur." Commander of 2d Division, 8th Army Corps, 31 May 1899 to 6 April 1900.

U.S. War Department. *Combat Lessons: Rank and File in Combat: What They're Doing, How They Do It*. 9 vols. Washington, DC: Operations Division, Combat Analysis Section, 1944–1945.

———. FM 7-10. *Infantry: Rifle Company, Infantry Regiment*. Washington, DC: Government Printing Office, 1944.

———. FM 7-15. *Infantry Field Manual: Heavy Weapons Company, Rifle Regiment*. Washington, DC: Government Printing Office, 1942.

———. FM 17-10. *Armored Force Field Manual: Tactics and Technique*. Washington, DC: Government Printing Office, 1942.

———. FM 17-32. *Armored Force Field Manual: The Tank Company, Light and Medium*. Washington, DC: Government Printing Office, 1942.

———. FM 17-32. *Tank Company*. Washington, DC: Government Printing Office, 1944.
———. FM 17-36. *Employment of Tanks with Infantry*. Washington, DC: Government Printing Office, 1944.
———. FM 17-36. Supplement No. 1. *Employment of Tanks with Infantry: Illustrated Problems*. Washington, DC: Government Printing Office, 1944.
———. FM 72-20. *Jungle Warfare*. Washington, DC: Government Printing Office, 1944.
———. FM 100-5. *Field Service Regulations (Tentative): Operations*. Washington, DC: Government Printing Office, 1939.
———. FM 100-5. *Field Service Regulations: Operations*. Washington, DC: Government Printing Office, 1941.
———. FM 100-5. *Field Service Regulations: Operations*. Washington, DC: Government Printing Office, 1944.
———. FM 100-15. *Field Service Regulations: Larger Units*. Washington, DC: Government Printing Office, 1942.
———. *Manual for Commanders of Large Units*. 2 vols. (Washington, DC: Government Printing Office, 1930).
U.S. War Department, Historical Division. *The Admiralties: Operations of the 1st Cavalry Division, 29 February–18 May 1944*. Washington, DC: Historical Division, War Department, 1946; reprint, Washington, DC: Center of Military History, United States Army, 1990.
Willoughby, Charles A., ed. *Reports of General MacArthur*. 2 vols. Washington, DC: Government Printing Office, 1966.

Articles

Ayotte, John U. "Planes, Tanks, Guns and Doughboys." *Infantry Journal* 50, 1 (January 1942): 24–31.
Barrows, Frederick M. "Streamlining the Offensive: The Evolution of the Panzer Division and Its Place in Blitzkrieg." *Military Review* 21, 80 (March 1941): 9–19.
Ingles, Harry C. "The New Division." *Infantry Journal* 46, 6 (November–December 1939): 521–529.
Jenkins, Reuben E. "Offensives Doctrine: Opening Phases of Battles." *Military Review* 20, 77 (June 1940): 5–16.
Krueger, Walter. "Preparedness." *Infantry Journal* 13, 6 (March 1917): 551–558.
Kluckhohn, Frank L. "Master of Amphibious Warfare." *New York Times Magazine* (31 December 1944): 11 and 32.
"Krueger of the Sixth." *Newsweek* 21, 9 (1 March 1943): 22–23.
———. *Newsweek* 27, 5 (4 February 1946): 58–61.
Lynch, George A. "Current Infantry Developments." *Infantry Journal* 45, 1 (January–February 1938): 3–9.
———. "Firepower … Man Power … Maneuver." *Infantry Journal* 46, 6 (November–December 1939): 498–505 and 606.
———. "Infantry in Offensive Combat." *Infantry Journal* 47, 1 (January–February 1940): 69–78.
———. "Infantry in Offensive Combat." *Infantry Journal* 47, 2 (March–April 1940): 185–193.
———. "Motorized Divisions." *Infantry Journal* 48, 1 (January 1941): 2–5.
———. "The Rifle Battalion." *Infantry Journal* 47, 5 (September–October 1940): 508–517.

——. "The Rifle Regiment in the Offensive." *Infantry Journal* 50, 2 (February 1942): 6–18.

——. "Some Reflections on Infantry Matériel and Tactics." *Infantry Journal* 45, 4 (July–August 1938): 291–300.

——. "The Tactics of the New Infantry Regiment." *Infantry Journal* 46, 2 (March–April 1939): 98–113.

——. "Tactics of Rifle-Company Elements." *Infantry Journal* 47, 3 (May–June 1940): 292–298.

Marusek, Peter. "Tanks and Infantry in Northern Luzon." *Cavalry Journal* 55, 4 (July–August 1946): 17–19.

"Old Soldier." *Time* 45, 5 (29 January 1945): 29–33.

Phillips, Thomas R. "The New Face of War." *Infantry Journal* 45, 5 (September–October 1938): 387–392.

Shallenberger, Martin C. "The Brunt of the Battle." *Military Review* 21, 82 (October 1941): 17–18.

Strand, Wilbur C. "The Infantry-Tank Team in Jungle Operations." *Cavalry Journal* 55, 2 (March–April 1946): 2–6.

Templeton, R. L. "Jungle Fighting." *Cavalry Journal* 56, 5 (September–October 1947): 16–19.

Wales, V. W. B. "Armored Units, Armament, Organization, and Characteristics." *Military Review* 21, 81 (June 1941): 103–108.

Walker, Gordon. "General Krueger: Mystery Man of Pacific." *Christian Science Monitor* (9 June 1945): 3.

Secondary Sources

Books and Articles

Adams, Michael C. C. *The Best War Ever: America and World War II*. Baltimore: Johns Hopkins University Press, 1994.

Allen, Robert S. *Lucky Forward: The History of Patton's Third U.S. Army*. New York: Vanguard Press, 1947.

Arthur, Anthony. *Bushmasters: America's Jungle Warriors of World War II*. New York: St. Martin's Press, 1987.

Ball, Harry P. *Of Responsible Command: A History of the U.S. Army War College*. Carlisle Barracks, PA: Alumni Association of the United States Army War College, 1983.

Bergerud, Eric. *Touched with Fire: The Land War in the South Pacific*. New York: Viking Press, 1996.

Bland, Larry I. "George C. Marshall and the Education of Army Leaders." *Military Review* 68, 10 (October 1988): 27–37.

Block, Maxine, ed. *Current Biography: Who's News and Why, 1943*. New York: H. W. Wilson, 1943.

Blumenson, Martin. "A Deaf Ear to Clausewitz: Allied Operational Objectives in World War II," *Parameters* 23, 2 (Summer 1993): 16–27.

Blumenson, Martin, and James L. Stokesbury. *Masters of the Art of Command*. Boston: Houghton Mifflin, 1975.

Bolt, William J., and David Jablonsky. "Tactics and the Operational Level of War." *Military Review* 67, 2 (February 1987): 2–19.

Bonn, Keith E. *When the Odds Were Even: The Vosges Mountains Campaign, October1944–January 1945*. Novato, CA: Presidio Press, 1994.

Briggs, Philip J. "General MacArthur and the Presidential Election of 1944." *Presidential Studies Quarterly* 22, 1 (Winter 1992): 31–46.

Cameron, Craig M. *American Samurai: Myth, Imagination, and the Conduct of Battle in the First Marine Division, 1941–1951*. New York: Cambridge University Press, 1994.

Cannon, M. Hamilin. *Leyte: The Return to the Philippines. United States Army in World War II: The War in the Pacific*. Washington, DC: Office of the Chief of Military History, Department of the Army, 1954.

Cerami, Joseph R. "Training: The 1941 Louisiana Maneuvers." *Military Review* 67, 10 (October 1987): 34–43.

Chwialkowski, Paul. *In Caesar's Shadow: The Life of General Robert Eichelberger*. Westport, CT: Greenwood Press, 1993.

Clendenen, Clarence C. *Blood on the Border: The United States Army and the Mexican Irregulars*. New York: Macmillan, 1969.

Cline, Ray S. *Washington Command Post: The Operations Division*. Washington, DC: Office of the Chief of Military History, Department of the Army, 1951.

Coakley, Robert W., and Richard M. Leighton. *Global Logistics and Strategy, 1943–1945*. Washington, DC: Office of the Chief of Military History, Department of the Army, 1968.

Coffman, Edward M. "The American Military Generation Gap in World War I: The Leavenworth Clique in the AEF." In William Geffen, ed., *Command and Commanders in Modern Warfare: Proceedings of the Second Military History Symposium, U.S. Air Force Academy, 2–3 May 1968*. Washington, DC: Government Printing Office, 1969.

———. *The War to End All Wars: The American Military Experience in World War I*. New York: Oxford University Press, 1968; reprint, Madison: University Press of Wisconsin, 1986.

Coffman, Edward M., and Peter F. Herrly. "The American Regular Army Officer Corps between the World Wars: A Collective Biography." *Armed Forces and Society* 4, 1 (November 1977): 55–73.

Collins, Arthur S. "Walter Krueger: An Infantry Great." *Infantry* 73, 1 (January–February 1983): 15–19.

Combat History of the Second Infantry Division in World War II. Reprint, Nashville: Battery Press, 1979.

Condon-Rall, Mary Ellen, and Albert E. Cowdrey. *The Medical Department: Medical Service in the War against Japan*. Washington, DC: Center of Military History, United States Army, 1998.

Connaughton, Richard, John Pimlott, and Duncan Anderson. *The Battle for Manila: The Most Devastating Untold Story of World War II*. Novato, CA: Presidio Press, 1995.

Cooling, Benjamin, ed. *Case Studies in the Achievement of Air Superiority*. Washington, DC: Center for Air Force History, 1994.

———. *Case Studies in the Development of Close Air Support*. Washington, DC: United States Air Force, Office of Air Force History, 1990.

Cosmas, Graham A. *An Army for Empire: The United States Army in the Spanish-American War*. Columbia: University Press of Missouri, 1971; reprint, Shippensburg, PA: White Mane Publishing, 1994.

———. "Securing the Fruits of Victory: The U.S. Army Occupies Cuba, 1898–1899." *Military Affairs* 38, 3 (October 1974): 85–91.

Costello, John. *The Pacific War*. New York: Rawson, Wade Publishers, 1981.

Craven, Wesley Frank, and James Lea Cate, eds. *The Army Air Forces in World War II*. 7 vols. Chicago: University of Chicago Press, 1948–1958.

D'Amura, Ronald M. "Campaigns: The Essence of Operational Warfare." *Parameters, U.S. Army War College Quarterly* 17, 2 (Summer 1987): 42–51.

Davis, Burke. *Marine! The Life of Lt. Gen. Lewis B. (Chesty) Puller*. New York: Little, Brown, 1962; reprint, New York: Bantam Books, 1964.

Davis, Vernon E. *The History of the Joint Chiefs of Staff in World War II: Organizational Development*. 2 vols. Washington, DC: Historical Division, Joint Secretariat, Joint Chiefs of Staff, 1972.

Dietrich, Steve E. "The Professional Reading of George S. Patton Jr." *Journal of Military History* 53, 4 (October 1989): 387–418.

Division Public Relations Section. *The 6th Infantry Division in World War II*. Washington, DC: Infantry Journal Press, 1947.

Doubler, Michael D. *Closing with the Enemy: How GIs Fought the War in Europe, 1944–1945*. Lawrence: University Press of Kansas, 1994.

Dower, John W. *War Without Mercy: Race and Power in the Pacific War*. New York: Pantheon Books, 1986.

Draper, Theodore. *The 84th Infantry Division in the Battle of Germany, November 1944–May, 1945*. New York: Viking Press, 1946.

Drea, Edward J. *Defending the Driniumor: Covering Force Operations in New Guinea, 1944*. Fort Leavenworth, KS: Combat Studies Institute, U.S. Army Command and General Staff College, 1984.

——. *In the Service of the Emperor: Essays on the Imperial Japanese Army*. Lincoln: University of Nebraska Press, 1998.

——. *MacArthur's ULTRA: Codebreaking and the War against Japan, 1942–1945*. Lawrence: University Press of Kansas, 1992.

Eaton, George B. "From Luzon to Luzon: Walter Krueger and the Luzon Campaign." *Valley Forge Journal: A Record of Patriotism and American Culture* 6, 11 (June 1992): 17–36.

——. "General Walter Krueger and Joint War Planning, 1922–1938." *Naval War College Review* 48, 2 (Spring 1995): 91–113.

Echevarria, Antulio J. *After Clausewitz: German Military Thinkers before the Great War*. Lawrence: University Press of Kansas, 2000.

Ellis, John. *Brute Force: Allied Strategy and Tactics in the Second World War*. New York: Viking Press, 1990.

English, John A., and Bruce I. Gudmundsson. *On Infantry*. Rev. ed. Westport, CT: Praeger Publishers, 1994.

Ekirch, Arthur A. Jr. *The Civilian and the Military: A History of the American Antimilitarist Tradition*. New York: Oxford University Press, 1956; reprint, Colorado Springs: Ralph Myles Publisher, 1972.

Falk, Stanley L. "Comments on Reynolds: 'MacArthur as Maritime Strategist.'" *Naval War College Review* 33, 2 (March–April 1980): 92–99.

Falk, Stanley L. *Decision at Leyte*. New York: W. W. Norton, 1966.

Faust, Karl Irving. *Campaigning in the Philippines*. New York: Arno Press and *New York Times*, 1970.

Finnegan, John Patrick. *Against the Specter of a Dragon: The Campaign for American Military Preparedness, 1914–1917*. Westport, CT: Greenwood Press, 1974.

Flanagan, Edward M. *The Angels: A History of the 11th Airborne Division*. Novato, CA: Presidio Press, 1989.

Frank, Richard B. *Downfall: The End of the Imperial Japanese Empire*. New York: Random House, 1999.

Gabel, Christopher R. "Evolution of U.S. Armor Mobility." *Military Review* 64, 3 (March 1984): 54–63.

———. *The U.S. Army GHQ Maneuvers of 1941*. Washington, DC: Center of Military History, United States Army, 1992.

Gailey, Harry A. *The War in the Pacific: From Pearl Harbor to Tokyo Bay*. Novato, CA: Presidio Press, 1995.

Gates, John Morgan. *Schoolbooks and Krags: The United States Army in the Philippines,1898–1902*. Westport, CT: Greenwood Press, 1973.

Geffen, William. *Command and Commanders in Modern Warfare: Proceedings of the Second Military History Symposium, U.S. Air Force Academy*. Washington, DC: Government Printing Office, 1969.

Goldman, Eric R. *Rendezvous with Destiny: A History of Modern American Reform*. Rev. ed. New York: Vintage Books, 1955.

Gole, Henry G. *The Road to Rainbow: Army Planning for Global War, 1934–1940*. Annapolis, MD: Naval Institute Press, 2003.

Gray, Millard G. "The Aitape Operation." *Military Review* 31, 4 (July 1951): 44–62.

Greene, Fred. "The Military View of American National Policy, 1904–1940." *American Historical Review* 66, 2 (January 1961): 354–377.

Greenfield, Kent Roberts., ed. *Command Decisions*. New York: Harcourt, Brace, 1959.

Greenfield, Kent Roberts, Robert R. Palmer, and Bell I. Wiley. *The Organization of Ground Combat Troops*. Washington, DC: Office of the Chief of Military History, Department of the Army, 1947.

Griffith, Thomas E. *MacArthur's Airman: General George C. Kenney and the War in the Southwest Pacific*. Lawrence: University Press of Kansas, 1998.

Hagan, Kenneth J., and William R. Roberts, eds. *Against All Enemies: Interpretations of American Military History from Colonial Times to the Present*. New York: Greenwood Press, 1986.

Hattendorf, John B., B. Mitchell Simpson, and John R. Wadleigh. *Sailors and Scholars: The Centennial History of the U.S. Naval War College*. Newport, RI: Naval War College Press, 1984.

Heefner, Wilson A. *Twentieth Century Warrior: The Life and Service of Major General Edwin D. Patrick*. Shippensburg, PA: White Mane Publishing, 1995.

Hofmann, George F. "Combatant Arms vs. Combined Arms: The U.S. Army's Quest for Deep Offensive Operations and an Operational Level of Warfare." *Armor* 106, 1 (January–February 1997): 6–13 and 51–52.

———. "The Tactical and Strategic Use of Attaché Intelligence: The Spanish Civil War and the U.S. Army's Misguided Quest for a Modern Tank Doctrine." *Journal of Military History* 62, 1 (January 1998): 101–134.

Hogan, David W. A *Command Post at War: First Army Headquarters in Europe, 1943–1945*. Washington, DC: Center of Military History, United States Army, 2000.

Holzimmer, Kevin C. "In Close Country: World War II American Armor Tactics in the Jungles of the Southwest Pacific." *Armor* 106, 4 (July–August 1997): 21–25 and 30–31.

———. "It Is Amazing that It Worked at All: Joint U.S. Operations in the Southwest Pacific in World War II." Society for Military History Conference, Madison, WI, 5–7 April 2002.

———. "Walter Krueger, Douglas MacArthur, and the Pacific War: The Wakde-Sarmi Campaign as a Case Study." *Journal of Military History* 59, 4 (October 1995): 661–681.

Hough, Frank O., and John A. Crown. *The Campaign on New Britain*. Washington, DC: Historical Branch, Headquarters, U.S. Marine Corps, 1952.

House, Jonathan M. *Towards Combined Arms Warfare: A Survey of 20th-Century Tactics, Doctrine, and Organization*. Fort Leavenworth, KS: Combat Studies Institute, U.S. Army Command and General Staff College, 1984.

Isely, Jeter A., and Philip A. Crowl. *The U.S. Marines and Amphibious War*. Princeton, NJ: Princeton University Press, 1951.

James, D. Clayton. "MacArthur's Lapses from an Envelopment Strategy in 1945." *Parameters: Journal of the U.S. Army War College* 10, 2 (June 1980): 26–32.

——. *The Years of MacArthur*. 3 vols. Boston: Houghton Mifflin, 1970–1985.

Jamieson, Perry D. *Crossing the Deadly Ground: United States Army Tactics, 1865–1899*. Tuscaloosa: University of Alabama, 1994.

Janowitz, Morris. *The Professional Soldier: A Social and Political Portrait*. New York: Free Press, 1960.

Kennett, Lee. *G.I.: The American Soldier in World War II*. New York: Charles Scribner's Sons, 1987.

Killigrew, John W. *The Impact of the Great Depression on the Army*. New York: Garland Publishing, 1979.

Larrabee, Eric. *Commander in Chief: Franklin Delano Roosevelt, His Lieutenants, and Their War*. New York: Harper and Row, 1987.

Leary, William M., ed. *We Shall Return! MacArthur's Commanders and the Defeat of Japan*. Lexington: University Press of Kentucky, 1988.

Leighton, Richard M., and Robert W. Coakley. *Global Logistics and Strategy, 1940–1943. United States Army in World War II: The War Department*. Washington, DC: Office of the Chief of Military History, Department of the Army, 1955.

Leuchtenburg, William E. *The Perils of Prosperity, 1914–1932*. Chicago: University of Chicago Press, 1958.

Levine, Alan J. *The Pacific War: Japan versus the Allies*. Westport, CT: Praeger Publishers, 1995.

Linn, Brian McAllister. *Guardians of Empire: The U.S. Army and the Pacific, 1902–1940*. Chapel Hill: University of North Carolina Press, 1997.

Long, Gavin. *MacArthur as Military Commander*. London: B. T. Batsford, 1969.

Lorelli, John A. *To Foreign Shores: U.S. Amphibious Operations in World War II*. Annapolis, MD: Naval Institute Press, 1995.

Luvaas, Jay. "Buna, 19 November 1942–2 January 1943: A 'Leavenworth Nightmare.'" In Charles E. Heller and William A. Stofft, eds. *America's First Battles, 1776–1965*. Lawrence: University Press of Kansas, 1986.

Manchester, William. *American Caesar: Douglas MacArthur, 1880–1964*. Boston: Little, Brown, 1978.

Masterson, James R. *United States Army Transportation in the Southwest Pacific Area, 1941–1947*. Washington, DC: Department of the Army, Historical Division, Transportation Unit, 1947.

Matheny, Michael R. "The Roots of Modern American Operational Art." Army War College, Department of Military Strategy, Planning and Operations Home Page, 1 April 2003, carlisle-www.army.mil/usawc/dmspo/Staff%20Publications/modern_operations.pdf.

Mayo, Lida. *The Ordnance Department on Beachhead and Battlefront*. Washington, DC: Office of the Chief of Military History, United States Army, 1968.

McCartney, William. *The Jungleers: A History of the 41st Division*. Washington, DC: Infantry Journal Press, 1948.

McMillan, George. *The Old Breed: The First Marine Division in World War II*. Washington, DC: Infantry Journal Press, 1949.

Miller, Edward S. *War Plan Orange: The U.S. Strategy to Defeat Japan, 1897–1945*. Annapolis, MD: Naval Institute Press, 1991.

Miller, John, Jr. CARTWHEEL: *The Reduction of Rabaul*. Washington, DC: Office of the Chief of Military History, Department of the Army, 1959.

———. "The Casablanca Conference and Pacific Strategy." *Military Affairs* 13, 4 (Winter 1949): 209–215.

Miller, Stuart C. *"Benevolent Assimilation": The American Conquest of the Philippines, 1899–1903*. New Haven, CT: Yale University Press, 1982.

Millett, Allan R., and Williamson Murray, eds. *Military Effectiveness*. 3 vols. Boston: Unwin Hyman, 1988.

Millett, Allan R. *Semper Fidelis: The History of the United States Marine Corps*. Rev. and expanded ed. New York: Free Press, 1991.

Milner, Samuel. *Victory in Papua*. Washington, DC: Office of the Chief of Military History, Department of the Army, 1957.

Morton, Louis. *Pacific Command: A Study in Interservice Relations*. Colorado Springs: United States Air Force Academy, 1961.

———. *Strategy and Command: The First Two Years*. Washington, DC: Office of the Chief of Military History, Department of the Army, 1962.

———. "War Plan ORANGE: Evolution of a Strategy." *World Politics* 11, 2 (January 1959): 221–250.

Nenninger, Timothy K. "Creating Officers: The Leavenworth Experience, 1920–1940." *Military Review* 69 (November 1989): 58–68.

———. "Leavenworth and Its Critics: The U.S. Army Command and General Staff School, 1920–1940." *Journal of Military History* 58, 2 (April 1994): 199–231.

———. *The Leavenworth Schools and the Old Army: Education, Professionalism, and the Officer Corps of the United States Army, 1881–1918*. Westport, CT: Greenwood Press, 1978.

Ohl, John Kennedy. *Supplying the Troops: General Somervell and American Logistics in World War II*. DeKalb: Northern Illinois University Press, 1994.

O'Neill, William L. *A Democracy at War: America's Fight at Home and Abroad in World War II*. New York: Free Press, 1993.

Papararone, Christopher. "Equivalent Theory of Logistics." *Army Logistician: Professional Bulletin of United States Army Logistics* (January–February 1995): 12–17.

Paret, Peter, ed. *Makers of Modern Strategy: From Machiavelli to the Nuclear Age*. Princeton, NJ: Princeton University Press, 1986.

Perret, Geoffrey. *Old Soldiers Never Die: The Life of Douglas MacArthur*. New York: Random House, 1996.

———. *There's a War to Be Won: The United States Army in World War II*. New York: Random House, 1991.

Petillo, Carol Morris. *Douglas MacArthur: The Philippine Years*. Bloomington: Indiana University Press, 1981.

Pogue, Forrest C. *George C. Marshall*. 4 vols. New York: Viking Press, 1963–1987.

Prefer, Nathan. *MacArthur's New Guinea Campaign, March–August 1944*. Conshohocken, PA: Combined Books, 1995.

Reardon, Carol. *Soldiers and Scholars: The U.S. Army and the Uses of Military History, 1865–1920*. Lawrence: University Press of Kansas, 1990.

Reynolds, Clark G. "Admiral Ernest J. King and the Strategy for Victory in the Pacific." *Naval War College Review* 28, 3 (Winter 1976): 57–66.

——. "MacArthur as Maritime Strategist." *Naval War College Review* 33, 2 (March–April 1980): 79–91.

Ross, Steven T. *American War Plans, 1890–1939*. London: Frank Cass, 2002.

Schaffer, Ronald. "General Stanley D. Embick: Military Dissenter." *Military Affairs* 37, 3 (October 1973): 89–95.

Schaller, Michael. *Douglas MacArthur: The Far Eastern General*. New York: Oxford University Press, 1989.

Sexton, William Thaddeus. *Soldiers in the Sun: An Adventure in Imperialism*. Harrisburg, PA: Military Service Publishing, 1939; reprint, Freeport, NY: Books for Libraries Press, 1971.

Shortal, John F. *Forged By Fire: General Robert L. Eichelberger and the Pacific War*. Columbia: University of South Carolina Press, 1987.

——. "MacArthur's Fireman: Robert L. Eichelberger." *Parameters: Journal of the U.S. Army War College* 16, 3 (Autumn 1986): 58–67.

Skates, John Ray. *The Invasion of Japan: Alternative to the Bomb*. Columbia: University of South Carolina Press, 1994.

Smith, Robert Ross. *The Approach to the Philippines*. Washington, DC: Office of the Chief of Military History, Department of the Army, 1953.

——. *Triumph in the Philippines*. Washington, DC: Office of the Chief of Military History, Department of the Army, 1963.

Spector, Ronald H. *Eagle against the Sun: The American War with Japan*. New York: Free Press, 1985.

Stauffer, Alvin P. *Quartermaster Corps: Operations in the War against Japan*. Washington, DC: Office of the Chief of Military History, Department of the Army, 1956.

Taaffe, Stephen R. *MacArthur's Jungle War: The 1944 New Guinea Campaign*. Lawrence: University Press of Kansas, 1998.

Taylor, Emerson Gifford. *New England in France, 1917–1919: A History of the Twenty-Sixth Division U.S.A.* Boston: Houghton Mifflin, 1920.

Trask, David F. *The War with Spain in 1898*. New York: Macmillan, 1981.

Twelfth U.S. Infantry 1798–1919: Its Story by Its Men. New York: Knickerbocker Press, 1919.

United States Marine Corps. *History of U.S. Marine Corps in World War II*. 5 vols. Washington, DC: Historical Branch, G-3 Division, Headquarters, U.S. Marine Corps, 1958–1971.

Van Creveld, Martin. *Command in War*. Cambridge, MA: Harvard University Press, 1985.

Vlahos, Michael. *The Blue Sword: The Naval War College and the American Mission, 1919–1941*. Newport, RI: Naval War College Press, 1980.

Weigley, Russell F. *The American Way of War: A History of United States Military Strategy and Policy*. New York: Macmillan, 1973.

——. *Eisenhower's Lieutenants: The Campaign of France and Germany, 1944–1945*. Bloomington: Indiana University Press, 1981.

——. "From the Normandy Beaches to the Falaise-Argentan Pocket." *Military Review* 70: 9 (September 1990): 45–64.

——. *History of the United States Army*. Enlarged ed. Bloomington: Indiana University Press, 1984.

——. "Shaping the American Army: Mobility versus Power." *Parameters: Journal of the U.S. Army War College* 11, 3 (September 1981): 13–21.

——. "The Role of the War Department and the Army." In Dorothy Borg and Shumpei Okamoto, eds., *Pearl Harbor as History: Japanese-American Relations, 1931–1941*. New York: Columbia University Press, 1973.

———. *Towards an American Army: Military Thought from Washington to Marshall.* New York: Columbia University Press, 1962.

Weinberg, Gerhard L. "Grand Strategy in the Pacific War." *Air Power History* 43, 1 (Spring 1996): 4–13.

Wiebe, Robert H. *The Search for Order, 1877–1920.* New York: Hill and Wang, 1967.

Williamson, William R. "Campaign Planning." *Parameters: Journal of the U.S. Army War College* 14, 4 (Winter 1984): 20–25.

Willmot, Hedley P. *The Great Crusade: A New Complete History of the Second World War.* New York: Free Press, 1989.

Wilson, John B. "Influences on U.S. Army Divisional Organization in the Twentieth Century." *Army History* 39 (Fall 1996): 1–7.

Winton, Harold R. "Toward an American Philosophy of Command." *Journal of Military History* 64, 4 (October 2000): 1035–1060.

Wright, B. C. *The 1st Cavalry Division in World War II.* Tokyo: Toppan Printing, 1947.

Young, Kenneth Ray. *The General's General: The Life and Times of Arthur MacArthur.* Boulder, CO: Westview Press, 1994.

Zedric, Lance Q. *Silent Warriors of World War II: The Alamo Scouts behind Japanese Lines.* Ventura, CA: Pathfinder Publishing, 1995.

Theses and Dissertations

Alspaugh, Lilyan Mae. "General Alfred M. Gruenther: Dedicated Spokesman for NATO." PhD diss., Michigan State University, 1969, United Microfilms International (UMI) Order Number 7014979.

Atwater, William Felix. "United States Army and Navy Development of Joint Landing Operations 1898–1942." PhD diss., Duke University, 1986, UMI Order Number 8718403.

Cameron, Robert Stewart. "Americanizing the Tank: U.S. Army Administration and Mechanized Development with the Army, 1917–1943." 3 vols. PhD diss., Temple University, 1994, UMI Order Number DA9512809.

Eaton, George B. "From Teaching to Practice: General Walter Krueger and the Development of Joint Operations, 1921–1945." Advanced Research Project, Naval War College, 22 February 1994.

Foster, Randolph V. "Armor in Jungle Operations." Military Monograph. Advanced Officers Class No. 1. The Armored School, Ft. Knox, KY, 1 May 1948.

Johnson, David E. "Fast Tanks and Heavy Bombers: The United States Army and the Development of Armor and Aviation Doctrines and Technologies, 1917 to 1945." PhD diss., Duke University, 1990, UMI Order Number DA9106619.

Johnson, Douglas V. "A Few 'Squads Left' and Off to France: Training the American Army in the United States for World War I." PhD diss., Temple University, 1992, UMI Order Number DA 9227482.

LaSaine, John T. "The Evolution of United States National Security Policy in Global Crisis, 1935–1940." PhD diss., Brown University, 1990, UMI Order Number 9101792.

Matheny, Michael R. "The Development of the Theory and Doctrine of Operational Art in the American Army, 1920–1940." Monograph Prepared for the School of Advanced Military Studies, United States Army Command and General Staff College, Fort Leavenworth, KS, 1988.

McEnery, Kevin T. "The XIV Corps Battle for Manila, February 1945." MMAS thesis, United States Army Command and General Staff College, 1993.

Nenninger, Timothy K. "The Fort Leavenworth Schools: Postgraduate Military Education and Professionalization in the U.S. Army, 1880–1920." PhD diss., University of Wisconsin, 1974, UMI Order Number 74-18, 946.
Odom, William O. "The Rise and Fall of U.S. Army Doctrine, 1918–1939." PhD diss., Ohio State University, 1995, UMI Order Number DA9534040.
Osterhoudt, Henry Jerry. "The Evolution of U.S. Army Assault Tactics, 1778–1919: The Search for Sound Doctrine." PhD diss., Duke University, 1986. UMI Order Number DA8710809.
Pollacia, Nick. "The Third Army Maneuvers, May 1940: The First of the Great Louisiana Maneuvers." MA thesis, Northwestern State University, LA, 1994.

INDEX

CPSIA information can be obtained
at www.ICGtesting.com
Printed in the USA
LVHW020339280622
722206LV00015B/516